Black Mecca

Black Mecca

The African Muslims of Harlem

ZAIN ABDULLAH

OXFORD

UNIVERSITY PRESS

OXFORD
UNIVERSITY PRESS

Oxford University Press is a department of the University of Oxford.
It furthers the University's objective of excellence in research, scholarship,
and education by publishing worldwide.

Oxford   New York
Auckland   Cape Town   Dar es Salaam   Hong Kong   Karachi
Kuala Lumpur   Madrid   Melbourne   Mexico City   Nairobi
New Delhi   Shanghai   Taipei   Toronto

With offices in
Argentina   Austria   Brazil   Chile   Czech Republic   France   Greece
Guatemala   Hungary   Italy   Japan   Poland   Portugal   Singapore
South Korea   Switzerland   Thailand   Turkey   Ukraine   Vietnam

Oxford is a registered trade mark of Oxford University Press
in the UK and certain other countries.

Published in the United States of America by
Oxford University Press
198 Madison Avenue, New York, NY 10016

Library of Congress Cataloging-in-Publication Data
Abdullah, Zain.
Black Mecca : the African Muslims of Harlem / Zain Abdullah.
    p.   cm.
Includes bibliographical references and index.
ISBN 978-0-19-531425-0 (hardcover); 978-0-19-932928-1 (paperback)
1. Muslims—New York (State)—New York. 2. West Africans—New York (State)—New York.
3. New York (N.Y.)—Emigration and immigration. 4. Harlem (New York, N.Y.)—Ethnic relations.
I. Title.
BP67.U62N483 2010
297.089'96607471—dc22   2010007426

Acknowledgments

A research project such as this takes many years and touches many lives. I would like to begin by thanking everyone who extended a hand, large or small. Each word of encouragement meant a great deal, especially during those times when the research or writing became daunting. This book could not have been written without the kindness of the people participating in the study. They opened not only their doors but their hearts, granting me access to their fears, hopes, and dreams. I am truly grateful to all of them. My deepest appreciation goes to Balozi Harvey (Zayd Muhammad), an African American Murid convert and president of the Murid Islamic Community in America. He graciously gave his time and made himself available whenever I needed him. He was so kind and congenial, and I only hope this work can measure up to his generosity and warm spirit.

While many gave assistance, I would like to give a very special word of thanks to particular people who were extremely generous with both their time and resources. From Senegal, they include Abdoulaye Thiam, Khady Gueye Djily, Imam Bassirou Lo, Abu Bakr Diouf, Adama Diop, Aissatou Ndao, El-Hadj Diagne, El-Hadj Ndiaye, Fatou Diop, Ibrahima Banda, Lamine Diene, Nogaye Mboup, Abdoulaye Kebe, Balla Diop, Momour Drame, and Selemane Coulibaly. Others from Senegal are Abdul Aziz Houle, Mohamed Hanne, Mamadou Diallo, Thiam Modou, Djibril Gueye, Omar Sarr, and Abdoulaye Windemraye. Many from Côte d'Ivoire (Ivory Coast) gave amazing help. They include Imam Soulaymane Konate, Soumaila Sanugo, Ibrahima "Sidi" Sidibe, Fatou Bakayoko, Abdulkarim Meite, Assetou Doukoure, Mamadou Kone, Mathedje "Mathy" Cisse, and Matilla Bamba. I also want to include here Ibrahima Sacko from Mali, Amina Gai from Gambia, and Fatimatou Sharief from Liberia. From Guinea, I want to thank Imam Bah Algassim, Mohamed Fofana Youla, Asmaou Diallo, and Ahmad "Mamadou" Sow.

Harlem became a home away from home because of the warm embrace I received from countless residents. Because of their hospitality, it occupies a special place in my heart. Harlem regulars taking an exceptional interest in this project include Imam Talib Abdur-Rashid of the Mosque of Islamic Brotherhood, Eddie Stafford, Ishmael Randall, Lanissa Aisha Renee McCord Sy, Amina Kane, Muhaimana Abdul-Hakim, Sadjah Sabree, and Jabril Howard. I thank them for their invaluable support. My gratitude goes out to many others assisting the work, particularly during the early stages. They include Luqman Abdullateef, Charles Muhammad, Janice Muhammad, Leelai Demoz, Professor Muhammad Abdur-Rahman, Salihou Mecca Gjabi, Zeinab Eyegye, Linda Boyd, Atanga Libutsi, John Kane, Munkaila "Mika" Abdur-Rahman, Leu Lui, Zelda Smith, Sydney Carter, Ida Sewell, Jeremy Rocklin, Gnoleba Remy Seri, Esq., and Verna Mungo. They all took an interest in the study and gave freely of themselves. I am infinitely grateful.

During the course of such a long journey, lives are found and lives are lost. Shaykh Abdul-Malik Abdul-Quddus, an African American fluent in Wolof and African Islam, had a gentle soul, a quick wit, and a ready smile. He was senselessly murdered after aiding an unknown victim one night in Harlem. His keen insight and readiness to assist were indispensable to me, and I sorely miss him. Friends Kweli Kinaya, a bright African American Muslim with a curious mind, and Veronica Calderhead, a native Canadian and Rutgers University–Newark librarian, showed ongoing interest in this research before their passing, and I have long appreciated their support. This work is certainly dedicated to their spirit.

A great many thanks go to the librarians and staff at Rutgers University–Newark and Temple University. The people working at these great institutions are among the best in the world. I have benefited more than I can say from their professionalism and enduring support. At Rutgers, I would like to extend special thanks to B. Joyce Watson, Elizabeth Ann Watkins, Maggie Harris-Clark, Helen Funnye, Dorothy Grauer, Carolyn Foote, Marlene Riely, Roberta "Bobby" Tipton, Yoshiko Ishii, Ka-Neng Au, and Natalie Borisovets. In the Media Department, Gerard "Gerry" Drinkard possesses a prophetic passion for justice, and he is a true treasure. I have appreciated his caring spirit over the years. At Temple, Fred Rowland is simply amazing. I have pushed all sorts of projects his way and he has never ceased to be helpful and encouraging, two qualities any researcher cannot do without.

Research assistance can be the bedrock of any study, and I am indebted to a number of generous souls who worked hard to push this project forward. Pamela

Zimmerman is a remarkable transcriber, and her tireless effort to complete assignments on time was a godsend. I also want to thank Judy Rogers, former director of Nah We Yone, for her assistance and for introducing me to John Wilkinson, who was a tremendous help in the field. The Department of Religion at Temple University often assigns graduate students to assist faculty in their research for a semester, and I would like to extend my thanks to Walter Isaac, Elizabeth Lawson, and Cindy Osueke. Natasha Nichols, a former student of mine at Rutgers, voluntarily offered research assistance, and I am truly grateful for her help.

I would like to give a special word of thanks to Wendell P. Holbrook, professor of African-American and African Studies at Rutgers University–Newark. Wendell was my teacher during my undergraduate years at Rutgers. When I sought his advice for graduate school, he became a mentor and trusted advisor. When I became a doctoral student, he invited me to teach at Rutgers, and we became colleagues and friends. Wendell, you have made a major impact on my intellectual development, and I value our friendship. Thank you. Another special word of appreciation goes to Clement A. Price, professor of history at Rutgers University–Newark. Clem, the friendship and compassion you have extended to me over the years have meant a great deal. Indeed, your example has taught me what it means to be a responsible scholar, teacher, and citizen. Let me simply say that I look forward to deepening our relationship in the future. Supportive colleagues are not always common. But the warm fellowship and ongoing encouragement provided by the members of my department at Temple University have been tremendous. They have helped to sustain me over several years as I researched and wrote this book, and I deeply appreciate their good cheer. Aminah Beverly McCloud of DePaul University and Paul Stoller at West Chester University have extended constant friendship and caring collegiality, and they are likewise deserving of my gratitude.

This work has benefited from several funding sources during the initial stages of the research. Awards from the Social Science Research Council and the Smithsonian Institution's Center for Folklife and Cultural Heritage and their National Museum of African Art were very much appreciated. The study was also enriched by a research fellowship with the Religion and Immigrant Incorporation in New York project, which was under the auspices of the International Center for Migration, Ethnicity, and Citizenship at the New School for Social Research. I also appreciate the support of Steven Gregory, director of the Institute for Research in African-American Studies at Columbia University, who invited me to become a visiting scholar, affording me a place to write or just to think while in Harlem. I would like to thank Theo Calderara, my editor at Oxford University Press, for believing in this project from the start. I deeply appreciate his patience, his readiness to answer any question, and his diligent efforts to bring the manuscript to completion. Moreover,

I value the ardent efforts and amiable character of Molly Balikov and Tamzen Benfield. Their hard work to expedite the production and release of this book was a real boon. I also appreciate the fine copyediting work of Wendy Warren Keebler.

My most important acknowledgment goes to my loving family and friends. There are no words to express my gratitude and appreciation for all the love, encouragement, and support I have received from them. You all have been the very foundation of my life. Thank you for tolerating my absences over the years. I can only hope that this work gives you a modicum of the joy you have given me.

Contents

Black Mecca

1

Prologue: A New Blues People

In 1983, the intersection at 125th Street and Seventh Avenue in Harlem was officially named African Square.[1] A sign was immediately hung on the corner post, placing it between the ones for Adam Clayton Powell Jr. and Martin Luther King Jr. This posting signifies that Harlem is a Black space—a cultural center where people of African descent live deeply, love passionately, and labor intensely. But the people who conceived of an "African Square" could not have anticipated a massive influx of 100,000 Africans into New York City by the early 1990s, not to mention the continued arrival of approximately 50,000 each year.[2] And, unlike in the past, when Africans migrating to the United States were Christian and English speakers, a great many today are Muslim from French-speaking countries. But since the Black saga in America is undoubtedly characterized by rupture and reinvention, the story of Africans in Harlem is a blues story. In his review of Richard Wright's *Black Boy*, Ralph Ellison speaks of the Black experience as an inner tale "filled with blues-tempered echoes of . . . Southern towns and cities, estrangements, fights and flights, deaths and disappointments, charged with physical and spiritual hungers and pain."[3] So, Africans migrating to New York are a new blues people, with their own song to sing and drama to act out. This, too, is Harlem. Their bodies clad in loose *boubou* robes and tasseled hats, they stroll up and down Harlem streets, their costuming proclaiming loudly, in the words of one Senegalese intellectual in New York, "We are here!" But they are more than merely present.

African Square sign shown here between ones for Adam Clayton Powell, Martin Luther King Jr., and West 125th Street. (Photo Zain Abdullah)

Africans have arrived with divergent views of the borough and its people. Some were exposed to American movies, which depicted Harlem as a neighborhood rife with crime and chaos. Others consumed Black popular culture or read the words of civil rights leaders. In other words, while some have already internalized negative images of Harlem before they arrived, many others consider it their very own "Black Mecca." They are attracted not only to its glorious past but also to its Black soul, its blues impulse. Because they are emigrating from African countries, they find that Black neighborhoods imbued with this sensibility can feel like home. Of course, the reality is often quite different, especially when class conflicts and cultural misfires go unresolved. Just like African Americans, however, Africans have a stake in making a place for themselves in Harlem, and this claim will force them to tell their own stories. Sometimes their narratives will overlap with African American accounts, and at other times they will be wholly unique and original.

Besides the ancestral links African Americans share with continental Africans, scholars are recognizing the extent to which Muslims were a significant segment of the enslaved population in North America. In fact, historians such as Michael A. Gomez argue that thousands of African Muslims were bound and brought to the American mainland.[4] This research has led to scholarly questions about the kinds of Africanisms or African customs that have survived slavery and been retained by Black Americans, especially naming and musical traditions. Indeed, some have investigated how the surname Bailey was conceivably an aberration of the West African Muslim name Bilali, a claim implicating the Black abolitionist Frederick Douglass, whose original family name was Bailey.[5] Others speculate that because the given name of Harriet Tubman, another African American abolitionist, was Araminta, which is strikingly similar to the common West African Muslim name Aminata[6] (or perhaps a hybrid or shortened version of it in the case of Arame, a female name in Senegal), West African Muslim culture might have shaped the life of this historic figure in some way. There also appears to be sufficient evidence to demonstrate the impact of West African musical forms on the blues, and scholars have explored the ways West African Islam has contributed to its formation. While research on Islam's role in Black culture is ongoing, it is reasonable to consider how musical elements in the liturgies of West African Muslims might influence, even tangentially, the harmony, melody, or rhythm of Black music.[7] Still, the aim of this prologue is not so ambitious. Despite these fascinating attempts to ascertain artistic connections between enslaved African Muslims and Black musical forms, I am interested in how Muslim immigrants from West Africa emerge as a new blues people in Harlem.

LeRoi Jones (Amiri Baraka) titled his now-classic 1963 book *Blues People*, in which he explored the development of blues and jazz as a way to talk about the epic journey of Blacks in America. For him, Black music embodies African American history. "The music was the score, the actually expressed creative orchestration, reflection, of Afro-American life, our words, the libretto, to those . . . lived lives."[8] For me, the blues is a metaphor. It is a way to begin a conversation about the sensibilities of a people—their dreams, fears, and hopes. This is not to say, then, that as the blues might imply, this is a story about the woes of another immigrant group. In many ways, it is about their resilience. "What is distinctive about using blues and jazz as a source of intellectual inspiration," says the African American philosopher and activist Cornel West, "is the ability to be flexible, fluid, improvisational, and multi-dimensional—finding one's own voice, but using that voice in a variety of different ways."[9] Seeing it through this lens, we can understand West African Muslim life in Harlem in terms of its elasticity, its defiance to be characterized in one way or another, and move beyond old immigration models in which immigrants were seen as isolated, bounded within their own enclaves, not connected to the world around them.

But obviously, Harlem, too, must change to accommodate these newcomers. Churches have reworked their "No Loitering" signs to include French translations, and African American *masjids* (mosques) have likewise added French wording to their announcements, especially on signs instructing newly arrived Africans about where to pay their donations. And the Islamic practices of West African Muslims have been modified somewhat. They strive to infuse their services with a blues sensation, or what Ralph Ellison called "an impulse to keep the painful details and episodes of a brutal experience alive in one's aching consciousness, to finger its jagged grain, and to transcend it."[10] While this character might be exhibited anywhere, it is most vividly displayed at annual celebrations. In this way, West African Muslim lifeways include particular characteristics central to the blues. These include the vocal musicality of the *athan* (call to prayer), the rhythmic chanting of prayers as a plea for mercy, the solo performances at Islamic events, the call and response of communal worship, and the duality of both *huzn* (sadness) and *fat-h* (victory) one can hear in Qur'anic recitations. All of this religious activity demonstrates a blues soul.

On one day in July, for instance, Africans begin arriving for an annual event well after one o'clock in the morning. The celebration is for Mame Diarra Bousso, the mother of Cheikh Amadou Bamba, a Muslim cleric from Senegal and the founder of the Murid spiritual order. Women wearing vibrant indigo robes and headwraps slip through the darkness and into the Harlem State Office Building, entering from a courtyard named African Square Plaza. Men follow, dressed in their own multicolored flowing garments. Black security guards, two men and three women, monitor their tedious walk past the checkpoint and then through the metal detector. People enter, greeting one another in Arabic, Wolof (a native language of Senegal), and some French, then scramble to the elevator. When the doors open, they pile in, and the car is quickly filled with an aroma of heavy makeup and a mélange of sweet-spicy fragrances. At the twelfth floor, they pour out into the lobby. Some stop to talk, while others dash into a rectangular room with three hundred chairs divided by a single aisle. The men have already filled the right side, and about fifty more stand chattering in the back. On the left, women sit twisting in their seats, chatting about this and that. As time presses on, the room quickly exceeds its capacity.

Waiting at a head table are five male speakers, although women are typically featured presenters at Mame Diarra events. As more people enter, the room tightens. "Please take a seat!" yells a female escort, extending her hand and torso in the proper direction. "There's plenty of seats," she urges. "Please, go sit down!" Some try their luck. Most, however, are much too engrossed in the prospect of being together, particularly for such an auspicious occasion. Besides, their relentless work schedules consume them, and they are unwilling to waste a single moment. Men and women cross the artificial gender divide, exchanging warm smiles, hugs, kisses, and laughs, like family members at a reunion. "*Sadaqa Jara! Sadaqa Jara!*" another female host shouts, as she and others walk around shaking black plastic bags, allowing people to stuff bills inside.[11] As more people arrive, the heat rises, and small bottles of water circulate freely. In the hallway, people strike poses with family and friends for pictures at ten dollars a shot. It's all reminiscent of preperformance activities at the Apollo Theatre, only a half-block away. Even at two-thirty A.M., people continue to arrive, looking fresh and vibrant. As the first speaker begins his talk, Mamadou, a Senegalese migrant in his thirties standing nearby, leans toward me.

"This is not like in Senegal," he says, as we stand hanging out in the back.

"Oh, what's different?" I ask.

"In Senegal," he says, "it's much bigger, and it's a real celebration. But here, we just try it. We are really just trying."

The presenter recounts the miraculous exploits of Amadou Bamba and Diarra Bousso. Melodious recitals of Bamba's *khassaïd* (poetry) generate frequent cries of "Ahhh!" and finger snapping from the crowd.[12] After forty-five minutes, the presenter breaks down crying and is unable to finish. Nearly blocking my view, Abdou, a devout teenage Murid raised in Harlem, suddenly turns around. "You see!" he says, glaring into my eyes. "The mother of Cheikh Amadou Bamba is like the Virgin Mary for us." He then spins back around. A male *jeli* (griot, or praise singer) in a purple *jalabiyya* (robe) rises from a circle of chanters, grabs the microphone, and regales the audience with recitals, walking slowly toward the head table. The crowd swoons, and a woman faints into *daanu leer* (a Wolof term for spiritual ecstasy). Women surround her, administering sips of water, but her eyes continue to roll madly.

The *jeli* resumes the chant but switches lyrics, as his piercing, harmonious tone heightens and changes rhythm. Returning to the circle, he joins the others and *serigne* Fallou Ndiaye, a renowned blind Senegalese reciter who came to New York just to participate. Ndiaye intensifies the recital. He begins his solo, and chanters join in on cue like backup singers. Fingers snap in applause. The chant is in Arabic, but its African tone carries the pitch up and down, seeming to send the entire room spinning. During the next two hours, the pace gets heavy, as the group moves swiftly through several traditional selections: *mawahib ul-quduus* (Gifts from God, the Most Holy), *matlab ul-shifahi* (The Happiness of Healing), *Mame Diarra* (biography). Elegantly draped in indigo gowns with rust tie-dye lining their collars, dresses, and headscarves, several women rise from their seats and move toward the chanters. The excitement mounts, and people begin stirring around the room. Others stand, then sit, not knowing which is better. When one woman reaches the circle, she turns slowly and dances for a moment, then throws a handful of money into a pile, making certain to time each toss to a break in the tempo. By four-thirty A.M., the energy still hangs in the air, and "*Sadaqa Jara!*" rings out once more before the program ends. Even though this event is only one of many for African Muslims, a group that includes several others such as the Fulani or the Malinke, it illustrates a blues sensibility. In other words, the chanter's voice fluctuates from high and low pitches to create an intense emotion. The sorrowful tone of the words forces a participatory response from the crowd. And, as with any blues singer, storytelling is a vital part of the performance.[13]

Murid woman tossing money into chanter's circle at a religious celebration. (Photo Zain Abdullah)

In her book *Firstlight*, Sue Monk Kidd argues that the ritual of storytelling allows us to endure suffering, because it sustains us through the pain and transforms it into hope. "Story," Kidd writes, "means 'to know.'"[14] She goes on to say that discovering our personal stories "is a spiritual quest. Without such stories we cannot be fully human, for without them we are unable to articulate or even understand our deepest experiences."[15] My primary aim here is to use story to convey a deeper understanding of African Muslims in Harlem. For if we are able to comprehend their tale, we just might gain a better grasp of ourselves. But in this case, the practice of story is no simple matter. The story I am attempting to tell is necessarily a compilation of multiple narratives. This text is crafted out of the stories I was fortunate enough to collect over many years of research. It is also based on my own story. I often jotted down cryptic notes after witnessing something, ducking into cafés or *masjids* in order to capture as much detail as possible. And obviously, writing up these notes more fully at home produced another layer to the story, making the entire enterprise a coproduction of sorts. In the end, *Black Mecca* is a patchwork quilt. But because this work does not focus on a single African Muslim community, it endeavors to weave together a number of sketches spread across cultural terrain, religious orientation, and social groupings.

I conducted ongoing fieldwork for this project from 2000 until early 2004, and updates were made until 2007. While the research took me throughout the New York metropolitan area, my main site was on and around 116th Street in Harlem. But because I was not merely interested in studying African Muslims by themselves or how they managed their lives within their own religious worlds, I adopted a multisited approach, which meant that I was forced to track "the people" and their interactions into different locales.[16] To understand their encounters with others, I was compelled to investigate the communities of their neighbors and conduct research at these locations as well. As much as possible, then, I tried to place African Muslims in conversation with their environment and the residents within it, giving the study, I hope, more texture. Another major aim of this book is to allow African and other respondents to speak as fully as possible, exposing readers to the depth of their voices. As a result, many hours were spent at various locations in the area: the Harlem Market, African *masjids*, African and African American restaurants, Laundromats, apartment stoops, celebrations, community programs, religious services, and the streets. In my attempt to identify people of African descent and others racially, I chose to adopt what some might consider an unconventional approach. Terms referring to racial identity such as *White* or *Black*, including derivatives such as *Whiteness* or *Blackness*, will be capitalized. Like other ethnic, national, or linguistic designations that refer to a population (e.g., Italian, Nigerian, Chinese, etc.), racial markers, I believe (while socially invented and conveying no innate biological validity), do nonetheless sharply identify the experiences, cultures, worldviews, and unique speech patterns of a people and, thus, may be capitalized. While people of African descent who are indigenous to the United States will be interchangeably referred to as African American, Black, or Black American, continental Africans or those born and raised in Africa will be labeled more broadly (when not referring to specific ethnic groups) as African or Black immigrant.

I attempted to center my observations at three African institutions in Harlem: Masjid Aqsa on Eighth Avenue near 116th Street (established in 1998); Masjid Salaam on 116th near Seventh Avenue (founded in 1998 but now defunct), and Masjid Touba on Edgecombe Avenue and 137th Street (purchased in 2001). Using this method, my aim was to link a series of "portraits," with each description unearthing a particular context and a unique story.[17] Except for prominent figures such as *imams* (Muslim leaders) or certain community activists, I use pseudonyms for my respondents. While some ethnographers have chosen not to follow this practice—instead using real first names for all participants, demonstrating what those researchers believe is a higher level of accuracy and liability—revealing this kind of detail would not only violate the privacy of my interlocutors, but it might also jeopardize their well-being, since many are undocumented.[18] To further protect their identity, then, I sometimes altered the locations of certain smaller events, the names of specific stores, and certain background particulars of some respondents. Still, I believe their stories are well represented here, and I hope readers will find them useful.

Also to that end, I would like to mention something about the readership of this book. I have researched and written *Black Mecca* with a broad audience in mind. That is, the book covers the apparent topics of Islam, Africa, and immigration, but it is also informed by other subjects such as multiculturalism, religious pluralism, gender, race, terrorism and national security, urban studies, sacred space, intergroup relations, globalization and transnationalism, gentrification, bilingualism, migrant labor, and so on. Because the work touches on so many areas, I worked to retain its narrative style, which meant using as little jargon as possible. At the same time, high-quality ethnography dictates that there should be a balance between good storytelling and well-placed social analysis. I hope the combination will satisfy both academic audiences and lay readers.

In addition to the subject areas mentioned above, researchers and students, for example, might find this work interesting for the way it challenges segmented assimilation theory in immigration studies.[19] While the segmented model recognizes how new immigrants are being absorbed into three different and perhaps disadvantageous sectors of American society, it has summarily ignored the role of religion. In contrast to traditional assimilation, in which newcomers are thought to enter the United States and follow a "straight-line" path into the dominant

Anglo-American culture, these scholars claim that today's immigrants are integrated into either the White middle class, the "downward" path of a Black and Latino underclass, or the ethnic community characterized by tight group solidarity and rapid economic advancement. West African Muslims in Harlem show us that contemporary immigrants might choose a different course altogether.

Nonspecialists might find *Black Mecca* of use in other ways. While Muslims are projected soon to become the largest religious community in America after Christianity, the public is still unaware of this group's diversity.[20] While there are various claims about the number of Muslims in the United States, acceptable figures vary between 4 million and 6 million, with Muslim migrants representing more than eighty countries, not to mention a sizable contingent of African American Muslims.[21] American Muslims also exhibit a huge range of religious orientations (from reformists to liberal/moderate to ultraconservative), class standings, and ideological positions. Yet, because of widespread, orientalist stereotypes of Islam and today's volatile geopolitics, Muslims are usually seen primarily as Arabs. These assumptions will clearly prevent the masses and policy makers from fully grasping this religious community. But America has fundamentally been a place where a panoply of ideas and characters can grow. While Barack Obama, the first African American president of the United States, is a Christian, his East African ancestry is Muslim on his father's side. In January 2007, Keith Ellison, the first Muslim elected to Congress and the only African American to hold this post from Minnesota, took the oath of office by swearing in on the Qur'an instead of the Bible. Moreover, Ellison used the two-volume translation of the Qur'an that had been owned by Thomas Jefferson himself. The following year, Andre Carson, another African American Muslim, assumed congressional office representing Indiana's Seventh District. With Islam discussed or represented at the highest offices in the land, I hope this work will help to dispel misconceptions about Muslims, particularly regarding religious pluralism in America.[22]

West African Muslims are pretty diverse themselves. While most West African immigrants to the United States have come from English-speaking nations with Christian leanings such as Nigeria and Ghana, the recent surge of African immigrants into Harlem originates in French-speaking countries. As a result of major changes in the U.S. immigration laws of 1965, which allowed an unprecedented arrival of new immigrants from Asia, Latin America, the Caribbean, and Africa, scores of Muslims from African nations were allowed to enter the United States. Following African independence in the 1960s, West Africans from former French colonies were encouraged to migrate to France as a source of cheap labor. By the next decade, however, the desire for African workers had waned, and France terminated legal immigration in 1974.[23] In the mid-1980s, direct flights between Dakar (Senegal) and New York were inaugurated.[24] With an economic crisis occurring in

Europe and devastatingly poor conditions in West Africa, the migration of West Africans to France was redirected to the United States.

The Senegalese were among the first Francophone African Muslims to arrive in Harlem, and they were followed by those from Côte d'Ivoire (Ivory Coast) and Guinea. But with national independence just beginning in the 1950s (and ending in 1975 for countries such as Cape Verde), many African Muslims largely think of themselves in ethnic terms. Most Senegalese Muslims in Harlem are Wolof and attend Masjid Touba. At Masjids Aqsa and Salaam, Ivoirian Muslims are primarily Malinke and Dyoula speakers, while those from Guinea are Fulani. While Ivoirians hold sway at these two *masjids*, some claim that the Fulanis from Guinea outnumber them. In terms of their religious identity, Senegalese Muslims are primarily Murid, belonging to a Sufi spiritual order called Muridiyya.[25] Ivoirian and Guinean Muslims customarily follow a less particular, more universalist version of Islam, although these dividing lines are often arbitrary; in practice, there is a degree of mixture.

West Africans' presence in Harlem and other places throughout the country is actually more substantial than official figures reveal. According to the U.S. Census Bureau's Current Population Survey, the total population of West Africans in the United States was approximately 167,000 in March 2000. A decade earlier, the U.S. Census reported that there were 2,287 Senegalese, 1,388 Ivoirians, and 1,032 Guineans living in the country. When compared with the 2000 Census, only a slight difference is discernible.[26] Because the Immigration and Naturalization Service only records legal immigration to the United States, its numbers are invariably much lower than those from the U.S. Census Bureau, which counts both legal and illegal residents. Some informal estimates claim that the Senegalese in New York number between 10,000 and 20,000.[27] Other unofficial counts place the number of Murids at 4,000 to 6,000 nationally, with 2,500 in New York.[28] Nonetheless, while official figures are generally too low, informal estimates are usually exaggerated. The U.S. Census for 2010 will undoubtedly reveal much higher numbers.

My overall approach was not to write a book about Islam or Muslims per se. Rather, I wanted to write about the lives of particular people, paying close attention to when and where Islam mattered. Instead of treating Islam as a given, I wanted to know when it was important and when it appeared inconsequential. Under what circumstances does Islam or these people's version of it make a difference in their lives? And how? This would alert me to its "real" meaning, I believed, and why it mattered. But since African Muslims are also racialized as Black immigrants, it's also important to understand when identities such as race matter in the scheme of everyday life, realizing that one is not necessarily constantly consumed by these markers. That is, what are the contexts that allow religious or racial identities to be made and remade in our lives? As in most ethnographic works, I have incorporated an array of materials and research techniques, including survey reports, organizational documents, formal and informal interviewing, and, of course, participant observation. But certainly, any decent work exploring the lives of a people will consider reference materials as well as fictional accounts, film, and visual art, and I have included these works when appropriate. Also, I did not try to structure the book chronologically. Sometimes life is precarious, giving us U-turns and sending us back to the beginning, so the chapters are arranged according to particular themes and ordered in a way I thought would give proper nuance or pull the story together.

So, what is *Black Mecca*'s story? First, as the subtitle suggests, the book is about African Muslims and their attempts to become a part "of" Harlem and not merely to dwell "in" it. In the early 1980s, urban anthropologists began to deviate from a perspective that treated immigrants as encased beings "in" cities. This book looks at how post-1965 West African immigrants create Islamic practices and institutions that inscribe their presence and negotiate their place as new members of American society. While Will Herberg's classic book, *Protestant, Catholic, Jew*, showed us how early European immigrants used religion to aid their integration into middle America, *Black Mecca* revisits this theme for West African Muslims grappling to avoid assimilation into a Black underclass.[29] Unlike similar works, this book does not simply cover these immigrants in isolation. It takes on the way they publicly engage others; shift their religious, racial, and ethnic identities; alter the urban terrain; and give new meaning to our world. I venture to tell a story about this experience.

Second, the various Muslim establishments that Africans have created do not merely sustain their survival in Harlem. They have erected an entirely new world. And while residents now affectionately call the area "Little Africa," this book recounts a story about an emerging "Black Mecca." [30] It is clearly unlike the artistic cluster of writers, thinkers, and activists of long ago. But for all intents and purposes, the area, by way of its new Black arrivals and Muslim religiosity, has become the new Black Mecca of Harlem. The blues chorus that these immigrants sing conveys their narratives of struggle, spiritual yearning, and redemption. And this, too, is the story I endeavor to tell.

2

America Dreaming

I

One cold evening in late February, I visit L'Association des Sénégalais d'Amérique (the Senegalese Association of America) on 116th Street. With brisk winds against my back, I pass quickly through the doorway and enter a mélange of Arabic, French, and Wolof greetings and replies: *"As-salaamu 'alaykum." "Wa 'alaykum salaam; çava?" "Çava bien; nangadef?" "Mangi fe."* Among a dozen members, the association president, Ibrahima Diafouné, sits at a wooden desk staring into his computer screen. He occasionally opens a drawer to retrieve a file, peeks at its contents, and thrusts it back inside. Ibrahima stands just over six feet tall, but his boyish smile welcomes any visitor. Pinned on the bulletin board against the right wall is a newspaper clipping from the *New York Post*. "Rescue at Sea," the headline blares.[1] I stand riveted, reading each line. Fourteen Senegalese men crossed the Atlantic in a yacht bound for New York. I spin around and ask Ibrahima for a copy but try not to appear overly anxious.

With a glint in his eye, he turns to an official. "Would you make a copy of that article for him?" he says.

Abdoulaye, a long-standing member in his sixties, watches from a nearby lounge chair.

"Do you know about this?" I ask naively.

"Yeah," Abdoulaye replies wryly.

"Have you been to see them?" I ask.

"Yeah, we've been there, and we're checking things out," he answers calmly.

I have learned that the men are being held in a detention facility, and because of my past work in U.S. prisons, I assume I will need a list of their names before arranging a visit.

"Do you have their names?" I ask.

"I'll give you a copy," Abdoulaye shoots back, almost anticipating my request.

Several days later, I call him and inquire about the contact information. He promises that he is working on it, but several weeks later, I still haven't received anything. While I am becoming antsy, I know that Abdoulaye is extremely efficient, and he has been inundated with work on a major Murid celebration scheduled for the following month.

In late March, I attend *jum'ah* prayer at Masjid Touba. After the services, I join others in the second-floor lounge. A few moments pass as people sit chatting about the day's events, and Abdoulaye enters the room. We smile and greet each other.

"I have the list for you!" he blurts out. I stare at him and wait. "It's in my bag," he says with a wide grin. He reaches over, grabs his brown leather satchel, pulls out a white sheet of paper, and hands it to me.

I quickly inspect the list, then look at him. "Can I keep this?" I ask.

"Yes, it's yours," he replies.

I look back at the names and try to imagine a face for each one. Then a deep sense of anguish sets in as I think about what brought them so far and why.

Before going to the Elizabeth Detention Center in New Jersey, I want to see if any individuals or organizations are already involved. This will help to facilitate my visit and allow me to benefit from their experience and insight. I learn that a grass-roots social-services organization, Nah We Yone—a Krio phrase meaning "It belongs to us"—caters to displaced Africans and assists them in their adjustment to American life. The group also has a program for Detention Center visits, and the executive director, Judy Rogers, an African American native of New York City, put me in contact with Robert, a regular volunteer.[2] He and I speak several times on the telephone and make arrangements to meet at the facility. Robert has spent some time in the Peace Corps in Senegal and speaks fluent Wolof. Because he works in Manhattan, he will take the bus from New York and meet me in Elizabeth. Since we haven't met face to face, our ability to recognize each other was uncertain. Usually, an idea of one's racial type helps in such situations, and it is strange being without this very American prop.

Since this will be my first visit, I decide to dress in business casual. I want to appear professional, especially in a prison setting, where uniforms and rank matter a great deal. As I drive to the center, I receive a call from Robert saying he is almost there. Once he leaves the bus stop, he'll walk the rest of the way, about half a mile.

As I approach the turn leading to the facility, I spot a White male walking briskly along the road. His blondish hair, orange cotton shirt, blue jeans, and tattered brown loafers are not an odd sight in this predominantly White, working-class district. But it is still rare to see someone with his profile walking along the highway. For a brief moment, it occurs to me that this man might be Robert. But by the time I whiz by, I am in no position to stop. Minutes later, I pull into the parking lot. The center is a one-story, mostly unmarked, beige-colored building. I enter a small waiting room with two rows of blue plastic chairs bolted to the floor. Two White women, dressed in dark business suits and speaking in what sound like Slavic tones, give me polite glances as they frantically pore over files. Just then, a White male walks in, a bit pale and disheveled—the same one I passed moments earlier.

Don't tell me this is the man fluent in Wolof—the national language of Black Senegal, I think as I stare at him. I stand up and walk toward him.

"Zain?" he says warily, extending his hand.

"Yeah. Robert?" I reply with a similar gesture.

Robert looks around the hall, appearing fidgety and unsure of where to put his hands. Perhaps I'm not exactly what he was expecting, either.

"I guess we should go sign in," he says. "Did you do that yet?"

"No," I answer. "I actually just arrived and was waiting for you."

We walk to the thick Plexiglas window and push our IDs through the slot. The guard on the other side slips us red passes and locks to secure our things in the lockers behind us. Minutes later, a steel door near the window clacks open, and a rotund corrections officer ushers us into a small room to be swiped for contraband. Having worked as a chaplain for the Department of Corrections, I am tentative about returning to this environment and worried about how I will respond. The clatter of metal doors opening and slamming shut still shocks my system. It floods me with memories. I suspect it is a sound one never forgets. After inspection, another door clicks, and the guard instructs us to walk through. We enter a short corridor with interview cubicles and glass windows on our right. Strangely enough, the empty booths make the scene appear even more ominous. On the other side of the hallway, a huge picture of the American flag appears on the block wall, with the words "God Bless America" above it. Superimposed on the flag is an American eagle, with the Twin Towers, a bridge, and New York skyscrapers as a backdrop. At the upper left, a fire department helmet appears, with the Statute of Liberty on the opposite corner.

"The inmates painted this after nine-eleven," Robert says.

I can't help but think of the irony. It is an astounding symbolic tribute to the value of freedom and the fight for liberty. Yet here we are visiting Senegalese men still incarcerated for fleeing economic repression and poverty.

We reach the end of the corridor, where another guard sits gazing into a monitor. On our right, a row of glass booths line both sides of the hallway. Each partition is equipped with a pinkish wired telephone hung within arm's reach of the plastic chairs. By this time, half of the fourteen men have already been deported.

Within ten minutes, Lamine walks through the door wearing a greenish-blue jumpsuit. He peers through the glass as he continues to approach our booth about halfway down the hall. He spots Robert and then sees my face, and his stiff lips widen into a full grin. Robert picks up the phone, begins telling him about my work, and introduces me. I greet him with "*Salaam*," and his broad smile stretches even more, making it hard for him to speak at times.

Born in the mid-1970s, Lamine has a youthful appearance. He is a devout Murid and Pulaar, a Fula-speaking people from the Senegal River Valley. He worked as a security guard and tailor, fixing boat sails at the marina in Dakar, Senegal's capital city. His obligation to care for relatives and unemployed friends stretched his meager finances to the limit. He had been living on one of the boats at the docks for several months when Modou, a *lebu* fisherman, asked that he join him on a journey across the Atlantic to America. Lamine believed this was an impossible proposition. And despite frequent conversations with Modou, Lamine never really believed him. Still, Modou insisted they must leave before *laylatul-kabir*, the night of the big feast of *eid al-kabir*, which many Muslims call *eid al-adha*, the celebration marking the end of the annual *hajj*. Besides Lamine, Modou spoke to others and chose each of the thirteen for his unique skills. Most were out-of-work mechanics who knew how to fix boat motors. Khadim, a small-scale businessman in his early forties, had already traveled to Thailand and Japan, buying and selling jewelry. He had even lived in the United States for four years back in the early 1990s but had returned to look after his ailing father. In fact, it was Khadim who dissuaded Modou from sailing to Spain, a more common trip but just as dangerous. Khadim argued that there were more opportunities to find work in America, and since he had already been there, he could act as a guide. He also contributed six hundred dollars toward food. Unlike other secretive voyages to Europe, costing hundreds and even thousands of dollars, no one had to pay for the ride, allowing them to save their money for other essentials.

The men all had significant family obligations. They had only basic Qur'anic training, and none was college-educated, which made chances of steady employment in Senegal dismal. They could no longer rely on the government, and the economy was less than adequate, providing little or no means for advancement. They had lost all hope, and leaving appeared to be their only option. This was also a strategy supported in the Qur'an. In one parable, angels ask the weak why they refuse to migrate to another land rather than remain oppressed.[3] Migration is central to the Islamic story and a powerful trope in the Muslim mind. But it is required only if Muslims are unable to alter their life chances at home. Still, migrating to a foreign land is no simple task. In order to obtain a visa to enter the United States legally, one must be sponsored by a legitimate entity in the country of destination. For workers, the American company must prove that few natives can perform the job. For those seeking education, the school is required to issue documentation of acceptance, and full payment of tuition is increasingly required. For visiting relatives or friends in the United States, the sponsor has to be self-sufficient and able to look after the guest during the stay.

Even with all of this, a visa will most likely not be issued unless the applicant can demonstrate independence, which assures American officials that the person will not try to remain in the United States permanently. This often requires the submission of documents demonstrating a commitment to the home country, such as a good job, bank statements with substantial savings, a spouse and children, property, a lucrative business, age beyond one's prime years, or, more commonly, a combination of these. As more people attempt to leave developing nations for the West, it appears more difficult for others to justify their travel to these countries. With such a mass exodus from Africa, some try purchasing a visa.[4] But they are rarely successful. This clearly breeds a climate of desperation, and reckless attempts to reach Europe or now America are ongoing. In late 2006, however, Spain began to partner with countries such as Senegal to curb unlawful entry, creating more liberal immigration policies and legalizing migration from Africa.[5] So far, this has reduced illegal migration to the Canary Islands. While thousands of Africans are still arriving unlawfully, the Spanish plan to sanction these immigrants has drastically reduced illicit migration. In the end, most Africans leave their countries with dreams fueled by globalized images of a Western utopia. As this representation becomes more sophisticated through advanced media technology, this sensational depiction of a western wonderland will continue to enliven the imagination of outsiders. This is especially the case for people in developing nations where economic conditions appear to be worsening.

On the day of the trip, Lamine was feeling queasy. At five o'clock that evening, Modou showed up with Saliou, a boat mechanic with ten years' experience. Saliou was in his mid-twenties and belonged to the Sufi order of Leyéene. The brotherhood was founded by Libasse Thiaw in 1883, and his followers are primarily located in the Cap-Vert Peninsula, Africa's farthest point west, just off the coast of Senegal.[6] Saliou also worked periodically for a transportation company. When his father died, he was responsible for two widows, the cowives of his polygynous father, and other relatives. Modou and Saliou approached Lamine, each carrying an overnight bag.

"Let's go, we must leave before *layatul-kabir!*" Modou coaxed.

His queasiness had gotten worse, but Lamine believed Modou's plan to sail to New York was a ruse and that they would simply take a ride around the marina and return to the pier. Lamine trusted Modou as if he were his blood relative and knew he would take care of him. By custom, since Modou had invited him, it was his duty to safeguard Lamine's well-being. The three climbed into the single-cabin, sixty-foot catamaran, *L'Onde Marine* (Ocean Wave) and slowly pulled away from the waterfront.[7] Modou had instructed the others to meet him at Goree Island. There were two reasons for this. First, he felt it was their legacy to follow the journey of their enslaved ancestors across the Atlantic. Second, leaving from Goree Island would place them directly on the sea, and he could navigate the voyage more easily by following the old slave-trade routes. It was December 12, and Lamine rode, nauseated, in the cabin. They docked at Goree Island to pick up the eleven others. They all understood exactly where they were going except Lamine. In fact, he believed they were headed to America only when they had traveled out of cell-phone range. Then he began to panic. By this time, he had come down with flulike symptoms. While many would risk losing a permanent job at home for the promise of more money abroad, Lamine was not willing to jeopardize his family's survival. But at this point, he had no choice. They were bound for New York.

The captain had estimated a twenty-five-day journey, so they had bought seemingly sufficient rice, blackeyed peas, yams for *fufu*, onions, cooking oil, dried fish, tea, and sugar. The yacht had a small stove, and they used it to prepare meals, eating two or three times a day. Most of the men were dressed in *boubou*, light cotton robes, but Modou wore a heavy jacket, and Khadim, having already experienced winter in the United States, brought along a heavy overcoat. To get them across the Atlantic, Modou relied on his knowledge of the sea along with the boat's navigation system.

Despite their preparation, the entire trip would take more than fifty days, double their initial calculations. The boat was obviously not equipped for a seafaring journey. And while it was slightly better than the small *pateras* used to smuggle Africans to Spain (a trip of five to ten days and without proper hygienic conditions), traveling in this manner posed a major health hazard, not to mention a tremendous threat to life. Lamine's body turned hot, cold, then hot again. The only medical ointment onboard was shea butter. The others rushed to cover him with the cream, then raised their hands to implore the heavens, making *dua* (supplication) for divine intervention.

"They were more worried than I was," Lamine says, smiling and lowering his head.

While they belonged to various spiritual orders, they were all brothers in faith and found themselves bound together against the constant threat of death. They also considered themselves pioneers of sorts, and they didn't want their efforts to help their families marred by the loss of a single life. About ten days later, Lamine was feeling better, but the rest of the trip was fraught with disaster.

About twenty days into the journey, they began to run out of food. They realized they would be at sea much longer and quickly rationed the remaining provisions. They ate once a day and then only enough to curb their hunger. On rare occasions, they would use a hook and dried fish to catch ocean fare. If they were successful, they would concoct Senegal's national dish, *thiebou jen.* They wished they could catch large fish, even the dolphins they watched swimming along the bow of the weather-beaten catamaran. But the sea was much too dangerous, and they feared being lost to the treacherous waters. In fact, the chance that their bodies might be lost to the sea and missing from family and friends deeply concerned them.[8] Around the same time, the boat's GPS system failed. Huge thirty-foot waves made the unit useless. During the day, Modou struggled to steer the ship west, and at night, he followed the stars.

Since they had left in the dead of winter, the frigid temperatures on the ocean were unbearable. The cabin was designed to accommodate just four people, but whenever possible, they all huddled together for warmth.

"There was always something to do, and it was just freezing, really freezing," says Laye, one of those remaining at the Detention Center. "Most times, though," he adds, "while someone slept, the others had to keep pumping water out of the boat." Laye, age twenty-seven, has completed elementary school, Islamic studies, and an apprenticeship to become a mechanic. He is Murid, but his family belongs to the Niassen, a branch of the Tijani Sufi brotherhood. At the time of the voyage, Laye had two brothers, a younger sister, a retired father, and a mother at home, and his temporary jobs, obtained by standing on street corners and waiting for sporadic work, were insufficient to support them and his distant relatives. His sacrifice was for his family and the future of his unborn children. "I would never take such a risk for myself," he says. "The captain saw we had dignity and wanted to help us."

Sometimes it rained every day, letting them capture drinking water in tea glasses as it trickled down the tattered sails. Even then, ocean storms made the trip feel as if they were on a roller coaster from hell, and salt water blended with fresh. On other days, it wouldn't rain for a while, and some were forced to consume sea water, causing their limbs to swell. The harrowing winds tore the sails continuously, and Lamine's hands were cracked and swollen from constantly having to mend them in the freezing cold. Unable to continue, he had to show others how to sew the ragged sails. Soon they could no longer be repaired. They were left with no way to capture drinking water, and they had drained their supply days ago. The sails were also their main source of power. The crushing waves wreaked havoc on the boat's spotty motor. It had only worked intermittently and needed endless repair, finally giving out about fifteen days into the trip. In addition to these mechanical problems, the men could find no rest from their daily turmoil.

"There was no room for sleep," Laye says. "Even if there was, there was so much to do at each moment and to watch out for, it was impossible."

Even death would not save them from their ordeal, especially considering that Islam deemed suicide punishable in the afterlife and dying at sea would deny them a proper burial. Besides, their families wouldn't have the closure they needed. Still, their lives hung in the balance.

"We thought we would die every day," Cherif explains. A Wolof man in his twenties, Cherif follows the Tijani spiritual order. He held a job in a gas station in Senegal, working at times twenty-four hours straight with two days off. But then he would be out of work again. It was the kind of meager existence he couldn't accept for his new wife and baby, forcing him to beg in order to feed his family.

"My life is for my family!" he yells. So he took the risk. "Every day, we think our life is finished," he says, still displaying a look of desperation. "Only God says life is not finished!"

They all prayed constantly, hanging on to life but waiting for death. Every night, they made *duas* for help and asked to be guided to shore. Sometimes this was done collectively before and after the *salah* (formal prayer), if conditions permitted. As they floated along during the night, some tried whispering intimate pleas directly into God's ear. Whenever possible, each recited his own unique Sufi *wird* (formulaic prayer) and made *thikr* (benedictions). They kept track of the days and performed weekly *jum'ah* prayers, forgoing the customary sermon.

When the engine completely failed, they decided to take a vote whether to return home or keep going. Modou appealed to his shipmates, believing it would be too dangerous to attempt a return, especially since the wind was behind them, and the tattered vessel was clearly in no shape for the trip. They agreed to stay the course. Despite it all, a major factor influencing their decision to continue was an abiding image of America as a land open to immigrants. Near the end of the journey, they had little food and no water. As their boat crept west, they struggled to hang on to life for nearly forty days. On one miraculous occasion, oranges appeared, floating on either side of the boat.

"We saw oranges, a lot, a lot," Lamine says excitedly. They reached over, each man holding himself in with one hand, grabbing the oranges with the other.

"There's no reason why we made it," Khadim says. "It was amazing!"

Fierce winds eventually pushed the boat toward Canada, but Modou refused to dock there. "We intended to go to America, and we're going to fulfill our intention!" he insisted. He pulled on the wheel rotating the rudder, and the boat slowly shifted off course.

As they traveled a day or so northward, the nights were still and opaque. Days before, they had been able to have a little light powered by a small generator, but by this time, it, too, was broken. On their final night at sea, Khadim lay awake in the cabin. A light twinkling in the distance caught his eye, and he immediately woke the others. Soon they recognized an Australian merchant ship, the Oriental Overseas Container Line (OOCL) *Melbourne*. Its crew had noticed the small boat bobbing in rough water and contacted U.S. Border Patrol. They were instructed to attempt a rescue. Still, the 770-foot vessel was unable to steer next to the crippled catamaran. The captain of the OOCL *Melbourne* intended to reel the boat in to a place where the U.S. Border Patrol and the Coast Guard could take over. They were eight hundred miles off the coast of Cape Cod, Massachusetts, and the ailing yacht was too battered to be saved. The men had to be lifted onto the ship by ropes, a rescue taking about eleven hours. The catamaran sank shortly after they were safely hoisted from it. Once on deck, the men were held in a room so their identities could be checked. Terrorism was a major concern and ruling this out was the first order of business. Despite the men's harrowing ordeal, reports indicated that they were in remarkably good shape, with only one or two needing to be hospitalized.

While the great majority of African Muslims arrive in America by much less dramatic means, this type of seafaring voyage out of Africa and into Europe is not uncommon.[9] This story demonstrates that migration involves more than the mere abandonment of poor material conditions in one country and access to better ones in another. It can just as likely be a journey infused with religious meaning, devotion to family, and a search for grandeur.[10]

II

During 2006 alone, nearly thirty thousand Africans emigrated illegally to the Spanish Canary Islands. More than half were from Senegal.[11] Such migrants endure multiple hazards, such as arduous treks on dangerous roads and through scorching deserts, rough sea voyages with barbarous *passeurs* or human traffickers, and, finally, formidable patrols on both sides of the African-Spanish border. African men from various countries make the trip, although they are occasionally joined by women. One organization Web site has reported just how desperate the quest for Europe has become. According to the story, a group of Africans were caught in Spanish Morocco as they were attempting to scale the metal wall into Spain. Just before capture, they threw a pregnant woman over, hoping that she and her unborn child would gain asylum.[12]

Starting in 1999, increased surveillance was introduced, with "the latest technology in long-distance radar systems, thermal cameras, night-viewfinders, infrared optics, helicopters and patrol boats," along with hundreds of newly hired officers.[13]

The shortest distance from Africa to Spain is about eight miles, if one travels through the narrowest point at the Strait of Gibraltar. With Europe in such close proximity, African migrants have tried to use small fishing boats, *pateras*, with the intention of sailing through the channel undetected. The new patrolling equipment has lessened their chances of success, and many have been arrested attempting illegal entry. Even on the rare occasions when these tiny boats survive the deadly waters, African expatriates sometimes die at the hands of smugglers, who may force passengers overboard to avoid being caught by authorities.

The outlay for the sophisticated surveillance is high, and the Spanish government has tried to enlist the European Union to help defray the cost. The Spanish have argued that since Spain is the first line of defense against illegal migrants entering other countries such as France or Great Britain, European nations would benefit from these new measures. Human-rights agencies and political detractors have argued against this expenditure, saying that the money would be better spent integrating African immigrants already in these countries. Both sides appear to have agreed on the need to check illegal immigration, bolstering Spain's position as guardian of the gateway to Europe. On the other side, Spanish social critics have wanted to draw more attention to those invisible, nondescript body smugglers who facilitate illegal entry in the first place.[14] Still, these approaches fail to address the migrants themselves, including both the existential difficulties they suffer and the spiritual forces they invoke along the way.

"*Barcelone aw barzakh*"—or "Barcelona or the grave!"—has become a rallying cry for African Muslims on this journey. It is a fatalistic yet powerful declaration combining the stiff realities of their material plight and the religious power they call upon. The word *barzakh* is Arabic and, according to Islamic eschatology, signifies the period in the grave when the soul waits for the day of judgment. If an individual has lived honorably, the waiting will be joyous and restful. On the other hand, if a person's life was marred by bad character and injurious behavior, the time will be agonizing.

African Muslims from various regions in West and North Africa tend to attempt to enter places such as Malta, Greece, Spain, and Italy and European territories such as the Canary Islands. Even in East Africa, thousands of Somalis die each year crossing the Gulf of Aden en route to Yemen.[15] With a major crackdown at the Spanish border, illegal migration has been redirected to the Canaries and their outer regions. This is a treacherous journey, and often fewer than half of these migrants reach their destination alive. In 2003, for example, a group of eighteen migrants left the western Sahara in a small boat, attempting to reach Europe through the Canary Islands. While the Spanish territory was sixty-seven miles away, their tiny vessel failed in rough seas, sending them adrift in the Atlantic Ocean for two weeks. Twelve drowned, and one woman and five men from Mali and Ghana survived, suffering multiple ailments including hypothermia, malnutrition, dehydration, and exhaustion.[16] In this particular case, twelve lives were lost, but when this is multiplied by the hundreds of voyages made, the Red Cross estimates that between two thousand and three thousand people die on these trips to reach Spain each year.[17] In an obvious increase from the death toll of 471 in 2007, 509 Africans died within the first ten months of 2008 trying to reach Malta and Italy, according to the U.N. High Commissioner for Refugees office.[18]

While the high death toll for these few locations (Canary Islands, Malta, and Italy) is unthinkable, adding fatality figures for the Spanish mainland and its Ceuta and Melilla enclaves, not to mention Italian islands such as Lampedusa, staggers the imagination. Because these are secret missions, countless bodies have been lost at sea, raising the toll further. And yet, despite the grim picture these numbers reveal, they miss the chilling tragedy of unspeakable horror these Africans face riding in these floating caskets many call *lothios* or "*pirogues* of death."[19] One story in the Spanish media reported the authorities finding a boat with thirty-three African survivors traumatized by a failed mission. An online news site recounted that the group "had set off a week earlier from the Moroccan port of Alhucema, but the boat's fragile motor boat broke down in rough seas." The story added, "Fifteen of the boat's occupants, including nine children aged under four, had died from hunger or thirst during the journey. The bodies of the children, rotting in the sun, were thrown overboard by their parents. One Nigerian mother, whose two children died en route, repeatedly asked Red Cross workers in Almería, 'Where are my babies?'"[20] A different disaster involved the rescue of a capsized boat off the coast of Motril in the province of Granada, as patrol teams pulled twenty-three people, including a pregnant woman, from the water. As horrifying as these stories are, the high level of risk people are willing to undertake cannot be fully explained by the lure of economic opportunities alone. Rather, the mere chance to improve the lot of their families drives them to these lengths, if they can only survive the journey.

Senegal is about 910 miles from the Canary Islands, a trip typically lasting ten days by fishing boat. These expeditions, however, cost more than the material sum paid to smuggling gangs, exacting payments between eight hundred and twelve hundred dollars for a one-way, unseaworthy slog from Senegal to the Canaries.[21] All pay an immeasurable price for the emotional and psychological damage they suffer along the way, not to mention the chronic stress of a hostile sojourn as undocumented persons, if they reach their destination at all. Under such treacherous conditions, religious faith sustains the travelers and fortifies those left behind. The Islamic idea of *barzakh* (grave), mentioned above, clarifies the meaning of life, reminding them of *qadr*, or the realization that every aspect of one's life is protected by divine destiny. They believe that Allah has preordained their *rizq* (livelihood), and they need only fulfill it through direct action. If their aspirations go unrealized, resulting in their demise, they can be certain that their return is to

Allah, finding comfort in the Qur'anic verse *"Inna lillahi wa inna elayhi raaji'un,"* or "Verily we belong to God and to God is our return."[22] This perspective clearly animates them, and it is this underpinning that sanctifies their journey.

A Senegalese migrant intent on making the journey customarily consults extended family members and asks for their prayers. This is followed by days of prayer and the blessings of one or more Muslim clerics. For someone like twenty-nine-year-old Ibrahima Seck, the benediction of his relatives and spiritual guide was perhaps more important than the resources his family garnered for his passage.[23] In fact, if he had been responsible only for his wife and two children, he would undoubtedly never consider making such a perilous voyage. Although he had been out of work for well over a year, he also had a college degree and could manage. But following the deaths of his parents, as the oldest son, he was now responsible for eight brothers, sisters, and cousins. Entire communities look to young men like Seck for adequate support. In preparation for the trip, the *marabout* or spiritual leader guides the migrant in the performance of ceremonial baths and ritual sacrifices such as charity giving.[24] This spiritual practice doesn't end in the country of origin. It continues throughout the journey and during the stay abroad.

In *We Won't Budge*, Manthia Diawara quotes his cousin Aicha, who received prayers from her *marabout* before making her trip to France. Because she was entering the country with false papers, the *cheikh* guaranteed that she'd have no problems, or he would exact no payment. "I did not pay him," Aicha said, "until I was safely here; then I sent him a thousand French francs." Explaining her divine reprieve from police harassment, she added, "He even said that whoever dared to ask me questions would have a serious misfortune fall on his head. Sure enough, only one policeman asked me a question, and even before he finished his sentence, he came down with an upset stomach and had to go to the bathroom."[25]

For seafaring migrants on *pirogues*, an interrogation by Spanish police would be a welcome fate, because it would mean they had survived a life-threatening ordeal and reached land. The few fishing boats completing the trip are so wrecked by the voyage that they must be destroyed. As the boats are lifted from the quayside for crushing, Arabic messages and prayers painted on the boats' hulls disappear with them. For some, however, international newspaper photos of these Islamic markings signal a safe arrival to family members scouring daily headlines back home.[26] The Islamic symbols traveling with economic migrants and the remittances relatives later receive create a religious circuit linking destinations with hometowns. As a household strategy, African migrants from Muslim families travel with more than material possessions. Crucial to their identity as new migrants is a new sense of knowing, a deep understanding that they are embedded within a continuous flow of spiritual resources in the form of prayers, incantations, and benedictions. As illustrated above, it was difficult for Lamine to understand how

Modou could talk about making any type of long-distance trip before *eid al-kabir*, a time when family support and spiritual blessings would be paramount.

Even those with good jobs fear losing them, realizing full well that finding another would be extremely difficult. Fifteen years ago, Moustafa faced a similar dilemma. He was born in a small village two hours outside Dakar, Senegal's capital city of two million people. At an early age, he was sent some distance away to live with his uncle so he could obtain a formal education in Ndar, also known as Saint-Louis. Later, he moved to Dakar to complete secondary school and college.

"If you lose your job in Senegal," Moustafa recounts, "it is very, very hard to find another one. So, it's just like, when you lose a job, people are going to go and pray for you. Because I see some people, they lose their jobs, and after ten years they couldn't find anything. So, if somebody loses his job in one family, everybody cries!" In such a harsh job market, his position with an airline company was a windfall. Just to apply for the job, 160 people took the exam, and he was one of four chosen. The salary was decent, and with flying privileges, he was able to visit a few European countries. But eventually, the day everyone dreaded came. Moustafa was called in for an unscheduled talk with his supervisors.

"It was one Thursday around twelve o'clock. I was told to come to the main office. When I get there, I see a couple of delegates and my direct boss and the director of my section. We were like five people in the department, and I was hired as the fifth one. They were all sitting and told me to have a seat." They explained that the company had filed for bankruptcy and they were downsizing. Since he was the last one hired, he had to be the first to go. Being the youngest and being single also worked against him, even though two-thirds of his salary went to a large family in another city.

"This is not fair!" Moustafa says he thought at the time. "Because I'm the youngest? I'm taking care of all my relatives, and my family is even larger than the family of my boss. So, why me?" It wasn't atypical for a young Senegalese man to be the only one working in a family of twenty to fifty people. But now he had to send home his younger brother, who had been living with him in Dakar, and fire the housekeeper, a middle-aged woman he supported out of kindness more than anything else.

Moustafa remembers that he stood up from the rickety chair, his face full of disbelief. "OK, it's fine" barely escaped his mouth, but he had stopped listening to his boss some time before.

"No, it's not," his supervisor said, "because we love you."

"I left the office and walked outside," Moustafa recalls. "I was, like, 'Wow!' This is the end of my life. My life is over. This is like the day of judgment." He began walking, veering off the pathway and into the street. The ocean waves crashing against the rocks steadily overtook the city chatter. He walked toward a boulder. After climbing on top, he removed his jacket and stared at the Atlantic Ocean, watching how the horizon met the sea at what appeared to be the ends of the earth. As he relaxed, his thoughts slowed just a bit. "What's on the other side," he thought. "Do I have to go, take the risk? And what will my parents do?" Although the bankrupted airline offered laid-off employees a few years' compensation, unemployment in Senegal was a frightening thought. And Moustafa, a well-educated man in his mid-thirties with administrative experience, knew the prospects were just as bad for him as they were for unskilled, uneducated job seekers.

Most African Muslims blame corrupt politicians for a lackluster economy, and they claim that many jobs are acquired through a system of blatant nepotism and special concessions doled out to friends. Many survive by upholding the religious value of *khidma* (service). With a Muslim population of about ninety-five percent, Senegal constitutes an intriguing mixture of both Islamic and African cultural values. This is not to romanticize Islam or African lifeways as unified entities reducible to a few tenets or customs. But it is important to illustrate specific points where religion and ethnic practice meet. In this case, the Islamic concept of *khidma*, a central value within Muridiyya and other African Sufi orders, underscores the need to perpetuate the common good within African societies, a sense of responsibility for oneself and service to others.

"It's a country where people believe," Moustafa says. "There are a lot of believers. And they're living well," he adds, leaving me curious, given the current state of the job market.

"They're living well?" I interject. "How would you describe that?"

"The problem is the economy," he replies. "It's a country that is seventy-five percent peasants. They're farmers. But it's a poor country because we don't have oil. We don't have a lot of resources like in Ivory Coast or in Nigeria. But it's a country where people help a lot. And you don't feel the poverty. You can see inside the country—on the south, on the north—you can see people, you know they're very poor, but you cannot feel it. I can say there is no homelessness in Senegal. Yep, no matter where you are and no matter where you go, if you see a person sleeping in the street, he is mentally sick."

As I listen to Moustafa describe a culture of mutual assistance, a necessary mechanism for assuaging the pangs of poverty in his impoverished nation, I wonder about poor towns such as Thiaroye, an old fishermen's village on the outskirts of Dakar with forty-five thousand inhabitants.[27] Senegalese fishermen claim that they have been devastated by their country's endorsement of the Fisheries Partnership Agreement, an accord granting European and American ships unrestricted access to Senegal's waterways. Many argue that European trawlers, massive ships used for commercial fishing, ravage the area and undermine the ability of local fishermen to compete. Instead, many have turned their fishing boats into migration vessels, a type of water taxi for moving human cargo to the Western world.

"So, you have a real extended family, where the community embraces one another and takes care of one another?" I ask.

"Yes," Moustafa replies. "People help each other a lot."

But I still wonder just how this concept operates, especially as it relates to poverty and homelessness in a place like Senegal.

"OK," I say. "Let's say someone visits a town in Senegal. Is there a general sense that even the stranger must have a home, that he or she must be attached to a family?"

"You can do that even yourself," Moustafa says. "You don't need anybody to tell you. Like, right now, if you want to go to Senegal, you see somebody you think you can trust, you go to him and say, 'OK, I'm an American. This is the first time I come to Senegal, but I just don't want to go to hotels. Right there, you have somebody who's going to take you to his house and give you everything. They're going to share."

"Do you have an example of how this works?" I ask.

"I remember one day, I was like fifteen years old," he says. "I was in Diourbel, my hometown, on summer vacation. One guy came after *maghrib* [evening prayer] and greeted my dad. They finish praying, and they talk a little bit. He said he was traveling, but the last bus going to Dakar left already. And he said he needed a place to stay until tomorrow. And this was the first time we saw this guy. My dad tell him, 'You're home! You can stay!' My mom brought him food. And later, my dad called me and said, 'Go sleep with your brother in the other room. Your room is going to be for this guy.'"

"That's quite amazing," I say.

"Yeah, and in the morning," Moustafa says, "he woke up, prayed with my dad, ate breakfast, and my dad accompanied him to the garage to take the bus. That happens a lot."

This conversation about *khidma* as an Islamic value and coping mechanism within village life speaks to how many African Muslims understand their civic and religious duty. While these stories abound—and more than a few Western visitors to Senegal have verified them—what matters most is how a value like *khidma* is incorporated into Harlem society. What does it mean in that space? To what uses is it put and why? Abdoulaye, a Senegalese tailor living in Harlem, feels it's important to recognize the line separating culture from religion. On one occasion, I ask him a general question about how African Muslims in America get along.

"Yes, yes," he begins. "They know Islam, and they try to be united. If anybody has a problem, they help them together. That's the Muslim way."

"So, Islam teaches you to be united?" I ask.

"The Muslims are supposed to be united," he replies. "That's the Prophet Muhammad's saying. All Muslims have to help, together—what I have, you want it, I have to give to you."

"Do you see that happening?" I say.

"Yes, now they cook together," Abdoulaye replies. "That's the African way. That's not Muslim," he says, looking at me sternly. "What I do is not just Muslim, that's our culture. You go to Senegal, you can eat or sleep at anybody's house. That's not religious. That's Africa. It has nothing to do with religion."

In this sense, the common good is not merely a religious dictate but also a cultural imperative. In other words, Islam animates these cultures at very specific times, providing a religious dimension to their cultural or ethnic lifeways.

For many countries in the developing world, people seem to fit into one of two social categories. The growing majority are perpetually poor, while fewer are moderately well off. A thriving middle tier is virtually absent. Under corrupt regimes and foreign regulations taxing local economies, such as Structural Adjustment Programs, it is a common assumption that the poor in Africa will remain so for the rest of their lives.[28] Even worse, the absence of either governmental or private investment packages for aging parents and relatives undermines the upward mobility of aspiring youth, whose enthusiasm for something better and meager resources wither under their responsibility to care for multiple households. Still, their sense of familial duty is more than a worldly obligation to kin. For many, their love and respect for family are a sign of Allah's mercy. In the Qur'an, a major attribute of God derives from the root word ra-hi-ma, a verb connoting mercy. In the basmala, the phrase beginning each chapter of the Qur'an, Allah is described with two forms of mercy: ar-rahman and ar-raheem.[29] The first refers to an all-embracing mercy, a kind of life-sustaining benevolence extended to all things. The latter, ar-raheem, denotes another aspect of mercy. This is a type of divine compassion inspiring personal growth and spiritual enlightenment. More to the point, both forms of benevolence share their root with the word rahim (womb), our mutual birthplace. This implies that Allah's mercy is best revealed through a genuine concern for the human condition, beginning with those closest to us.[30]

Being a dutiful Muslim and tending to relatives and poor members of the community do not always fall on the shoulders of young men. Conscientious Muslim girls also aspire to ease the burdens of their needy parents and friends. Born in the city of Dakar, Khady's father passed away when she was just a year old. "They loved each other dearly," Khady says of her parents. But her father's untimely death left her mother an impoverished widow with eight children. According to Senegalese custom, Khady's uncle was expected to look after the family. But his international business ventures prevented this, as he eventually relocated to Paris. Her mother soon remarried, giving Khady and her seven siblings a new stepfather and several half-brothers and -sisters. The decision was made to send Khady to live with her grandfather, a relatively affluent airport employee and construction worker. As she became acquainted with her new surroundings, Khady befriended her neighbor Sophie, a Senegalese Catholic. They shared many things, but most significant was that both of their fathers had died. This deepened their friendship. If nothing else, they both understood paternal longing, and they needed each other. Children taunted them for losing their fathers, compelling them to skip school at times.

For African housewives, the premature death of a husband often means immediate destitution, unless she manages to have a marketplace business or a wide support network. "I felt really sorry for her," Khady says of Sophie. "She had nothing, and her mother couldn't rest. So, I found a way for her mother to sleep at night." Because Sophie's oldest sister had received a partial scholarship to study in France, her mother struggled to send her money abroad. Khady had been helping Sophie's family, sneaking food to them when she could. But now she had another strategy.

"I took Sophie to live with me," Khady explains, although she was just a youngster herself of about nine or ten. "I told my grandfather, 'Listen, my girlfriend came from Paris for vacation. Can she stay with us for a while, because her mother, she don't have much? She's my girlfriend, and I have a whole room to myself.'"

Khady was one of eight girls living in her grandfather's house, a three-story building with space enough for each to have her own room. A devout Muslim, her grandfather agreed, as long as there would be "no smoking or drinking," something Khady quickly guaranteed wouldn't happen. Her grandfather admired Sophie's meek manner. "And she was in the family," Khady says, smiling proudly. "She lived with me for three years." In traditional societies, where the division of labor is typically split between men as breadwinners and women as housekeepers, African Muslim women could participate in *khidma* and perpetuate the common good by manipulating household resources. In Khady's case, she managed to appropriate her grandfather's means in order to extend a tremendous measure of compassion and service to her neighbors, despite her young age.

Sophie's mother always told Khady that God would reward her one day. When Sophie's older sister finished school in Paris, she met and married a young American and had two children soon after. They moved to the United States, where her husband was a lawyer, while she struggled to get her medical license. As the toddlers grew, she called her mother for advice. They decided they would ask Khady to take a full-time job caring for the children in the United States. It would pay well, she'd have her own quarters, and they would even hire a maid, saving her from any other household chores. Khady would have full access to the house, not as a worker but as a respected and loved member of the family. It was the least they could offer her for all of her kindness. Khady was just thirteen and needed her mother's approval, but it was the opportunity she wanted.

"I used to feel sorry for my mother," Khady says, lowering her eyes and staring stoically. "Because I was seeing a woman with seven children . . ." She pauses and thinks. "So, I never liked to hang out. I always have to work. It's all I think of, work,

work. That's why my education, well, I really don't have much, because when I was young, I was thinking, 'Oh, I cannot go to school. I have to just work to help her.' And I stopped school and I start working. I used to go to my neighbors or tell my mommy's friends, 'If you want to go to the party, you want to go to church, to a wedding, I keep the kids so you can pay me something—give my mother something for her to provide for us.'"

One of Khady's uncles sent money to her mother from time to time, but the challenge of overcoming poverty with many children was difficult. "Let me go!" Khady begged her mother. "I can make money and send it to you." Hearing these compassionate words from her teenage daughter, the mother broke down crying.

In those days, the early 1970s, few continental Africans were living in the United States, and not much was known about life in America. Most traveled to either France or England, since they were the primary colonizers in West Africa. "Today," Khady says, "you don't even have to pay someone to go to the United States. They will just go." But during that time, her request was unimaginable.

"Why should I let you go?" Khady's mother said. "You're just a young girl, and I don't even know this place."

Khady said, "Well, I don't know where the place is, but if you pray five times a day, you should believe Allah is everywhere. And who is going to take care of you if Uncle dies?"

With tears in her eyes, Khady's mother was overcome with her daughter's concern.

"Mom, I just want to go to make you happy," Khady said to her mother. "I want you to go to Mecca. I want to build you a house. And I want you to have nice things."

"And I did!" Khady boasts today, her face humbly beaming. "It was my dream to take care of my mother and brothers and sisters. I came here [to the United States], worked, built a house, and she went to Mecca in 1982."

Like the African migrants Paul Stoller describes in his striking ethnography *Money Has No Smell*, industrious African Muslim women like Khady became "travelers [who] dreamed of economic adventure and fashioned themselves as jaguars—young, solitary, sleek, adaptable, knowledgeable, and daring."[31] The anecdotal accounts from African men and women such as Moustafa and Khady are revealing but not for the obvious reasons. In other words, the recollections of their early life in Senegal, the details of their stories, matter less than the meanings they draw from them. Not only do these narratives speak volumes about how they imagine home, but they also provide clues about how these images shape their identities in the diaspora, including what still matters to them and in what contexts. As they struggle to find their way in Harlem and other places, the notion of an extended family, which often includes fictive kin, remains crucial, especially as *khidma* is employed to cement bonds across ethnic lines or, as Khady's story illustrates, between Muslims and Christians. Still, it is only one of many elements needed to navigate the meaning of their presence in America.

III

The Murid celebration of the Grand Magal takes place in Touba, Senegal, and it marks the anniversary of Cheikh Amadou Bamba's exile by the French colonial government. In 1895, Bamba was deported to Gabon by European officials until 1902, because they feared his growing popularity as a Muslim cleric would undermine their authority. He was later exiled to Mauritania from 1903 until 1907 and, finally, to a remote area of Senegal, before being permitted to return in 1910. His deportation, however, produced unanticipated results. In exile, he wrote volumes of religious treatises, and legends spread about his nonviolent defiance of colonial rule, including how he survived torture, deprivation, and assassination, which quickly expanded his following and transformed him into a saint.[32] Today, thousands of Senegalese abroad return home to commemorate the event. Those who cannot make the pilgrimage celebrate in their places of settlement, such as New York. In honor of Bamba's exile, Murids in Harlem perform personal and collective acts of worship throughout the day—making *thikr* (recitations), reciting the Qur'an, chanting Bamba's *khassaïd* (religious poetry), or performing special *duas* (supplication). The real celebration doesn't start until much later, at twelve or one the next morning, and lasts until about five. Until this time, most perform religious rites in their shops, while driving in cabs, or at home. Murids who are not working will go to Masjid Touba on 137th and Edgecombe.

On the appointed day, I meet Abdoulaye at L'Association des Sénégalais d'Amérique. He serves as chairman of the African and African American Relations Committee at Masjid Touba, and we have planned to walk to Masjid Malcolm Shabazz together for the festivities. Masjid Touba often rents space at the much larger Shabazz for big events. L'Association is a home away from home for Abdoulaye and countless others, a place where he spends many hours strategizing and organizing events for Africans and Black residents.

I reach the office doors, with their French-style brown-stained wooden crossings, and peek in. Abdou, an official, is sitting on a bar stool at the counter to the left of the entrance.

"*As-salaamu 'alaykum,*" I say, opening the doors.

"*Çava? Wa 'alaykum salaam, çava bien?*" Abdou replies. He squints as he tries to bring my face into focus. After a brief pause, he says, "Oh, how are you? I haven't seen you in a while," and his eyes drift back to the *African Sun Times*.

Before I can tell him I'm looking for Abdoulaye, I spot him sitting on a couch against the right wall. The association office teems with people. Free African newspapers litter the tables, along with flyers and pamphlets advertising all sorts of services for African immigrants, such as special health-care benefits and translation assistance. In a space just twenty-five by seventy feet, parts are sectioned off for computer classes and English lessons.

"Heeey!" Abdoulaye yells.

He rises to meet me, and we embrace. I notice a large poster on the wall above where he was sitting, advertising a beachfront housing development in Dakar. As I admire the colorful drawing of housing units with ocean views, Abdoulaye begins talking about his former life in Senegal.

"People called me American," he says with a huge grin. "I used to have Afro, wear bell-bottom pants. I make my own bell-bottom pants, and belt tight like Jimi Hendrix. I bring my customers, and I make them bell-bottom pants."

"What about African styles? Do you make African clothes, too?" I ask.

"Yes, but I love to dress like African American," he replies. "I want to be African American!" he says, and his eyes widen with enthusiasm. "I want to come to Harlem to hang out together. That's my dream," he says, then pauses. "I used to wear the Afro. I used to glue my hair, that's why I have Afro."

"Oh, you had a wig?" I ask.

"No," he answers. "I used to go to the barber shop to get the hair, because my hair too soft. I get the African glue to glue my hair. At that time, no wig. Maybe they have it, but it not come to Africa," he explains. "Anytime African Americans do something, when Africans see me, he say, 'That's your people!'"

Others adopt different aspects of African American culture. Cheikh, a Senegalese in his mid-forties, watched his brothers and cousins in Senegal pretend to be members of the Black Panther Party, and he'd join them in wearing the clothes.

"When I was very young," he explains, "my older brothers, they used to come with the hat and put it on one side, and one glove, and say they represent the Black Panthers."

"You learned about that?" I ask.

"Yeah, in school," he answers. "They tried to explain it. I don't understand anything, but when I go out with my beret, I'd say, 'Yeah, I'm a Black Panther!' For me, they were just fighting for the rights of Black people in America."

Many African Muslims have shifted their focus from opposing colonialism to fighting racism. In his *In Search of Africa*, Manthia Diawara discusses how the mimicry of Black popular culture was a very powerful part of 1960s youth culture in his home country of Mali. The symbols of Black life and culture were believed to transform them mysteriously into African Americans. They even pretended that they did not speak French.[33]

Abdoulaye Thiam, in *boubou* robe, instructs young computer users at L'Association des Sénégalais d'Amérique, the Senegalese Association of America. (Photo Sharjeel Kashmir)

As Abdoulaye finishes his story, we walk out and begin making our way down the street. In Senegal, especially in the early 1960s, Abdoulaye didn't have much access to American television. His main sources of Black American culture were the stories told by his uncle (a World War II veteran) and the occasional movie but mostly music. As we talk, he slows down and turns toward me.

"Jimi Hendrix, Jimmy Cliff. That's what I buy every month," he says. "A forty-five and a thirty-three [vinyl records]. I would listen to them all the time. And I loved Jimi Hendrix! I have Senegalese money, forty-five dollars, and spend all of it on records. People say, 'You're American!'"

By the time Abdoulaye met African American tourists and famous Black musicians in the early 1970s, his uncle had already instilled in him a sense of Black pride. The uncle told Abdoulaye how he learned about the transatlantic slave trade from his grandparents. He was taught how Africans were captured and brought to the Americas, but he didn't know much more. While he was a soldier in Germany, Abdoulaye's uncle discovered Black Americans and demanded that White officers release them, allowing them to return to their original homeland. Needless to say, his request was denied. But stories like these told to young Africans during the '50s and '60s fueled their imaginations about America and Black people. For Abdoulaye, these tales fostered a bond between him and Black Americans.

We reach Adam Clayton Powell Boulevard and wait for the light to change. It's after eleven o'clock at night, and holding a religious event at this hour seems strange to me. I'm always stunned to hear how late Murid celebrations begin. The flyer stated that this particular affair would begin at eight and last until five in the morning. Earlier in the day, I called Abdoulaye to check on the time for the event.

"What time should I get there? It starts at eight," I asked. "I guess nine or so would be good, huh?"

"About twelve or one!," he shot back.

"What? One o'clock! Are you serious?"

His voice remained unchanged. "Yeah, about one o'clock."

Most Islamic programs in the United States end shortly after or even before *isha* prayer, generally at nine o'clock in summer and at six in winter. Most reserve the rest of the night for sleep until *fajr* (dawn prayer) or perhaps a break in the night for *tahajjud*, a special kind of devotion performed between midnight and daybreak. In Harlem, West African Muslim communities have adapted their practices to fit the demands of their never-ending work schedules. As they reach for the American dream, they are attracted to the opportunity to have two or three jobs, even while attending college.

We cross the street and walk down to the *masjid* entrance. Cheikh is standing at the door, dressed in a long white *boubou* with gold trim. We greet, and I ask him about Aminata, a mutual friend from Senegal.

"Oh, she was working," he says. "But she went home to prepare for tonight. She should be here soon."

"Working this late?" I ask. "What kind of work does she do?"

"She's a home health aid worker," he replies. "She also works at some agency. I'm not sure where."

Aminata had secretarial training in Senegal and worked in a large company there. In America, she was forced to reinvent herself and, like many newly arrived immigrants from Francophone West Africa, had to begin from a much lower position on the socioeconomic ladder. Cheikh anticipates my curiosity about Aminata's work schedule.

"You see," Cheikh says, "in Senegal, you work, and for a family of fifteen or twenty people, you have only two hundred dollars a month, because over there, they pay monthly. It's very hard. When they tell you, 'Oh, in America, it's very easy to have like five hundred dollars a week.' It's worth it; even if you were working over there in a suit and a tie and in an office with AC and things like that, you're going to leave [for America]. Why have two hundred dollars a month, give your family one hundred dollars a month, when you can give them the whole two hundred dollars and keep two hundred dollars in savings and live well in America. Why not go to a place where you can have six hundred dollars to a thousand a month?"

Given this scenario, it's not difficult to see how continental Africans dream of coming to the United States. And it would certainly be a dream if it were in fact so easy for them to earn that kind of money. But the hard work it takes to realize that dream is invisible. With countries such as Senegal and Côte d'Ivoire receiving millions of dollars in remittances, significantly augmenting their GNPs, would-be migrants will have a difficult time believing their economic dreams could not be fulfilled in America.[34] Many African Muslims talk about watching internationally syndicated television shows such as *Dynasty* and *Dallas*, which portray lavish American lifestyles, giving them the idea that life in America is simple and trouble-free. For younger Africans, rap videos fill their imaginations with what they believe is possible in the United States. Unlike in Abdoulaye's time, Africans migrating to the United States during the past two decades often arrive full of fantastic notions about what they will find. Because their economic prospects are so dire, commercial films such as *Coming to America* portray positive Black images, giving them a measure of hope, even if it is highly romanticized. The desire to believe in a world strong enough to lift them from despair is so strong, as several Africans explain, that some believed that Americans could even float. This kind of imagining represents an intriguing paradox, since the notion of flying as a way to escape oppression was envisioned by enslaved Africans yearning to return home.[35]

Cheikh and I continue talking for a few more minutes. At twelve forty-five in the morning, the night stands as a perfect backdrop against pastel gowns emerging out of limousines and moving swiftly into the building. Senegalese men and women strolling toward the *masjid* appear to float along the walkway, their feet hidden under the drapes of their long robes. Everything feels so free at this late hour—as if the city has surrendered itself to the sacredness of the occasion. Every once in a while, a car appears, slowly moving up or down the street. It's going to be a long night, and I want to check nearby restaurants for closing times, just in case I miss the food at the celebration. I've attended these events in the past and figure this is a good strategy. I walk into the Blues Café and extend greetings. A young woman in her twenties and a tall, thin teenage boy dressed in a white African robe walk over to greet me. I notice a man with a white *boubou* sitting with a plate of grilled lamb over a mound of white rice. He lifts his eyes carefully, looking in my direction, but quickly diverts them to gaze out the window.

"What time do you close?" I ask.

"Oh, we stay open late," the young man replies. "Yeah," he says, looking into space, pausing to think. And then he announces, "Three o'clock! Yeah, three o'clock!" Not only are these late hours good for business during the all-night vigils, but they also provide a valuable service by catering to those with irregular work schedules.

As I prepare to leave, Aminata walks in, dressed in a shiny, peach-colored dress with a matching headwrap.

"You made it!" I say. "How was work?"

"*Al-hamdu lillah* [praise God], it was fine. How are you and your family?" she asks, smiling graciously.

Aminata, in her mid-forties, is married to Samba, a Senegalese street merchant in his early fifties. They have four children and are making plans to return to Senegal as soon as they can save enough money. As we talk, I think about Khady and how she worked hard on menial jobs to purchase a house for her mother.

"How are things back home?" I ask.

"Good," Aminata replies. "We built a house for my children, and we are working on another."

Besides the film and television images Africans consume about life in the United States, the most powerful symbol of American rewards is the conspicuous display of material success reaped from remittances.

Aminata places a takeout order of *thiebou yap* (lamb with cabbage, carrots, cassava, and red broken rice), and Samba joins us. He hears our conversation about life in America for Senegalese migrants and begins to reminisce.

"When I was home," Samba says, "I see people go to America for like two or three years. They come back to my country, and they're driving nice cars, they build houses for their parents, having all these luxury things. You might even see a friend who was in school, and he was even behind you in class, you were better than him. He comes back, and he's driving a Mercedes or a Hummer, building a two-story house, two floors, getting married, spending lots of money, gold and things. All because he left the country!" He speaks loudly. "I say, 'Whoa! It must be true what they say about America. I'm here working in the company. Everybody envies me, like, oh, he's working at this big company'. But I couldn't buy a little land. I said to myself, 'Maybe that's the place I have to go.'"

American currency has maintained a high rate of exchange in West African countries. Combined with the low cost of living in places like Senegal, this makes it much easier to purchase homes. Unlike in the United States, land is not expensive, and there are generally no property taxes. Mortgages are also virtually nonexistent, especially when, for example, one can build a modern three-story house in West Africa for fifty thousand dollars. The same structure would cost many times that in America. With the influx of foreign home buyers, some of this is beginning to change, and the costs are escalating. Mortgages are even becoming prevalent in Ghana. By the same token, a greater increase of West African immigrants in the United States means that their earning potential will be severely challenged, especially as they vie with their countrymen and other immigrants for the same jobs. While the recent instability of the American dollar has caused some to reconsider their stay in the United States, there is no indication that this will alter their view of the American dream or their strategy for becoming successful here.

Aminata pays for her food and grabs the plastic bag, and we all walk out together. She appears still to be thinking about our conversation. "Ya know," she says, squinting her eyes and looking across the street at Shabazz, "we used to think this was the best place on earth. Yep, in Senegal, when you see kids even playing in the street, most of them they call themselves American. They call you 'Cana.' I guess it comes from 'Americana.' If you do something good, if you try to look good, they say, 'Oh, yeah, you're a Cana, you're an American. Yeah, because we just love America so much. And people, they take American names like James Brown, Michael Jackson, or 50 Cent," she admits. "You can see even now if you go. When I was there, you walk in the street in Dakar, you see people dressed up like 50 Cent [the rapper]. We used to learn about slavery, and I knew I had blood over here. When I was coming here, I was, like, 'I'm going to see my people, my cousins, I never met. Part of my blood is here in America. I love it so much. So, when I get here, I was like, 'Oh, wow, I'm in heaven.'"

Manthia Diawara writes about trying to imagine what life was like for Black people in America. He remembers stories he was told about "a land of wealth and prosperity, where even the poorest had toilets, showers, and bathtubs in their ghetto houses."[36] He muses about the American women he has seen in movies. America is the place where "a black woman could transform herself into white, Chinese, or Indian if she liked," as evidenced by African American models on glossy magazine covers.[37]

The night grows later, and I see a crowd gathering in front of the *masjid*. Aminata, Samba, and I cross the street, enter through the front doors, and proceed past the security desk. We extend our farewells and promise to continue our talk later. As I ponder their words and consider the image they had of America before their arrival, I think more about the role these portrayals play in the lives of West African Muslims in Harlem. While Aminata's depiction appeared to be consistent with other stories I've heard, even from immigrants from other African countries, I wonder how this particular way of imagining America affected their strategies for migration and then settlement, especially after discovering that things were drastically different.

One evening in May, I am asked to give a talk at Masjid Aqsa about my research. It is an invitation I am reluctant to accept, because I am still in the early stages of gathering data and not prepared to make any conclusions. An ethnographic project such as this is a path of discovery, possibly revealing snippets of insight along the way. But I feel obligated to return their kindness, as they have tolerated my constant presence and nagging questions about their dreams and fears. I decide to give a brief talk on the early presence of African Muslims in the Americas.[38] It will expose the community to new ideas about its historic relationship to the country and allow me to discuss the contemporary relevance of my work.

On the evening of the talk, I sit on the carpet in Masjid Aqsa, waiting for the arrival of Imam Soulaymane Konate. The building's double glass doors and office balcony betray its former life as a furniture store. People sit around, reading the Qur'an or performing *sunnah*, voluntary prayers before *maghrib*. A few perform *wudu* in the washroom downstairs. I don't see Konate, but I figure he'll show up soon. A full-time cleric, he's never too far away. Several minutes later, he walks through the door, his orange and black-and-white print African robe fluttering against his body. He walks swiftly, shaking hands on his left and right, listening to people who stop him with requests every few steps. With eyes cast downward, he grimaces as usual. But he finally breaks free and scurries to his balcony office at the rear of the *masjid*.

Konate's workplace strikes an interesting contrast to the office of Imam Bassirou Lo, the imam at Masjid Touba. Newspaper clippings relating to African Muslims adorn the wall, and two framed pictures are on Konate's desk. In one, he poses with a wide smile next to a government official. He wears similar clothing in both but

Imam Soulaymane Konate in his balcony office at Masjid Aqsa. (Photo Zain Abdullah)

stands alone in the second with an all-white outfit—a thick turban, laced *jalabiyya*, and an overcoat—while holding a wooden cane. Lo's office, in contrast, is replete with well-placed pictures and flyers, each reflecting some aspect of Murid belief and practice. In certain respects, the iconography in their offices speaks volumes about the distinct roles they play in their communities and the larger society. While Konate certainly addresses a range of religious issues for his congregants, his role as a public figure and community advocate is paramount. Lo, however, is much more of a spiritual advisor, a clerical task he is afforded due to the work of social-service and political associations within the Murid order.

Konate returns from his office and leads several hundred people in prayer. Abou approaches me to see if I am ready for the talk. Abou is in his late forties and from Côte d'Ivoire. Before coming to the United States in 1989, he graduated from a local college, then taught high school English for four years. Since his arrival, he has held different jobs, often more than one at a time, while attending college. Several years ago, he managed to complete another undergraduate degree in finance and economics from Baruch College. It was Abou who arranged the lecture. I get up, and he escorts me to a chair in front, then hands me a microphone.

"What's the title of your lecture?" he asks, while leaning toward me. It is a good question, but I haven't thought about it, especially since we haven't talked for more than a month.

"Ah, just tell them it's on West African Muslims in Harlem," I reply. I have jotted down a few notes, and I have prepared a series of enlarged pictures of enslaved African Muslims from the early eighteenth and nineteenth centuries. I punctuate my talk with photographic posters of Ayuba Suleiman Ibrahima Diallo of Maryland in 1730, Omar ibn Said of North Carolina in 1807, Yarrow Mamout in Washington, D.C., in 1819, and Abdul Rahman of Mississippi in 1828.[39] With the women behind a sheer curtain in the rear, the men sit on the carpet in front and jerk with excitement after viewing each display. As I mention their towns of origin, places such as Timbo, Futa Jallon, and Futa Toro, the audience is visibly intrigued, yelling out these locations almost before I can speak them. They are astounded by copies of the original Arabic works written by enslaved Africans. I end my talk by mentioning the dehumanization of Africans during slavery, a process that included the stripping away of native languages and ancestral names. Out of this degradation, however, early Africans managed to forge new identities and reinvent their traditions.

Following the talk, people rush up to shake my hand. An elder walks up, grabs my hand, and, with a slight smile, peers into my eyes. I attempt to rise for a show of respect, but he gently pushes me back into my seat. I'm finally able to stand, and I see a man in his early thirties slowly walking toward me. His hands mimic signs of explosion on both sides of his head. Sekou, an itinerant merchant from Guinea, has been moving between the United States and his hometown for many years.

"You talk really made me think," he says in broken English. "I had never thought of it that way before. Just a little light can do a lot," he says, then repeats it a few times. He explains how the information presented in the talk forced him to see himself and the community differently.

Shortly after my conversation with Sekou, I gather my things and walk outside. A few Africans stand on the sidewalk by the curb, discussing my talk, while some lean against parked cars. Another person sits in a white plastic chair, leaning back to lift the front legs from the ground. Omar, an Ivoirian barber in one of the nearby salons, sees me as I walk over to greet him. At the same time, Ibrahim walks up. He's from Mali and teaches Arabic and Islamic studies at the *masjid*.

"Hey," Omar bellows, as he turns to face the others. "You should have heard this brother inside! He was throwin' down, telling it like it is, man."

They look at me curiously.

"He was talking about Africans here a long time ago," Omar says, spinning his body around to address all of them. "Man, he was breaking it down! I'm telling you!" I know Omar is cosmopolitan, with his trendy clothes and Bohemian manner. But I have never heard him use Black English before.

My talk seems to have met two inherent needs of this community. First, it addressed their concerns about the lack of an Islamic tradition or viable culture in America. While many admire the United States for what they believe are its riches and promise of material success, few believe that Americans are God-fearing people.

"Before I come to America," Moussa, a Muslim immigrant from Côte d'Ivoire, said to me on one occasion, "people tell me nobody believes in God here. I come here and find lots of churches, lots of mosques. That's not true!"

The early history of African Muslims in this country links them to an Islamic tradition stemming back to the nation's founding. In this sense, it validates their religious practice and legitimizes their sojourn in America. In other words, the shame some feel for spending so much of their time in a non-Muslim country can be refuted, in part, because of this early Islamic presence. This type of history also rewrites their saga in America, bringing them closer to African Americans. Not only do they share a racial category and an ancestral link with Black Americans, but now their connection could quite possibly extend to an Islamic heritage. For many, this gives them a new sense of belonging in what has sometimes been considered a hostile environment.

As we stand outside talking, Abou emerges from the *masjid* and joins us. The others leave, but Abou and I continue the conversation.

"How do you think Muslims back home feel about America?" I ask. "And how do you think they feel about Black Americans?"

"Well," Abou answers, "their concern is not black and white. Their concern is, are they going to practice their religion there? Because the first people who went to France came back and said, 'Oh, if you don't drink alcohol when it gets cold over there, you'll die. So they have that negative attitude, when you say you're going to any White country."

"They think you're going to lose your religion?" I ask.

"Yeah, that's the concern of our parents when I came over here. But after I came here, we start making *salatul-taraweeh* [Ramadan prayers], and we sent the video cassette back home. Before that, a lot of parents didn't want to send anyone over here."

"When was that?" I ask.

"In '89 or '90," he replies. "That's the year we started having *layla al-qadr* [special Ramadan night prayer]. It was almost a dozen of us—maybe eight brothers and one brother's wife. In the fifth year, we brought Cheikh Foufahna. He's a big *cheikh* in the whole of Ivory Coast right now. We video-recorded him with us, reciting and preaching. And when people saw him with us, they now believed it was not something fabricated, because they know the *cheikh* will never falsify something."

"And so African Muslims began to send their relatives here?" I ask.

"Yeah," he answers. "They were refusing because they thought they were going to lose their religion. Now they realize they can practice Islam in America. That's why from 1993 till now, it's a million Ivoirians coming over here."

While the danger of losing one's faith does not affect the migration decisions of all Muslims from Côte d'Ivoire, it certainly speaks to the fact that the decision to migrate to another country is based on more than the mere calculation of material gain. For many, the retention of one's religious belief and practice is just as important, if not more so, than the acquisition of wealth. In this regard, the "good life," or real success, for these African Muslims means availing themselves of America's economic opportunities without sacrificing their Islamic sensibilities. This perspective belies the notion that the sole preoccupation of all African immigrants is earning money. I am not suggesting that African Muslims adhere to some transcendental practice of Islam, either before or after migration. Islam plays various roles in their complex lives. While some attend the different African *masjids* seeking spiritual awareness and redemption, others come solely for the ethnic and social camaraderie.

I had commissioned an African American Muslim, Fatima, to take pictures of the event to document the occasion. I walk toward the main entrance of the *masjid*, stopping to peer through the door Muslim women use to enter the *musalla* (main prayer area). A six-foot wooden shoe rack partitions off the women's area. Green curtains hang on a cord from the end of rack to the far wall, totally enclosing the section from the front. During well-attended programs, the curtains are usually drawn. At other times, they might remain open. As I stand outside, straining to look through the door, I see Hadjjah Raissa staring at me. Since Fatima arrived late, I was unable to give her the camera before my talk and assumed that my plan had failed.

"Are you looking for the young sister?" Raissa asks.

"Oh, yes, I am," I reply, feeling somewhat dismayed.

"Now, you know she can't go to the brothers' side," she says, admonishing me with only the hint of a smile. "Why did you have her try to photograph you?" she adds sharply.

A college graduate and a successful businesswoman in Côte d'Ivoire, Raissa now works as a merchant in the downtown district. At the *masjid*, she's a major official in charge of Muslim women. The name Hadjjah is an honorific indicating that she has completed the *hajj*, the annual pilgrimage to Mecca. I have learned that Raissa and others admonished Fatima as well, preventing her from entering the men's side to retrieve the camera.

Because of her work schedule, I rarely get a chance to talk to Raissa at length, so I decide to take the opportunity. We began a brief conversation about the talk.

"What is funny is that I never thought about coming here," she says. "Maybe for vacation but never to live. I was thinking more of maybe Canada or Europe, but I didn't want to go to France."

"What made you come?" I ask.

"The reason we're all here is the same thing," she replies. "Most of us did not come here because we love America. We came here for economic reasons. Poverty is rampant back home. We have leaders who don't know anything about good governance. You see so many people here, and the life they had back home is so much better than the life they're living here. But they don't have the choices. Because of economic reasons, they have to be here and support their family back home. We love America. But we would come to visit and go back. It's not about coming here."

For African Muslims from middle-class families, migration is animated less by personal poverty than by the desire to fully realize their earning potential. They are far better off than those West African families reduced to eating one meal a day. In fact, many contrast the sizable houses they lived in back home with their rat-infested apartments in New York. The more fortunate ones relish the relatively "stress-free" work or school schedules they had, allowing major breaks in the middle of the day, with no obligation to work around the clock.

Raissa pauses to think. "Actually, we used to be scared to come to America— oh, really, to come to Harlem."

"What do you mean?" I ask.

"We used to watch movies about Harlem, and there would be burning buildings and killings. That scared a lot of people."

Images from Blaxploitation films of the 1970s, filled with gangsters, pimps, and drug dealers, were often consumed by Senegalese, Ivoirian, and other African viewers. Films such as *Cotton Comes to Harlem* (1970), *Shaft* (1971), *Black Caesar* (1973), *Gordon's War* (1973), and *Harlem Nights* (1989) informed their poor views of Harlem and its people. In essence, two contrasting images of Black life were possible for African viewers. There was the one portraying glamorous Black stars in blockbuster movies and fashion models displayed on billboards and periodicals. The other depicted Blacks as criminals on French news and syndicated television shows or in the Blaxploitation films. But perhaps this does not constitute a contrast at all. On the one hand, a portrait of wealthy America sends a powerful message around the world denoting its overwhelming success as a nation. With the end of the Cold War and the fall of communism, this portrait champions America as the place of winners. On the other hand, negative images of Harlem appear symbolically to separate Black America from the rest of the country, marking it as dangerous. In the end, these images signal to immigrants those people they must avoid if they are to reap the rewards America has to offer. But, as the next chapter will illustrate, their ability to gain the opportunities they seek will in many respects depend on how well they get along with local residents.

3

The Black Encounter

I

It's Friday, so I make my weekly trek to West Fourth Street to catch the A train to Harlem. Standing on the platform, I lean over and perform the ritual stare up the tracks, looking for a beam of light. The train arrives, passengers push their way on and into narrow spaces, which gets me thinking about Africans and how they navigate their place in Harlem. I also think about the question posed by Countee Cullen, the Caribbean poet of the Harlem Renaissance, who asked in his 1925 poem "Heritage," "What is Africa to me?"[1] Why has this question been so important? And what will its answer reveal?

When the doors open at 14th Street, four teenage boys squeeze their wiry bodies through. Two appear to be African American, and the other two, I guess, are Latino.

"I thought he was African," one Black teenager blurts out.

"Naaah," another answers.

The train rolls forward, and its clacking nearly mutes their voices. The young boys stop to ponder the identity of their school's new security guard. Their silence is broken when the same boy repeats, "I thought he was African."

The others wait intently for more.

"But he wasn't," the boy says, "'cause I asked him."

Two immediately begin interrogating him. "What was he, then? Is he . . . or is he . . .?" The other boy refuses to guess; instead, he is prodded for a direct answer: "What? What? What is he?"

The young man withholds the answer, seeming to enjoy the suspense. His smirk loosens, and he carefully positions himself. "He is Black!" he blurts out.

One of the Latino boys notices me following their conversation, then lowers his eyes and head. He turns to the one who began the conversation and speaks in low tones, forcing me to read the silent motion of his lips.

"Oh," the other responds aloud. "You knew?"

The Latino boy then alerts the others that I'm watching. They carefully turn their heads toward me, glance in my general direction, turn back, and change the subject.

This story illustrates an important point about how identities are formed in everyday situations. More directly, this scenario speaks to a particular West African and Black American encounter, one that forces them and others to rethink the boundaries that mark their sense of belonging. This engagement also raises new questions about one's relationship to Africa, especially when Africans and African Americans hold divergent views of the continent, often disputing what role it should play in their lives. Even so, while the reinforcement of boundaries marking identities can occur within formal institutions, such as the workplace, the daily rehearsal of identity is very often played out in casual settings like this one.[2]

As my train approaches Times Square, I decide to switch to either the 2 or 3 train, which both stop at 116th and Malcolm X Boulevard, the old Lenox Avenue. The corner is a vortex of African bodies gyrating within multicolored flowing robes, Islamic *kufis* (Muslim caps) and headscarves darting about, and hip-hop gear pulsating to the rhythm of a "perfect" beat.[3] I emerge from the station, turn around, and notice Leslie's Hair Salon across the street. Along with businesses such as restaurants and Laundromats, African hair shops are sites where Blacks and Africans interact regularly. Although this is much more the case for women looking for perms, braids, or in-vogue hairstyles, unisex barbershops are gradually becoming places where African and African American men meet as well. While Blacks are usually customers, West African women either work for an American proprietor or, more recently, own their boutiques. I cross at the corner and stroll up to the salon's picture window. Peeking inside, I see more than a dozen African women dressed in traditional attire, with three or so treating hair at each station. As I stand there, a Black woman comes stumbling out, yelling at the African worker.

"Come out, bitch!" she hollers. "I'll cut your motherfuckin' throat!"

"You better gimme my money!" the African worker shouts as she emerges with others trying to hold her back.

With her hand in her pocketbook, the first woman stands outside the door, repeating her threat.

While the situation illustrates just how explosive things can get between long-standing residents and newcomers, the underlying factor appears to be financial rather than cultural. But Jamal, a twenty-three year-old Black security worker at the shop, holds a different view.[4]

I am struck by Jamal's composure during the scuffle, as he sits back in his lawn chair on the sidewalk and watches things unfold. He has lived in Harlem since the age of seven, and he appears to have grown accustomed to such outbursts. As things cool down, Lenny, a Black man in his early thirties and a salon employee, leaves the shop and joins us outside. They begin talking about the fight and their view of Africans in Harlem.

"They're not like us," Jamal says, shaking his head and rocking in his chair. "They're different."

"Ahhh," Lenny says. "Don't get me started on them. They're some nasty people!" he bellows. "And ruuude!"

"But I don't know how to explain it," Jamal says, staring into space. "I guess it's just cultural differences."

"Yeah, I don't know," Lenny gripes. "I do know they don't mess with me, 'cause they know I'll tell 'em 'bout themselves. But they are some nasty people."

"What do you mean by nasty?" I ask.

Lenny thinks for a moment. "Ya know, just nasty," he replies.

I wait for more.

"They throw trash and stuff all over the floor, and they have an attitude," he adds.

In Jamal's mind, these conflicts are about cultural differences, ethnic behaviors that clearly separate Africans from Blacks. But is this the divide he is unable to explain? That is, are differences between culturally distinct groups in pluralistic societies necessarily divisive, and do they automatically lead to conflict? Whether Jamal can justify his statement or not is immaterial. What is worth exploring is how he recognizes differences between the two groups. He is convinced that "they're not like us," and he assumes that "culture" might be the reason. New immigrants obviously possess values and worldviews that differ from those of native residents, and they behave differently as a consequence. However, cultural differences in and of themselves do not create boundaries, forcing people to see themselves as separate and distinct. What creates and maintains a divide is the social importance or cultural meanings people attach to these differences. In fact, "culture" and the way it is objectified—by which I mean how it is reduced to a "thing" with a specific set of values or behaviors—appear to structure relations between African Americans and other immigrants as well. Robert C. Smith's work on Mexicans in New York illustrates how *mexicanidad* (Mexicanness) or, more precisely, *ticuanensidad* (Ticuaniness) constructs a boundary of cultural difference between Mexicans and their Black and

Puerto Rican neighbors. According to Smith's respondent, Blacks and Puerto Ricans actually suffer socially because they are seen to lack "culture" entirely, not so much for having a different culture. What makes this curious is how often residents cite culture as the reason groups cannot get along or succeed.[5]

While Jamal evokes culture as a way to mark the boundary that set Africans and Blacks apart, Lenny defines these differences in a way that gives meaning to the cultural border. He uses the word *nasty*, a term many Black residents use to describe Africans. In *Harlemworld*, John L. Jackson Jr. quotes Paula, a thirty-eight-year-old Black woman who accuses Africans of acting as if "they are royalty" and claims, "They all nasty." He also refers to an eighteen-year-old Black Latina, Elisha, who asserts, "All they want us for is so they can braid our hair and give us extensions."[6]

On a different occasion, Lateefa speaks to me about her experience.

"We're walking down the street," says Lateefa, a Black Harlem resident in her forties, "and you see the ones that want to braid your hair. One woman, one time, grabbed me."

"And what happened?" I ask.

"I told her, 'No! No thank you. If I need my hair braided, I'll get an appointment.'"

In a place where scores of hair salons compete during an economic downturn, some Blacks feel prodded by African salon workers (many undocumented), who are desperate to remit money regularly to needy families back home. Still, behaviors like these could be misconstrued by residents. As Jackson's work suggests, *nasty* is a term applied to those Africans who might appear antisocial and perhaps fail to interact with Blacks beyond business. These areas, however, are clearly fault lines where a high level of distrust exists. It's a site where even services provided by African hair braiders are held in contempt. Lenny struggles to define what he means by calling Africans nasty and later associates it with unclean work habits. Being nasty, though, could actually mean all sorts of things. Whatever it means, it becomes important when it creates the type of social distance one might desire to maintain between groups.

The Harlem Market near Malcolm X Boulevard straddles 115th and 116th Streets. Its main entrance greets shoppers with an elaborate dome of red, yellow, green, and orange stripes. Local customers and tourists from around the world come to purchase African artifacts, fabric, and designer items from Senegalese, Ivoirian, Malian, and Guinean merchants. One can spot a few African American vendors as well. I take a break from Jamal and Lenny and venture to the market to visit with Kebe, a Senegalese tailor. I almost pass Anta's booth, Mustafa's World of African Art, but notice Candy, a Black woman from Colorado in her mid-fifties, inside. I walk over as she and her daughter, Stacy, rummage through a table of hand-carved wooden masks. They are hoping to find the appropriate artifact to fill a spot on a wall of African masks in Stacy's apartment.

After ten minutes of quibbling over which color and markings would complement the wall, Anta has grown frustrated and asks, "Are you sure you want African art?"

"Oh, yeah, of course," Stacy answers. "This art is a link to my heritage."

"Yeah!" Candy says. "That's for sure."

"OK, do you like the color on this one?" Anta points to a mask.

When they have completed their purchase, I begin explaining my research as we walk toward the entrance.

"How do you feel about African products?" I ask, "and African Americans who—"

"African Americans!" Candy yells, cutting me off. "No, no!" she says. "They are African and African American." She points to an African merchant standing outside his shop. "I'm Black!"

She explains that while she embraces her African heritage, she firmly believes that labeling herself African American fails to recognize the struggles Black people endure daily. To her, the modern Black diaspora takes precedence over an age-old African past. More important, her identity choice reinforces a boundary between the Africans whom she referred to as African American and herself as a Black woman. This is not to suggest that all Blacks make these distinctions between themselves and their African counterparts. What constitutes this difference, however, is not always clear. That is, while Candy is resolute in her sense of the line that separates her from continental Africans in Harlem, others are less certain.

After leaving Candy and Stacy, I think it would be a good idea to see Jamal and Lenny again before continuing up 116th. Back at Leslie's Hair Salon, I notice how the sight of so many African women, clothed in stunning colors and indigenous styles, interjects a type of Black cosmopolitanism into the urban landscape. At once, it defies the notion of a monolithic Blackness and forces a reimagining of the Black self. Like Countee Cullen's refrain, "What is Africa to me?" it complicates one's presuppositions about where the boundary between Black and African identity lies.

"Who owns the salon?" I ask Jamal. "I mean, is the salon African or African American owned?"

"What do you mean?" he says, looking up at me with grimace from his lawn chair.

"Well," I reply, straining to help him understand my categories, "is the shop owned by Africans, or is it owned by African Americans?"

Still confused, he struggles to answer as Lenny watches. Jamal pauses and thinks a bit more. "The shop is Black owned," he shoots back. "Yeah, yeah!" he says. "It's Black owned!"

As it relates to identity and its demarcation, Jamal has a great deal of difficulty determining the difference between African and African American. For sure, many continental Africans in Harlem subscribe to both an African identity and, for those who consider America another homeland, an African American one. In fact, some African restaurants and clothing stores, such as "Kaloum Restaurant of African American Food—Serving All African and Guinean Cuisine" and "B.B. African American Fashion," clearly include the words *African American* as identity markers. Some would even argue that as African immigrants become U.S. citizens, they are actually replacing Blacks as the "new" African Americans.[7] Accordingly, asking Jamal to choose between an identity that is either African or African American is not giving him two distinct choices at all. To him, Africans could easily fit both categories. However, as the need to distinguish between the two groups increases, the classification of "Black" as an identity marker moves farther away from its association with Africa. As a symbol in the construction of a Black identity, Africa gradually becomes inconsequential. Rather than emphasizing African *roots*, then, many Blacks in Harlem foreground an experience stressing their diasporic *routes*, preferring to recognize their New World encounters and current realities. In this sense, Jamal believes that the term *Black* makes the proper distinction. At the very least, it does not include the word *African* and, thus, appears to answer the question.

After the conversation at Leslie's Hair Salon, I end up on Adam Clayton Powell Boulevard near 112th Street, walking toward 125th. The Cheikh Amadou Bamba Day parade moved up this thoroughfare several days ago, and I want to know how residents viewed the event. As a public display of an embodied Africanity in Harlem, paraders were subjected to the gaze of Harlem spectators, and a nonverbal, symbiotic encounter ensued between the observers and the observed.

Three men are sitting on their apartment stoop. They appear relaxed, and one periodically goes to the trunk of his car for a cold beer. I ease my way toward them, greet everyone, and offhandedly talk about the August heat in New York City. Apartment stoops and the casual talk occurring there reveal a great deal about how people informally send messages about identity. The informality of the location makes it an important place for an ethnographic investigation. Under more formal conditions, people are less apt to reveal everyday feelings about themselves or others.

"You want some?" one of the men asks, holding out a wet Heineken.

"Oh, no thanks," I answer.

Unlike the Senegalese *boubou* outfit I wore in the Bamba parade, I'm dressed in a pair of khaki pants and a yellow pullover shirt. I knew I'd be talking to Harlem residents about their perceptions of Africans, and I wanted to remove anything that might prevent an open response.[8]

One of the men on the stoop is Jimmy, an African American middle-aged re-tiree from the trucking business and a Vietnam veteran. The other two are Black Hondurans. Edwin, the older of the two, also served in the United States military and has been in the country for thirty years. The other, Eddie, is in his late twenties and has been living in Harlem for about twelve years.

Without addressing anyone directly, I began a conversation. "What do you think about the African parade?"

"Fuck 'em!" Jimmy spouts off.

"What?" I say, more than a little stunned.

"Fuck 'em," he repeats. "Tying up all that traffic like that!"

Although unexpected, Jimmy's response reveals his assumptions about Afri-cans in Harlem. His subsequent dispute with Edwin and Eddie raises related issues about Blackness and notions of belonging.

"They don't care 'bout you," Jimmy says. "Don't you know that?" He glares at me. "You don't know that!" he exclaims. "You Black, right?" He checks my identity and admonishes me, too.

"Well, yeah," I say.

"Well, you don't know that?" he mocks, gawking at me.

"I'm trying to understand what you're saying," I answer.

"You think they care 'bout you!" he yells. "Shiiit! They don't care 'bout you."

Jimmy's statement that "they," meaning Africans, do not care about "you," a general reference to all Black people, speaks to his recognition that there is a clear difference between Africans and Blacks. In fact, it is a distinction that, in his mind, should be evident. "You don't know that!" he snaps, as though it is the kind of difference I am supposed to understand intuitively, much the way Blacks and Whites in the Jim Crow South or elsewhere just knew about the racial boundaries separating them. I am expected to recognize this borderline just as clearly. If my memory has failed me, Jimmy does his best to remind me. Moreover, he reaffirms not just that Blacks and Africans were different but also that they each belong to a distinct category. He reminds all of us, in fact, that "they" are not "you." That is, his quick probe—"You Black, right?"—is his way of reminding me of the category to which he and I belong.

Finally, the notion of caring is used to underscore the reason a demarcation exists between Blacks and Africans. Because he claims that Africans did not "care" about Blacks, they are regarded as outsiders. According to Jimmy, the very fact that "they" are Africans automatically means they don't care. The idea of caring—or, in this case, not caring—allows certain Blacks to assign a particular meaning to an African identity. It helps to define the nature of the boundary between them. Caring or the illusion of it is an essential bond that people share as members of the same group. Moreover, because it reflects a certain affinity that members have for

African American spectators gaze at Murid women marching in the Cheikh Amadou Bamba Day Parade. (Photo Zain Abdullah)

one another, it can create a deep emotional attachment. In the way Jimmy uses it, caring is an important resource in the formation of a Black selfhood. Many Harlem residents (especially Blacks) have intimated to me that they believe Africans are exploiting them. Whether these feelings are accurate or not isn't the point. What is at issue here is the way Blacks use the notion of caring or uncaring as a resource for self-identification and as a way to create social distance.

At the same time, the idea of caring speaks to how one group relates to another, how members' interactions demonstrate their compassion, love, or concern for one another. The act of caring, then, is a critical barometer for determining which groups belong in Harlem, or perhaps any other Black community, and which ones do not.

Edwin and Eddie chime in to dispute Jimmy's implicit denial that they have a right to be in Harlem—or even in the country, for that matter.

"No, no, no," Eddie interjects, vigorously shaking his head. "See?" he says over Jimmy's rantings. "I don't believe that—"

"What are you running away from?" Jimmy shouts.

"What do you mean?" Eddie says.

"Why are you here?" Jimmy says. "You gotta be runnin' away from something."

"Look, I'm tellin' you." Edwin chimes in and turns toward me. "A lot of these people get locked up, and they can't fulfill their constitutional right to vote. I can vote! So, I'm more of an American than they are."

Edwin's response speaks volumes about the kind of tensions that exist between immigrants and native-born populations. For global cities like New York, the pace of work is fast, and few have the time or the energy to foster neighborly relations, particularly for immigrants working at low-wage jobs around the clock. At the same time, globalization has allowed many of these migrants to become transnational citizens of sorts, maintaining dual and triple identities that situate them in Harlem and somewhere else simultaneously. Many of these immigrants—or transmigrants, as some would call them—feel less pressure to integrate fully into local communities and have a sense that they will return home eventually.[9] However, most African Muslims rarely return. Extremely harsh working conditions and the economic exploitation they suffer severely frustrate their plans. Needless to say, their dissatisfaction increases, and despair sets in, which causes tension in their interaction with residents. As more settle down and attempt to make a life for themselves in urban neighborhoods such as Harlem (and some are beginning to relocate to smaller cities and the suburbs), arguments about belonging will most likely increase.

The foreign status of Africans and other immigrants such as Edwin and Eddie is used as a marker to define difference. Jimmy's question, "Why are you here?" is not merely addressed to these two Hondurans. Rather, it is essentially a question

ⁱnts, particularly those who have come and settled in Harlem. As a
cheap labor or simply as competitors for inadequate housing and
ⁱs, immigrants often pose a threat to low-income urban residents.[10]
on that immigrants in Harlem are "running away from something"
serves to give residents like him a feeling of dominance. According to this view, no
matter what strides immigrants (including Africans) make in the United States, their
perpetual exile or immigrant status contradicts the belief that they are surpassing
Blacks. On the other hand, immigrants may see themselves as law-abiding citizens
pitted against Black criminals. According to Edwin, this explains a major difference
between them and some Black residents. That is, many immigrants have internalized stereotypes depicting African Americans as criminals or people caught in a
cycle of destructive behavior. Edwin states that because "these people get locked
up," even he—as a first-generation immigrant—can exercise his American rights
more than native-born Americans can. As Edwin would have it, African and other
Black immigrants are often afforded a better sense of belonging than native-born
Blacks. Still, while both sides employ immigrantness as a resource for the construction of their identity, the meaning they attach to it is not the same.

"They don't like us!" Jimmy shouts. "They don't like Black people! But they
have to deal with us, and they don't like that shit."

"What do you mean, we don't like Black people?" Eddie snaps back. "We are
Black!"

"But if they don't like us, why are they here?" Jimmy says sarcastically,
ignoring Eddie's retort.

"They don't embrace the country, but we embrace the country." Edwin turns
to look at me again. "They got their priorities all mixed up. Look! You've been in
this country longer than me," he says, scolding Jimmy. "And what do you have that
I don't have?" he adds as Jimmy stops, looks away, and begins staring into space.
"We have the same thing!" Edwin yells.

"All I'm saying," Jimmy repeats like a mantra, "is they don't like us, so why are
they here?"

Jimmy's statement that Africans and other immigrants "don't like Black
people" is telling. In fact, other Black Harlem residents express similar sentiments.
Some say, for example, "If they are so much better than us, why are they living with
us?" These assertions are generally made after Blacks discuss what they believe to be
a haughty or "nasty" attitude displayed by Africans. The "here" of which they
speak, of course, is Harlem, a place that has been recognized as the capital of
Black America since about the 1920s. As a symbol of Black identity, it has played
a powerful role in the Black imagination the world over.[11] With this connection
between place and identity, the very idea that Africans don't "like" Black residents but continue to live in Harlem is inconceivable.[12] In their minds, the two

are inseparable. In other words, one cannot live with Black people and not love Black people.

Stereotypes often exacerbate these tensions, though. Edwin's accusation that immigrants "embrace the country" while Black Americans do not is a common view among Africans. It's the idea that Blacks do not take advantage of the opportunities America offers. While Africans may view themselves as industrious and prudent, they picture many Blacks as mirror opposites, ungrateful and lazy. Edwin's assertion that Blacks "got their priorities all mixed up" furthers this argument. He continues to say that instead of buying "expensive items like cars" and remaining in an apartment for "twenty years," they should concentrate on purchasing a house. To prove their carelessness, Edwin chides Jimmy, saying, "What do you have that I don't have?" By distancing themselves from a Blackness they imagine to be at the bottom of the social ladder, Africans and other Black immigrants mediate this divide by constructing another one that answers their needs as newcomers. Native-born Blacks, at the same time, create their own boundaries against an immigrant backlash.

Eddie's retort that he is Black is poignant, but I believe it misses the point, at least in this context. To put it simply, Jimmy and other long-standing residents refer to the kind of Blackness shaped by an American nightmare, an ongoing horror from which there has been little or no relief, particularly for poor residents. It has afforded many Blacks a bottom-up view of America, or what writers such as Oscar Zeta Acosta and Pedro Pietri might call a "cockroach view" of the world. Edwin, by comparison, speaks of a dream most Black immigrants seek to attain but few Black residents experience.[13] Much of the tension between Black immigrants and Black residents, however, appears to be centered around a number of misplaced expectations one group has of the other. It's not unlike the class divide that already exists among African Americans. A growing, upwardly mobile Black middle class ascribes to the dream of full integration that Martin Luther King Jr. envisioned. At the same time, a rapidly expanding Black underclass suffers the nightmare of disenfranchisement that Malcolm X articulated.[14] In this way, there is certainly not one America, and some of today's immigrants are being integrated into a particular segment of it, a very different one from that in which their Black counterparts struggle.

On my way back to the train station, I see Jamal and Lenny lingering outside the salon. I walk over, and, following a brief chat about the day, Lenny picks up on our earlier conversation.

"And they call themselves Muslims?" he says. "I don't know what kind of Muslims they are, because the Muslims I know aren't nasty—and they're not rude! Muslims are clean people and polite. I don't know what kind of Muslims they are."

Lenny already has a positive image of Muslims in Harlem. Malcolm X led the Nation of Islam's Temple 7 on 116th and Lenox Avenue (now Malcolm X Boulevard) since the mid-1950s, and its "do-for-self" philosophy" and Black Power rhetoric seeped into the community, transforming whole segments of Black thought and culture. Similarly, Islam and Muslim culture are an integral part of West African life. But Harlem is new terrain for these Black immigrants, just as their presence creates a fresh encounter for longtime residents. Alternative histories must be rehearsed and old memories reimagined for both West African Muslims and Black residents.

As a child, Sadjah, an African American now in her forties, grew up in the "Nation." "We were all in the same community," she remembers. "So that just felt really great. I loved the reverence with which people held us. People would come to the [Nation's] Salaam restaurant, and if they weren't dressed properly, they would always ask, 'Can I come in here?'"

As a religious expression of the Black Power movement, the Nation adopted an Islamic sensibility and advocated Black pride and a love for self that was uncompromising. While most did not become registered members, thousands of Blacks supported the group's efforts by patronizing its businesses, attending services, and purchasing its newspaper, *Muhammad Speaks*.[15] African American Sunni or orthodox Muslims have likewise influenced the Harlem community in very significant ways. As Lenny bellows above, residents see Muslims as "clean" and "polite" people.

There is another critical point about the relationship between Muslims and non-Muslims in Harlem. The great majority of the native-born Black Muslims are converts. This fact cannot be understated when we consider the kind of affinity residents have for them. In a real sense, they were already cousins, friends, or associates and viewed as belonging to the "same community," as Sadjah asserts. The Muslim identity of African immigrants, therefore, fails to obviate strained relations between them and Black residents, regardless of the latter's admiration of Islam and Black Muslim culture. In contrast to their affinity for indigenous Muslims, the Islamic identity of Africans is disregarded, especially in this case, and they are deemed outsiders. For some residents, however, the Islamic character of Africans is uncertain. Much of this ambiguity relates to the fact that Muslims in America and around the world are generally profiled in terms of Arab types, and the dark skin of Africans often precludes their membership in the Muslim world, at least in the minds of many Westerners (and some Muslims).[16]

In conversations with residents about Africans in Harlem, some will occasionally interject, "They're Muslim, right?" Others might conduct a more impromptu check. After *jum'ah* prayer at Masjid Touba, for example, forty or so Senegalese are gathered outside, all decked out in traditional African and Islamic clothing.

Strolling by, an African American man slows his pace just enough to ask, "Is this a mosque?"

"Yeah, it is," I answer.

"Good!" he replies, then crosses the street and struts up the block.

It is different for Lenny. Since the Africans at the shop claim to be Muslims, too, the only way he can maintain his wayward depiction of them is to reject their religious claim. In this sense, even if they are acknowledged as Muslims by others, the fact that he is unaware of their "kind" places them in a strange and unusual category. Either way, the legitimacy of their Islamic affiliation is at times brought into question by outsiders in the Harlem context.

II

The Touba Khassayitt shop anchors the Murid community in Harlem. It supplies members with books, pamphlets, cassette tapes, CDs, and DVDs covering all sorts of religious topics. The posters it sells of Cheikh Amadou Bamba and other clerics offer devotees a divine visuality, a panoply of images that sacralize their newly acquired, media-saturated landscape. I enter its door on 116th Street near Eighth Avenue (better known as Frederick Douglass Boulevard).

"As-salaamu 'alaykum," I say. "Çava?"

Standing behind the glass case, Osman lifts his bald head slightly and returns a curious, lukewarm greeting. As I come into view, a smile slowly accents his face. The interior is small, about twelve by fourteen feet, with shelves arranged in three rows, each leading patrons to the checkout counter. Wooden ledges along the wall are filled with books and extend from the floor to the ceiling. Prayer rugs, incense, and other Murid paraphernalia protrude here and there, forcing one to take second looks from time to time.

"Can I help you?" Osman asks.

"Well, I'm just looking around," I answer. "You have some nice things in here."

His face lights up, and he immediately begins a conversation about Islam and Muridiyya. Then silence hangs in the air. I glance up and notice his intense glare, as if he were preparing to say something important. As he talks about the virtues of Cheikh Amadou Bamba, he carefully walks around the counter and stands in front of me. He leans forward and says, "You know our Cheikh is Black!" He pauses, staring into my eyes, as I wait for the rest. "And not an Arab, and that's better, because he's for us."

It seems strange that, believing me to be a Muslim, he would try to convert me to Muridism. Converting non-Muslims to Islam is one thing, but converting to a different version of it is something else.[17] It is also striking to hear an Afri-can make a racial appeal to religious conversion. I would have been better pre-pared to hear this from someone in the Nation of Islam or another proponent of Black Islam, since, in one way or another, wrestling with the confluence of race and religion has become central to the African American Muslim experi-ence.[18] Still, Osman's appeal raises a number of questions for me regarding Africans' notion of Blackness. It also forces me to think about just how much or in what ways this racial consciousness shapes their religious beliefs and prac-tices. This is not a question about theology. My concern here is about the lived reality of Islamic, Black, and African experiences in Harlem. That is, how do West African Muslim immigrants create a new life for themselves in Harlem? When does Islam matter, and when is it a nonissue? When does race matter? And when and in what ways is an African sense of self important? In sum, how do West African Muslims imagine themselves and their life with others in Harlem?

As night falls, I leave Touba Khassayitt and walk around the corner for *maghrib* (evening prayers) at Masjid Aqsa. For *jum'ah* (Friday) services, nearly eight hundred congregants cram into spaces on three floors (basement, main entrance level, and a top floor, entered only from an external stairwell). On this particular evening, more than one hundred worshipers show up. The majority of attendees are from Côte d'Ivoire, but a large number come from Guinea, fewer from Senegal and Mali, and some from countries such as Togo and Burkina Faso. African American Muslims come in small numbers. Upon entering, people place shoes in racks along the right wall. A few shoes litter the floor but are pushed into corners. People enter dressed in both African robes and Western attire, and some proceed to the back staircase leading to the ablu-tion area downstairs. Others perform *sunnah* (extra prayers), while some sit on the green pile carpet reciting the Qur'an or chanting liturgical formulas with the turn of each *thiker* bead. Shortly, the *athan* sounds, signaling the time for prayer. Fifteen minutes later, Imam Konate descends from his upstairs office and steps in front to lead. He faces forward, and the fabric on his white *ibaaya* (religious cape) settles from his exaggerated twists and turns as he checks to make certain each person is lined up correctly. Both hands rise to his shoulders, and he makes the *takbir*. "Allaaahu Akbar!" he announces, and the congregation follows until the *salah* is complete. After the prayer, he moves quickly, preparing to leave before he must return for *isha*, the final prayer of the day. I decide to walk out with him.

Assetou, an Ivoirian woman in her mid-thirties, also walks outside. She slips behind a table set against the *masjid* wall at which she sells ginger, sorrel and tama-rind drinks, along with other food and clothing. We notice each other, and I greet her: "*As-salaamu 'alaykum*, Assetou. How are you, *ça va*?" Smiling, she returns the greeting, and I walk over to purchase a drink.

"What have you been doing these days?" I ask.

Her smile drops slightly as she attempts to follow my words. "Oh," she says, and pauses briefly. "I'm fine, everything good. And you?"

"*Al-hamdu lillah* [Praise Allah], I'm good," I say, and her smile widens when she realizes she has answered correctly.

While Assetou was intimately familiar with the Islamic greeting and comfortable returning it, she was more hesitant when the conversation switched to English because of her poor command of the language. Black residents often read this reluctance or hesitance to respond, not to mention other avoidance strategies such as Africans averting their eyes when passing Blacks on the street, as not only rude but also demeaning. The avoidance strategy of Africans and the Black response signify one in a series of cultural miscues, or what I call cultural misfires, occurring between them. Assetou and I have developed a certain level of trust over the years. She knows I'm not going to rush her or think less of her if her English isn't perfect. Although they often speak four or five languages, many Africans believe their lack of English fluency exposes them to Black ridicule. This is a major source of conflict.

Imam Konate and I walk to the corner of Frederick Douglass Boulevard, turn right, and continue down 116th. Our conversation is frequently interrupted by greetings to and from African men, women, and children moving in both directions. One could attribute their openness to the *imam*'s presence, but I've had similar experiences when walking along the same street alone. The Islamic greeting "*As-salaamu 'alaykum*" reorients the social compass as people move through congested urban space. This simple exchange not only establishes a quick and immediate symbolic connection, but it also communicates feelings of respect, safety, and memories of home.

"Africans used to get beat up all the time," Imam Konate says, shaking his head in pity.

"Beat up?" I say. "Why?"

"Yeah, somebody would ask them the time, and if they didn't know what he was talking about—they couldn't understand him—the guy would say, 'Damn African!' And pop him. Bam!" He slams his right fist into the other.

"Did that happen to you?" I ask.

"Nooo!"

"Why not?"

"Because I know how to protect myself. I would look at them and say, 'Look! I'm a nigga like you, and you messin' with the wrong person. Plus, I would have my three fifty-seven [gun] on my hip, and they wouldn't mess with me. But it used to be baaad. Real baaad."[19]

During the early days, African Muslims in Harlem felt extremely vulnerable. If assaulted on the street, they were either undocumented and could not report their attackers to the authorities, or they were legal immigrants but did not possess the language skills to explain the situation. Finding a professional interpreter would have been another solution, but that is costly. And more often than not, family or friends with better capabilities could not afford to leave their jobs to translate, especially if they, too, were working illegally or afraid of losing their jobs. African Muslims in Harlem have often avoided African Americans because of this early conflict, while some have tried disguising their African identity by "acting" Black.[20] Obviously, a misreading of this behavior by long-standing residents frustrates relations between them and their African neighbors.

On another occasion, while leaving Baobab Restaurant on 116th near Masjid Malcolm Shabazz, I run into Aminata, a thirty-year-old Sudanese woman and an activist in the African community. She has been living in or around Harlem since the early 1990s.

"How's your research going?" she asks. "Do you know what's a major concern?" she continues before I can respond. "Relations between Africans and African Americans."

"I see a cultural gap," I say. "Sometimes Africans might avoid talking to Black Americans because their English isn't very good. They don't even look at Blacks when they pass them on the street—or even nod."

"Well," Aminata gripes, "I don't think it's that."

"Oh, really?" I say. "What do you think?"

"Sometimes they might not nod because, if they do, there is an obligation to stop and hold a conversation with that person. In African culture, you don't just speak and keep walking. That's rude! You have to ask about their family and everything. Sometimes I'm conducting a case study, and before I can get into the case, I have to spend fifteen minutes just in introduction. I have to ask about her children, family, her health, et cetera, before we can talk about why I came."

"Do you speak their languages?" I ask, attempting to understand the diversity of her clients.

"No," she replies. "It's just"—she nods her head up and down—"'Ah haa, wow [yes], ah haa,'" she says, showing how she responds. "It's about listening, whether you understand or not. There's also etiquette for meeting an elder or a person of a different gender. So, Black Americans might not understand this. They might think they're being rude."

"This is a cross-cultural problem, because to African Americans, it's rude," I add.

"All Africans go through this," she says. "It's a shock!" She raises both hands, fingers tense and spread out. "It's a culture shock!"

Much like Jamal, Aminata feels that cultural differences separate African Muslims from Blacks, but she thinks that the problem could be rectified with a better grasp of these issues and ongoing exchanges. Yet the problem runs deeper. Conflict between the groups stems in large part from the negative images African Muslims have consumed prior to their migration.

"In Africa," Konate says, "they used to teach African people about Black Americans here."

"How was that?" I ask. "In the movies?"

"Yeah, yeah, the movies, because what they used to say about Black Americans . . . is that they are criminals," he replies.

"Is this coming from your teachers or television, too?" I ask.

"No, no, from television. Because the television used to sell this type of image. Yeees," he says softly, pausing to reflect. "But while you are watching the movie, the bad roles are for Black people. Always! And we didn't know they were telling lies. We didn't know that!"

While Imam Konate has learned to be critical of these negative portrayals, most of his countrymen and other African Muslims migrating during this early period were less analytical and accepted poor images of Blacks and Harlem.

"When I came here," Konate admits, "the next day, we came to Harlem. Right here, somewhere on 119th, they used to have a little African restaurant there. My brother would say, 'Let's go to the restaurant and see if we can eat.' I said, 'I can't! I saw . . . Black Americans. Just take me home. They're going to kill me! Just take me home! I don't want to stay here.'"

While crime and street violence have certainly been rampant in particular areas, others speak of this fear as an exaggeration perpetuated by their countrymen in order to orient new arrivals properly.

"When I first came from the plane," says Mamadou, an Ivoirian man in his late twenties, "I was, like, 'Oh, no! This is where people shoot each other.' I'm telling you, I was scared. And when I got to Harlem, my uncle's, like, 'Oh, no, don't go out by yourself.' But it's, you know, exaggeration! When they tell you their story, it gets you more scared."

For other Africans, African Americans were seen as kindred spirits. Prominent figures such as Muhammad Ali, Martin Luther King Jr., and, for those with greater access to Black literature, Malcolm X signified the highest levels of Black achievement, which reflected quite positively on America. As the world watched athletes such as Carl Lewis or Marion Jones run for Olympic gold, African Muslims also tuned in and felt as if they were running with them. When Blacks in the United States pumped their fists in the air to James Brown's "Say It Loud—I'm Black and I'm Proud," clenched hands went up all over West Africa as well, just as Senegalese Muslims and others swayed with African Americans to the sultry sounds of Marvin Gaye.

African Muslims wear traditional clothing as a way to assert their African presence and infuse urban space with a new Islamic ethos. Nothing makes Africans more recognizable than this ethnic apparel, especially when their fabric flutters in the wind like a national flag. In fact, many African Americans purchase African fabric or custom-made pieces at the Harlem Market because this affords them a clear measure of distinction. Unlike the time when Africans were wary about being identified as foreigners in Harlem, their African clothing plays a crucial role in the performance of their identities in public. My casual meeting with Salimou illustrates this point.

One sunny afternoon in July, I am standing with Adamou, a Senegalese vendor in his thirties, while he sells books and DVDs on 125th Street and Seventh Avenue. Looking up the street toward Lenox, I notice a dark African man, thin and about six foot one, dressed in a multicolored *boubou*. As he approaches us, his smile widens. We embrace and exchange greetings. Salimou, a Guinean in his forties, works as a Muslim chaplain, teaching Islam to inmates for the New York Department of Corrections. We met some time ago at an African affair, and, as was the case then, he makes it a regular practice to dress in African clothing.

"Still wearing your African outfits, huh?" I say.

"Of course!" He leans back with both arms stretched out. "I love iiit!" he howls. "You see, African American *imams* don't like dressing in African clothes. They suffer from an identity crisis. They don't know who they are. So they try to follow another culture—Arab culture. But when I dress in African clothes, it tells everybody I'm African!"

This brief conversation raises an interesting point about the way clothing can mark racial and religious boundaries, helping the wearer negotiate meaning.[21] In other words, Salimou's African attire clearly signifies an African identity, one that marks a boundary between him and others. On the other hand, he also believes that to be a Muslim of African descent and not wear African clothes constitutes some sort of "identity crisis." In this sense, wearing African clothing is a sartorial performance of two overlapping identities: African and Muslim. In Harlem, though, Black observers view these sartorial performances quite differently.

On a cloudy day one August, I walk to Adam Clayton Powell Boulevard to see if I can talk to more residents about the Bamba Day parade. As I approach a bench set on an island between 116th and 117th Streets, I notice an older African American man resting. I ask him if he saw the parade, but he claims he "wasn't around." A drizzle soon turns into a heavy rain, and I take shelter under a nearby scaffolding, where several others are waiting. Dean, a young African American in his twenties,

A Black resident watches two Senegalese Muslims walk toward him in African attire. (Photo Zain Abdullah)

paces back and forth, making repeated calls on his cell phone. As he completes his last call, he steps up to the metal bars where I stand facing the street.

"Did you see the African parade out here on Saturday?" I ask.

He tilts his head toward me and says, "No, I wasn't around."

"Do you think Harlem has changed?" I ask.

"Changed?" he replies. "Yeah, it's changed." After looking up and down the street, he glances toward me again. "You work for the *New York Times* or something?"

"No," I answer. "I'm writing an article on the parade and working on a book."

"Ah-huh," he says.

"Do you think Africans are a part of that change?" I ask.

"What do you mean?"

"Well, you see a lot of Africans in the community who didn't used to be here. What do you think about that?"

He rises from leaning against the bar and squares his shoulders. "There are the ones that wear traditional clothes," he says. "They stick to themselves. I don't know if they think they're better than us or what. As for the others, they are the Americanized Africans, the ones you see at the club."

To Dean, Africans dress in ethnic clothing not merely as a marker of distinction, a way to be African in Harlem, but also as a sign of superiority. In John L. Jackson Jr.'s *Harlemworld*, Elisha, an eighteen-year-old Black Latina, criticizes them for how they publicly wear "their African shit and act like they still in Africa."[22] In a similar vein, Ann Miles, in *From Cuenca to Queens*, finds that even migrants from Ecuador living in Queens, New York, wear their native attire as a protection from the harmful effects of street life. Idealizing her old country ways above her newly adopted "MTV" urban world, a woman named Rosa "proudly wore the traditional *pollera* [wide pleated skirt] that identified her as a *chola* [rural folk]."[23]

Without such garments, African Muslims in Harlem struggle to identify their countrymen or -women in the public sphere, which for most is a communal space. After leaving Imam Konate on 116th Street, I cross the street to visit the owner of Darou Salam, an African variety store near Seventh Avenue. Standing in front of the shop, I pull out my pad to jot down the address and other particulars about the business. Just then, an Ivoirian man using the public telephone notices me. He hangs up and walks over, speaking Malinke.

I say, "Are you speaking Fula?"

He pauses and stares at me. "Oh, no," he replies. "I thought you were someone from Ivory Coast, my country—you look like someone from my country. How are you doin'?"

"*As-salaam 'alaykum*," I reply.

"*Wa 'alaykum salaam*," he answers.

We smile, shake hands, and depart.

As an African American researcher, I am frequently told by African Muslims in Harlem that my caramel-colored complexion and somewhat narrow facial features identify me as Malinke or Fulani. For lonely African migrants, these misadventures with Blacks who might resemble relatives or hometown friends are disconcerting.

"Sometimes you can watch in the street," Ndiaye, a Senegalese store manager, says. "And you see some people, and they look like your own blood, but you don't know. Yeah, I was, like, 'He looks like my cousin.'"

Some speak of their Atlantic crossing as a transmutation of the soul. Harlem becomes a time warp transposing them to a place where they feel they are walking in the footsteps of ancestors. Ibrahim, a Senegalese French and Arabic teacher in his early forties, confesses that "the first days when I get out and I walk, it's like, really, I was so, so, sad." He describes how he could feel the past suffering of his enslaved ancestors, as he painfully struggles to make a life for himself on the streets of New York. While the historical past of American slavery joins Africans and Blacks at the hip, their separate imaginings of this event and its horrors result in a new type of divergence between them.

It's customary to see Africans sitting in folding chairs on sidewalks outside their favorite restaurants or variety stores. They form a semicircle, taking care not to block pedestrians, and talk about the day's events or catch up on the latest gossip from back home. One day, I notice Talla, a Senegalese merchant in his late forties. He and some others are set up directly in front of Touba Inc., a shop where his wife is co-owner. A seat is available next to him, and as I walk up, I take his warm smile as an invitation to join them. The four middle-aged men, dressed in elegant *bou-bous*, form what seems to be a traditional elders council, the kind one would see holding court under an African baobab tree. As Talla and I begin talking, an African man in his twenties walks over and prepares to sit in the once vacant seat. He pauses and looks surprised to see me. I immediately offer my chair.

"No, no, no!" he says vigorously.

"Oh, no, please take it," I say.

"No! It's OK, stay, stay," he counters, pumping his hands as if to push me back into the seat.

I return to my seat and notice Alice, the owner of a thrift store next to Touba, moving used clothes and shoes in black plastic bags out of the shop. Then she returns inside to organize more bags. Alice is a fixture in the community. At seventy-one years old, she's spry and well connected in municipal politics. I leave my seat, peek through the window, and watch her meander through a maze of about twenty large plastic bags on the floor.

She steps back outside, and I notice the wording on her white T-shirt: "They stole us from Africa, and so you owe us reparations. Now pay us." I look at the words intently, trying to get her attention. Suddenly, she stops and returns the stare.

"Oh, I'm trying to read your shirt," I explain.

She looks back at the bags and resumes her routine, picking one up and moving it to a different place. "That's right, they owe us! Forty acres and a mule," she says, staring at the clothes protruding from one bag. "I want my forty acres and a mule. Do you know what I mean?" She diverts her eyes for a moment to look directly into mine. She looks back and mutters, "Forty acres is a lot."

"And forty acres is worth a lot more today than it was then," I say.

"Yeah, that's right!" she says, still scanning her inventory.

"How long have you been in Harlem?" I ask. "Were you born and raised here?"

"I came here in 1951," she answers. "I was born in South Carolina."

"You must have a lot of stories to tell," I say.

"Yeah, a lot of stories," she answers, staring into space.

"This place must have changed, huh?"

"Yeah, now we have Africans here," she grumbles. "Huh, they can walk around here with their nose up in the air like they better than us. They must think they're better than us or something. I don't know what's wrong with them." She begins a tirade about the problems between Blacks and Africans in Harlem. "They think they're better than us? I tell them, 'You sold us into slavery!' They say, 'Ah, no, ah, ah!' But I tell 'em, 'Ah, yes, ya did!' They don't want to hear it, but I tell 'em."

Other African Americans also implicate Africans in the slave trade, charging that Africans (without distinction) acted in compliance with those who captured and bartered other Africans. More important, this allegation renders African Muslims blameworthy and constitutes another obstacle to better relations. African Muslims, on the other hand, might deploy the stigma of slavery to distance themselves from Blacks.

At a different location, African Americans run in and out of Babou's variety store on Malcolm X Boulevard. A huge red vertical "99 Cent" sign, swinging loosely on windy days, helps to signify the place as hot zone of activity. I walk in looking for WD40. I swiftly walk past Ibrahim, a middle-aged Muslim from Ghana. He is a dark-skinned man with a scraggly salt-and-pepper mustache, and his squinty eyes peer out from under his beige baseball cap.

In Ghana, Ibrahim received his pharmaceutical certification and worked as a technician supplying hospitals and stores with medical products. "I had a major position," he says with bravado. He was also a police officer back home. "See, look at my picture with my uniform!" he announces, reaching back into his pants pocket and pulling out his wallet. He fumbles, searching through several flaps. He finally shows me an old photograph. Its brownish tint can't obscure how proud he looks. His police cap is perched high on his head, and the uniform outlines his well-built frame. Now, standing behind a counter at the elevated bag-check station, he holds his torso erect in his white-and-blue-striped linen shirt. At least it makes him look more official.

"Wow!" I remark, looking at the picture. "You were big back then. Your neck was massive."

"I know," he murmurs. "See what the stress of this place will do to you?"

Stress can be debilitating, but the photograph was clearly taken some years ago. At the same time, I know exactly what he means. And despite the poor image most Americans have of Africa, many Africans complain about the higher quality of life they have sacrificed by staying in the United States.

An African American man, six feet tall and in his early twenties, steps up to the counter. He pulls a pink laminated card out of his pants pocket and slaps it on the counter. Ibrahim takes it, spins around, and starts looking for the man's bags on the floor behind him.

"Do you have any WD40 oil, you know, the kind to oil small things?" I ask.

With a thick Ghanaian accent, he replies, "Ah, I don't think so." He looks up and across the aisles. "No, I really doubt it," he concludes. Ibrahim locates a few bags and plops them on the counter.

"He probably don't even know what you talkin' 'bout!" the young man spouts off, grabbing his bags and scurrying for the door.

"What you mean I don't know what I am talking'?" Ibrahim says, turning quickly to find him, eyes reddened and lips pursed. "What do you mean?" he repeats. "Who are you to say I don't know what I'm talking?" he continues, catching only a glimpse of the younger man's back as he leaves the store. "You bitch!" Ibrahim blurts out. "What do you mean? I'm more educated than you. You fuckin' bitch!"

He turns toward me, his chest heaving in and out. "How can he say I don't know? How does he know? He knows nothing!"

"Well, don't worry about it," I say, trying to calm him.

But he continues. "They think just because we're from Africa, we don't know nothing. Why do they think that? Do you think just because we are from Africa, we don't know anything? The other girl, African American, she told me, 'Go back to your country!' What do you mean?" he asks rhetorically. "You can't go back to yours!" As he reimagines his earlier exchange with the young woman, he shuffles his feet from side to side. "I can't tell you go back to yours. At least I know where to go. I know exactly where to go. I could go back home. She can't! Slave daughter!" he yells. "Talkin' about 'I was born and raised here.' So what? Do you know where you're from?" He pauses briefly, then bawls, "Slave girl! I don't understand these people and why they say that. And she's African American."

In this context, the issue of belonging underscores a major fault line between some Africans and African Americans. Among other things, it involves ideas about where home is. It involves the contested nature of what Africa means and how or when it matters. Ibrahim was told to "go back" to his country, and he in turn chided the African American girl for not knowing her real place. If we take Ibrahim's ranting at face value, he believes the young lady did not see his country as home or perhaps didn't even view Africa as home. African children report similar incidents with their African American peers. Some African youth in American cities even undergo physical abuse and are ridiculed for being from Africa. The *Philadelphia Inquirer* reported a case in which a young Liberian boy was accosted by his Black schoolmates, attacked, and told to "go home."[24] While the motive for the attack was unclear, a major concern is what this might reveal about how young Black Americans view their new African neighbors. Moreover, what does this say about the state of Black consciousness on the ground, inside inner-city Black communities, places very distant culturally from the halls of academe, where the notion of Blackness is customarily debated and rehearsed? By labeling the young woman "slave girl," Ibrahim evokes a dividing line that for many African Americans conjures images of past betrayal and deceit, a sentiment that causes some Blacks in Harlem to distrust African Muslims altogether. Africans claim they don't understand this version of events and are mystified that such a reading of history can so adversely affect their current relationship. While few admit personally hearing African Americans accuse them of "selling them into slavery," most state (but only after further investigation) that they heard this from "an African cab driver," who presumably heard it from a Black customer during casual conversation. Despite the fact that most African Muslims in Harlem appear to have learned about these accusations secondhand, it has become an issue that has strongly affected the way the two groups see each other and interact. This does not apply in all cases, however, and many African Americans and Africans in Harlem have found ways to mediate the boundary and bridge the divide.

III

Some see Islamic ethics as a way to address the rift between Africans and Blacks. "This feeling of brotherhood, I didn't find it when I come here—really," says Mamadou, a Senegalese substitute teacher. "I didn't find it. . . . But I don't lose hope. They're going to get closer and closer because in fact they are brothers. You understand? We are all Black—OK! You don't have to accept the differences. I think the problem between African Americans and Africans is about suspicion. Everybody [Blacks] looks at you as if you [Africans] did something bad. It's like you wake up in the morning, everybody's watching what you did yesterday. Nobody wants to talk to his neighbor. And that's so bad! You understand?"

I ask, "What do you mean by suspicion?"

"Suspicion is when you think someone is bad, just because you have it in your mind. And really, you do not try to get information for that." He pauses for a moment, then blurts out, "Suspicion of what? We have to say it, suspicion about slavery. Even God doesn't want suspicion."

For many African Muslims in Harlem, race and religion are not mutually exclusive. While African Americans and Africans may have "differences," and they may have difficulty reconciling divergent versions of Blackness, Mamadou appeals to a divine solution by arguing that God doesn't condone the suspicion that appears to divide them. The Qur'anic verse that speaks to this issue occurs in *sura al-hujarat*, the Apartments. It's believed to have been revealed in the early period of Islamic history following the Muslim *hijrah* (migration) to Medina, a region some two hundred miles north of Mecca. The *ayah* (verse) states, "O ye who have faith! Avoid much suspicion [of one another]; for suspicion in some cases is a sin; and spy not on each other, nor speak ill of each other behind their backs. Would any of you like to eat the flesh of his dead brother [or sister]; Nay, ye would abhor it. And be conscious of God. Verily God is Oft Accepting of Repentance, Most Merciful" (49:12).[25]

This *ayah* underscores the need for what Muslims call *'imran*, social ethics or societal values that serve the common good. More directly, it also highlights three major factors that bear on the experience of African Muslims in Harlem. First, the verse occurs during a crucial time in the relationship between the *muhajirun* (migrants) and the *ansar* (host population) in seventh-century Medina. The community was rapidly expanding, and growing tensions threatened to tear it apart unless some rules of ethical behavior could be established. African Muslims feel that a similar situation exists in Harlem, and the suspicion of which Mamadou speaks generates discord. Second, an underlying theme is brotherhood, calling community members to abstain from unwarranted distrust of one another. But if we consider the thirteenth verse that follows it, at least two levels of brotherhood emerge. On the one hand, verse 12 enjoins the new society to enter into a fellowship based on faith. Verse 13, on the other hand, addresses all populations, reminding the reader that human diversity itself is part and parcel of a divine scheme and should not breed enmity.[26] In this sense, Mamadou refers to African Americans as "brothers." It is a coalition based not on ethnic differences but, in the context of Harlem, on what is believed to be a common Blackness. As he states on a different occasion, "What difference does it make to divide Black people up? You know you're not White." In this way, Mamadou and other African Muslims in Harlem view themselves as members of two interrelated brotherhoods: one for believing

Muslims and another that unites them as Black people. The final point of this verse and Mamadou's reference to it involves reconciliation. Because God accepts repentance, as the verse states, he maintains "hope" that African-Americans and Africans will find some resolution. Still, Muslim immigrants from West Africa have attempted other ways of bridging the gap.

On one excursion to see African merchants, I jump on the 2 train to 125th and Lenox. I make a left and walk toward the Apollo Theatre. Across the street, the Bamako Products sign catches my eye, so I cross the street. Various African textiles are prominently displayed in the window. In the front of the store, fabrics and outfits fill shelves from the floor to the ceiling. Peering from the back is a brown-skinned man with a bald head. I enter, and it seems almost as though he was expecting me.

"How have you been?" he says, grinning with a warm and familiar look.

Unsure of myself, I tautly reply, "Fine. How've you been?"

An eerie silence follows, and he searches for a way to place me. "Ohhh! I thought you were from my country."

"Yeah, I get that a lot," I reply.

Yousuf, a Malian in his early forties, runs the store with his son, Gebi. He worked for the United Nations but actually came to the United States to complete his degree in economics at Columbia University. He became a stockbroker but decided to open his own business because he didn't want to "kiss anybody's ass." Eclectic styles and colors fill the store, and a mild exotic aroma titillates my senses.

"People might think some of these pieces come from India or somewhere like that," he explains. "But there are all kinds of African cloth. You have cloth from West Africa, East Africa, South Africa . . ." He walks to one shelf and pulls down a gorgeous, multicolored, fine silken fabric resembling an Indian sari. "Like this one," he says. "It's from East Africa. It looks Indian because of the mix of cultures there. *Cobba* is something I can't get here because it is too expensive. It comes from Central Africa, and they make it from the bark of a tree. They beat the bark until they get a very fine fiber from it and then weave it into a cloth. But you can get it at Bloomingdale's for eight hundred dollars." He sees me looking at the Mudd cloth. "Now, Mudd cloth," he continues, "is used for camouflage in Africa. The hunter wears it as a camouflage to catch his prey. People don't know it, but it's camouflage. It's heavy, but the colors help the hunter blend in with the environment. Here, people wear the Mudd cloth as a form of resistance against White culture. They also wear it as a fad and to show some distinction."

As the conversation shifts to include African material culture in the diaspora, I take the opportunity to steer it in the direction of Black and African relations.

"Have many Malians migrated to the United States?" I ask.

He pauses to think. "No, I don't think so."

I then share a sentence from an unpublished essay I wrote stating that contact between Africans and Harlem residents is primarily limited to business transactions.

"No, no, no!" he says, shaking his head in disagreement. "This is not true. We didn't come here just to do business. We came here to give Blacks their heritage back! We came here to teach you what you lost! We don't even call you Black Americans. We call you cousin." He calls his son from the back room. "What do we call Black Americans?" Yousuf says to him.

Gebi thinks and asks, "In what language?"

"No, in any language," Yousuf says. "What do we call Black Americans?" he repeats.

His son spouts a word in Maninka.

"You see?" Yousuf says. "Cousin!"

Gebi nods in agreement and returns to his work.

"All Africans are taught this in Africa, but when they get here, they turn to making money. They forget," Yousuf explains. "Even the hair braiders. They are teaching women not to process their hair and to return to their original selves. They are teaching you the African ways. This is the reason I'm telling you the stories of the fabric, to educate the people about Africa. I don't just sell African fabric to make money, but of course we need to make money, but I sell African fabric to educate."

He turns and notices a book vendor on the sidewalk outside his shop. Jabari, an African American in his early fifties with salt-and-pepper locks, is at his stand, moving books from one shelf to another.

"Ask him!" Yousuf cries. "He'll tell you" He leads me outside to meet Jabari. "Tell him! Tell him Africans came to America to teach Blacks their long-lost African ways!" Yousuf shouts.

Jabari continues to rearrange his book display. "They came here to make money," he says calmly and with only a slight expression.

"No, no!" Yousuf says, and we listen as he repeats everything again.

"They came here to make money," Jabari repeats with the same stoic look. "Immigrants come to another country to make money, not teach!"

As a cultural broker of sorts, Yousuf has positioned himself and, indeed, all Africans as role models whose task it is to help Blacks reclaim their lost heritage, a job not without its economic rewards.[27] To be sure, African immigration to the United States is largely motivated by economics and, to some extent, educational pursuits, as it is for thousands of others. Still, African Muslims arrive on these shores with more than financial dreams. Whether they realize it or not, they also contribute new religious and cultural capital, or what I call ethnic fragments, that many community members have come to appreciate. George, a thirty-five-year-old African American street "hustler," states how much he enjoys "seeing" the various cultures, by which he means the African clothing and restaurants and the outward display of their religious practices. Attending African *masjids* has afforded African American Muslims a sense of belonging they never experienced at Arab or South Asian places of worship. In this case, they share more than a generic Muslim affinity. For Black converts, Muslims from West Africa embody a profound Islamic identity without Arabocentrism, something that has customarily relegated Blacks to the margins of mosque life and leadership. These Islamic and traditional exchanges give African Americans a chance to redesign their spiritual frontiers and cultural habits. For some, this encounter constitutes a mediation of their differences and a revisualization of their Blackness.

At the Harlem Market, Kebe's booth stands near the 115th Street entrance. He has been in the country for nearly seven years and has worked several jobs. But his tailor shop does reasonably well. I arrive at the sliding glass door of his booth, and I find it closed, which is quite unusual. I look inside and see Nya, her eyes lowered and fixed on a sheet of paper in her hands. Sitting relaxed in a tattered swivel chair, she looks up and notices me peering in. She immediately begins waving at me, gesturing for me to pull back the door and enter. I open it halfway.

"Hi," I say. "Is Kebe around?"

"No," she answers. "He went to get some *white* bread for his food. He'll be right back." She repeats, "he just went to get some *white* bread."

Besides her vernacular tone, her exaggeration of the word *white* for the kind of bread Kebe was getting disclosed her American sensibility. And this piqued my curiosity. Over the few years I've known Kebe, he has never left his shop in the hands of anyone except one of his countrymen who could watch it from an adjacent booth. I step inside the narrow booth and stand by the door.

"Are you from Harlem?" I ask.

"Yes," Nya replies.

Kebe suddenly returns, extends greetings, and slides into the seat at his sewing machine. "Do you want some?" he asks, placing the bread on the small table near his food.

"Oh, no, thank you," I say. "I just came by to see how you're doing."

I turn and look at Nya. She is dressed in a white African outfit with elaborate rust and brown embroidery laced around the neck. Her hair is wrapped in the same fabric. Nya works as a teacher's aide at a school for troubled youth and says she wears her African clothing daily. It symbolizes her commitment to African religion and culture and plays a crucial role in her spiritual life.

"How do you feel when you wear African clothes?" I ask.

She raises her head slowly, eyes gleaming. "Oh, I feel reeeally good when I wear African clothes. When I first started wearing it, I wasn't sure how people were going to respond. But people really loved my clothes, how beautiful they were, and they appreciated the style and design. It's to the point now, if I wear something else, something not traditionally African, people get upset and say, 'Where's your African clothes?'" She pauses for a moment. "I have some great pieces. Right, Kebe?" She turns to look at him. "Kebe will tell you. Right? Tell him, Kebe! Don't I have some bad clothes?"

Kebe nods halfheartedly and keeps sewing, taking a piece of food when he can.

"I just thank the African brothers for taking care of me," Nya adds.

"What do you mean?" I ask.

"I thank African tailors like Kebe for hookin' me up with these bad clothes. I'm telling you, the brothers are here to hook me up."

Nya's reaction reflects that of many others who view Africans as an important cultural and, at times, spiritual resource. As a devout Muslim, Kebe feels that Nya's traditional African religiosity, involving multiple deities, violates his strict Islamic monotheism, which explains his less than enthusiastic response about the spiritual implications of her African dress. Even so, Blacks welcome religious and cultural engagement with African Muslims as a way to authenticate their sacred and ethnic practices. Yet some African Americans reveal their ambivalence about the nature of their encounter and struggle to come to grips with the divide.

On nice days, people regularly hang out in lawn chairs, on apartment stoops, or they can be found leaning against scaffoldings. A barbecue pit next to an apartment building emits the smells of American fare. Before going to Masjid Aqsa, I stand on 119th and Seventh, lingering but intently listening to teenagers talking near one of these urban picnic tables. While the girls laugh at younger children chasing one another, they also listen to the boys talk about other neighborhood children, basketball, cars, and how they want to make money. I decide to cross the street and turn to face the traffic light.

A voice rings out. "You all right, man!"

I turn left and spot Lee, a bald African American man in his mid-thirties, about six foot one and husky. "Yeah, I'm all right," I say.

Lee looks busy, even jittery, making small steps almost in place, looking left to right and up and down the street. His T-shirt clings to his body, and he uses a handkerchief to wipe sweat rolling into his pencil-trimmed mustache and beard.

"Look!" I blurt out as we wait either for the light to change or for traffic to lighten. "I'm writing a piece on the African immigrants. How do people feel about Africans in Harlem?" I ask, watching his eyes roll around and his body pace back and forth.

"They don't fuck with us!" he answers abruptly. "That's how we feel about them. Yeah!" he says, shrugging his shoulders. "They don't fuck with us," he repeats, taking a few steps forward. "Unless we're in a cab."

Stunned, I shadow him, moving forward. "What do you mean?" I ask.

He paces, still looking up and down the street, as though he's expecting someone. "What?" he says.

"What do you mean when you say unless you're in a cab?"

"Hey, look," he says, "you got two dollars?"

"What?"

"Let me hold two dollars. I'm trying to get a cab. I know you got two dollars," he says.

Two dollars, I think. *"Damn! People ask me for change, a quarter, even a dollar. But two dollars!"* We reach the middle of the street, and I go into my pocket and pull out some dollars bills, peeling off two. "OK, here you go," I say.

He takes them and says, "Now, you wanna know 'bout Africans, right?"[28]

A white Chevy SUV pulls up.

"Yo, my man!" Lee yells out.

A thin African American man in late twenties jumps out. "Yo, what up, B? How you?"

Lee walks over, and they hug.

"I've been looking for you, man," the driver says. "Where you been?"

"You know, man," Lee answers, "trying to do my thing out here. You know how it is? Look, B, hit me off with something. I need a couple of dollars."

Without hesitation, the other man reaches into his pocket, pulls out some bills, and hands them over.

"Ah-ite [all right], my man," Lee says.

The other man leaves, and Lee and I walk toward a corner bodega. Lee still peers up the street, then turns to me.

"OK, now, what you wanna know?" We enter the store. He looks around, then reaches his hand toward me again. "Yo, man, you got two dollars? I need to get this [lottery] ticket."

"Come on, man," I say. "I just gave you two dollars." I repeat my question about the cab.

"OK," Lee says. "They try to charge us like they know more than us—like they from here. And they don't wanna hear shit from us. We try to tell 'em that it doesn't cost that much to go to a place. And they try to tell us what it cost."

We leave the store.

"Oh, yeah," Lee says, resuming his stares up and down the street. "The other problem is, if we try to sell them something, they don't buy from us. Don't ask me why," he adds quickly. "I don't know." He wipes his brow and swipes the sweat from his chin. "OK, they got 116th locked down, right? All they want from us is for us to spend our money. Other than that, they treat us like we're nothing—especially the females. If you talk to 'em, they don't say nothing to you." He stops to think. "I asked a couple of my African people why they do that. They're not doing the boyfriend thing, but still, you can speak if somebody says something." His face tightens. "Fuck 'em!" he yells. "Then again," he says as his demeanor eases, "I can't say 'fuck 'em,' 'cause they our people and shit. We should come together," he announces. "Look, I'm out."

Lee pivots and crosses Seventh Avenue. People like Lee appear unsure about the ongoing conflict between Africans and Blacks in Harlem. They feel that their common ancestry as African people should allow them a greater sense of unity, self-determination, and accomplishment. But they also speak disparagingly of the other group. Some handle this ambivalence in another way altogether.

After Lee departs, I walk to 116th Street, turn right, and make my way toward Eighth Avenue and Masjid Aqsa. I look to my right and peer into Halima's hair and nail salon. Several African women are sitting and chatting, without customers, at two nail-care stations, while a male barber cuts a young man's hair. Assuming that they are Muslims by the name of the shop, I enter and greet everyone Islamically. I ease over to the barber, someone I see from time to time at both African *masjids*, Aqsa and Salaam. I think this will be a good time to introduce myself and perhaps begin a conversation about Harlem.

"Can I help you?" the barber asks in a lukewarm tone. A Senegalese in his early thirties, Omar is slim and dresses in somewhat trendy New York Village gear, with a body-hugging untucked black shirt and snug jeans. His own hair is styled in a short Afro twist, which seem to accent his dark, slender face and deep eyes.

"No, well, I just wanted to stop in and give my *salaams*," I answer. "I'm working on a book that looks at Africans and African Americans."

"What do you mean?" he shoots back.

"Well," I reply, "I want to understand how Africans and African Americans get along in Harlem."

In the past, I would begin introducing myself this way, and it was received very well by both Africans and American Americans. I also found that punctuating my speech with a series of Islamic expressions, such as *insha-allah* (if Allah wills), *masha-allah* (it pleases Allah), and *al-hamdu-lillah* (praise Allah), appeared to grant me greater access and thus more cooperation. So, during this informal conversation, I have no reason to think otherwise.

Suddenly, Omar bursts out, "You come in here talking all this '*insha-allah*' and '*masha-allah*,' what are you talking about?" I listen as he gears up for more and continues cutting. "We all the same!" he yells. "There's no African and African American, we're all the same," he repeats.

His Black teenage customer interjects. "I know what you're saying," he admits. "But it doesn't matter, 'cause we're the same."

Omar yells, "What are you?"

I try to think where he's going with this question, and it reminds me of Jimmy's way of checking my identity, but I don't answer fast enough.

"What are you?" he repeats.

"I'm Black," I reply.

"Well, then," he says. "You asked me that question like you're White or something!"

I glance at the African women workers on my left and notice them following our conversation, leaning toward one another to chat in low tones after each exchange. I'm not sure what they understand, but they seem to be enjoying the show. While I initially adopted a conventional interviewing strategy, allowing Omar to respond with little interference from me, I now decide to follow another approach. In *White Women, Race Matters*, Ruth Frankenberg discovered that being interactive with her interviewees produced better results, since the idea is to get respondents to forget they're being interviewed and answer as naturally or openly as possible.[29] Not wanting him to think I am intimidated, I look him straight in the eyes and smile.

"What's your name, brother?" I say.

His face relaxes, and he smiles, calmly answering, "Omar."

We continue talking about Black unity, and I explain that my purpose is to understand as much as I can. Fifteen minutes later, we shake hands.

"I'll come back and see you," I say.

"OK, that'll be good," he replies.

This episode reveals an emergent viewpoint in Harlem. A contingent of Africans and Blacks increasingly talk less about their differences and more about a shared Blackness. Then again, this new outlook is not devoid of internal scrutiny and introspection. That is, once they acknowledge the inconsequential nature of their cultural differences, both groups recognize the fact that every group has "good" and "bad" people, and making the decision not to condemn an entire population for the actions of a few is what matters most.

For some Black Americans, especially those who see their relationship with Africans as a competition for scarce resources, the separation between them is irreconcilable, and they view Africans (and recently, Whites and other gentrifiers) as "invaders." Many African immigrants, too, view native-born Blacks as incorrigible slackers, lazy, uneducated, or woefully ignorant of the "real" Africa. They believe that Blacks see them as "animals," recent arrivals from the wild "jungle." Other African Americans, seeking to connect with their ancestral homeland, foster cultural and Islamic exchanges with their African Muslim neighbors. Their actions engender collaborative projects and bridge building. In these cases, African Muslims position themselves as either cultural brokers or Islamic *du'at* (missionaries). For local Blacks uninterested in appropriating African culture or Islam, the line separating them is intolerable. In this context, Africans and Blacks find one another in cabs, at local stores and restaurants, or during business transactions, but these relations are often tense or potentially confrontational, often resulting from long-held stereotypes that force a misreading of each other's intentions. Still, there appears to be a strong desire for reconciliation on both sides. In the midst of this, Africans and Blacks increasingly talk of their racial sameness and downplay any cultural differences. While this viewpoint clearly indicates a shift in consciousness, it has yet to produce significant partnerships between the two groups. It has, however, appeared to reduce conflict during their daily interactions and has the potential to improve relations. These three dimensions of the Black encounter reveal the multilayered nature of how these relations play out in places like Harlem, and they are shot through with religious sentiments, class struggles, racial formations, and other constructs. The next chapter will explore a challenge requiring a different type of resolution: language.

4

The Language of Heaven

I

Mohamed stands still, staring at the pictures. He begins to sweat. Minutes pass, but they feel like hours. He is confused and unable to react, his eyes moving from one image to another and back again. He understands how they are arranged or that they're organized in sequence. But little else makes sense. Finally, he has made up his mind.

"May I help you, sir?" says the young Latina, interrupting his thoughts.

How do I say this?" he thinks, and his heart races.

"Hello, sir!" she yells. He looks at her, then back at the picture. "May I help you?" she says again.

He turns around, scurries down the aisle, and heads out the door. He's back outside and still hungry.[1] As we sit in the Senegalese restaurant La Marmite, named for a lidded French casserole dish, Mohamed explains his first encounter at McDonald's.

"You just stand there," he says, speaking for himself and other new-comers from French West Africa. "Trying to say which food you have to order, because you don't know the language."

And not knowing whether or not the food is *haram*, or religiously unlawful, complicates matters even further. Mohamed is twenty-six, and his English has greatly improved since he first arrived in 1998. Before finishing high school in his native Côte d'Ivoire, he received a track scholarship to compete in the United States. Even then, not many restaurants like La Marmite were available.

During the early days of West African Muslim migration, single men divided their lives between work and the *masjid*. There was little time to cultivate a social life. Their daily existence was dictated by the classic "myth of return," the ardent belief held by most immigrants that they would garner riches in a few short years and return home to share the goods. Greatly inspired by this dream, most began their first years in America living in sordid conditions. In their minds, it was worth the sacrifice, especially since it was only until they struck it rich.

"When I came over to meet my husband," Aissatou says, "he was living on 45th Street, between Eighth and Ninth. There was a place named Hildona Court Apartments." Now in her mid-forties, Aissatou first arrived in 1986, when she was twenty-three. Her husband migrated several years before, but his merchant business was failing. "There was fifteen people in the apartment—one tiny bedroom apartment," she says.

"Fifteen people!" she yells. "Because there was only one person who spoke English, who was capable of talking to the person who owned the hotel to rent the room. The rest of them don't know how to speak English. They don't have no documents. They don't know how to find apartment. They don't know how to apply for apartment."

"That's why it's fifteen people in the apartment?" I ask. "How did they live there? I mean, where did they sleep?"

"There was one bedroom," she replies, "the kitchen with the living room together, and a bathroom."

"Wow!" I reply.

"Yeah," she says. "They put one bed in the room—three people sleep in the bed. They put a mattress on the floor—three people sleeping on the mattress. That's six. In the other [living] room, the same thing. That's twelve. One sleeping in the door where you enter; the other one's sleeping in the other door; one's way over, almost in the bathroom." She pauses. "I ask them, 'How are you guys living in here?' They say, 'What do you mean?' I say, 'Are you sleeping on top of the TV or what? You have a thousand suitcases piled on top—are you sleeping in the suitcases or what?'"

Once Aissatou arrived, she encouraged her husband to leave. They rented a room in a hotel and soon found a more permanent place.

Not only are African immigrants generally unaware of how expensive it is to live in the United States, but they are also often naïve about the difficulties of navigating the cultural terrain of a dense, complex metropolis like New York City. Just ordering a hamburger at McDonald's can be a major challenge for Francophone Africans. Fifteen Senegalese men shared a small one-bedroom apartment because they lacked the language skills to search for something better, even *if* their immigration papers were in order. With all the risks and sacrifices, what is it exactly about the American dream that compels them to stay and endure so much? One middle-aged Senegalese man responds sharply to a similar query: "Wouldn't you? If you believed you were on your way to heaven, wouldn't you take the risks?"

While the idea of an American paradise might sound fantastic, it shows why so many Francophone Africans feel less intimidated about traveling to a "new world," a place nearly four thousand miles away and dominated by a different language and culture. Ibrahim, an Ivoirian-born Arabic teacher in his late twenties from Mali, comments on this point. "It was like heaven on earth," he says. "In Africa, let's say maybe seventy or eighty percent think people in America walk on the sky, people fly—where you can take the money from the street like that!" he says, swiping the air as if scooping up cash. But at the same time, few thought there would be language barriers in this heaven. And for a predominantly semieducated, merchant class, the linguistic difficulties they face are quite formidable.[2]

Mohamed and I met several years back, when he was organizing the new African Day parade in Harlem.[3] Since these public events were a crucial part of the culture in Harlem, we began a conversation and scheduled a time to meet.

A little way up from the African restaurants on 116th, La Marmite looks quaint and exclusive among other nondescript American shops. It is on Seventh Avenue between 133rd and 134th, and Mohamed doesn't live far away. On the day of our appointment, I stand by the glass door, peering out to see if I can spot him. I can hear French news on the satellite station blaring behind me. Commentators are reporting about an Egyptian-based Swiss Muslim philosopher, Tariq Ramadan, and his visit to Senegal to talk about Islamic morals. Another story is about Fedération Nationale des Associations Feminine, a Senegalese women's rights organization, announcing its special gala in New York.

Most of the African restaurants blast French programming of some sort on mounted television sets. A few others play African music videos from time to time on flat-screen televisions. Either way, playing French news or African tunes as background noise links Francophone Africans to home, despite the fact that many are unschooled and not very fluent in French. The sounds from this type of programming strike a more familiar chord than do English shows, and the constant flow of French words or African voices in Senegalese eateries, for example, helps to ease the discomfort of culture shock. Besides the customary practices they perform at African *masjids*, which likewise help them to maintain ties with their respective countries, these restaurants give them a cultural refuge within a larger Anglophone world.

I finally see Mohamed, five foot eight and stocky, with a tannish complexion and a three-inch Afro. He waits at the corner for the light to change. It's a warm afternoon in early October, and the raised collar on his light blue pullover complements his loose-fitting jeans and tan sandals. It is a scene right out of his social world at the Riviera, a ritzy neighborhood in Abidjan where he would hang out with well-to-do kids, eating fish and plantain. He strolls across the street, carrying a brown leather portfolio, and eases up to the door. I push it open just as he reaches for the handle.

"*As-salaamu 'alaykum*," I say, and he repeats the greeting. We walk in and take a nearby table.

"I didn't like English very much," he says in the midst of our conversation.

"Oh?" I reply. "Why not?"

"I started in English when I was in Ivory Coast, but it was, like, the British kind. When we used to have the English class, I used to skip my classes, because it was so difficult for me. When I come to the United States, I was, like, wow, easy!"

"But why didn't you like it back then?" I ask.

"Oh, because I used to have a bad grade in English. It's hard to learn English in the French-speaking countries. Because if there's nothing to make it fun, students are not going to be interested. It was all grammar. And you only have an hour or two hours of English, probably like two times a week. And there's nobody around you can speak English with. After the English class, that's it. It's back to French."

A number of factors influence the acquisition of a second language. The authors of the book *Learning a New Land* identify five challenges to learning English for immigrant children in the United States.[4] While their longitudinal study tracks youth from China, Central America, Mexico, and the Caribbean (including Haiti), their findings are instructive for thinking through the kinds of issues Mohamed and others face. According to the authors' research, high competence in one's native language and knowledge of another language are positive factors for learning a new one. Most French-speaking West African Muslims in Harlem possess relative fluency in at least three or four languages, which include two or three native tongues and a European one, not to mention varying levels of Arabic.[5] Because of the vast diversity of their countries of origin, a half-dozen or so official languages are often recognized, along with many more spoken by each ethnic group. In Côte d'Ivoire, for example, there are some eighty languages, and this is small in comparison with a country such as Nigeria, which apparently possesses more than five hundred.[6] Despite the potential influence of such a rich vernacular environment, most experience difficulties learning English in the United States because they lack exposure to the American version. Those who took English classes in high school learned the British variety. For some, this only requires a minor adjustment after they arrive, but others encounter greater problems. Either way, exposure to native speakers is the key, as the phrase "less contact, less learning" denotes.[7]

Multilingual sign on the inside door of a Murid religious store. It includes Arabic, English, Wolof using Arabic script called *ajami*, and French. (Photo Zain Abdullah)

When Aissatou first entered that small one-bedroom apartment where her husband stayed with fifteen other men, she thought deeply about her life in Senegal—their spacious house and their maid, her highly respected administrative position, and her loving family and community. But her husband's plan to raise enough money to send for her was passing the three-year mark, and she had grown weary.

"I am a Muslim! I'm a woman!" Aissatou bellows, "and it's impossible to sit down for three years or more and not know when my husband is going to return. He doesn't have documents. It would be very hard for him to come home and go back to the U.S. How long I'm going to wait?"

Aissatou knows Wolof and learned French in high school, and she managed to take some English as a second or third language. But her English skills were extremely poor when she came to the United States. Even so, she was determined to be with her husband. It was, she believed, her Muslim duty.

Since she was married, her family sanctioned her trip. If she were single, especially during this early period when the African immigrant community was small, her relatives would have not allowed her to travel alone except under very special circumstances, such as a short-term business venture or a brief visit.

"Even if he has a small place where he's able to slip his feet and put his head," she says now, "I'm able to stay with him. I don't care what place it is. If he's sleeping in the street, let's sleep in the street together. If he has a place, let's sleep in the place together."

Because of her professional background and her ties with the Senegalese consulate, the visa to travel to the States was granted. She also took the trip with seven other people, easing the physical and religious burdens of traveling alone.[8] While Aissatou braced herself against the uncertainties of harsh living in America, there was absolutely no way for her to expect many difficulties beyond this, especially relating to language or culture. The social or cultural alienation immigrants feel is often unrecognized by the native population. But it is just as likely to be ignored by migrants themselves, as they and their families fail to consider survival needs beyond financial ones.

Aissatou's husband, Salimou, owned a store in Senegal, but he lost the business to hard times. This is what compelled him to try his luck in America. Aissatou had substantial savings and drained her three bank accounts, leaving one hundred dollars in each to keep them open. She brought the rest of the money with her to invest in Salimou's vending trade. She also joined him in selling items on the street. Aissatou arrived in September, and three months later, she was pregnant.

"That was a horrible thing," she says, almost repentantly. "Because pregnancy and struggling"—she pauses to reflect further—"I just got here, and you think you're coming to help your husband, and then the pregnancy. I don't know the hospital; I don't know how to get birth control. As a Muslim, you have to keep it. No abortion! I have to keep the pregnancy."

"Do Muslim women practice contraception in Senegal?" I ask.

"Yeah," she replies. "We do, like, normally, after women get their period and when they're breastfeeding. But before, a lot of women don't take birth control. They say it's against Islam. But now, so many children are struggling with men who have so many wives. They start taking birth control, because you'll have one thousand children. And you're not able to feed those children. You make those children suffer. It's now time for development. The country is moving forward. We have to change!"[9]

Because her husband couldn't miss work, Aissatou was forced to seek prenatal care on her own. She ventured to Urban Hospital, but no one understood her because her English was so poor. On one of her early visits, she stood at the reception desk, feeling lonely and dejected, and eventually broke down crying. A Filipino doctor instructed her not to return again without a translator.

"But you know," she confesses, "I don't know my rights. I don't know what to do."

On a few occasions, Barbara, a hospital coordinator who knew some French, would help. At other times, another doctor, Maria, translated when she was available, but getting an appointment with her was nearly impossible. Aissatou finally found a French doctor who would sometimes translate for her over the telephone. With all of this plotting, there would be times when Aissatou would reach the hospital at eight in the morning and wouldn't leave until three.

"Because I have nobody to talk English and French with me," she says, "I have to be there. And this is the reason I went back to school to learn and try to help the people."

She attended the Learning Center on 122nd Street and took ESL (English as a second language) courses. The school administered an English literacy test and gave her the results.

"My English was poor, but my mouth was strong," Aissatou says, referring to her first language assessment. "But you know, the pregnancy was real hard for me, and those people have to help. I don't know how to apply for Medicaid, because at the time, there was only ten Senegalese in the country. I am the third one who has a baby."[10]

Her English slowly improved, but the hospital bills were piling up much faster. She was told to go home, because her husband couldn't afford to make payments.

"I said, 'No! I'm not going nowhere!' And those people helped me. They helped me to get Medicaid to cover all my bills."

Now, Aissatou is co-owner of a variety shop on 116th Street, and since her English has greatly improved, she has volunteered to help African immigrants at the hospital.

"I used to be an interpreter, using French with people from Guinea and Wolof with people from Senegal," she says.

While this story illustrates a particularly difficult period for her, Aissatou and other African Muslims in Harlem see their hardship as part of a divine scheme. In other words, they tend to make sense of their adversity in religious terms. By observing their struggles and thinking through their narratives, we are able to comprehend how and where religious meaning emerges in their lives.

Aissatou tells me, "If I'm going to suffer or if I'm not going to suffer, it's going to be something I must learn in my life. A person has to struggle a little bit in your life, especially Muslim women. If God give you everything and you think everything is there for you, it's not! You have to struggle to know how to handle your life."[11]

Whether this struggle occurs at fast-food establishments, African eateries, or public institutions, the struggle with an English-speaking world is about more than new vocabulary words or the mechanics of grammar. It's also about how these people traverse a new land and the ways Islam helps them make sense of it.

In *Jaguar*, a novel based on ethnographic fieldwork among Nigerien migrants living in New York, African Muslims coming to America are instructed to rely on a linguistic network of Francophone immigrants. Issa, a main character in the book, is given similar advice before he leaves Abidjan for the United States: "They told him to look for any French-speaking African taxi driver as soon as he arrived at the airport."[12] This person would bring him to the appropriate place. For many

African Muslims under French colonial rule, however, the diligent use of Islamic Arabic and their adamant refusal to learn French were acts of resistance. Many older African immigrants, influenced in the early days by their elders to shun all things French, still haven't learned the language, preferring to remain within the sanctum of a Wolof- or Malinke-speaking world. "There is a great tendency to use Wolof when Senegalese speak among themselves," writes Donald Martin Carter, discussing Murid migrants in Italy. "'French is not our language,' some would say in the midst of conversation, and the conversation will then slip into Wolof."[13] The extent of one's Frenchness also signifies a religious divide, marking a difference between rural folk schooled in Islamic etiquette and urban dwellers formally educated under the French system.

This difference constitutes a generation gap between French-educated young people and their Wolof and Islamically trained older compatriots. "This places many of the members of the urban Da'ira (Islamic and mutual benefit circle) at a decided disadvantage in the urban world in which the language of the state bureaucracy is dominant," Carter argues. "In the urban Da'ira of Senegal, then, often the Marabout or some other member of the group educated in French will act as translator and advocate for those with language difficulties."[14] This case, however, is certainly not peculiar to Senegal. In Harlem, one Muslim official talked about how Muslim elders in Côte d'Ivoire had a similar reaction to French colonialism, preventing children from formally learning French or attending government schools. While implementing a strictly Islamic training regime apparently helped Ivoirians struggle against cultural imperialism, he admitted that it left them ill prepared for political office or other professional positions. In the mid-1980s, this posed a major problem for Africans migrating to Western countries such as the United States. Because they lacked French fluency, not only were Wolof-only or Malinke-only speakers shut out of an emerging Francophone network of Africans extending mutual aid to one another, but they were also unable to benefit from French-speaking Haitians and their knowledge of the city.

II

It's late morning at the Harlem Market. Warm words fill the air. "*Bon jour*. How are you? *Çava? Al-hamdu lillah*, praise Allah." English, Arabic, and French gestures blend evenly into one another. With so many African languages spoken at the market, French might become a common way to exchange greetings and chat about the day's events, depending on the fluency of the speakers. But African vendors are not in business to socialize, and French at the Harlem Market is bad for business. The great majority of their patrons speak English, and their ability to sell their products relies on how well they communicate in the native parlance. Because the market is often patronized by tourists, the atmosphere differs distinctly from that at other African businesses along 116th Street. Shoppers at the market expect to have a conversation about the African art, fabric, or trinkets before their purchase. Seekers of exotica or Africana are not simply purchasing a generic piece of wood or cloth. They also buy the storytelling or the lore told by the vendor about the meaning of each object. In their search for the appropriate African artifact, the story behind each purchase gives the patron a sense of discovery, a sensation of the hunt and capture. The two discourses of storytelling and discovery increase the value of the African products and help to guarantee a sale.[15] Without the rudiments of the language, however, selling the most basic merchandise can be frustrating.

The morning wears on, and Khadi prepares for the tourist bus as she sits on a stool outside her shop. Black African dolls with rich multicolored dresses adorn her table. She designs the figures and their costumes and has quite a reputation for her knowledge of the craft. Her store, Mustafa's World of African Art, is co-owned by Anta, a young Senegalese man with extensive experience in the international tourist market. The tight twenty-by-ten-foot space is filled with all sorts of wooden artifacts. Hand-carved African masks fill virtually every space, hanging on the walls near the ceiling and on the beams.

Now in her mid-thirties, Khadi arrived in the United States with her husband in 1991. The shop is named after her son, who was born in Harlem the following year. In Senegal, she completed secretarial training and performed typical office duties such as typing and filing. She still finds it hard to imagine her life as a merchant. But without an adequate grasp of English, she is forced to sell African art to make a living. Khadi is extremely pleasant and has a ready smile, but a discussion about her prospects in America, especially as compared with her former life as an office professional, appears to dampen her jovial spirit.

"We have problems with English," she says humbly, "because grammatically, it is the opposite of French. And that give us hard time to learn English."

Directly across from Khadi's art shop is Mame, a Senegalese woman selling clay pots and earth-tone sand pictures of African landscapes. When Mame's daughter, Zeyna, was in New York, we spoke frequently about African immigrants in Harlem. After Zeyna relocated to California, Mame and I continued talking about these issues.

"Don't forget," I'd repeat often, "I want to talk to you about selling 'wood' [African sculpture]."

"Yes, yes," she'd reply, "any time, any time!"

Although she customarily avoids any formal interview, especially with a tape recorder, she always invites me to share a meal or to join daily chats. On one of these occasions, a young Jamaican customer ventures into the market. He passes Khadi's shop and walks over to Mame's earthenware. Picking up one after the other, he turns with one in his hand and spots Mame ready to assist him.

"Do you have pots to put plants in?" he asks.

"What?" Mame replies. "I don't understand."

He repeats his question, this time a little louder and with greater agitation. Mame turns to Khadi, who is watching from her booth. She walks closer.

"What? What does he want?" Khadi asks.

"I don't know," Mame replies.

The customer looks at both of them. "Can I use this for plants?" he barks, raising the pot in one hand.

Mame and Khadi stare at each other and then at him, and I try to help. "He is asking if he can use this for plants, you know, a plant," I say.

They both look at me, bewildered. Khadi shrugs her shoulders with her hands up. "I don't know," she answers.

The Jamaican customer replaces the pot and scurries off, meandering throughout the market.

It isn't that Mame and Khadi don't understand the English words in and of themselves. They have a problem understanding the diction of their customer, since it is couched in a thick Jamaican accent. The long and varied U.S. immigration history, with its recent influx of new migrants from Asia, Latin America, Africa, and the Caribbean, has greatly intensified an already diverse cultural environment. And the African presence adds a countless array of new languages and sounds to the American tapestry. But this also means a concomitant rise in English accents, old and new dialects intermingling in settings where both natives and newcomers interact. In *No Shame in My Game*, an ethnography about the working poor in Harlem, Katherine S. Newman shows how service workers in multicultural settings must learn to navigate various dialects of English, street slang, and nuanced behavioral patterns. "Monolingual Spanish speakers fresh from the Dominican Republic have to figure out orders spoken in Jamaican English," Newman says. "All of these people have to figure out how to serve customers who may be fresh off the boat from Guyana, West Africa, Honduras."[16] African American patrons have their own expectations in the marketplace, and this adds a burden on African merchants who find it hard to respond adequately to their demands. Some residents feel a slow response from an African vendor, a twisted facial expression, or a suck of the teeth is disrespectful, and conflict often ensues. Many customers find it incomprehensible that they can own and operate a business, no matter how crude, and not understand their idiomatic English or interpret their bodily gestures.

"People don't realize how hard it is to make it in New York without the proper language skills," Khadi says. "People in Senegal may choose English as a second language, but that doesn't mean they really know it. They might be able to even understand what you're saying but can't really speak back."

On a different day at the market, I stop by Essa's African fabric and clothing booth near the bazaar's rear entrance. Unlike the custom-made items sewn by Kebe, the Senegalese tailor just a few booths away, Essa's pieces are off the rack. I stroll up and noticed him inside, selling a garment to a woman. The walls are packed with an assortment of colorful fabric, a mounting arrangement stacked from the floor to near the ten-foot-high ceiling. Beautiful African designs hang from a single rack against the right wall. After his customer leaves, he steps out of his stall and extends *salaams*. He customarily wears African clothes, particularly garments from his homeland of Mali, but this day he is wearing a casual button-down shirt, jeans, and a dark blue Yankees baseball cap. He looks like a real New Yorker.

"Why aren't you wearing your African clothes today?" I ask him in early December.

"Too cold!" he replies abruptly.

I say, "Some people wear warmer clothes underneath and still wear their African clothes on top."

"Yeah, I know," he replies, "but I'd rather just wear one or the other."

We are soon joined by Ismael, a forty-year-old African art merchant born in Niger but raised in Côte d'Ivoire. Like Khadi, Ismael has a quick, warm smile.

Actually, Muslims believe the smile is an important part of the Islamic greeting. The Qur'an states that a person receives ten blessings for every good deed, as long as the intention to perform an honorable act is upheld.[17] Extending the greeting of peace, *as-salaamu 'alaykum* (May the peace of Allah be with you), constitutes a prayer, a dutiful act, and its divine recompense is tenfold. Other benedictions are often added, such as *rahmatullah* (Allah's mercy) and *harakatuh* (Allah's bounty). Similar to the way *karma* is understood, the Islamic salutation intends to infuse goodness into the world. Regardless of one's native language, Muslims customarily repeat this Arabic formula.[18] Moreover, the prophetic tradition encourages regular acts of charity (*sadaqa*), stipulating that even a smile is a gift one gives to another.[19] Saluting one another with *salaam* and a smile represents a very basic part of the Islamic tradition. African Muslims, however, are learning that these religious practices are not always transferable to other social contexts. This is especially true outside of a communal environment.

"I used to smile at the people downtown when I talked to them," says Seydou, a Senegalese educator who moved his family out of New York to Newark, New Jersey, in the mid-1990s. "And they would say, 'What the fuck are you smiling at?' So I stopped smiling at people. Then other people would tell me I have nice teeth

The rear entrance of the Malcolm Shabazz Harlem Market on West 115th Street. (Photo Zain Abdullah)

and should smile more. So I didn't know what to do. I think they think I am trying to get over on them or something like that," he concludes.[20]

Verbal communication is not the only dynamic West African Muslims must navigate in these places. And while cultural context and social class are important factors to consider during their interactions with others, body language such as smiling might signal unintended meanings to others unfamiliar with culturally specific gestures.

As Essa, Ismael, and I chat, Barbara, an African American in her thirties, walks up. Essa had been expecting her, because he needs a favor. He has asked her to model a few clothing items so he can photograph them and show potential customers. Although he is from Mali, Essa speaks little French; Bambara is his native tongue. He gives a Mudd cloth overcoat to Barbara, and she immediately slips into it. Essa and Ismael look at it, face each other, and begin talking in Bambara. Barbara becomes visibly agitated, looking around nervously and peering into nearby shops.

"Look!" she finally yells. "Speak in English! I don't know what you're saying!"

Shocked, they spin around and stare at her.

"Yeah, yeah," Ismael says. "Speak in English."

"Yes, you're right," Essa replies. "We should speak in English."

People feel alienated when others talk about them in their presence and particularly in a foreign language. This is especially true for Americans, who routinely expect others to know English but exert little effort to be bilingual. But this behavior is particularly ostracizing when it occurs under conditions where relations are already strained, as they are between Blacks and Africans. Even for African American Murid converts, their relationship to the Wolof language structures their place within the Sufi order particularly and Islam more generally.

Similar challenges occur outside the market. Some of this burden is eased because newcomers receive a great deal of assistance from those who are more established. Many Senegalese street merchants maintain a network of mutual support. In some African traditions, this is called *susu*, a system in which micro loans are made within the circle. Members of a group deposit a particular dollar amount into a pot. Each member has a limited time to invest it and turn a profit, returning the borrowed amount for use by the next person. For Senegalese Muslims in Harlem, however, a few added features are in place. If the recent migrant has no place to live, an appropriate place will be assigned. The day after arrival, the initiate is brought downtown to learn how to buy merchandise, which is purchased for him. But the newcomer is not required to pay back any of the money for the initial installment. The very next day, he is placed on the street as a vendor.

"If you don't know how to speak English," Aissatou says, "they'll translate it for you and talk between you and the customer."

Sidiki, a street merchant from Guinea in his late twenties, sees English as a social necessity. He speaks seven languages, including French and several African ones, moderately well. In Guinea, he studied French in high school but was forced to drop out in tenth grade when his father died, leaving his mother without support. While in high school, Sidiki scoured the French news for stories about America, which were plentiful. The teacher frequently called on him to apprise the class of the latest information about America. His older brother migrated to the United States earlier but was killed driving a gypsy cab (an unlicensed taxi) in Boston. Although Sidiki wants to attend school, he is forced to spend hours on the street hawking items such as winter gloves and scarves or women's summer wraps. Unable to take English as a second language in high school, he learned it on the streets when he arrived. Merchants like Sidiki have a tougher time managing what they see as an inordinate number of rules and laws. And with poor English, many feel trapped at every turn.

"For us in Africa, selling in the street is legal," he says. "You know, the people are selling movies in the street, they're selling T-shirts in the street, everything in the street. But if you don't know English, you're in trouble. 'What [does] that mean?'" he says. "OK, sometime they can make some law if you don't read the newspaper in English, you don't get the TV in English, you're not going to know about it. When they give you ticket, you say, 'Hey! Why?' And they tell you, 'No, no. It's illegal, it's from the law.'"

Keeping up with the latest news from Guinea is much easier, since it is broadcast on television or radio in French.

For an African vendor on the streets of New York, even knowing conventional English could prove useless. On one of his regular vending days, Sidiki has an African American male customer. He is selling movies, and the patron inquires about the quality of the films.

"Yo, is this one good?" the customer says, pointing to a movie on the table.

"Yes!" Sidiki replies, unsure about what the man is asking. He speaks much too fast for Sidiki, and he doesn't want to appear ignorant and make matters worse.

The customer looks around then returns to the same DVD. "This one is bad?" he says.

"Yes!" Sidiki says again.

"Yo, man!" the customer yells. "Everything is yes!"

"I'm sorry for my language," Sidiki mutters to himself.

"This motherfucka, man!" the man bellows. "Everything yes-yes." He walks off.

Sidiki doesn't know what the man is saying, especially his profanity, and goes to ask his Puerto Rican co-vendor, Pedro.

"He says you are a motherfucker, that's all," Pedro tells him.

"What?" Sidiki responds. "My mother? I'm going to kill him! Nobody talks about my mother! My parents! No!"

Pedro interrupts. "No, no, no! In America, you don't fight him over that!"

"No, no!" Sidiki insists. "Nobody can curse my mother!"

For many, profanity is an idiomatic part of street language. In this context, however, it is no longer enough to listen for simple speech patterns. Street vernacular compels Sidiki to conform to a different type of listening. Verbal communication in this situation is quite different, but Sidiki will have to adapt if he wants to remain a street vendor.

"I know the language when they come," Sidiki says. "When they tell me, 'Hey, fuck you,' I just say no, forget it. I'm not going to listen to them."

Ironically, he doesn't blame his patrons for their profanity. Instead, he believes that many who exhibit this behavior are products of a harsh environment. The entire situation has compelled him to return to school to improve his English. This, he believes, will allow him to give them *da'wa* or impart his sense of Islamic morality and traditional African values.

African Muslims have been compelled by what they believe is an Islamic mandate to learn English in order to preach the *deen* (religion).[21] Learning English will undoubtedly make them more marketable and help them get along better in their day-to-day activities. But for them as *du'at*, or callers to the faith, learning English takes on a whole new meaning. In addition to selling clothing and other items on fold-up stands all over Harlem, others invest in the wholesale purchase of Islamic books and tapes in English, selling them in front of the *masjid*. Merchandising this religious material in English forces them to learn the content of these products. As they become more familiar with the language and style of these materials, they believe their English fluency will improve their ability to make *da'wa* (propagation) and introduce Islam to Harlem residents. In very important ways, their religious aspirations have motivated them to learn English, much more than the promise of advancement in their menial jobs or material gains ever could. Beyond this, African Muslims without proper English grapple with the vagaries of American life in ways locals can hardly imagine.

While some women are street merchants, most, particularly young women, seek a different vocational path. They, too, face similar linguistic challenges. Aicha was born in Korohko, Côte d'Ivoire, and her parents moved to Abidjan when she was just two years old. Since many Muslim women in Côte d'Ivoire marry at an early age, there are rarely opportunities to complete their education beyond basic Islamic instruction. Others work in the marketplace selling food or other items. As a young businesswoman in Côte d'Ivoire, Aicha operated her own import-export agency. She also ran a modest restaurant. She arrived in the United States in 2000, when she was twenty-six years old. Although she knew some French, Mandingo, and other African languages, her English capacity was limited to one phrase, *Good morning*. She learned a few other words, such as *me*, *English*, and *no* from television during her first few weeks in the country. When Aicha first arrived, she stayed with several Ivorian men in the Bronx. Lacking English, she was confined to the house, because there was no one available to escort her around. Her roommates also didn't encourage her to venture out, especially since she was performing all of the household chores such as cooking and cleaning. She quickly grew restless. *This is not my life!* she thought to herself, crying and watching the men leave for work each morning. Aicha was an industrious businesswoman in Côte d'Ivoire, and the three weeks she remained inside after her arrival were intolerable. One day, despite her roommates' warning, she waited for them to leave and went out for a short walk. Outside and alone, she entered a very different world and was unable to read the street signs.

"That's a big difference," she says today. "We don't have a number on the street back home. We have like a building number or apartment number. But not like here."

She thought she could walk several blocks, turn around, and make it back to her apartment building. Unfortunately, that didn't happen.

"I went one block, two blocks, three blocks, and then when I turned back," she says, "all the buildings were like the same! I can't remember my building number."

She began to panic. Before long, she had wandered more than ten blocks. Aicha lived on 151st Street but found herself lost somewhere near 164th. As the sun set, she grew frightened.

"I don't speak the language," she now explains. "I don't even know how to ask someone. And I saw a cop in the car, I start crying."

The police car pulled over, and the window rolled down. "Are you OK?" the officer asked.

"But I didn't even know what 'Are you OK?' means," Aicha recalls.

"Good morning!" she replied.

"What?" the policeman said.

"Good morning!" she repeated.

At that moment, the officer knew something was wrong and instructed her to get into the car. *Oh, no!* Aicha thought to herself. *They're going to send me back to my country! Why am I talking to the policeman?* The words were thundering in her ears: *They'll send me back to my country!*

"Get inside the car!" the officer commanded.

"Me, English, no!" Aicha said. "Me, English, no!"

She was finally escorted into the car and driven to the police precinct at Yankee Stadium. At police headquarters, a dark-skinned officer walked toward her.

As Aicha sat crying, her mind continued to race: *Oh, no! I'm going back today! Why did I go outside and walk?"*

"Do you speak French?" The officer asked, then repeated, *"Parlez-vous le français?"*

Aicha looked up in amazement. *"Oui,"* she replied, then immediately asked if they were sending her back to Côte d'Ivoire.

The French-speaking officer, Pierre, was Haitian, and he assured her that she was not being deported. Aicha told him the only fact she knew: her apartment wasn't far from Yankee Stadium. Pierre walked her outside. A block or two away, they spotted Aicha's friends frantically looking for her.

"I think that was a lesson," she says today, "because I didn't even know the money. They didn't tell me all those things, they just left me and went out."

This story speaks volumes about where most Francophone Africans begin culturally in the United States, regardless of their social status or educational level in their home countries. Because the French system is markedly different from the American, African immigrants from French-speaking countries undergo a culture shock barring them from simple communication. For an active adult and a successful businesswoman in her own country, it is devastating to enter a new society and not be able to function on the most basic level. Of course, Aicha's male counterparts contributed to her feelings of isolation, as they exploited her services and discouraged her from learning English or even walking outside. "But you know," Aicha says, "they were always scaring me, saying you're going to get in trouble." It's dreadful for an adventurous, twenty-six-year-old woman to end up in America and be confined for three weeks. She already took a huge risk coming to the United States on her own, for, as Aissatou has mentioned earlier, most African Muslim women would only receive family approval to stay if they were coming to join a husband. "And where you are going to put that young woman?" Aissatou asks. "The man's house is not safe. For women to be struggling, the young women, she's going to do something she doesn't want to be doing." Aicha's living predicament made matters worse, and soon she became pregnant out of wedlock, a scandalous affair in traditional societies. Without the proper language skills and cultural bearings, African men and women like Aicha seem like lost children in a concrete jungle. And each day they fight to regain a piece of their adulthood.

While language acquisition is crucial for fully integrating into a society, it is not the only requirement for upward mobility. Like any other group, African Muslims rely on their own cultural capital—the knowledge, experience, meaningful relationships, or even attitudes they muster to advance themselves socially. After three months of living in the apartment, Aicha could take no more. She soon met Aminata, a woman from Abidjan, who helped her find a school with an ESL program. So, after her male roommates left for work at eight in the morning, she prepared to go to school without their knowledge. She had seven hundred dollars in savings, and the school allowed her to pay one hundred dollars every month. For the next three months, she traveled for several hours both ways to attend classes. But she made it back to the apartment before the men returned at around ten each night. The more Aicha learned English and moved around the city, the more she met people. Eventually, she discovered there were free ESL classes at the nearby Bronx Community College. She enrolled. At around the same time, she began looking for a job, and Aminata helped her once more.

Aicha began working at KFC and continued taking classes at the community college. "When I start working," she says now, "it was hard for me to do both things." In the meantime, she moved into another apartment. After a while, she discovered she was pregnant and was forced to leave school. Life instantly became more difficult, but the state-sponsored medical assistance she was eligible to receive helped a great deal. "Thank God," Aicha says, "I knew a little bit of the language. So I was doing everything by myself, going to all my appointments by myself, because when you're pregnant, you get free Medicaid." During her days at KFC, Aicha's English slowly improved. In *No Shame in My Game*, Katherine S. Newman found that while low-wage jobs in the fast-food industry offer little advancement, they do allow poor English speakers to improve their language skills, especially in such a rapid-fire work environment.[22]

Some highly trained African professionals needing to improve their English start out at such establishments. Rama, for example, obtained her medical degree in Senegal, where she worked in the local hospital. Because her brother was living in New York and entered her name in the lottery, she was granted a visa to enter the country. But she wasn't interested, since she was already leading a very respectable life at home. Her brother convinced her that American opportunities could give her and her family an even brighter future. "I was good at English in school," she says. "But when I came here, it was like Hebrew to me. Believe me! It wasn't the English I knew." She studied her brother's ESL books and later took a class for conversation. "I had to learn fast," she says. "My first job was at McDonald's. So I think that helped me a lot, too." Once her English improved, Rama moved quickly from McDonald's to a Planned Parenthood office, a place where she could use her knowledge of medicine and human anatomy.

Others come with more technical expertise and just need help with applications or examinations. For taxi and limousine workers, the English on the driving test can be intimidating. So, when a motor vehicle office was opened on 125th Street, long-standing African immigrants more familiar with the governmental system devised a strategy. "They have a driver's license in Africa," Abdoulaye says of his

Senegalese countrymen. "You come here, the test is in English. That's why we have difficulty getting a license." There are only a few differences between the American and Senegalese guidelines, such as driving on the right instead of the left. But "a stop sign is a stop sign," Abdoulaye says. An examination in French would greatly accelerate entry into the job market. Abdoulaye met with the administration, and the test was redesigned for French readers.

Aicha's job at KFC was preparing food. Angling for a promotion, she jumped to perform any task requested of her. But she also realized that any advancement would require a better command of the language. While she tried to practice her English on the job, her Haitian manager refused to comply and spoke to her in French only. "She was very, very mean," Aicha recalls. "Never really helped me out with learning the register or other things." But while her communication was limited, she used another resource, a cultural asset and religious device. "Thank God," she says, "I can say I'm really a smiling woman. So I always smile at people. And that helped me! Every time the boss came, I'm the only one who has her teeth out." James, the head manager, certainly noticed. "'That girl,'" Aicha says, repeating his words, "'she's good to be a cashier, because she's always smiling. This is the kind of cashier we need—somebody who's always smiling like that. This is what our customers like.'" James asked Aicha's direct supervisor, the Haitian manager, to train her for the cashier's job. She adamantly refused, arguing that Aicha couldn't speak English. "I was crying," Aicha says. "So he called me, and we have a little conversation. He could understand me a little bit. But he was, like, 'Oh, she can do it with the English she's speaking.'" Before long, Aicha was sent to the KFC training site to learn the registers.

Because first-generation African migrants work schedules affording them little time for English classes, most are functionally illiterate. However, the stories of Aicha, Rama, and Abdoulaye demonstrate how they and other immigrants use their cultural or religious capital to transcend, at least to some degree, these communication barriers. Besides these workplace issues, their anxieties about the importance of French, English, or African languages significantly influence who they become in Harlem.

III

In the United States, the largest groups of African immigrants are from English-speaking countries such as Nigeria and Ghana, and they have also been in the country the longest. Most are Christian, but some practice traditional African religions, and some practice both simultaneously. Their migration is also shifting the religious landscape in the States. African Christians have a linguistic and religious affinity with Americans, and this has helped to ease their integration into American society. However, because of their British orientation and racial designation in the States, their path has been fraught with its own unique challenges. Still, they appear to have fared much better than their Francophone counterparts. I would argue that this is largely a result of their higher level of formal education and class status rather than their presumed cultural similarities.[23] Some French-speaking Africans feel that their English is better than that of Anglophone migrants, since they have their first real experience with English after they arrive and learn speech patterns directly from Black Americans or other indigenous residents. Although they are unable to "pass" fully for African Americans, Manthia Diawara remarks, they take much satisfaction in knowing that even Nigerians, for example, "could not speak English like natives."[24] Whether their English is spoken with a British or a French accent, which necessarily includes a tinge of African cadence, is perhaps inconsequential. But the various paths they take to make American English an integral part of their character will shape their lives in important ways.

One Friday, I go to Masjid Aqsa to meet George, an African American Muslim in his mid-sixties. He attends African *masjids* on a regular basis. When I arrive a little late, he is nowhere in sight. There are about twenty or thirty Africans scurrying about, preparing for *asr*, the afternoon prayer. Some are downstairs performing ablution, ritualistically washing their faces, hands, and feet, while others sit on the carpet reading the Qur'an and waiting for the *iqama*, the call to stand for prayer. A few others sit huddled in small circles and talk softly about the day.

Since *asr* is performed at around midday, local shop owners, street vendors, or taxi drivers routinely slip in and out, whenever they can steal away from work. Others might make prayers during the workday within the confines of their stores, forcing customers to wait in front of locked doors displaying signs: "I'll Be Back." A patron might also enter a shop only to find a draped woman "thikering," reciting Allah's praises, or prayerfully prostrating behind the counter.

Since it is Friday, the weekly *khutba* (sermon) and prayer for *jum'ah* services have just finished, and the static energy from nearly eight hundred attendees still hangs in the air. After removing my shoes, I step onto the carpet and walk to the back stairwell and down one flight. As I enter the second prayer area, I notice Moussa, an Ivoirian *imam* from Masjid Salaam, walking toward me with a huge grin. He is about five foot seven and slender. With each step, the sway of his long brown *jalabiyya* and bright white knitted *kufi* make him look authoritative.

"*As-salaamu 'alaykum*," he says warmly, grabbing my hand. After my reply and before it's possible to say anything else, he adds, carefully enunciating each word, "How you doing? You all right?"

"Yes, I'm fine, how are you?" I say.

"I'm fine," he answers. "And how are you?" he repeats.

Just then, I begin to recognize something. Imam Moussa is actually parroting my speech. He is a full-time employee at the *masjid*, and most of his days are spent speaking to African members in French, Malinke, Djoula, or other languages. He rarely has a chance to practice conversational English. Under normal circumstances, this mimicking might have been annoying, but his efforts are commendable. As water splashing from *wudu* stations a few feet away becomes more audible, I am reminded of the time for prayer and end our brief conversation.

"OK," I say, "we'll talk later."

Again, he carefully mimics my words. "Yeah, we'll talk later." And then he asks if I would be willing to teach the community English. I smile and fumble my speech, trying to figure out how I could justify the time. "Think about it," he says, interrupting my stutter. I stop and stare at him. He smiles and repeats, "Just think about it."

While Masjid Aqsa generally offers Arabic language instruction, English classes are often held down the street at L'Association des Sénégalais d'Amérique (the Senegalese Association in America), enrolling perhaps a half-dozen students at any given time. Teaching English at the *masjid* would provide a valuable service, particularly since it might attract those who are willing to take classes in a more familiar environment and if they were offered at nonstandard times such as after *fajr* (dawn prayer).

Most are forced to make significant sacrifices to remain in class, especially since low-wage jobs require more hours or an extra income just to earn a decent living. Sadjah, a longtime Harlem resident and an African American Muslim, taught an ESL class for Africans at Masjid Malcolm Shabazz, but she found it hard to retain students.

"It wasn't a bad experience," she says. "It was just that I don't think they understood the concept of *class*. I would give them a syllabus, and every week, I would have new students. I would say, 'OK, where's so-and-so?' 'Oh, he had to go to the store, or he had to fix this, and I'm taking his place today.' But they're very respectful, and they're very willing to learn." The Western classroom setting has a linear structure, which automatically supports a value system of individualism and personal competition, whereas other societies see learning as a collective enterprise. In this view, a friend substituting for an absentee student doesn't necessarily mean the missing person is no longer involved in the learning process. In fact, this is perhaps preferable to missing class altogether, obtaining notes, or getting an impersonal recording. This is not to condone student absenteeism. Rather, it reminds educators to be aware of the cultural context of learning and how it takes shape across societies. First-generation African immigrants are not just learning vocabulary and grammar in these sessions, but they must also acquire new under-standings of classroom structure and the culture of education in America.

The children of African Muslims born and raised in the United States have similar difficulties. Ibrahim instructs Arabic language classes at Aqsa. While he teaches both adults and children, his sessions for youngsters take up most of the day on Saturdays and Sundays. He also taught Arabic for several years in Mali and apparently gained quite a reputation as an extraordinary teacher. But teaching both continental and American-born African children poses a unique challenge.

"When I first started teaching the children here, I was so confused," he admits. "Because I was thinking, like, they're African, right? And it's going to be some edu-cation like back home. But I see they're so different. When you say, 'Sit down,' they get up. When you say, 'Get up,' they sit down. The kids think they're smarter than you. 'I was born here, an American! I'm better than everybody. He come from Africa. And the way he talk, you know his African accent, he don't speak English. So I'm smarter than him!'" Ibrahim sneers in imitation of the students' mocking. "But it's so different from the way we teach back home. You don't use nothing [to get their respect]. But when you talk and your eyes get red, everybody know that it's serious, and they're going to be quiet."

In this case, these American-born African children have internalized preju-dices against those with African accents. The consequence of failing to shed one's accent is the disparagement of one's peers, even at the *masjid*.

After *wudu* at Aqsa, people return upstairs and perform the prayer. George has also returned and is leaning against the wall. Imam Moussa is still sitting in the front prayer line, from which he rises and begins making an announcement in French. He is instructing Francophone Africans about where to get help for problems with immigration. By this time, the congregation has swelled to more than one hundred, and Africans from non-French-speaking countries such as Somalia are also present, along with more than a few Yemenis. Because French appears to be much more consequential in Côte d'Ivoire (with a politically strong Christian population of 32 percent compared with 38 percent for Muslims), the predominance of Ivoirian leadership at Aqsa is also reflected in its common use of French. In contrast, the Senegalese at Masjid Touba, whose home country of Senegal is 98 percent Muslim, use French officially, but they mostly communi-cate in Wolof. It's not surprising, then, that American Muslims at these places are complaining more about feeling ostracized, especially when no translation is provided.

I stand up and go over to where George is sitting. His broad features and brown complexion prompt me to ask about his birthplace and whether he's from the Caribbean.

"Oh, no," he replies with a slight smile. "People always think I'm African or from Jamaica or somewhere." Born in South Carolina, he has lived in Harlem since he was a teenager. Although he is clean-shaven and dresses in Western attire, he says, "They come up to me and start speaking their language all the time." His small Afro, however, makes him somewhat conspicuous among African men who mostly wear crew-cuts.

We begin talking about the sizable attendance of daily prayers at Aqsa. I guess it shouldn't be surprising to find urban mosques with one hundred or so at *fajr* prayer, a similar number in the afternoon, and a larger group at night. In fact, it's reasonable to expect such attendance at a city-based *masjid* where a large population of immigrants works and lives. Besides, the *masjid* is a vital sanctuary for Francophone Muslims who find it hard to fit into other places in the city.

"These people are something else," George blurts out.

"What do you mean?" I say.

"Nah, I mean, they really try to make you comfortable, make you feel at home." But even he feels alienated at times, except on special occasions when fluent English-speaking Africans give an Islamic talk. "There is one guy who gives lectures here," George says. "When he's here, it's really packed. You should see it! And he knows English well. He'll talk to you in American English. I don't know, he must have been around Americans—Black Americans!—'cause his English is too good, he speaks too much like us."

As *maghrib* (sunset prayer) approaches, more people begin entering the *masjid*. George looks to his left, toward the door. "There he is, right there!" he says. Babacar walks toward us, stopping every few steps to greet people. He appears quite popular. I wave my hand, flagging him over to our spot against the wall.

"Don't tell him what I said!" George quickly whispers as he leans closer to me.

"No, I won't," I say.

"I don't want him to know I was talking about him," George says with a grimacing expression.

Babacar reaches us and, with a wide smile, extends the peace.

"I see you're a good teacher," I say. "Where did you learn?"

"Oh, thank you," he replies. "Senegal."

"And where did you learn English?" I ask. "You speak well."

George perks up a bit and leans forward, making sure he doesn't miss a word.

"In Senegal," Babacar shoots back.

"In Senegal?" I repeat.

"Yeah, well, everyone is required to take a second language in school, and I chose English."

"OK," I respond, knowing that George expected a better explanation. "But you must have practiced it when you came here, because . . ."

"Oh, yeah, yeah," Babacar confesses. "I did. The English here is not like what I learned back home. You have to practice!"

Babacar is also a graduate student at Columbia University, studying in a dual MD/PhD program. His American English is flawless, except for a very slight accent. At the same time, it differs considerably from that of African merchants who have much thicker inflections and pepper their talk with "yo," "man," and "what's up" to sound more ethnically "Black." In either case, whether it is an American English spoken by Western-educated Africans or a Black vernacular voiced by African street merchants, both efforts reveal an attempt to reinvent their African sense of self as they search for their rightful place in Harlem. This also speaks volumes about an internal conflict over how language marks the boundaries of what it means to be African in New York.

The fact that African Muslims are learning American English does not mean that everyone has relinquished his or her investment in Frenchness, not to mention the high profile it conveys in this community.

After *maghrib*, we prepare to leave. Twenty-five people at a time jockey for the door. Others, already there, begin pulling their shoes out of the rack and slipping them on. Lamine, a Senegalese man in his late forties, stands by the entrance and appears to wait for us. Wearing a stylish blue dress shirt and black slacks, he obviously just came from work. Like many first arrivals, he started out working in a convenience store and as a street merchant. Now he works in an art-supply store in upstate New York. "It's practical art," he told me at an earlier time, "or what people call crafts." As we walk up, he greets us. He overheard our conversation about learning English and wants to make a few remarks. He explains that while speaking French in Senegal has a particular social status, Africans who use it in New York are ostracized and ridiculed.

"One African radio announcer," he says, "told French speakers to get out of here."

"Why?" I ask.

"Well," Lamine replies, "they would say, 'This isn't France! This is New York! So stop speaking French!' French-speaking Africans in New York are looked down upon." He grimaces. "Shit! They don't want to hear French. There're in New York, man! It was different when we were going to Paris, of course. But in New York, French is the last thing you wanna hear."

All the same, while African professionals might try to speed up African integration by demanding that others drop French, many with fewer opportunities to study English hold on to French as a common mode of communication within a polyglot community. Moreover, French is a vital part of their various identities, and they came to America not to abandon this part of themselves but to add to it. Most imagined America to be heaven on earth, an earthly paradise, a place filled with opportunities. By now, they have become intimately acquainted with its dark side and yet still recognize its many benefits. However, their ability to obtain the rewards they seek depends a great deal on how they transcend the language barriers before them. Like many other immigrants, they come to America with more than a tremendous fortitude to work. They also bring their religious resources. And they use this religious capital to find their way in Harlem society.

5

A Sacred City

I

The morning air crackles with excitement as the courtyard at the Harlem State Office Building swells with hundreds of African Muslims—men, women, and children decked out in their best *boubou* wear and head-wraps. As they maneuver into position, one can still hear prayers humming with the circular motion of *thikr* beads.[1] A procession slowly takes shape and stretches for at least three blocks. Paraders line up in military-style formation, breaking every seven lines with twenty-five abreast. The rhythm of the urban landscape succumbs to the vibrancy of African clothing designs. Banners with Qur'anic wording, Black pride slogans, and photographic posters of Cheikh Amadou Bamba and other clerics are interspersed among the crowd, with American and Senegalese flags whirling in the breeze. Every year on this day, traffic gives way to a sensory blend of sightly robes, sweet perfumes, and choral chants. With such fanfare, no one can deny the special significance of the day. In fact, David Dinkins, as Manhattan borough president, issued a decree in 1988 declaring July 28 "Cheikh Ahmadou Bamba Day" in New York City.[2] Since that time, a parade has been held to commemorate the occasion, but the festivities last more than two weeks and include rallies, communal prayers, breakfast gatherings, and lectures at several locations including the United Nations.[3]

Before arriving at the parade site, I walk up 116th from Lenox and eventually run into Sami, an Ivoirian and a recent college graduate who works for Chase Manhattan Bank. He wants to show me a new African restaurant just up the street from Masjid Salaam. As a *masjid* board member, Sami is well known, and our stroll is frequently interrupted with *salaams* from passing Africans. He has been in Harlem since the early days.

As we walk, he begins muttering to himself. "There sure are a lot of Africans in Harlem."

"Yes," I answer, reminding him of my presence, "there sure are."

But the repeated Islamic greetings we receive within a two-block walk reveal much more than just the predominance of Africans in Harlem. They also demonstrate the overlapping presence of a new sacred domain. One cannot define any city as a single place. Rather, the Islamic institutions, businesses, associations, and lifeways add another layer to the multiple worlds already operating in Harlem. In her critique of research models for studying urban life, Setha M. Low stresses the need to reframe the city in terms of images and metaphors. The image of a sacred city speaks to the ways urban religion helps people mediate "between the cosmological universe and the experience of everyday life."[4] In sum, African Muslim activity creates a new tier of urban sacredness, a middle world where the vagaries of Harlem life are symbolically reworked as they struggle to navigate the complexities of New York City.

After leaving Sami, I scurry to the corner of Seventh Avenue and 114th and see a crowd of Africans draped in traditional clothing moving toward Central Park. Unlike in previous years, paraders will gather in the park and then march up Seventh Avenue for a huge rally at the plaza. I turn the corner and attempt to blend into a stream of multicolored robes. Talla, a local Senegalese merchant in his late forties, appears in the crowd, and I stop him to snap his picture. The air is festive, and cameras flash repeatedly to capture smiles. Even members of a "suspect community" (a Muslim population under some measure of surveillance), who might be shy about posing for a picture on other days, or strict Muslims who are less than sanguine about the prospects of being photographed, suspend those fears.[5] The speckled sight of African Muslims moving north on both sides of the boulevard's median alters what I call a "street sense" of public space, the ordinary urban sights, smells, and sounds one expects to experience daily. The Bamba Day parade challenges this sensorial order, at least temporarily. "*Allahu Akbar!*" rings out, "*Allaaahu Akbar!*"[6] With hands cupped behind his ears, a man wearing thick dreadlocks, a checkered dashiki, and a black money belt stands prominently on the corner of 112th making the call. Two others with similar hair and attire are squatting on the ground, one swaying to the low chant of his *thikr*. As followers of Ibrahima Faal and a sect within Muridiyya, their appearance seems to punctuate the more commonplace sight of long pastel *jalabiyyas* (robes) and crew-cut hairstyles.[7] More curious is that eight-thirty in the morning isn't the time for *salah* (formal prayers), when one usually hears the *athan*. Still, the resonance of the call clearly serves to sacralize the event in time and space.[8]

Murid men gather at Central Park North and Seventh Avenue to begin the Bamba Day parade. (Photo Bassirou Lo)

Beyond the African Muslims' sartorial display, the auditory nature of the *athan* marks this unique moment as their own. In fact, sound, more than any other performative element, constituted a subversive act for Black Harlem paraders in the late 1920s. "The sound and noise that white New Yorkers heard as cacophonous and atavistic," Clare Corbould asserts, "were to Harlem's black residents a way to claim space as their own."[9] Moreover, making noise on the street in the Jim Crow South, for instance, wasn't always permitted, and, as Zora Neale Hurston wrote in her novel of the period, institutional racism attempted to relegate Black laborers "tongueless, earless, eyeless conveniences all day long."[10] As recent Muslim immigrants from a French-speaking country, most Murids lack adequate competence in English and Anglo-American culture. This casts an eerie shadow over their mouths, bodies, and sights.

At the same time, what makes this display so compelling is not the pomp and circumstance typically associated with these events. There are no brass bands or sparkling floats. There is not even a *djembe*, or African drum, a common sight at such cultural affairs. Girls dressed in bathing suits twirling batons are clearly absent. Celebrities and hand-waving beauty queens riding in convertibles are nowhere to be seen, and major elected officials are likewise not in attendance. But in the absence of trumpet blasting, elaborate moving stages, or commercial vendors, the parade achieves a level of purity.[11] That is to say, a public performance without these dazzling, temporal elements dismantles Harlem's hectic streets, briefly transforming them into simple places marked by religious yearning. Most witnesses speculate that the parade is "something African" but can't figure it out. Why would Murids continue to organize a police-escorted parade that no spectator understands? As "street theater," the Bamba Day parade creates a type of "liminal" space or a place where performers can reinvent themselves in ways not possible under normal conditions.[12] It also affords them an opportunity to contest competing identities as they attempt to negotiate perspectives on what it means to be Black, African, and Muslim.

While the event has not attracted much media attention in the United States, a Senegalese television crew arrives each year to record the entire affair, and it is aired for several weeks in their home country. Through satellite television, Murids all over the world participate in the public spectacle. Murids living in other American cities travel to New York to take part in the activities, each group with seven across holding banners that identify their particular town. As paraders gather at the park entrance, the procession expands and there is a gender and generational divide. Men are followed by a contingent of children and scores of fashionably dressed women, regaling onlookers with religious songs, dance steps, and their own sacred imagery and slogans. Unlike other grandstanding parades, where the entire thoroughfare is blocked off and spectators line up behind barricades, police block

traffic on the right side of Seventh Avenue, stopping cars from crossing the intersection, as marchers reach each corner. As the procession moves forward, trained
reciters unleash piercing chants of Bamba's *khassaïd* (poetry) that reverberate
through the streets. This grants them a singular and dominant voice, dramatizing
their presence in Harlem.[13]

As the march begins, I turn to walk with them, darting between sections and
snapping pictures. Flashing red and blue lights lead several limousines and marchers
up the street. And a large banner appears less than a quarter of a mile into the
parade:

> OUR BLACKNESS SHOULD NOT BE AN OBSTACLE
> TO OUR KNOWLEDGE AND OUR PERFECTION.
> ALL MEN WERE CREATED EQUAL.
> CHEIKH AHMADU BAMBA.

The saying is attributed to Bamba, but its tone is clearly reminiscent of a familiar
theme in Black American history. This moving signage creates a "visual episte-
mology," in the language of Allen and Mary Roberts, or a social narrative that interjects new ways of seeing Blackness.[14] In this case, the banner is particularly interesting
in how it advocates a Murid approach to racial equality. It also makes a striking
appeal to racial legitimacy by referring to "Our Blackness," a declaration at the outset
that Murid followers are part and parcel of the larger Black world. The notion that

Chanters of Bamba's *khassaïd* (religious poetry) march in the parade while reciting
aloud. (Photo Zain Abdullah)

"Blackness" should not obstruct one's life chances is a dilemma that has historically played out across the Black diaspora. The fact that Bamba is credited with this saying links African Muslims' racial struggle to other Black resistance narratives. Not only does it incorporate their voice into New York's racial politics, but, more important, it also affords them their own unique place in the overall fight against Black inferiority. Moreover, attributing this statement to Bamba means that their *jihad* (struggle) against racial discrimination is sanctified as an Islamic act.

On an earlier occasion, I asked Amadou, a Jamaican-born convert and New York professor, about the meaning of the banner. "Well, they're under the assumption," he explained, "that there is a microfilm in England of Cheikh Amadou Bamba, and they are saying that Gandhi had access to some of those things. And Gandhi may have been influenced by Cheikh Amadou Bamba's thinking. So if Martin Luther King was influenced by Gandhi, you can see there's a cycle." This idea is part of an attempt to retell and lay claim to a crucial part of Black history. For African Americans, the saga of slavery and civil rights provides a powerful narrative for defining the contours of a viable Black identity. The suggestion that a Black African Muslim saint, rather than the Indian sage Gandhi, is responsible for key civil rights ideas modifies this crucial aspect of Black history. Such a proposition turns the foundation of a Black Christian-based movement on its head, asserting instead that its origin is African and Muslim. While some might believe that the claim is entirely untenable, what matters most is not its accuracy but rather how Murids employ it to explain a new Black presence in Harlem. This statement indigenizes their presence, moving them from the margins to the center of Black America. Moreover, it puts forth a counter discourse that complicates monolithic notions of Black identity.

The procession continues steadily up the boulevard, and one section is led by more than fifty grade-school children, all dressed in African clothes, some wearing *kufis* (men's caps) and *khimars* (headscarves) while others are without. I jump on top of the street divider to take a photograph. About five children are carrying what Susan Slyomovics calls an "ambulating sacred text":[15]

> ISLAM = Peaceful Progress
> in Submission to Allah.
> Bismillah = Shaykh Ahmadou Bamba,
> Servant of the Messenger Spiritual Pole for Our Time.

Shifting the discourse from racial to religious, this banner attempts to redefine Islam within a post-9/11 context and to legitimize Muridism within the Muslim world. This is just the second parade after the 2001 attacks, and the sign immediately equates Islam with peace, an important proposition that many hope is not lost on a non-Muslim audience. Because the banner is held by Muslim children, it likewise challenges the notion that Islam is a violent religion that indoctrinates youngsters to hate the West. For Muslim observers, the sign illustrates that their peaceful advancement relies on their obedience to Allah's will, a statement that simultaneously voices their condemnation of terrorism and affiliation within the mainstream Muslim community. "Bismillah = Shaykh Ahmadou Bamba" maps out their specific religious path. The term *bismillah* is a grammatical contraction combining three Arabic words to create the single phrase "in the name of Allah." Not only does each Qur'anic chapter (with the possible exception of one) begin with it, but Muslims also often invoke this phrase before beginning any action to gain divine favor. The equal sign joining the *bismillah* and Bamba, then, distinguishes Murids in Harlem as a Muslim community with its own religious sensibility and history. "Servant of the Messenger"— or *khadimou rassoul,* as he is called in Arabic by Murids—designates Bamba as a devout follower of the Prophet Muhammad. The final line proclaims that Bamba is the "Spiritual Pole for Our Time," an honorific referring not only to his exemplary position among *taalibes* (disciples) but also signifying his elevated station as *qutb* (universal spiritual guide). This final point does more than place Muridism within the mosaic of a growing religious pluralism in America. As a procession is "designed to compete with the existing environment around it, becoming for a time the dominant element," the banner dramatizes a major way Murids stake their own claims for Islamic legitimacy and religious authenticity within Harlem and elsewhere.[16]

As the children pass, I notice a much larger placard slowly coming into view. Most posters are in English and of modest size, two and a half feet wide and held by seven or so people. In contrast, this one incorporates several languages and nearly spans the entire width of the street. It is at least five feet wide and is carried by no fewer than fifteen paraders, clearly designed to be the most visible banner in the parade. It says:

> Visite annuelle du Serigne Mourtalla Mbacke—Ibn Khadimou Rassoul
> aux Etats Unis du 25 juillet au 03 aout 2001
> sous l'égide de Murid Islamic Community avec la participation
> de la Assurances CNART—assistance et Taxa Wu—des Garanties
> Adaptées a vos besoins—
> avec CNART Assurances—vous pouvey courir le monde.[17]

Mostly in French, it also includes English, Wolof, and Arabic transliteration. Because of its multilingual character, the sign could not be a message to French speakers alone and certainly not to the English- (or Spanish-) speaking community of Harlem. As a colossal centerpiece, it clearly addresses those who share their ability to navigate these polyglot worlds. Even for those Murids steeped in Wolof society and not particularly well versed in postcolonial French, the culture is still very much a part of their tradition, and they know how to negotiate it. In the end, the sign's various components reflect the cosmopolitan or diverse nature of African Muslim identity. It embodies their personhood, and it is certainly an association few can claim.

For all intents and purposes, the wording on most banners is aimed at out-siders, an attempt to engage the public in a discourse about Blackness, Islam, and Africanity. However, there is also an internal dialogue occurring between Africans and African Americans. As the parade continues, I decide to look for Balozi Harvey, an African American Murid convert in his early sixties and the president of the Murid Islamic Community of America (MICA). It was he and Charles Kenyatta, a main supporter of Malcolm X, who lobbied for the Bamba proclamation and eventually founded the parade. Harvey's appointment as president of MICA is apparently the first time an African American has led an African organization of this kind. As president, he primarily helps Murid offi-cials make administrative decisions and instructs them on matters of policy. Other African Sufi groups such as the Tijaniyya have formed an American branch, and Black converts are certainly members. Yet the extent of their lead-ership has been the designation of a devout African American member, Seyed Ali, as chairman of Black American Tijanis. The fact that a Black convert heads an African Sufi organization with thousands of members in America, among an estimated three million worldwide, is quite noteworthy.

I finally spot Charles Muhammad, another African American Murid and a committee leader for the parade, and ask him if he has seen Balozi.

"He's leading one of the sections!" he yells out. "He's being interviewed by Senegalese reporters."

Realizing that I must have missed him, I rush back toward the front and see Balozi talking into a handheld microphone as an African television crew walks backward to record his conversation. He sees me run up, I fire off multiple camera shots, and he smiles with approval.

This particular year, Balozi wears a black *boubou* and a green *kufi*, a striking color pattern very different from that worn by African Murids. In fact, I notice that other African American Murids have chosen similar tones. Unlike everyday wear, processional clothing is part of a spectacle, a ceremonial act intentionally per-formed to dramatize the entire event. While costumes could be chosen to reflect a group's collective identity, differences in dress can also reveal internal struggles over contrasting interpretations of what defines the community.

"Well," Balozi explains during a later interview, "that particular day, I knew a lot of the [African] brothers were going to be in white, and I decided Afro-Ameri-cans should be in a different color [black and green], so they could be seen by the people who were on the street." He pauses to think and continues, "See, America is our village. We can never forget America as being our village. This is where our ancestors, those we know of, are from—those we've buried and struggled with. We have African ancestors in Africa, too. Unfortunately, most of us can't even tell you who they are, but we know they exist because we know how we got here."

While Balozi refers to native-born Blacks as Afro-Americans, he strongly believes that Black Americans ought to be viewed as simply Africans in America. In this way, he struggles to maintain the ancestral connection Blacks have with the continent without losing sight of what he calls their American village. So, in addition to his administrative role with MICA, he has instructed all participants to wear traditional African clothing, which includes a pants set with a one-piece loose-fitting robe. This gives paraders a uniform appearance and helps to reinforce the visual image of a single and undifferentiated African identity.

At the same time, the special color coding for African American Murids illustrates their attempt to delineate a different view of African identity in the diaspora. In other words, with Black immigrants entering cities such as New York from around the world, competing versions of an African heritage will be affected by a whole range of social and cultural factors, not to mention an array of racial, ethnic, and religious concerns peculiar to each group.[18] Despite the spiritual camaraderie Balozi and other Black Americans share with others in MICA, they clearly seek to differentiate their African American identity from that of Senegalese marchers. And yet Balozi's strategy to recognize his Black American ancestry masks a religious divide between Black Muslims and African American Christians. In sum, existing within overlapping diasporas often means having a foot in one cultural field and a hand in another, revealing how identities can be porous in ways that frustrate our intellectual maps.

In his exploration of what this murky terrain might mean for continental Africans, Ali Mazrui advances the concept of a triple heritage. This model examines how many Africans are forced to manage Islamic, traditional African, and Western cultures.[19] The rapid migration of African Murids into Black communities such as Harlem, however, pushes us to reconsider the usefulness of a three-way model, requiring us to rethink ways of grasping and talking about an African identity that is fluid and multilayered. I would argue that as African Muslims are integrated into Western nations that have pluralistic societies, they often encounter populations of African descent with their own views of what it means to be Black. African Muslims also face other kinds of Muslims with perspectives and practices that differ from their own. In the end, the notion of a triple heritage must also take into account the complex nature of each heritage and what this might mean for African Muslims who must invent new identities in their response to living in such diverse settings.

At the first parade after 9/11, American flags appeared everywhere, much more than in previous years. In certain respects, the twirling sight of these emblems contrasted the stunning display of African garments. With the Senegalese flag also present, the intention was not to simply disappear into the panoply of American multiculturalism. For international migrants in a global age, the presence of both flags amplifies the transnational fields they traverse daily. As transnational migrants, the parade's cornucopia of sights and sounds circulates around the globe, linking Murids in places such as Paris, Milan, and Berlin with those in Atlanta, Chicago, and New York, including those watching in the African cities of Touba, Bamako, Fez, and Cairo. It's a process that produces a Murid "glocalism," a linkage between the local and global spheres by way of traveling saints, monetary donations, and Islamic networks.[20]

"It's important that people know we do it in America and not in France," Abdoulaye says as he comments on all the flags. "One day you do it in Japan," he says, "maybe one day you do it in Paris. That is why we have the flag."

The prominent display of Senegalese flags announces a new African presence. And given mounting divisions based on class and ideology within the organization, displaying the national standard gives members a common symbol with which to transcend their differences, at least for the time being.[21] National flags are more than just colorful pieces of cloth waving in the wind. In a single moment, they capture the totality of one's heritage—historic victories, bitter defeats, popular dishes, the national anthem, and an idyllic landscape instantly conjured up in the mind's eye.

The American flag plays another role at the parade. Ritual elements are often combined with other materials to convey a meaning that is a bit more textured. For this purpose, the Senegalese flag alone is insufficient, and the American flag is needed as a way to allay outside fears and internal anxieties about the Senegalese presence in America. For some, the Muslim affiliation automatically labels them a "suspect community" in a post-9/11 world, a political climate in which associating with the "wrong" faith can place one under constant surveillance. The American flag signifies an attitude of deference that African Murids feel toward the host country, a gesture they hope will assuage an anti-Muslim backlash. Assatou, a Senegalese Murid in her mid-thirties, expresses her feelings about the flags' meaning.

"Thank God we are not doing anything bad," she says. "We are good people. You have to love yourself, yes, it is good. But also it's good for you to love the person who opens his arms to you in respect. Because all of us here, today, have a passport, the right to work, the right to live. We bought a house, bought a car. I mean, we don't know when we are going to leave, so the thing is for you to respect your own people and your own flag, because we are African, Black people. But when you pull out the Senegalese flag, it should be right there with the American flag, next to it, because that is a part of respect."

Demonstrating their appreciation for the opportunities they have in the United States is crucial. Still, both immigrant and native-born Muslims have felt extremely vulnerable after the terrorist attacks, and Assatou's feeling about leaving the country (or perhaps being forced to go) mirrors the sentiments of other African Muslims.[22]

Being Muslim, however, is not the sole reason Assatou and other West Africans feel insecure in New York. These Black immigrants are still haunted by the images of slain West Africans such as Amadou Diallo, an innocent victim killed by New York City police in a hail of forty-one bullets. Being Muslim and Black doubly marginalizes these newcomers. Assatou's contention that one must "respect your own people and your own flag" is a safety mechanism, allowing her to return home if things get too dangerous. Because Senegal is a predominantly Muslim country, the Senegalese flag represents a different kind of space, a place where they feel Muslims are not hunted and Blackness is not criminalized. Much of the meaning inherent in this symbolism might be lost on New York spectators. Still, the blinding imagery of thousands of Black bodies clad in elaborate African clothing, interspersed with twirling Senegalese flags and floating Islamic banners, stamps a new African sensibility onto the urban landscape.

As the procession reaches 116th Street, it enters a unique domain of African and Islamic variety stores, restaurants, fashion boutiques, associations, and *masjids*. Some bear the names of towns in Africa, while many adopt a religious tone, bearing the name of the Murids' holy city of Touba. Large photographic posters move along the parade route. Unlike some other Muslims, who ban the graphic representation of divine figures, Murids have developed a figural tradition allowing them to "live in intimate association with images of their religious leaders."[23] There is a single 1913 photograph of Cheikh Amadou Bamba, and his image is pressed onto button pins, stitched into clothing, mounted on walls and moving vehicles, and painted on glass surfaces. Bamba and the *marabouts* who have inherited his mantle are considered holy ones, saints, both living and deceased, women and men. Murids the world over seek their *baraka*, a word often translated to mean blessing, grace, or divine favor. Because of its wide usage, it can encompass a whole host of other meanings, such as good luck, bounty, material prosperity, and other kinds of good fortune. It is believed that Murid saints possess the ability to bestow *baraka* in the same way people possess other human talents such as wit and humor, physical prowess, or the gift of song. Consequently, some clerics have more than others.[24]

Touba is likewise endowed with *baraka*, and since Bamba founded it as a religious site, he and the city are considered one and the same. In fact, he is customarily referred to as Serigne Touba, or "Venerable Touba," and the sacredness of Bamba and Touba is also transferable to other clerics. So, when Murid leaders visit their *taalibes* in New York or elsewhere, the announcement "Touba is coming to town" is made repeatedly.[25] Moreover, Touba orients their consciousness and helps the devout Murid navigate the social world. When pictures of Bamba or the city's Great Mosque hang on shop walls, Touba appears. Touba and the *baraka* associated with it can be duplicated and transported around the globe.[26] Thus, the hagiographical image of Serigne Touba along with other clerics and sanctified objects imbue paraders and their businesses with esoteric power. The sacred space created by the parade allows Murids to enter a divine realm, a place where they are redeemed from the existential hardships of daily life. For them, this moving iconography etches new imaginative grids onto the city's streets, and it creates a new spiritual geography in Harlem.

By the time I reach the end of the march, the women's section looms large and displays a magnificent fusion of spiritual fervor and splendor. Because parades are not gender-neutral, the women's station can often reveal something about their social location within their communities. In his work on Italian parades in Brooklyn, New York, Joseph Sciorra has argued that "these processions are also public representations of the family, with separate marching units consisting of men, women, and children on display."[27] Yet, while their parading place might reflect a particular familial hierarchy, it doesn't illustrate the way Murid women manipulate these constraints through their engagement with "living" saints. With great emotional attachment, many Murid women rely on these saints to grant them *baraka* and a communion with God. During intense moments of devotion and divine inspiration, some even enter a state of *daanu leer*, a Wolof word for spiritual ecstasy.[28] At the Bamba Day parade, their liturgical dance, chants, and moving hagiographies create an extraordinary setting in which to "bring the saints . . . down to earth," caring for them, living in fellowship with them, being completely transformed by them.[29]

On the day following the parade, Khady, a Senegalese woman in her late forties, describes how she "cried for the whole day." "People say, 'Why are you crying?'" she says. "I say, 'I never thought this day would come. I want this parade because I don't have it back home . . . and you don't see the *cheikhs* [saints] in Touba.' When you go there, and if you are not close to them, and you don't really know the leaders, you don't see them. You just hear the leaders' voice, or you hear that the leader said this and that. But in this country, you sit with them, you eat with them. It is a blessing [*baraka*] to sit next to them. Something good must be in this country because we do not have it back home. Today, when he [the *cheikh*] came, I fixed breakfast for him, we ate lunch together, talked together. I never had it until I come to this country."

This reverence for the cleric or saint does not automatically imply complete submission to male authority, but it reflects a religious commitment to the divinity he and other *marabouts*, men and women, represent. In fact, "social life is set up and animated in reference to women" in Senegal, especially in urban areas where they have established powerful associations, earned sole proprietorship of multiple businesses, and customarily control the economics of the household.[30] Religiously, many belong to *dahiras* (Murid circles), which handle both the religious and the social needs of the community. They also join mixed-gendered *dahiras* where they may hold high offices, although most are members of all-female circles.[31] Each *dahira* is devoted to a male or female saint, and the *taalibes* are committed to supporting the *marabout* with *addiya* (annual tithes or monthly remittances). The aim of this economic support is to allow the *marabout* more time to increase spiritual power and influence. But the "religious capital" Khady has gained abroad affords her priestly access, something unimaginable in Senegal.[32] Arjun Appadurai recounts an anecdote about a family trip to India to visit a Hindu priest, who, for months, had already been performing rites in Houston, Texas.[33] Similarly, African saints travel around the world to maintain good relations with their *taalibes*. Because Touba receives thousands of dollars of *addiya* from their followers abroad, many of whom belong to a new class of wealthy businesspeople, Murid *cheikhs* spend a great deal of effort trying to uphold high levels of allegiance and group solidarity. Greater access to Murid saints, then, endears the laity to the leadership and heightens religious fervor.

While men have traditionally controlled the leadership within Sufi *tariqas* (orders), the Murid have acknowledged women saints such as Sokhna Magatte Diop, who, as a *marabout*, has several *dahiras* and bestows *baraka* on her followers.[34] She was even declared a Murid *caliph* (supreme leader). Other women directly related to Bamba have been revered as saints, such as Sokhna Maïmouna Mbacké (1925–1999), who has both male and female disciples.[35] However, Bamba's mother, Mame Diarra Bousso (1833–1866), is the most important saintly figure for Murid women. A *dahira* has been formed for her in New York.[36] Mame Diarra is a source of hope and inspiration for Murid women, and her hagiographical narratives serve to guide them in all aspects of life, including business.[37]

The images of Mame Diarra parading up Seventh Avenue demonstrate visual piety, and Murid women are transformed by them with a single gaze. There is a mystical encounter, a transmission of divine energy that moves from icon to observer. They walk, chant, wave signs, and embody the stories of the saints in a reenactment that releases a religious aura, a process collapsing time and space into a hagiographical present. During the march, Murid women also reenact the caring spirit of Mame Diarra directed toward her son, Amadou Bamba, as he walked to propagate the faith.

"The parade is very special," Khady recounts. "I heard Cheikh Amadou Bamba used to go all over the world searching, trying to find someone who wanted Islam, someone who would read one of his books, and so we march. It is a blessing [*baraka*] because, in those days, Cheikh Amadou Bamba didn't have cars, no buses or nothing. He was walking. So he walked to teach people to do the right thing, to teach them what the Lord wants us to do. We get a blessing [*baraka*] from walking—to help people. So we walk to represent him on his day."

As they carry Bamba's portrait, they are walking with him, caring for him during his struggles. In fact, they are supporting him, as Mame Diarra Bousso did when, according to legend, she would miraculously appear after her death to console and encourage him in times of great need.[38] More important, the ritual displacement of these images enhances their divine power. By moving saintly portraits from the privacy of the *masjid*, house, or sacred space to the street, Murids create what Edward C. Zaragoza calls a "symbolic dislocation."[39] Removing a sacred image from its house of worship (or places designated for sanctification) magnifies the saint and forces participants and spectators to renew their relationship to it. Because the religious symbol enters a domain outside its normal location, their association with the image is exaggerated, and the new encounter renews for them the sacredness of the object.

For Murid women in the procession, the acquisition of *baraka* is paramount. The parade is "special," Khady announces, because "we get a blessing [*baraka*] from walking." Despite their position at the back of the parade, women's high visibility has transformed the nature of Muridiyya itself. The "Islam of the brotherhoods and *marabouts*," Coulon Christian asserts, "has become primarily the religion of women."[40] Some argue that the religious dynamism of Senegalese women in particular constitutes an "*Islam au féminin*," or a woman's Islam.[41] Although the Senegalese journalist Codou Bop argues that the distribution of *baraka* and religious authority might be disproportionate between Murid men and women, we cannot disregard their successful efforts to offset this imbalance.[42] For example, while the possession of *baraka* has traditionally been male-dominated, Murid women in New York have much more earning potential and can challenge the constraints of conventional gender roles. They have used their economic position and religious networks to support *marabouts*, both male and female, who uphold them and address their concerns. This increased capital empowers their chosen saints and strengthens the religious and social status of these women. But what makes the life of Bamba, his mother, and early Murid figures so exemplary is their effort to be religious in a mundane world.

II

After the paraders reach the Harlem State Office building, a rally begins. The head of the Murids holds court under the canopy outside the front entrance. He is joined by a delegation of more than thirty, mostly Senegalese, including an honored chair for Balozi, with Charles occasionally making introductions, and a few local politicians. Speeches are made about the virtues of collaboration between Harlem and West Africa, and awards are presented. Others find areas on the concrete for a chanting circle and recite Bamba's *khassaïd* before a standing audience. Hundreds more withstand the blistering July heat on the plaza, socializing with family and

Women march carrying posters of (from left) Mame Diarra Bousso, Bamba in 1913, and Serigne Saliou Mbacke. (Photo Khady Gueye Djily)

friends, and applaud on cue at the end of talks. As the rally ends, the crowd peters out. Some must return to work, but many others continue with the rest of the schedule.

As African marchers make their way back down Seventh Avenue toward 116th, they gradually reenter a realm more commonly known for its roving display of African fashions. It's a place where the aromas of Guinean food capture the senses, and Wolof men gathering to chat in front of African boutiques conjure images of urban life in a Senegalese city. Convenience stores, import/export businesses, and agencies line the streets bearing the names of their spiritual leaders (Mbacké), an area in Muslim West Africa (Kara), or the Muslim world (Aqsa). The *athan* is called, and Ivoirian Muslims and others dressed in Islamic attire scurry to pray in nearby African *masjids*. After religious rites are performed, committees with African delegates hold meetings to discuss any number of issues affecting African Muslims and the community at large. Other Islamic events and celebrations add to the West African Islamic ethos permeating the area. This scene involves a set of discursive practices I call *masjid* life. Unlike special events such as the Bamba Day parade, these actions are embedded in the ongoing routine of social life, essentially positioning the *masjid* or several *masjids* at the center of their activities. That is, the *masjid* operates as a type of compass, giving West African Muslims a center around which to orient their lives.

Since it is Friday, the *jum'ah* prayer is to begin at one in the afternoon, and people jump into cabs and private black cars headed to Masjid Touba, the Murid's House of Islam. All of it is happening so quickly that Mahmoud, an African American Muslim convert in his late forties, and I barely have a chance to gain our bearings. Abdoulaye yells over to us from the street, "Come on! We have a ride for you! Are you going to the mosque? Come on—get in!" Before we can answer, we glance at each other and quickly enter through the back doors of a waiting cab. Abdoulaye jumps into the front, then turns to face us. "Don't worry about it! It's been paid for," he says, and spins back around. It is the first event in a network of activities that will accommodate all of our material or religious needs. In this circle, money is obsolete, which is an amazing feat to witness in New York City. Murid businesses appear to be true angels of *baraka*.

The *masjid* is a lofty three-story brownstone that has been totally gutted and renovated. Set on the corner of 137th and Edgecombe, it's on a well-kept, tree-lined street with a scenic view of Morningside Park a few yards from the train station. Our driver rides up to the entrance, lets us out, and speeds off.

"Cheikh Balozi," as he is affectionately called, walks up and with each step receives reverential greetings and handshakes from respectful congregants. As I move to greet him, I am struck by the level of dedication Murid men demonstrate outside, kneeling on the concrete sidewalk with thin prayer rugs. They even form short prayer lines, wedged between parked cars. Still others cram their wiry bodies into narrow spaces along the edge of the building, just inside a two-foot brick wall along the perimeter. The open door of the attached garage reveals a fifty-by-thirty-foot space filled with African women and children dressed in their best outfits.

"Is it that crowded inside?" I ask Balozi.

"I guess so," he answers. "Come on, I'll get you a seat inside."

I explain that I want to wait outside and will see him later before prayer starts.

Abdoulaye is standing by the curb, and I walk over to him and begin to watch things unfold. "Let me take some pictures," I say.

"Yes," he says without diverting his eyes from the swelling mass. "Take some pictures!"

I aim and take shots from different angles and from across the street. My only trepidation is whether or not to snap pictures of women directly. Although I am Islamically dressed in a *jalabiyya* and a *kufi*, which I believe preclude any ideas that I am some strange photographer or rogue reporter, I still feel uneasy. There are more than a few African *masjids* in Harlem, and these communities hold varying opinions about exposing Muslim women to the public gaze. Along with extremely conservative groups, there is a growing Salafi (ultraconservative) trend among African Muslims in New York, and many adhere to a strict policy of *hijab* or separation for women. But the overall range of Islamic practice is wide and runs along a continuum from the very moderate or liberal to the ultraconservative. This is not to suggest that a single community can be pegged as one or the other, because religious orientations differ within *masjids* as well, though not too sharply. Still, I don't want to offend anyone or sully my reputation.

I see Maryam, an African American Murid with three children who is married to a Senegalese. I get her attention and gesture that I'd like to speak to her. She rises reluctantly, then takes a few steps toward me, taking a brief glance to her right and left.

"Do you think you can take a few pictures of the sisters for me?" I ask.

"You can take it," she replies with a stern look. "It's all right. You can take it," she repeats, staring at my surprised expression.

"Oh, OK," I respond, and begin backing up.

I kneel, take a few more shots of the men, and tilt my camera to include the women, never pointing it at them directly. Still unconvinced, I get up and walk over to Abdoulaye for a second opinion.

"Would it be OK to take pictures of the women?" I ask as he stands chomping on his gum.

"Yes," he says, turning to look at me firmly as I wait for more. "Why not? Yes, go ahead, take pictures of them. They don't care."

While I eventually do take pictures of the women without incident, it is interesting to note how issues like this can be used to define the range and scope of Islamic values and practice in Muslim communities. At a different time, African women at Masjid Aqsa felt differently about gender separation and the maintenance of single-sex spaces. This reveals a great deal about the role religion plays in structuring gender relations within these communities.

At the *masjid*'s second-floor entrance, a four-foot portrait of Bamba meets visitors, practically levitating midway between two stairways, one leading down and the other up. His black image peering through an exceedingly white garment, with the tail end of a wrap partially draped over his mouth to indicate piety, sets a mystical yet spiritual mood. The main prayer area is downstairs on the ground level, where spiritual leaders and officials are given preference. Two security guards in green and reddish-brown *boubous* monitor the entrance. They also arrange seating for late arrivals. These prayer quarters are carefully supervised, because high officials are scheduled to deliver talks and eventually the day's sermon. It is a sacred place of immense spiritual reward, especially if one manages to stand in the first row of the prayer line. I proceed downstairs and stand at the door. Peeking into the hall for someone I can recognize, I see more than one hundred people sitting on a well-matted green pile carpet.

"Is it crowded in there?" I ask, holding my glance toward the inside.

Both guards step forward. "What did you say?" one asks. I repeat my question, hoping to signal my desire to enter. "Yeah," he announces sternly. He pauses for a moment, then says, "Oh, what's your name?"

"Zain," I answer.

He grabs my arm and pulls me just past the door. With his right hand still grasping my arm, he raises his left and signals to Balozi. Balozi nods once, and the guard ushers me inside and squeezes me between two people.

With a heat wave outside, people sit crunched together in a fifteen-by-thirty-foot space, which raises the temperature inside to sweltering heights. The timid breeze slithering through small windows does little to assist two small oscillating fans. Still, sitting in this sanctified space, a place where men listen reverently to the Qur'an on tape, swaying to their own Qur'anic recitation or personal *thikr* and extending respectful gestures to one another, more than compensates for the conditions. Murids speak of a type of spiritual euphoria that removes one from a bodily awareness in these situations, and this feeling certainly permeates the room.

Suddenly, the *athan* reverberates against the walls in a melodic African tone, which signals yet another strand in the mosaic of a growing American Muslim presence. After talks and a sermon in Wolof, which are followed by translations in Arabic and English, people stand for prayer. I struggle to find a place, but my shorter frame is squeezed out of the line from between two six-foot-three Africans. Without saying a word, one reaches back and pulls me to the prayer line tightly between them, shoulder to shoulder, foot to foot. I give an appreciative nod. After an audible *salah* (prayer), the supplication by the *imam* is silent. This seemed commonplace for Murids but is out of the ordinary for other Muslim groups in New York, African or otherwise. In those cases, collective supplications are performed aloud and receive resounding *amens*. For Murids, the invocation, or *dua*, is how the redemptive healing of *baraka* is dispensed, and there is an *amana*, a trust between a Murid and a spiritual guide, just as a physician is entrusted with the care of a patient.

As people file out one by one, I walk upstairs and see Mahmoud on the second-floor landing. Standing before a closed door, we begin to chat about the services. The door periodically opens and closes to let people in or out. After several minutes, I hear, "Come!" A tall African man cracks the door open with one hand and guides us inside with the other. As the door closes, I look into a furnished room on my right. Cheikh Mouhammadou Mourtada Mbacké is propped up on a king-size bed as he dispenses *baraka* to a few men and women kneeling on the rug beside him. As they approach the side of the bed separately, a personal request is whispered to the *cheikh*. He then lifts his right hand in prayer. "OK, next!" and it is our turn. We rise a little from where we are sitting on the rug, move forward, and wait. Looking unsure of ourselves, we are told to ask for whatever we want. We comply, and the *cheikh's* hand rises. Two Murids swiftly escort us out, and within minutes, we find ourselves back in the hallway, contemplating the timeless, surreal moment most Murids can only imagine.

People occupy every room with devotional acts, infusing the entire building with reverence and awe. The recitation of Bamba's *khassaïd* seeps into the air from downstairs like a Gregorian chant in a Catholic cathedral. I go down to witness more. Twelve young men sit cross-legged in a circle, each with one hand covering the right ear for better tone, with Arabic poetry books in their laps or on foot-high book stands. Their raised voices echo in unison and mesmerize onlookers.

Abdoulaye appears, looking around almost frantically. He spots me. "You!" he says, pointing. "Come on!" I follow him outside and into a waiting car. Mahmoud is already there with two other African American Muslims. Someone mentions that we are going to the United Nations but will stop on 116th Street to eat first. We jump out of the car and walk into Africa Kine restaurant but discover that they are out of *thiebou jen*, Senegal's popular fish-and-rice dish. Back outside,

Abdoulaye flags down another black car, and the driver whisks us to another eatery. After lunch, another car takes us to attend the sessions at the United Nations.

What is crucial to recognize here is the extent to which Murids are embedded in a well-orchestrated and sustained network of *masjid* life. From the morning to the evening, little is said, but everyone appears to know exactly what to do. There also doesn't appear to be a prominent leader settling expenses at restaurants or with cab drivers. And yet everything is handled with extreme precision and without a single dollar exchanged, at least that I could see.

Another small example of this network occurs during the official brunch for Cheikh Mourtada Mbacké at Balozi's six-bedroom home in New Jersey. The event is a permanent part of the Bamba Day activities. But the arrival of stretch limousines, diplomatic vehicles, praise singers, and an entourage of thirty to fifty people, augments the quiet suburban street, lined with huge oaks and no sidewalks, in what the town residents aptly call the Village of South Orange. The affair brings together some local politicians, businesspeople, and predominantly African American guests across the class spectrum. The entire entourage arrives, socializes, eats, prays, and leaves so swiftly that American guests haven't even taken the first course yet. They actually were there for a couple of hours, but their coordinated yet unspoken efforts frustrate the kind of lingering most Americans expect at social gatherings. For Murids, their Islamic faith complements the communal spirit. In other words, they think of themselves not as individuals but as members of a collective. Even when praying or acting alone, their actions are envisioned as part of a larger whole.

At the United Nations, guests are greeted by members from the Senegalese consulate and receive badges. The lectures are held in official chambers, outfitted for special delegates and wired for simultaneous translation. About one hundred African Americans attend the English session, along with a smattering of Africans. A young Asian woman sits in the front row, never moving, and remains attentive during the entire two-hour session. Among several Murid scholars, Cheikh Ahmadou Dieng, chairman of the faculty of English and Humanities of Cheikh Anta Diop University in Senegal, speaks about French efforts to conquer Muslim lands and the "strength" of Islamic resistance. He asserts that Cheikh Amadou Bamba believed Islam would give the "Black man" dignity, which presents an interesting parallel with the ideology of the Nation of Islam.[43] He continues to say that the "Black man was inferior to no one" and that they should take a leadership role in the world. Others speak about *khidma* (servicing humanity) and *taqiyya* (God consciousness) as important concepts in Muridiyya. In his attempt to link Muridism with the Black experience, one speaker makes numerous references to Martin Luther King Jr. and the civil rights movement. "What's all this Martin Luther King stuff?" an African American Muslim woman in her late twenties yells. "Somebody better tell him about it!"

This outburst raises an interesting point about the separate Islamic orientations of African Americans and Africans. African Muslims experience the United States through the prism of migration, which suggests that they hold a very different vision of America from that of many African American Muslims. King's dream that everyone, regardless of race, would experience full integration and equal access to resources and opportunities clearly underscores the reason continental Africans came to the U.S. In fact, this explains why most of the African restaurants owned by Muslims prominently display King's portrait. Even on the rare occasion when a picture of Malcolm X adorns their shop walls, which obviously reflects their admiration of Malcolm as a Black Muslim, it's not the fiery one most are accustomed to seeing. One African restaurant displays a picture with Malcolm's side profile and a hat tilted over his brow, a much less revolutionary posture. By comparison, most Black Muslims are poor and working-class, and their experience in America is not inspired by the idealism of King, not to mention the Christian character of his message. Rather, African American Muslims, among millions of other disenfranchised Blacks, relate much more to the harsh realism of Malcolm X. So, while Bamba's spiritualism gives Murids a religious foundation and Black pride, the social philosophy of King fuels their dreams for economic advancement and educational opportunities.

III

After leaving the Harlem Market one day, I cross Lenox Avenue and begin walking up 116th. As I approach Masjid Malcolm Shabazz, I slow down and head in the direction of an African American Muslim street vendor. Another older African American, sitting on an apartment stoop with two other men, sees me and begins beaming with anticipation.

"Hey, *salaamu 'alaykum*, brother. How are you?" he yells.

I return an enthusiastic greeting.

"I got some tapes," he shrewdly interjects with a gleam in his eye.

I politely reject his offer and change the subject. "So, how've you been?" I say, as though we've known each other for years.

Saleem, or George 3X, as he was known in his Nation of Islam days, just celebrated his seventy-ninth birthday and has lived in Harlem for more than thirty years. We begin talking about his younger days.

"We were pioneers!" the vendor shouts, and I turn to follow the voice. "We were pioneers before these others were pioneers!" he yells again.

One of the men on the stoop nods in agreement as he continues looking into his newspaper and turns to the next page. The street vendor looks excited, walks in front of his stand, and bellows out a few more statements. I walk over to hear more. He casually returns to his fold-up table, where he sells white cotton athletic socks, African "Black" soap, and other small items.

"So, you're a pioneer, huh?" I say.

"Yep . . . that's right," he says, tightening a stern look, his lips pursed and his head and eyes moving only slightly in my direction. "One time, we sold one thousand *Muhammad Speaks* each out here!" he exclaims. Founded by Malcolm X in 1960, the Nation of Islam's *Muhammad Speaks* newspaper reportedly sold some five hundred thousand copies at its height and became one of the most successful Black papers in the United States.[44] For their accomplishment, salesmen were sent to Chicago, the headquarters of the Nation of Islam, and treated to dinner with the chief minister, Warith Deen Mohammed, in 1975. They also had their names changed to Islamic ones. He was given "Omar Muhammad."[45]

"Are you from Harlem?" I ask.

"Yep, born and raised," Omar says, rocking sideways.

"Do you think the area has changed?"

"Yeah, it's changed," he replies. "For the better! Different cultures is good for Harlem."

"What about African Americans and Africans?" I ask. "How is that working out?"

"We all get along. Huh, they respect me," he says sternly. "I was out here [vending] before they came with their stores. They see me workin' here every day. So they know that I'm not lazy. Some of them know that I made *hajj* [pilgrimage] twice. So they give me respect for that. But I'm doing my part!" he shouts. "I'm holding it down. They know I'm not lazy."

As a former member of the Nation of Islam, Omar followed the group's transition under Warith Deen Mohammed. Still, Nation followers were trained to buck racial stereotypes depicting Blacks as idle or lazy. They were indoctrinated into a strict religious culture and taught to be industrious and morally upright, extending respect to all. As a lifelong Harlem resident, Omar watched as many African Muslim merchants revitalized the area by taking over empty stores. It was all too reminiscent of the days when they, too, operated their own stores, restaurants, barbershops, and supermarkets in the area. As a new Black Muslim presence in Harlem met an old one, Omar's attempt to maintain their respect as an assiduous worker and a pious person, who performed the pilgrimage twice, was crucial. This scenario, however, reveals an interesting dilemma for the relationship between African American and African Muslims.

As Omar implies, Black Muslims from Masjid Malcolm Shabazz revere the Nation of Islam's achievements and overall legacy, and they expect others to acknowledge and respect them for pioneering an Islamic sensibility not just in Harlem but nationwide. Just two doors away from the *masjid* entrance, a huge, almost life-size black-and-white photo hangs in the picture window of the Shabazz Brokerage Agency. The image portrays the no-nonsense posture of Malcolm X and Captain Joseph X, who led the Nation of Islam's paramilitary unit, accompanied by an entourage of four or five staunch-faced men, crossing Lenox Avenue in the late 1950s. The photograph is a testament to their long-standing presence in Harlem, their industriousness, and their efforts at Black upliftment.

"They don't realize all this didn't just pop up," comments Kabir, a Shabazz member in his fifties and a former manager of the Harlem Market. "We've been here for over sixty years. But they [Africans] don't respect us." In addition to the Nation of Islam's history, Kabir is referring to a respect for recent undertakings such as the several businesses adjacent to the *masjid*, various new housing and construction projects under way, and the political clout they've mustered resulting in their official jurisdiction over the Harlem Market.

Kabir considers it a matter of the correct *adab*, or protocol. "Allah just put us here before them," he says. "We didn't plan it that way. We were put here to prepare the way. Now you can come and set yourself up and do well." In Kabir's view, the earlier presence of Black Muslims in America was a matter of divine providence (*qadr*). And since God planned it this way, Africans, as he would have it, ought to respect the sacred order of events and acquiesce to African American Muslim leadership as it stands. "They deal with African American Muslims not because they like to," he continues, "but because they must. They want to lead themselves, but they know they have to deal with us. If I were in their country, say Egypt or Saudi Arabia, they wouldn't let me come there and lead them! But Africans come here and don't want to follow African Americans."

Whereas many Black Muslims express these sentiments, they also feel, as do their non-Muslim Black counterparts, that there is tremendous potential for galvanizing their resources or "coming together" and that this will prove extremely beneficial. However, more than a few Black Muslims at Shabazz complain that this collaboration between them has been thwarted because African Muslims do not "respect" them. By the same token, while Kabir blames a system of white supremacy for the way Africans internalized negative images of Black Americans, he also believes that the African presence in Harlem has affected their view of themselves and the continent. "We had a glorious idea of Africa in our heads," he explains, "until we met *real* Africans from the continent. That helped to change our view of things."

For Kabir and other Black Muslims at Shabazz, it's one thing to imagine the glories of an Islamic West Africa and envision a shared history with African

Muslims. It is quite another to meet Muslim immigrants from West Africa in impoverished and now gentrifying neighborhoods, competing for power and scarce resources. The change Kabir mentions certainly does not move in one direction. The encounter forced him and others to reexamine their own circumstances. "They come here and immediately set up businesses," Kabir argues. "And we were here all of the time and still on the street selling items. If it rains, we're out of business." He chuckles. "When they see this, it proves what they already have been taught about us." Of course, his speculation fails to recognize the recent expansion of a Black middle class, which by no means started with the gains of the modern civil rights movement. Still, some argue that with greater access to wealth, executive positions in corporate America, and a deeper, more systematic integration into White suburbs, the Black middle class has abandoned its poor neighbors in the inner cities, leading to the demise of voluntary associations that used to offset inadequate public services.[46] At the same time, a Black underclass has grown exponentially, and perpetual poverty has been extended across several generations, plaguing a much larger segment of the Black population.[47] In contrast, many African Muslim immigrants have arrived in the United States as middle class, already endowed with a higher socioeconomic status than their Black counterparts. They are also well embedded within religious and familial networks, bolstering their status in the diaspora or, at least, allowing them an ethnic safety net. Kabir explains how they formed a business alliance with African Muslims. Despite what he describes as "cultural problems getting in the way," he and others feel that their common adherence to Islam will ultimately serve to unify them.

The "change of view" Kabir expresses implies one kind of response from some African American Muslims. More important, this idea of change masks a crucial aspect of the cultural dislocation between them. Like many Black Muslims at Masjid Malcolm Shabazz, African Murids see no distinction between their identity as Black people and their Islamic practice. Because of their own racial and religious struggles against French colonialism in Senegal and France, they are comfortable with Black themes in the sermons at Shabazz, and they actually appreciate the inclusion of "race talk" in the services. Still, Murids attending Shabazz for services or renting space there for various celebrations faithfully wear *boubou* dress, prepare Senegalese cuisine, and perform reverential gestures for their saints that often last until the next morning. In contrast, the cultural setting at Shabazz tends to be significantly different. While Murids are Sufi and uphold an ethnic spirituality, Black Muslims at Shabazz are religious in ways that focus on the social conditions of their community. As indicated by the U.S. flag on their Muslim newspaper, the *Muslim Journal*, their religious orientation has in many ways become mainstreamed and has adopted a vernacular character. In contrast to the elaborate Senegalese robes of Murids, the dress for Black Muslims at Shabazz has American features, a kind of Islamic modernity, with men wearing blazer jackets, dress shirts, slacks, and *kufis*, while the women dress in loose business suits or dashiki kaftans with decorative head-scarves.

"When our *cheikh* was in New York, he didn't get the same honor and respect their people are getting right now in Senegal," Robert, an African American Murid convert, argues while standing in front of Shabazz. "Shabazz security even removed the *cheikh*'s car, when it was in front of the mosque. And when a conflict broke out, one of the security guards told me, 'I'm tired of this bullshit!' He was tired of having to change and deal with the Africans and their customs."

Robert's interpretation of a kind of cross-cultural fatigue between Black and African Muslims at Shabazz is revealing. But the details of the event matter less than what his reading of it means. In other words, although the two groups share a fundamental belief in Islam and the critical way it ought to speak to their racial concerns, their respective cultural sensibilities prevent the collaboration they both apparently want and need. Still, African Muslims primarily from Côte d'Ivoire and Guinea have their own peculiar experience in Harlem.

While giving the Friday *khutba* at the Mosque of Islamic Brotherhood, Imam Talib Abdur-Rashid an African American Muslim in his mid-fifties dressed in a modified form of African-Arab clothing criticizes African Muslim immigrants for becoming too Americanized, something he argues was evident by the FUBU jeans and designer clothes they wear. Later, Imam Talib is approached by one African explaining that they didn't just start wearing hip-hop gear in America. In fact, they have been keeping pace with Black American styles and other aspects of Black popular culture for many years. "Coming in contact with African immigrants has challenged our ideas of Africa and Africans," Imam Talib admits. "It caused us to readjust what we understood from reading and watching television."

According to African Muslims at Masjids Aqsa and Salaam, they began attending the Mosque of Islamic Brotherhood in the early 1990s, when the Friday preacher at Shabazz exhorted all Africans to "go home!" Unlike Murids, they didn't particularly like the centrality of Black themes in the sermons and frequent call-and-response rejoinders from attendees. They also felt harassed by *masjid* security, as they were often stopped and questioned before entering and forced to sign in and out. The fees they were charged to use Shabazz for social gatherings or meetings were also considered less than brotherly. Seeking a more "orthodox" climate, they first moved to the Arab-led Islamic Cultural Center of New York on 96th and Third Avenue. But that was too far from their homes and shops, and parking was much too scarce, especially for cab drivers. At the Mosque of Islamic Brotherhood, they found a blend of traditional Islamic practice, African heritage, and Black pride, and they were not charged to use the space. They still required a religious institution that could speak to their multilingual needs and migratory complexities. And a contingent of mostly Ivoirian Muslims rented a loft area on 116th near Seventh and opened Masjid Salaam in 1998. The ground floor of an old furniture store on Eighth near 116th was leased the same year, and a similar group founded Masjid Aqsa.

Both *maghrib* (sunset) and *isha* (night) prayers at Aqsa and Salaam are attended by at least one hundred people each day. The other prayers—*fajr* (dawn), *thuhr* (noon), and *asr* (afternoon)—are well attended but not nearly as large. Most arrive just before the *athan* and form Qur'anic reading and *thikr* circles. Younger men in their twenties sit with older men twice their age, poring over the meaning of scripture or helping one another memorize several verses at a time. Some sit alone, holding the Qur'an in one hand, staring off into space with silent lips moving, and periodically checking the text for accuracy. This round of devotions dramatically infuses their never-ending work schedules with religious meaning, allowing them to feel human under what many feel are demoralizing conditions. Unlike the contentious encounters between African and Black Muslims at Shabazz, the Mosque of Islamic Brotherhood, Aqsa, and Salaam have attempted to build bridges. Imam Talib, for example, gives the *khutba* at the African *masjids*, and they return the favor. Before they left the Mosque of Islamic Brotherhood to form their own institutions in 1998, they even consulted with Imam Talib and mosque members for advice. They wanted to ensure that good relations would continue between them.

While members at Shabazz are trying to forge a business alliance with Africans, Imam Talib and African Muslim leaders have formed a different kind of partnership: a Harlem *shura*, or Muslim consultative board. This gives them a joint platform for addressing concerns within the community. Like Kabir and others who believe their shared religion will eventually help to improve business relations between them, they, too, believe that Islam is a major unifying agent facilitating their efforts to reach across an ethnic divide. "We're gonna *lock* up Harlem!" Imam Talib exclaims, expressing his desire to collaborate with African Muslims to better the neighborhood.

The first major point of cooperation between the Mosque of Islamic Brotherhood and Africans occurred following the Amadou Diallo murder in 1999. Because Diallo was a Muslim immigrant from Guinea, both Aqsa and Salaam were directly involved in the case. Masjid Malcolm Shabazz had strong ties to city hall, and African Muslims initially went to Shabazz for advice. However, some claimed that Shabazz was apathetic, taking much too long to address their political concerns.

They grew tired and sought out Reverend Al Sharpton, who immediately ignited a huge media blitz and a series of demonstrations. "In the beginning, the

Majlish-Shura, the National Islamic Advisory Council," Imam Talib explains, "assigned me and Hasan Ali Rasheed to get close to the Diallo family. We didn't want Sharpton to take control of the situation." Hasan Ali Rasheed was the *imam* of Shabazz at the time and, according to reports, was extremely responsive. Unfortunately, Imam Hasan died during this period, and many claim that the next administration at Shabazz adopted a very different posture. Still, as Imam Talib became a staunch advocate for Diallo, the incident helped to solidify a deeper bond between Black and African communities in Harlem. But Imams Talib and Konate are both very clear about the extent of their involvement in the case. In a Friday sermon several weeks after the murder, Imam Konate stressed to listeners that ethnic allegiances were unimportant. "Diallo was not my brother because he was from Guinea," he announced, "but because he was a Muslim! We should rally around his killing because he was a Muslim, not because he was our countryman." Around the same time, Imam Talib made a similar statement at the Mosque of Islamic Brotherhood. "I love my immigrant brothers because they're Muslim," he proclaimed during a sermon, "not because they come from Africa. Their immigrant identity is not always in agreement with their identity as Muslims." Together, these statements signify a concerted effort to focus on the Islamic faith they share, rather than on their cultural sensibilities, which they also value, as a way to understand each other and manage the needs of their respective communities.

When one enters the Harlem Market, the pace of daily life changes, and another rhythm takes over. Most African merchants go about their day waiting for patrons to enter their stalls, rearranging their products from time to time after a customer has rummaged through them. Some sit back in fold-up chairs, chatting about a host of events, including the latest gossip. Others seem always to be haggling with potential buyers. Despite the secular nature of this business arena, African merchants break up their days with a regular cycle of formal prayers (*salah*). In a place like Harlem, it's not unusual to see Muslims performing the postures of their daily devotions. What strikes me, however, is how these liturgical actions seem to fit naturally into the cultural fabric of the market. Rather than announcing the time for prayer and interrupting the flow of the environment, one or several persons simply rise, go to perform *wudu* (ablution), return to spread out their *musallas* (prayer rugs), and pray. In this way, their actions enact an Islamic spirituality that seeps into one's soul over the course of the day. As Rebecca Sullivan notes about the meaning of wearing the nun's habit, actions like these reflect religiosity as a "state of being rather than a value of piety," refuting any attempt to quantify faith.[48] In other Muslim markets in the United States, each prayer becomes a huge spectacle and almost tears into one's consciousness. In these instances, a *mutawa'*, or religious disciplinarian, blasts an announcement that merchants and patrons should stop all activity and rush to worship. Although this approach plays an important role in those communities, the manner in which these rituals are performed at the Harlem Market illustrates a major way in which *masjid* life is sustained. What is even more noteworthy is the way these Islamic practices influence the public arena.

During one Ramadan, I have been at Masjid Aqsa for several hours and decide to walk around to Salaam. This day, I am dressed casually, in black slacks, brown shoes, and a rust-colored jacket. I also wear a white *kufi*. At the corner of 116th and Eighth, I cross the street. As I approach Sopey Cheikhoul Khadim, the Murid supply shop, I see an African American girl in her early twenties leaning against a parked car in front. Shelly is about five foot seven and thin. She wears a snug brown puff vest and mustard-colored Timberland boots, with the hood of her orange sweater covering her hair. In the spirit of Ramadan, two three-foot-high black speakers on the ground by the shop entrance pour out *at-tarteel*—slow, measured, and rhythmic tones of the Qur'an. Unlike the spectacle of chanting Bamba's *khassaïd* for several hours during the parade, the daily engagement of Qur'anic sounds forces an interaction between African Muslim culture and public space. Besides the way traditional African attire marks territory, capturing the visual senses of the community, or how African cuisine signals identity through smell, the aural pulse of Qur'anic recitation diffuses into the city streets, competing with hip-hop sounds pounding out of passing cars, apartment windows, boom boxes, or stores looking to attract young customers.

Shelly's hands are stuffed into her vest pockets, and the car she leans against rocks slightly from the pumping motion of her legs.

"You all right?" she says before I have a chance to speak.

"Yeah, I'm all right," I reply. "How are you?"

She cuts her eyes to take another look at me, then looks away. "All right." The words ease out.

"You live in Harlem?" I ask.

Her eyes and head tilt quickly in my direction. "Yeah, I live here."

"Do you know what's playing on the speaker?" I ask.

"Yeah, it's the Qur'an, right?"

"Yeah, you're right."

"How do you feel about it playing out loud like that?" I ask as Shelly's legs stop rocking and she thinks for a moment.

"It's soothing," she says. "I like it. It makes me feel good."

"Really?"

"Yeah, it does," she says.

"What are you doing, just hangin' out?" I ask.

She immediately interrupts her stares up and down the street and turns to look at me. "I sell weed!"

Damn! I think to myself, and I wonder how she could expose herself in that way. *What if I were a cop?*

"What do you do?" she shoots back.

"I teach college. I'm a professor," I reply. "I'm here because I'm writing a book on Harlem, African Muslims in Harlem."

"Oh, word?" she says. "That's what's up. You want some weed?"

"No, that's all right," I say. "I'm fine."

"I know a lot of professors who smoke weed," she says. "You sure you don't want some."

"Oh, yeah, I'm sure," I say.

I watch as Shelly stashes brown paper bags filled with money and drugs in the bottom crack of a lamp post. "Are you in school or something?" I ask.

"I go to school for hair," she says.

Her response jolts me, and I wonder when she has time to attend classes or practice her trade, especially if she spends so much time on the streets.

"This is just a hustle to make extra money for school," she says. "I can't get financial aid, so I do this to make money." Her tense body suddenly begins to relax. "I really want to go to Spelman," she adds, nodding her head up and down.[49] "You know, in Atlanta?"

"Yes, that's great!" I say.

As we talk, Africans walking in and out of stores stare at me stoically. I suspect many believe my *kufi* identifies me as a Muslim, and they have a difficult time understanding how I can be talking to a non-Muslim woman or a known drug dealer, especially during the holy month of Ramadan.[50]

"Will you give me a recommendation for school?" she blurts out.

"Of course I will," I answer, and reach into my jacket to give her a card. I tell Shelly I have to go, and she pushes off the car, steps forward, and gives me a hug.

"Thank you for talking to me," she says, and I leave.

As a young woman selling marijuana on the streets, Shelly gives testimony about her perception of the Qur'an that certainly speaks to the extent to which an African Islam is altering Harlem's cultural field. In other words, while many might believe that the divergent worlds of drugs and religion do not meet or, perhaps, should not overlap, this episode illustrates a context in which Qur'anic tones reach into the inner space of a young drug peddler. Together, West African migrants animate a Muslim life that sustains an Islamic discourse, by which I mean the public performances, daily practices, street talks, and sensory perceptions that create a sacred city in Harlem.

IV

A few days after the Bamba Day parade, I go to Masjid Salaam to look for Babacar. The *musallah* (prayer area) covers an open space of about eighteen by thirty feet on the second floor above several stores, including an Ethiopian deli. The two other stores directly beneath the *masjid*, a variety shop and a restaurant, are owned by African Muslims. Standing in front of the entrance, I begin my trek up the narrow, dank hallway and climb the fifty-odd steps. A small pile of shoes clutter the landing, but most are brought inside as worshippers enter through one of two doors on the left or right. As at other *masjids*, shoes are placed in a wooden rack attached to the wall near the door. I enter the *musallah* and spot Mamadou, a twenty-five-year-old Senegalese who's been in Harlem since his early teens. I usually run into him at the Mosque of Islamic Brotherhood, down on 113th and Nicholas. It is a surprise to see him.

We greet each other, and I sit on the green carpet next to him. He looks tired and explains that he has been working at a variety store to pay the bills. He also has been working on a project he hopes will make some "real" money.

"I'm designing these car rims," he says. "I have some pretty good designs."

"Have you ever thought about going to school for it?" I ask.

"Yeah," he replies. "But I never did. I'm trying to get the design ready and get it out there. I used to do music."

"Music?" I ask. "What kind of music?"

"You know," he says. "Hip-hop, rap. But I found out music was *haram* [forbidden], so I stopped. I used to do it for some time. It was hard to stop at first. But once I found out it wasn't Islamic, I just gave it up."

"How did you learn it was *haram*?" I ask.

"We have classes," he replies, "and some of the brothers here teach us about the *deen* [religion]. We read books by 'Uthaymin. This is the way of the Salaf."[51]

"Well, you know," I reply, "there are different ways the *fuqahaa* [Muslim jurists] have interpreted this. Some say music itself isn't *haram*, but it's a matter of what it makes you do or not do that's the problem."

He listens but remains silent, nodding from time to time. "Yeah," he finally says, "someone else told me that."

As we sit and talk, I remember three African American Muslims I passed on the street earlier that day. Their attire and manner indicated that they were Salafi, followers of a growing ultraconservative movement now influencing Mamadou and more than a few African Muslims in Harlem. Their scraggly, untrimmed beards reached their chests, and they wore closely shaven mustaches. Walking in a semi-regimented pattern, each wore a solid black, brown, and gray *jalabiyyah* (robe)

Masjid Salaam, now defunct. (Photo Zain Abdullah)

down to the calf, leaving his high pants legs barely visible. I quickly extended the Islamic greetings as they reached within a few feet of me. Without breaking their stride, they quickly looked and muttered a brief reply, a typical response from some Salafis when greeted by outsiders.

The *athan* sounds for *maghrib*, and several hundred people line up. The mix is an appealing sight of exotically scented men wearing African clothes, business attire, and hip-hop gear. They glance down at their feet, moving their toes in place to make sure the rows are straight, a habit encouraged as a sign of faith. Daily prayers here are well attended, and the size of the congregation reminds me of the weekly *jum'ah*, a time when one can count more than six hundred congregants with thirty or forty rows spilling over onto the sidewalk below. After the prayer, one or two people stand at the door yelling, "*Fi sabi-lillah, fi sabi-lillah!* [For the sake of Allah!]," holding black plastic bags full of bills. As native-born Americans approach the doorway, I notice the bag is pulled back slightly, so as not to impose this fund-raising effort on guests.

As people disperse, I see Babacar in the corner reading some papers. I walk over to him, and he looks up.

"Ah! Where have you been?" he says, and rises to hug me.

"Oh, I went to the Cheikh Amadou Bamba Day parade," I reply. "Did you go?"

He tries to resist but can't help twisting his face in disapproval. "I was reading their publication," he says. "They don't practice Islam. They put their *cheikh* above the Prophet Muhammad and the *cheikh*'s writings above the Qur'an."

"Yeah, well, perhaps some do," I reply. "But I attended the UN event, and they had a lineup of scholars on the panel."

Babacar agrees that the "educated ones" don't practice this, but perhaps those from the rural area do. "They kiss and rub their hands on the car of the *cheikh*," he adds. "What is this?" he yells.

"All groups have different levels of religious practice," I say. "And this covers a wide range of behavior."

He agrees, and we eventually move on to a different topic.

Many African Muslims in Harlem consider the behavior of Murids to be blasphemous, especially their deep reverence for their *cheikhs* and their teachings. Most of these Africans, however, know very little about the group except what they witness from a few followers. Still, a borderline between orthodoxy and heterodoxy, true believers and deviants, underscores a major way African Islam is partitioned in Harlem.

Once, at the Harlem Market, I sit eating with two African vendors, Mousa and Djibril, both from Côte d'Ivoire. Despite the many times we have eaten together and conversed, Djibril feels the need to check my Islamic identity. As we hover over and reach our hands into a single aluminum container of food, he turns to Mousa and asks him in Malinke if I'll be fasting for Ramadan.

"Yeah," Mousa replies, and turns to me. "You fast Ramadan, right?"

This Muslim identity check, similar to the inspection of my racial identity in chapter 3, corresponds to the ways others are categorized by religion. Djibril's question reveals an attempt to divide Harlem into *dar al-Islam* (insider) and *dar al-harb* (outsider), exclusive realms that Muslims inhabit and others do not.[52] Questions about Islamic practice in African Muslim communities represent another way of marking religious territory or signifying who belongs and who does not. But in this case, it is through proper or improper Islamic behavior, as in the case of the Salafis or the condemnation of Murid religiosity.

At times, internal fissures develop along other lines. As I leave Masjid Salaam, I enter the hallway, stopping on the landing to put on my shoes. About midway down the stairs, I hear a commotion. "Fuck you!" blares out in an audibly foreign accent. Suddenly, "Fuck you!" sounds again but with greater force. I reach the entrance and see ten Ivoirians holding back one of their countrymen. He begins to pace, turning at times to point at a Somali Muslim who apparently has co-opted two white plastic chairs, exclusive places set up by Ivoirian Muslims to sit in front of the *masjid* and socialize. "It's about the chairs," Amreet, another Somali announces after I ease closer to ask about the conflict. He might have been right; even so, the chairs not only represent a generic Muslim territory but also signify an ethnic space that fellow nationals share, along with a niche where Ivoirian males bond and rehearse their masculinity. It is this hidden meaning that makes the infraction of appropriating the chairs by non-Ivoirians so explosive.

On the day of this year's Magal celebration, a commemoration marking Cheikh Amadou Bamba's historic exile, I drive toward 125th from 116th, looking carefully for celebrants and spotting several here and there. All in all, people appear to be moving about casually, as if conserving energy for the long night ahead. I have decided to wear my blue *boubou* with the gold trim. As I pull up in front, I can hear people yelling, "Qur'an twenty-eight! Qur'an twenty-eight!" This is an indication that the Qur'an has been recited twenty-eight times within a few hours. During the fasting month of Ramadan, the entire Qur'an is read aloud, divided into one thirtieth part for each day. The fact that the entire book has been read within several hours, not to mention twenty-eight times, is intriguing. For Muslims, the reading of the Qur'an carries immense rewards. According to a prophetic saying, reciting one letter is worth ten blessings multiplied by whatever special value a letter already possesses. For religious purposes, then, reciting the sacred text numerous times signifies a tremendous act of worship. And it can only serve to magnify the religious significance of the Magal as well. In order to accomplish this feat, more than two hundred people read it collectively, with seven or eight groups and each person within each circle reciting a thirtieth part. Reading any scripture multiple times as a liturgical exercise generates massive spiritual energy. Moreover, this communal act speaks volumes about Muslims' collective sense of themselves. Even as each Murid engages in individual acts of devotion, he or she views this solitary deed as a means by which the entire faith community benefits.

I walk through the front door and am greeted by a *masjid* official, then swiftly brought upstairs to the second-floor lounge. People spend hours watching the Magal by satellite TV, which airs routine lectures and images of crowds moving about. Sounds of "Ahhh!" ring out in unison as bodies jolt in response to statements about the meaning of the Magal. Young and old sit in chairs or on the carpet, all glued to the screen. Some shed tears as passionate preachers recount Bamba's trials and legacy.

Hamadou, a fourteen-year-old, turns to look at me. "Bamba had the *sunnah* [religious practice] of Muhammad very well," he says. "So, for us, Bamba is an example of how to practice the *sunnah*."

This year's Magal theme is "*Role de Emigration*." Viewers weep when they are reminded by lecturers of how Bamba designated Touba as a place for the sole worship of Allah. When Touba was just a place in the desert, one speaker announces, Bamba predicted it would be a special site for monotheism. While Mecca had a history of "pagan worship," he says, Touba would be a sacred place without this past and thus completely dedicated to the one God. Speakers also quote Bamba's predictions that Murids would raise *masjids* all over the world, especially in the West. For Murids in New York City, they are the living embodiment of Bamba's vision. Their migration is not merely for economic gain but also has a divine mandate.

After several hours, I get up and walk outside for air. Suddenly the *athan* is called. As I turn to go back into the *masjid*, I notice several white *kufis* appearing out of the dusk. I look closer and see about seven Africans wearing traditional attire. Since the *athan* has just been called, I assume they are coming to pray. They reach the corner where I am standing, and we exchange *salaams*. Then they cross the street, passing Touba altogether. I quickly turn around and see more coming. I have grown accustomed to seeing Africans walking in droves toward the *masjid* and then entering. But their passing it completely surprises me. I then realize that they are Fulani Muslims from Guinea on their way to the newly established Futa Islamic Center on Eighth near 138th. According to informal reports, there are perhaps more Fulani from Guinea in Harlem than Malinke from Côte d'Ivoire, but they have just recently begun to set up their own religious institutions. Still, this calls to mind an important fact about the range and scope of African Islam in this part of New York. While there are times when African Muslims reach across ethnic divides to support one another, their daily religious encounters follow a very distinct cultural path. During these times, their Islamic practices remain separate and do not overlap. Where an African American Muslim might attend several of these African *masjids* throughout the week, most Africans frequent *masjids* where their ethnic groups are well represented. This is not merely a religious decision but a matter of familiarity. Each African *masjid* will accommodate particular languages and customs, and unfamiliar newcomers find it difficult to adjust.

One African *imam* expresses a similar problem when I ask him whether he is going to attend the Magal. He speaks at least five languages, but he says, "I was invited, but I don't understand Wolof. Why should I sit there when I don't understand anything, watching their mouths move? Someone mentions Serigne Touba, and everyone yells, 'Ahhh!' Or someone says 'Bamba,' and they all yell out, 'Ohhh!' What is this?" These comments clearly mark particular fault lines separating West African Muslims. African languages such as Wolof for the Murids, Malinke or Dyoula at Masjids Aqsa and Salaam, and Fula at the Fulani's Islamic Center constitute a series of borderlands, cultural frontiers in which members construct a deep sense of belonging. The Murid's invitation illustrates crucial times when these communities have attempted to transcend this ethnic divide. Each of these African Muslim groups, however, represents an integral part of a religious space that has become a kind of sacred city in Harlem. But this does not indicate the end of their struggles, and the next chapter looks at what it means for African Muslims to engage in personal *jihads* (struggles) of their own.

6

Harlem *Jihads*

I

Cities are alive. Streets swell in the sweltering heat. Sidewalks crack in frigid temperatures like hardened lips. The air carries an array of smells and sounds. But this is merely the brick and mortar, exterior and corporal existence. In her classic work *The Death and Life of Great American Cities*, Jane Jacobs urges city planners to reject a modernist, form-over-function approach to urban design.[1] She argues for the life of cities by drawing our attention to its human component, a vibrant complexity that enlivens urban form and regulates a city's soul. Harlem is animated by the flow of a people, and it is only in that context that we can understand African Muslims.[2] But like the people inhabiting them, cities change. And the rapid pace of gentrification in West Harlem is changing its character, its mood. For example, the exchange of passengers riding uptown on the number 2 or 3 train was always predictable. During rush hour, they would board or disembark like clockwork, with each stop calculating the distance between Black, Latino, and White neighborhoods. Standing on a crowded 2 train from midtown, Harlem-bound riders were certain to get a seat after 96th Street. This station stop marked the dividing line between White Manhattan and Black New York, including the *barrio*.[3]

One early evening in July, the actions of a lone White woman in a business suit disclose just how much this simple arrangement has been overturned. As the train leaves 96th, only a few seats become available. At any other time, half the car would be vacant. I notice a thin, blond-haired woman, impeccably dressed in a black knee-length skirt and jacket. Her brown leather briefcase is set on the floor, pushed up against her black stilettos. The train reaches 110th Street, the first stop on the Harlem border, and she doesn't budge. The tone sounds, and the doors close. We continue up Lenox Avenue, and I gather my things, preparing to leave at 116th. As the train comes to a full stop, the woman carefully rises, walks through the doors, and makes her way toward the exit. I walk behind her in utter disbelief. It is 2001, but this is the first time I have witnessed a White businesswoman presumably returning home to Harlem, especially in the evening. If this were anywhere above 145th Street, I would have barely noticed. But this is West 116th Street, an avenue renamed for Malcolm X, whose prescient voice still reverberates, rallying Black crowds to maintain control and ownership of Harlem. The woman eases by the subway art depicting Minton's Playhouse, the 1930s club where modern jazz or bebop allegedly began. I wonder if she feels what the artist attempted, an effort "to capture the lyricism and spirit of the African Diaspora within the Harlem community."[4] I watch as she enters shaky ground, a tense turf where relations between Africans and Blacks are volatile, and I also wonder if she, a new Harlem resident, feels any tension.

Brian, a White male in his early thirties, echoes White fears of residing in Harlem. "I'd love to move into the area," he remarks during a visit to the Harlem Market. "But I don't know how people would respond to a White man living in the community." A nurse at a New York hospital, Brian came to Manhattan from Boston ten years ago and lives just below 110th Street. His love for African culture brings him to the market, and he occasionally goes to 125th Street with friends to shop for bargains. While he applauds the way Harlem appears to be "changing," he is still not ready to make the change himself. We stand there chatting and staring at the mahogany African birthing chair from Ghana he has just purchased. "Just like in some White areas," he says, "Blacks might not be welcomed." He pauses and thinks. "But people have treated me so nicely," he adds with astonishment.

Brian's hesitance to relocate to Harlem is exactly what amazes me about this young woman. As she walks up the stairs to exit, I trail her outside, wondering what her thoughts are about a young Black male walking behind her and if she senses any danger. If she doesn't think of it, I certainly do. But this is the quagmire of race in America, especially when racialized bodies cross paths. It puts everyone on alert, even if you make a conscious effort not to give it any credence. Regular encounters (either real or imagined) produce a type of "racial fatigue," a term Shelby Steele uses in his award-winning documentary on the murder of Yusef Hawkins, a Black teenager who was killed by White youths in Bensonhurst, Brooklyn, for being out of his "proper" place.[5] In this way, territory is racialized, and I wonder if the young woman feels out of *her* place. As she walks along the pavement, her every step appears deliberate, almost calculated, and her stride is straight and even, as if she hopes no one will notice her. Still, her presence means a great deal more. Sociologists use the term *White flight* to describe Whites abandoning suburban or urban neighborhoods under the encroachment of desegregation. They fear that the quality of their homes and public services such as schools will decline with the integration of African Americans, Jews, or other minorities. Studies in the early 1990s have shown that while a sample of Blacks preferred to live in equally mixed, Black and White areas, Whites surveyed were not willing to move into a community that was more than one-fifth Black.[6] So what does it mean when the reverse happens? "Fleeing the more expensive parts of Manhattan," Robin D. G. Kelley remarks, "whites are integrating Harlem in large numbers." He adds that "whites moving into black communities tend to push property values up, thus pricing many longtime black residents out." Kelley quips, "It's funny how we never call this process integration; instead, we use the presumably race-neutral 'gentrification.'"[7]

Yet Blacks seem unable to explain the presence of White gentrifiers and their brazen disregard for the age-old racial boundaries. "White people aren't even afraid to walk around Harlem anymore!" Dean blurts out as we sit on a bench talking about changes in the community. Just twenty-five years of age, Dean is already able to remember a different time in Harlem. The renovation of abandoned, dilapidated storefronts by Africans clearly represents one kind of change. In fact, one could argue that their overwhelming presence, not to mention the visibility of Africana, has helped to allay white fears. "You see them four o'clock in the morning out here," Dean continues. "I mean, I can understand it for those Whites who've been in Harlem. They're a part of the community. But you have all these Whites who are just moving in."

Dean hustles as a real estate broker of sorts, helping people, Black folks specifically, to find a "decent" apartment or just a room. With large-scale construction under way, low-wage, working-class Blacks and Latinos are being ousted and displaced to other boroughs with less expensive housing. Some Harlem developments are required to designate specific units for affordable housing, but this is far from adequate. Dean points to one newly renovated building on Adam Clayton Powell Boulevard. "It's full of White people!" he yells. Even more than the change brought about by the huge influx of African Muslims, longtime residents are largely concerned with the apparent takeover of Harlem by young White and Asian urban professionals. This is the change most poor and working-class residents dread, because it threatens to uproot their already tenuous lives.

As Dean and I talk, people walking by frequently interrupt us to greet him. Another local resident, an African American man in his late twenties, sits by us.

From time to time, he nods in agreement, bearing silent witness to Dean's truth telling. Between post-civil-rights-era ghettoization and the milking of property by absentee landlords and a recent upscale gentrification, Harlem and its residents have been flung from one extreme to the next in a relatively short period. "You used to see people on the street playing and hanging out," Dean says. "Living in Harlem used to be very different than it is now." Like most Black cities under the sway of gentrification, Harlem is in transition. But it has always been in motion, from the swing of Duke Ellington's orchestra in the early 1930s to the current bends and twists of ballerinas at the Dance Theater of Harlem; from the whirlwind of Marcus Garvey's United Negro Improvement Association advocating Black liberation in the early 1900s to the Million Youth Marches of recent years. Its movement, however, is not a solitary thing but includes brown and black and now yellow and white bodies keeping it in motion. What, if anything, does this reveal about its present condition? At the very least, we can say that for each group, Harlem has its own meaning.

Harlem is beginning to resemble a series of "ecological niches," living areas extending from the center of town, each corresponding to a particular lifestyle and economic status.[8] West Africans predominate on certain streets, while trendy upper-middle-class professionals meander in and out of others. Some, like Dean, might imagine Harlem as a single community with multiple families and fictive cousins, while many more envision separate communities linked by a series of familial networks.[9] Harlem advocacy groups argue for tenants' rights and fight for improved housing and better urban renewal. And for these activists, the city is a battleground between powerful planners and residents.[10] With advanced capital and religious circuits linking Harlem to countries around the world, many immigrants and entrepreneurs imagine the city as an urban node connecting the local with the global. For thousands more, Harlem can represent a montage of advertisements, as everyday residents struggle against the increased commercialization of their neighborhoods. Each vision of the city represents one way researchers have attempted to understand the range and scope of human activity in the metropolis. At the very least, these attempts move us away from one of two typologies: the "melting pot" (an assimilationist view that group differences will eventually dissolve into a single, homogeneous nation) and the "salad bowl" (a multiculturalist perspective arguing that retaining ethnic affiliations is crucial for integration).

These diverse perspectives on city life suggest that while one approach might help to describe an urban activity, a single lens can rarely capture the ebb and flow of even what Jane Jacobs calls a "street neighborhood," much less a place as large as Harlem.[11] To grasp this complexity is to attempt to understand the various contexts that African Muslims must traverse daily. Finding their place in Harlem is

A mural on 132nd and Seventh, with an African woman on the right, stating, "Support Community Struggles; Better Housing, Education, Unity, Equality." (Photo Zain Abdullah)

more than acquiring a physical address, and they must quickly learn new ways of living among very different populations.

On 111th Street, for example, a couple of blocks from the Mosque of Islamic Brotherhood, I park my car and begin walking toward the mosque. The street resembles many others in the area, with a line of old and newly renovated brownstones and a few recently constructed, upscale buildings for a highly professional clientele. It is almost the Harlem I knew in the early 1980s—except for a new round of faces streaming by me. White men in their mid- to late twenties or early thirties, dressed in cotton shirts, nylon jackets, jeans, and Rockport shoes, stroll up and down the street. Now and then, one spots a young White woman jogging in spandex. As I reach the corner, I glance into the Laundromat and see a young Asian woman loading a washing machine. I turn onto St. Nicholas Avenue and nearly bump into a well-dressed Indo-Pakistani man being pulled by a black-and-brown cocker spaniel and a smaller black Scottish terrier.

In just a quick walk around the block, it becomes all too clear how the gentrification of Harlem signals its suburbanization.[12] Not only did Mayor Rudolph Giuliani use massive police force to clear street merchants from 125th and sanitize it for big business, but he also dispatched huge contingents of undercover officers on "buy and bust" missions to eradicate narcotics for Harlem's new middle-class residents, "despite a steady decline in drug use and violent crimes."[13] As retail rents soared, local Black businesses began to fold, and Harlem's 125th Street, the epicenter of Black America for almost a century, was being turned into "an outpost of corporate America with gleaming office towers and big-box stores."[14] At a time when even local residents find it hard to handle the transformation occurring in their neighborhood, West African Muslims appear to be likewise swept up by a cycle of change and frustration. All of them emigrated from Black countries, and some believed they were entering an all-Black neighborhood. While they evidently come from cultures where, to some extent, ethnic differences have been worked out, the Harlem they now enter is a highly contentious one, and they will necessarily be forced to learn new strategies to live alongside not just Black, Caribbean, and Latino residents but also affluent Whites and second- or third-generation Asian and South Asian professionals. In the past, one consolation for immigrants entering a new urban locale was that both residents and newcomers could slowly learn each other's ways and adjust accordingly. But with the rapid influx of immigrants and gentrifiers, not to mention the concomitant changes within the urban economy, the city is like a moving train forcing newly arrived Africans to adjust all too quickly. Yet at the same time, Jerilou and Kingsley Hammett observe, "New York is on its way to becoming a 'theme-park city,' where people can get the illusion of the urban experience without the diversity, spontaneity, and unpredictability that have always been its hallmarks. Like the suburbs New Yorkers so long snubbed, the city is becoming more private, more predictable, and more homogenized."[15]

After reaching the Mosque of Islamic Brotherhood, I watch several young African American men hanging around the building and outside stores. They keep tabs on the coming and going of cars and people. An Asian woman, wearing loose-fitting jeans and a white blouse, emerges from a brownstone. Our eyes meet suddenly, and it appears that she pauses to read the situation out front. Tearing her eyes away, she walks briskly to a BMW 525 parked across the street. The motley crew of newcomers seems to bob in and out between pedestrians, residents in work clothes, and children just released from school. But more than a few with ravished, drug-ridden bodies, numb from the devastation of street life, walk a different path up and down the block. Black and Latino hip-hoppers occupy another part of Harlem, a mere backdrop like everything else. But it seems these separate worlds never collide.

As I stand outside the mosque, a three-story corner brownstone, a black car pulls up in front, and Imam Talib scrambles to get out. He is dressed in his customary white *jalabiyyah* (robe), black *'ibaya* (preacher's overcoat), and white *kufi* (Muslim cap) with black turban. It is *jum'ah*, and I am glad to see him, particularly because his presence means I won't be late for the sermon. He greets me with a quick smile and walks toward the front stairs. Two small Muslim children with *kufis* and robes patiently sit on the top landing, waiting for their parents to return from prayer. Imam Talib climbs the steps, but before pushing open the door, he turns toward the children and extends a warm greeting and a huge grin. "*As-salaamu 'alaykum*," he says, elongating his words and leaning backward to see their faces. They bashfully turn to look at each other but remain quiet. And Imam Talib gives the same greeting again. They look at him and mutter, "*Alaykum, alaykum*." He glances back at me. We both laugh, and I hurry up the stairs to follow him inside. This cultural fragment is another part of Harlem few have a chance to witness. With several hundred anxious attendees waiting inside, Imam Talib has remembered the golden rule and performed an act of kindness. While these small acts do much to characterize a community, they are very often missed by the public.

During his sermon, Imam Talib speaks about the importance of prayer. He also relays a story about an African American man who spotted him walking outside and yelled, "Hey, I need to come to the mosque and get some of those rituals!" Imam Talib, clearly agitated, shouts at his congregants, "We don't do rituals here! We do *'ebaadah* [worship]!" While I can appreciate his concern not to have others trivialize their religious devotion, reducing its spiritual significance to empty rhetoric, there is clearly another side to the incident. The rapid pace of gentrification, job scarcity, low-wage employment, governmental crack-down on the informal economy, and numerous other disorienting forces erect an impenetrable wall against the community. The image of hundreds of Black men with saintly names praying and moving in military-style formation is ex-actly the "ritual" some African American males desire, especially when such dev-astating circumstances appear to undermine their manhood. For a community torn apart by the onslaught of urban renewal and high-priced development, this kind of weekly or daily show of unity, spirituality, discipline, and purpose is certainly empowering. If nothing else, it sanctions their presence and renders them visible. In 1952, Ralph Ellison wrote *Invisible Man*, a highly acclaimed novel about the alienation and social dislocation of African Americans in 1940s New York.[16] Because Whites refuse to "see" him, the protagonist is an unnamed Black man in search of his identity and place in society. Conversely, not only do Islamic liturgies at the Mosque of Islamic Brotherhood validate these people's presence within their own neighborhood, but they also name them, a recognition Ellison's character sought, by granting converts a new identity with Arabic or African qualities. In this context, ritual acts are a matter of combating an awkward dis-possession of oneself. It's an Islamic dispensation of sorts and demonstrates vital ways religion can speak directly to social conditions.

After the prayer, I give a ride to Rahim, an African American Muslim in his late fifties. He is going to meet with Ghafur, an official at the Mosque of Islamic Brotherhood and founder-director of a nonprofit organization. Ghafur's office is on 133rd Street, and they are getting together to hammer out details for a new AIDS/HIV program. Government funds are available, and they feel they have a shot. Rahim gets out of the car ahead of me, and I watch him step through the glass door of a ground-level storefront office. Its side entrance anchors a five-story brick apartment building facing 133rd. I enter ten minutes later. I haven't seen Ghafur in some time, especially outside of the mosque. Usually, he's managing mosque affairs and we have quick chats between tasks. I rarely see him without his *jalabiyyah* and never without his *kufi*. Now, as he walks over for a brotherly hug, his black slacks and yellow short-sleeve polo shirt are an interesting change. Plenty of Black Muslims consistently don some form of religious clothing as a signifier of their Islamic identity. They feel bombarded by countervailing cultures and mixed commercial messages, all competing for a single audience. The Islamic *thobe* and headscarf many African American Muslims wear buffer them from the cultural hegemony of outside forces. Yet Ghafur's business attire signals his compliance with a world beyond the mosque. His language differs as well. Now—when he is not speaking of spiritual matters and the realities of the unseen—his speech is peppered with phrases such as "proper office management" and "corporate accountability." This code switching might appear inconsequential on the surface, but it underscores the polyvalent discourses prevalent in Harlem (even within a single individual), and it allows us a glimpse of the cultural dexterity needed to survive in this field.[17]

I leave them for a walk up Malcolm X. I want to get a takeout meal from Spoonbread Too on 138th, but I am more excited about witnessing the pageantry of the boulevard. It is a warm August afternoon, and such a stroll captivates the senses. The pulsating beats of African tonal languages play off the cadence of Haitian Kreyol and West Indian dialects. And Spanglish—English interposed with Spanish—punctuates the atmosphere from time to time. Black Americans of varying hues, class backgrounds, and idiomatic slang color the urban canvas with their own unique spirit. White and Asian newcomers slip in and out of restored buildings and trendy shops as culinary aromas fill the air. I continue up the boulevard, and two young African American women strut by in stretch jeans that leave nothing to the imagination. Each clack from their pumps accents their curves and mesmerizes gawking male hip-hoppers. They stand more than six feet tall in their four-inch heels, and their ponytails swing in the opposite direction of their torsos, which are stuffed into unforgiving spandex tops. At times, they turn toward passersby for a word or two without breaking stride. All the while, flowing African robes and headdresses are interspersed into the metropolitan showcase, adding color and a tinge of the sensational.

At the corner of 135th, the Schomburg Center for Research in Black Culture, an affiliate of the New York Public Library, displays a thirty-foot-wide cloth poster hung high on its exterior wall, beckoning pedestrians to remember the "Black Image." Like the medley of street vernacular, the *haute couture* shops, the mysterious aromas wafting from kitchen exhausts, and the body language of promenading young women, the Schomburg's sign is one of many social texts to read and interpret. Each segment is part and parcel of a larger testimony about Harlem life. Every block or so, street peddlers move close enough to make their own pleas. "Marlboros! I got dem Marlboros!" one says. Bystanders chat with friends on corners, watching the traffic of people and cars, or pass the day with their favorite street merchants. These Black vendors are modern-day *griots*, urban storytellers, and people gather around them to debate an array of social issues. Their TV trays, floor mats, or fold-up tables carry everything from kitchen knickknacks to apparel, from old photographs of Harlem's yesteryear to thirty-year-old vinyl albums of jazz greats. Others have Afrocentric clothing, Muslim oils, incense, and natural soap. Similar to the curbside conversations Mitchell Duneier skillfully writes about in his ethnography *Sidewalk*, residents at these sites rake over the meaning of their lives in Harlem and critique the larger world.[18]

Just below 134th Street, Jameel, an African American Muslim merchant in his early thirties, peddles bottled perfumes and other trinkets on a card table draped in white cloth. His oval wire-framed glasses make him appear erudite, even against his stubble mustache and long, untrimmed beard. Jameel just graduated from the College of New Rochelle with a 3.6 grade-point average. He was advised to talk to me about graduate school just before we met last year. His white *kufi* glistens in the sun as he bends over into the *ruku'* position while making prayer on his mat. He returns to a full standing posture, then drops into *sadjah*, with his hands, knees, and forehead on the ground, whispering the customary *tasbih*, "*subhana rabbiyal-'ala*" (glory to my Lord, the Most Lofty). He finally sits back on his knees into *jalsah* and completes his prayer.

"*As-salaamu 'alaykum*," I say, reaching around the table to shake his hand. He puts on his glasses and returns the peace. As we begin chatting about graduate school, Sherman, the thirty-year-old son of a close friend, walks up. He works at a child-care center while he's finishing his undergraduate degree at Medgar Evers College in Brooklyn. I haven't seen him in some years, and we grab each other for a hearty hug. We all stand there talking about education and the process of becoming a lifetime learner. At this point, Denny approaches the table. He lingers to hear our conversation, nodding his head in agreement at times. A burly six foot three, Denny is wearing his square wire-framed glasses and gripping a hardcover book tightly against his chest. Although he was raised in Harlem, he completed college in Massachusetts. Now, the more he hears us, the more he becomes visibly excited, nodding repeatedly and shuffling his feet in place.

As Duneier discovered about the street vendors he studied in Greenwich Village, "sidewalk life is crucial because the sidewalk is *the* site where a sense of mutual support must be felt *among strangers* if they are to go about their lives there together."[19] People like Jameel and Duneier's respondent Hakim, among others, are what Jane Jacobs calls "public characters."[20] In terms of street culture, these individuals help to facilitate the flow of urban activity within dense commercial areas. Their stands operate as community stations mediating the local news or the urban danger of which Duneier writes.[21] But they are also important places where Harlemites can contest their marginal status or simply use these concrete platforms to speak truth to power. While the conversations at these locations may resemble what urban theorists such as John L. Jackson Jr. describe as rumors or conspiracy theories, especially among the unschooled, vendor tables can also supply young street intellectuals with a free and open stage to excoriate the status quo.[22] For university-educated men, the prim space of the college classroom is woefully inadequate for a multidimensional exploration of their social grievances.[23] Instead, these public talks often take the form of an intellectual rap session or a literary yet cultured call-and-response melee. As such, they include both academic discourse and popular imaginings, which inform each other throughout the conversation.

The book Denny is holding is Harriet A. Washington's *Medical Apartheid*, which won the 2008 National Book Critics Circle award for nonfiction.[24] Washington is a fellow in ethics at the Harvard Medical School, among other places, and for Denny, her book has all the evidence he needs.

"This book proves everything!" he yells, interjecting himself into the conversation as we turn toward him.

"What book is that?" I ask. He carefully tilts it so I can read the title, but just barely, and flings it under his arm.

"Oh, you got it," Jameel says.

"Yeah!" Denny exclaims. "And it wasn't easy, either. This tells you what they did to us from slavery to the present. Tuskegee and shit! How they experimented on us and shit. This tells about all their fucking asses," Denny says, his face twisting hard.

"Oh, OK," I say.

"Yeah, yeah," Jameel adds. "That's right, it does."

"It talks about how these motherfuckers created AIDS, too!" Denny shouts.[25]

"You mean as biological warfare?" I ask.

With the Schomburg Center for Research in Black Culture in the background, an African American Muslim sidewalk merchant performs his role as public character. (Photo Zain Abdullah)

"Biological warfare, chemical warfare. Yeah!" he barks back. "They're doing this shit 'cause they know their time is up. They know that shit. The White man's time is up, and they want to bring as many of us with them as they can. These people walking around are stupid—talkin' 'bout 'Nobody reads books anymore.' What rock did you climb up from under, man?" he asks rhetorically. "Stupid! These people out here don't know nothing." Denny peers down the street, turning his body toward 133rd. "No, but they're gonna let Liberation Books go," he continues, looking for the store's sign. "That place is a historic landmark! And these people around here gonna let it be destroyed. They talkin' 'bout she owes six hundred dollars in back rent. He padlocked the place and said all the books in there belong to him now. How's that? All those books in there?" he says mockingly. "What's he gonna do with all those books? He should donate it to the schools, a nonprofit organization or something."

I wait to see if he will mention the Schomburg Center, especially since we are within earshot of the building. I interrupt him, saying, "What about the Schom—"

"Or the Schomburg!" he interjects, cutting me off. He faces in the direction of the building. "But I don't know," he says with a perplexed look. "That place is too much with the New York Public Library now. They have all these signs saying it's a New York Public Library now."

Actually, the Schomburg has been affiliated with the NYPL since the mid-1920s, I think silently.

"But yeah!" Denny says, breaking my thoughts. "I guess they can give it to them, too."

Sherman remains quiet, but he is clearly disturbed by Denny's line of reasoning and particularly his profanity, and he squints his eyes with each curse.

"I used to teach in the school system," Denny says. "But these bastards wanted a minstrel show for our kids. They wanted to show them *Stomp the House—*"

"*Stomp the Yard,*" I interject.

"Or some shit like that," he continues as if he didn't hear me. "I wanted to show them *Nothing but a Man.*[26] It's very good, man. I'm telling you, it's good! But these motherfuckers outruled me. I left. I don't have time for that shit."

With a black bookbag strapped to his back, Sherman tenses up his body as he listens to Denny. Suddenly, things change.

Denny says, "Did you see *White King, Red Rubber, Black Death?*[27] It's about the couple of million people they killed in the Congo."

Sherman perks up, and I notice his backpack move up as he straightens his back. "Yeah!" Sherman yells. "That's a very good film."

"Is it a documentary or a feature film?" I ask.

They pause and think. "It's a documentary," Denny replies. "They murdered a couple million people," he adds.

"No!" Sherman interjects. "Twenty million!"

Following this exchange, I leave, saying "As-salaamu 'alaykum" to Jameel and "Peace" to Sherman. Denny interjects with "Hotep!" and I reply with the same.[28]

As I walk, I think about Sherman's point of intervention into the conversation. As he listened to Denny, it appeared he was trying to differentiate between two separate narratives or, as I see it, interlocking truths. On the one hand, there was the discussion of Washington's award-winning research to uncover Black victimization at the hands of powerful medical researchers. Jameel was also interested in this, and Sherman listened with great interest. Then there was also the talk about a government conspiracy to use AIDS as biological warfare against Black people. During the conversation, Denny also talked about the reality of UFOs and a video documenting the government's attempt to cover up their existence. Be it AIDS, extraterrestrial beings, or something else, the importance of this account does not lie in its truthfulness. In other words, it operates as a testimony underscoring power dynamics between two parties, whether documentation is readily available or not. In Black public sphere, the narrative focuses on the inability of governmental agencies to deceive Black people about their victimization. In this regard, Denny referred to the Tuskegee syphilis experiment, in which Blacks were led to believe that they were being treated for the disease, when all along they were given a placebo allowing White researchers to track its various stages instead of treating them properly. Narratives like these caution others to be wary of powerful institutions, medical or otherwise, even if they claim to have their best interests at heart. In sum, the story conveys a truism about the relationship among knowledge, power, and victimization. Washington's research and perhaps the documentary *White King, Red Rubber, Black Death* represent a truth based on documentation. By the same token, stories about government conspiracies might appear apocryphal, but they are based on the truth of past victimization, an "emotional truth" that unlocks a human component of knowing, an unconventional way of seeing the world, rather than historical accuracy.[29] The two truths, then, inform each other and operate in tandem.

In the end, African Muslims have more than one Harlem to traverse. Their success in navigating the various dimensions of this terrain depends on many factors, including the ability of each person to manage lifestyle changes, adjust to new intergroup relations, and withstand a larger system of racial hierarchy, immigrant scapegoating, and a Muslim backlash. On the ground, these Muslim migrants are immediately faced with issues of gentrification, including the political and economic dynamics inherent in this process, the stress and strain of an immediate racial encounter, and the Black image as it relates to street drama and a public discourse of interspersing truths. All of this reflects new struggles, urban *jihads*, raging in a place like Harlem. African Muslims, too, bring their own ideas about citizenship and knowledge of how to negotiate state power. They are already accustomed to particular ways of living and thoughts about the good life. And they have long ago discovered strategies for working across differences, notably those identities pertaining to ethnicity, religion, and colonial and postcolonial notions of race.[30] Their new *jihad*, though, is to find fresh approaches to these issues in order to survive and grow in America.

II

Newcomers to cities are forced to alter their individual pace—resetting their bodily clocks, shifting their thinking, and recalibrating their spiritual awareness. For some, this adjustment is interminable, and they falter endlessly under the pressure to change. For most African Muslims, however, the trial of finding their place in Harlem signifies a new kind of *jihad*—an intimate struggle with the self. While *jihad* has been translated as "holy war," Islamic sources view war as neither holy nor unholy. Rather, wars are deemed either just or unjust. Other Arabic words such as *harb* or *qatl* translate more appropriately as "war" or "fighting," respectively. *Jihad*, first and foremost, refers to the repeated act of struggling with one's ego, an internal wrestling with the machinations of our inner selves. This is referred to as the greatest struggle, *jihad al-akbar*. The same intense effort to grapple with the injustices or wrongdoing within the soul can be directed externally to fight against social oppression. But this outer form is considered the smallest struggle, or *jihad al-asghar*. This is certainly not to suggest that external effort is not important; since many African Muslims in Harlem personally strive to avoid unsavory behavior, they must also exert a great deal of effort against outward forms of injustice and discrimination.

Social injustice might equally frustrate the life chances of more than one group in America. But this doesn't mean that each one will have a similar experience. Black American artists such as James Baldwin and Richard Wright tired of U.S. racism and, in the mid-1940s, expatriated themselves to France, a place they felt had much less discrimination. During the same period, African immigrants in France were treated with disdain and subjugated to the lower rungs of French society. More than a generation later, West African Muslims migrating to the United States from France speak of discrimination in ways that conflate race with immigration, providing us with a comparative view of social oppression.

Bintou, a Senegalese woman in her mid-thirties, was born in Dakar, where she completed high school, and then she attended college in Paris. In the midst of a pregnancy and a failing marriage, she managed to finish her associate's degree from Borough of Manhattan Community College and her bachelor's from Baruch College. She majored in business administration and has worked for years in public health and HIV/AIDS prevention. Among several other tasks, she volunteers in a program at the United Nations to combat female genital mutilation.

On one evening, I have spent much of the day at Masjid Touba and am running late for my appointment with Bintou. As I drive from Edgecomb Avenue toward 116th, I dial her number.

"Where are you exactly?" I ask after greeting and informing her of my whereabouts.

"You can get out on 116th and Lenox," she says.

"No, I'm driving, so I can come to you," I say.

"Oh, OK," she says. "Do you know where 116th and Lenox is?"

"Yes," I reply, "but what's the name of the shop?"

"I'm at Omou's Hair Salon—"

"Oh, Omou's," I say, cutting her off. "I know where it is."

"You know Omou?" she says, sounding surprised.

"Yes," I say, "I know her well. I'll see you in a few minutes."

"Oh, OK," she says warily, and hangs up.

I park near Baobob, a Senegalese restaurant on 116th near Malcolm X, and walk briskly to the corner. The light changes, and I cross over to Omou's salon, one store in from the corner and a few doors away from the Harlem Market. Pushing the door open, I notice Omou, a genteel Senegalese woman in her thirties. "*As-salaamu 'alaykum*," I say with a huge grin. It has been a year or more since we last talked. She smiles warmly and gives *salaams* as she walks out from the back room. Omou worked for an African hair-braiding salon on 125th but left to open her own booth at the Harlem Market. After a successful run of several years there, she moved to her current location, a fully equipped space with six stations and plenty of mirrors.

After pleasantries and a brief chat, I ask her about Bintou. "Oh, yeah, she's right here," she says. "Bintou!" she calls out.

A petite brown-skinned woman emerges from a rear office. She is wearing a light green African kaftan top with a long dark green skirt. Although Bintou is an observant Muslim, her hair is unwrapped. "*As-salaamu 'alaykum*," she says with a gracious smile.

"You know Bintou's my sister-in-law," Omou interjects, and then she invites me to meet her husband. For all the years I've known her, I had no idea Omou was married.

After I meet Lamine, a cordial man in his forties from Dakar, Bintou and I enter the storage room to have a conversation. As we talk, Bintou's cell phone rings constantly, and she finally turns it off. I have discovered that many Africans with cell phones are in constant contact with family and friends at home and abroad, including in France, Italy, and Germany. With advancements in technology and greater accessibility of cell phones, African immigrants around the world are engaged in a global telecommunications network, fostering not just transnational identities, where a one-to-one link exists across countries, but also "glocalized" identities, in which the global and the local merge the two realms into a single space. Being connected in this way alters the nature of their migratory experience, and it is a major factor differentiating old and new immigrants and their relationship with their countries of origin.[31]

With the cell phone off, we continue our conversation uninterrupted. We discuss Bintou's first impressions of New York. But I wonder how African views of America might be different for those who have never been to a Western country before migrating to New York.

"I'd already been in Paris," Bintou says. "So, after I arrived, I see it looks a little bit like Paris for me. I said [to myself], 'OK, what I see here is totally different from what I see on the TV."

"Did you and other Senegalese Muslims have any negative images of Paris?" I ask.

"Well," she says, "before, people were going to Paris without a visa. You just have your ticket, you go to the airport, you go to Paris. It was easy. But immigration from Senegal to Paris and from Senegal to the U.S. is totally different."

"What do you mean?" I ask.

"The U.S. is more comfortable for African people to live here," she replies. "Better than living in Paris."

"In what way?"

"In Paris, you always have your passport, everywhere you go," she responds. "You're afraid to be deported. You're afraid to be sent back home. In the U.S., you leave your passport in your house. Nobody is going to ask you where you're going; nobody tells you if you're legal or you're illegal; nobody knows if you're legal immigrant or you're illegal immigrant. But in Paris, Senegalese people are afraid."

With harsher restrictions on African immigration to France, the fear of harassment, imprisonment, or deportation is mounting. In a political climate tense from the threat of terrorism, France remains on constant alert. Under such conditions, African Muslim immigrants are prime and perennial targets. Under much stricter laws, even legal residents and citizens have their rights violated. "The reinstatement of the law of 'acceptable behavior' in peacetime is truly racist," Manthia Diawara argues in We Won't Budge, "because it encourages racial stereotyping of blacks and people from Muslim cultures as illegal immigrants and criminals."[32] African Muslim immigrants in Paris walk the streets in fear of being targeted, forcing them never to leave their homes *les san-papiers*, or without proper documentation.[33] "Even though our great-great-grandfathers fought over there in the war, helping France, they still call their great-grandchildren 'immigrants,'" says Mariam, a Muslim in her early forties from Côte d'Ivoire. Being forced to walk around with a passport puts one in a perpetual state of flux and produces acute fear and anxiety, something no democracy can withstand over time. "When you have children here, they're American," Mariam continues. "But it's not like that in France. There, they call you 'Franco-Ivoirian.' But here, we're all Americans. When you see Black people in France, you know they're from another place. But in America, they have Black, they have Asian people, they don't know the difference between the American Black people and African Black people," she says. "So when you come to this country, you can put your passport in your suitcase; they're never going to ask you for papers or something like that. In France, when the police see you, you're Black, they're going to arrest you and ask you for your ID."

Mariam's point about the permanent foreign status of African Muslims in France, not to mention the fierce criminalization of both their Black and Muslim identities, is well taken. And while many U.S. citizens promote their ethnic heritage as hyphenated Americans, there is virtually no expectation that anyone will be checked on the street for immigration papers. Violations of immigration laws are usually fought with raids on particular establishments. But while both legal and illegal African migrants in the United States are not overly concerned about this kind of open harassment, they still feel extremely vulnerable, and many fear they could be deported at any time. In *Money Has No Smell*, Paul Stoller discovered that while perhaps half of the African Muslim traders from Niger were undocumented, their trepidation about being thrown into detention and deported was totally unfounded, as he was unable to verify a single incident. Still, they transformed themselves into "ghosts," as it were, avoiding formal medical appointments, dealing in cash transactions only, refusing to have bank accounts, and shunning any type of registration procedure. Stoller also observed that their fear was less about detainment than about returning home as failures, a fate worse than death given the utopian image America commands in these countries.[34]

"When one person gets deported," Bintou says, "you can't imagine how that makes us feel back in Senegal, how that affects a whole neighborhood; many people might be involved in taking care of that person, hoping they will make it." The fear of being detained or deported, then, has very little to do with a missed opportunity for personal attainment and everything to do with gaining divine grace, uplifting the family, and preparing a world for one's progeny.

While African Muslims in the United States are not typically harassed because of their immigration status or their Islamic identity, since the stereotypical Muslim is an Arab, they are routinely profiled in terms of race, especially while riding in cars. This is where their escape from French maltreatment is turned on its head in the United States.

"We have a lot of our Muslim brothers in immigration jail for nothing," Mohamed explains to me on one occasion. Now twenty-seven, Mohamed arrived in the States from Côte d'Ivoire when he was seventeen. Since that time, he's seen how Black Muslim immigrants have been racially profiled and end up languishing in detention. He feels it is because they are uninformed and need to understand how to handle themselves when they are pulled over by the police. While this is a tough sell since the police killings of innocent Black immigrants such as Amadou Diallo and Osmane Zongo, most of these arrests, Mohamed believes, could have been avoided if people had been carrying the proper identification. Unlike in Paris, immigration status in the United States will most likely not be an issue, and a passport is generally unnecessary. But for Black people in urban America, Mohamed believes it is imperative to carry some form of ID, understand their rights, and conduct themselves appropriately—not jumping to rash conclusions or being uncooperative. Even with these precautions, he questions the logic of their arrest and wonders why non-Black immigrants are not treated in a similar fashion.

"In most cases," he says, "when I ask what happened, they say, 'We were in the car; the police stopped us and asked for our ID; because we don't have ID, they sent us to the immigration.' I'm, like, this doesn't make sense! There's nothing criminal. This is something I'm working on right now, because they don't stop the Chinese like that and send them to the detention center."

After my conversation with Bintou, I walk back to my car for the drive home. Despite the racial profiling African Muslims face in America, many are elated at the chance to escape the harassment they experienced as immigrants in France. In many ways, they feel a great relief from the pressure of being hunted as outsiders, eternal pariahs with racial and religious marks on their heads, regardless of how long they lived there. While racial discrimination is certainly a problem, it is much different from what they experienced under years of colonization. Whether at home or abroad, then, belonging is crucial. Africans need to find their place within America, because finding a place for each migrant means finding a place for their relatives and loved ones as well. Even though they are viewed as Black people in America, they are not targeted as foreigners and can assert their right to belong like any other American. This is one of several steps toward empowerment and incorporation. Even with this reprieve, the fear that they might be deported haunts them daily, and this is where their internal struggle, their *jihad al-akbar*, lies.

III

On one of my visits to the detention center in Elizabeth, New Jersey, I am accompanied by Assane, a forty-five-year-old Senegalese French and Arabic instructor. Born in Dakar, he was raised in Saint-Louis, a city of more than half a million people and the old colonial capital. With a bachelor's degree in French and a master's in law, he had a reputable job as a high school teacher before migrating to the United States in 2000. In New York, he hasn't been able to secure a permanent job, so he works as a substitute teacher in the public schools and tutors the community in Qur'anic Arabic. His face is clean-shaven, revealing a smooth, dark complexion and making him appear younger. But his inability to find full-time work is clearly wreaking havoc on his health. Even his easygoing manner cannot obscure his bloodshot eyes, weary from a lack of proper rest and nutrition. But Assane has agreed to assist me during the visit. After meeting at the train station in downtown Newark, we drive to the detention center in my car. As usual, Assane is jovial and full of smiles, but this time, I sense some nervousness. We park and begin walking toward the building.

"Did you bring a picture ID?" I ask.

He glances at me with a far-off look in his eye. "Uhh, yeah, yeah, I have it, uhh, I have it," he stammers. As we approach the door, Assane grabs my forearm. "I hope you won't get me in trouble in this place," he says with an edgy smile hiding his tremor.

"Oh, no," I say. "I would never even ask you to come here if that were the case."

His tight grip on my arm eases, and he lets go. We enter through the glass door and stand in line behind three young Spanish-speaking men.

As we wait, two women walk up behind us. They look around the small room nervously. As one begins grumbling, her companion stands still, looking at her from time to time but remaining silent.

"Can I bring my cell phone in? And what about this pen?" the first woman asks, holding up a black ballpoint.

"You can put it in a locker," I reply, pointing to the stack of gray metal compartments behind us. "The pen should be all right."

I turn back to look at Assane and notice his blank expression, as though thoughts are racing through his mind. He tries following my brief exchange with the woman, but the people in front of us are taking some time, and he looks stressed.

Just then, the woman turns toward Assane, her eyes scaling his face. "Are you Haitian?" she blurts out.

"No," he says. "I'm from Africa."

"What part?" she asks.

"Senegal," he replies, half smiling.

"Where are you from?" I ask her.

"Guess!" she says. "Can you guess?"

"I can't tell," I say.

Assane offers, "Dominican Republic."

"Yeah," she says.

By this time, the other men are done, and we step up to the thick security window.

The Corrections officer looks up sternly, peering through his large rectangular glasses. "Have you been here before?" he asks.

"Yes," I shoot back immediately, and push my license through the tiny slot under the window.

He stares at the computer screen, then back at me. "You a lawyer?" he asks, his eyes piercing through his wired-framed lenses.

"No," I reply, and remain quiet.

He quickly repeats robotically, "You been here before?"

"Yes," I reply with a similar sternness. "I've been here before."

Having worked in penal institutions as a chaplain, I know all too well the intimidation factor inherent in this line of questioning, so I decide to play along. Assane, however, is not amused.

"Oh," the officer says, changing his tone. "I just ask so I can find your name and duplicate it, that's all."

"You're coming to see him, right?" the officer says, twisting the computer screen on its swivel to show us a photograph of Mamadou. I have already identified him on my list as the next person to visit.

"Uhh, yeah," I reply, squinting my eyes and leaning forward to get a good look.

Assane remains quiet, and it is as if I can feel his body trembling. But he composes himself, and we complete our visit with no problems.

As we leave the building and begin walking toward the car, Assane lets out a sigh of relief and grabs my arm again.

"That was good," he says. "But maaan, let me tell you, when we were standing talking to that woman, my legs were shaking. You don't know; I was really nervous."

"Because of your status?" I ask.

"Why do they want all this ID?" he says. "And what are they checking? I thought someone might come out any moment and say, 'OK, let's go, we got you!'"

"Is it because you're not legal?" I repeat my earlier question.

"No!" he yells. "Even people with legal status don't want to come here. It's not if you're legal, it's *how* you became legal."

His response makes me think of the Dominican woman inside and the claim of the detainees that Senegalese migrants never come to see them. To ease his concerns, I change the subject.

"It must be a lot of blessings to come here and help them, to visit them," I say. "Like the *hadith* [Islamic traditions] about visiting the sick."

"Yes," he says as he begins to relax and reflect on the visit. "Islam says you get a lot of blessing visiting the sick and visiting people like this. You get blessing from God. This is good to get, we need this."

This episode, in part, illustrates how navigating the U.S. terrain involves much more than an industrious work ethic and staying out of trouble. The threat of deportation remains a constant fear, even for "legal" persons who have somehow managed to obtain permanent residency. Regardless of whether one is documented or not, many believe the opportunities they seek by coming to America will also come with freedom from fear. Assane has explained that caring for another person is a major value in many cultures of West Africa. It is how people demonstrate their humanity. But it is also an Islamic mandate, as when the Prophet Muhammad exhorted Muslims to extend as many acts of charity as there are bones in the human body. Tending to the needs of the dispossessed is more than a devotional act. It is a sacred embodiment or an internalization that seeps into the very sinews of the body. This means that the act of alleviating suffering conflates the sacred and the profane, the spiritual and the material realms of our lives. Because they fear expulsion, many African Muslims feel unable to extend this cultural courtesy and religious obligation to their fellows, which traumatizes them and saddles them with a heavy burden of guilt. This predicament also triggers a rupture in their being, separating them from their religion and their culture at the same time. For most, a dislocation like this is a kind of exile.

Jacob K. Olupona has written perceptively about the African religious experience and how it configures the rise of a new pluralism in America.[35] While the religious presence of these recent migrants is altering our sense of the sacred, African immigrants often toggle between belonging and disjuncture. "These immigrants, who have just escaped dire circumstances," Olupona writes, "suddenly find themselves in exile, having escaped one kind of oppression only to find themselves at the mercy of another."[36] Ogbu U. Kalu argues that because migration is such a life-altering process, Nigerian congregants in the United States are caught in a "paradox," stuck between experiencing America as a promised land, a procedure he calls "crossing Jordan," and the agony of exile.[37] One might see this tension as "two warring ideals in one dark body," as W. E. B. DuBois described it.[38] But the travails of their exile are not predicated upon a need to reconcile two competing identities, African and American. In fact, they are already negotiating multiple identities and are ensconced in several different societies. African Muslims in Harlem are clear about their sojourn in America and the economic rewards they seek to uplift their families back home. But most pay a huge price for these opportunities, and a major strategy is to engage in a personal struggle against the effects of exile and use their religious capital, or their Islamic wherewithal, to galvanize members and resources against social marginalization.

Even though Muslim immigrants from West Africa have worked hard to establish their own *masjids*, Islamic schools, and religiously sanctioned businesses (all within the past two decades), their efforts obviously pale in comparison with their Islamic life back home. This is not to suggest that their religious efforts in Harlem have not been a tremendous resource for members over the years. It does, however, compel us to consider more intently the extent of their exile in the United States and ponder deeply what this religious dislocation means. Karen Armstrong, in her memoir, *The Spiral Staircase*, raises a vital point about the otherworldly dimension of this displacement. "Exile is, of course, not simply a change of address," she writes. "It is also a spiritual dislocation." She adds: "Cut off from the roots of their culture and identity, migrants and refugees can feel that they are somehow withering away and becoming insubstantial. Their world—inextricably linked with their unique place in the cosmos—has literally come to an end."[39] While Armstrong was referring to her own dislocation when she left the Catholic convent and entered a secular world, African Muslims necessarily find themselves ripped from a religious support system and thrust rather quickly into a non-Islamic environment. Many falter in the process, forced to reconsider the meaning of freedom and democracy in America.

On one occasion at Masjid Salaam, we perform the *isha* prayer, and I decide to find a quiet corner to review my notes. I start walking toward the back of the *masjid* and see Assane leaning against the wall with his legs stretched out. He looks tired but still manages a smile. I set my leather shoulder bag on the carpet, sit down beside him, and lean back. When he first arrived in the United States, Assane worked at odd jobs, usually menial tasks. He has a wife and children in Senegal, and he sends them money as often as possible. His substitute teaching position pays pretty well but hardly enough to cover living in New York, remittances to relatives abroad, and savings. He taught high school French for thirteen years back home, though he has never been to Paris. "Senegalese speak better French than the French," he announces. He makes what he can by teaching the Qur'an to West African families, and he holds long-distance sessions with one Senegalese woman, a health-care aide, on his cell phone. "She calls me whenever she gets time, and we read the Qur'an together over the phone," he says. "I would prefer to have a student face-to-face, but she's some distance from here, and this is the only way she can do it."

I begin rummaging through my bag, looking for my pad and pen. Then I pull out the latest *Azizah* magazine, a periodical chronicling the experiences of American Muslim women, and place it on the rug beside me. The issue features an African American Muslim college student on the cover. The reigning homecoming queen at North Carolina A&T, she is pictured in fashionable Islamic clothing with her crown on top of her *khimar*. Assane glances over at it. "Wow!" he says. "This is something. May I see it?" He can hardly flip through the magazine fast enough. He calls to a Senegalese friend, a biological researcher at Columbia University, for a quick look. He then snatches it back and continues looking through it. "Look at this," he says, reading the article titles and showing the glossy pictures. "Um, um, um, this is something!" he repeats loudly.

"What do you think about it?" I ask nonchalantly.

"Oh!" he replies, removing his glasses. "You see," he says, then pauses to stare straight ahead. "We need things like this. Muslim women need to be heard. We need to show what our women think, instead of having them be silent or not heard. So, I like this. I like it a lot."

Obviously, such a diverse community of West Africans is stratified across the class spectrum, and it constitutes a wide continuum of religious orientation as well, from the very liberal to moderate to extremely conservative. And while the progressive views of Assane regarding women reflect his middle-class standing, other professional Muslim communities in the United States might be quite patriarchal.[40]

A lull in the conversation reminds me of my notepad, and I start flipping through the pages.

"It's hard to make it in this country!" Assane blurts out, and he begins a tirade about the challenges Africans face in America. In fact, it is more of a soliloquy, and I become almost invisible to him. "I don't think I belong here," he says. "This is not my country! I don't think so! No, I don't think so." He finally turns to glance at me. "I've been here five years. And still no work visa or work permit. Do you think they think this is a human being, with a family, who needs work? No, they don't! They tell you there is a backlog. What is that supposed to mean? Would they accept that? Not five days, five months—five years! What is this?" He rolls his head back against the wall. He looks away from me again. "I come to this country, and they talk about human rights. How is this human rights? I think this is not human rights. It is all words! That's all, all words!" he repeats, "I don't think this is my country. I think I should leave. I don't think I belong here." Tilting his head toward me, he stares into my eyes. "See, you don't know what we go through in this country. How do they expect us to survive? This forces us to do illegal things. If I can't work, I must do illegal things to get money. How do they expect us to survive?"

Just then, an African doctoral student at Columbia University walks over and greets us. They begin speaking in French about strategies to get a work permit. As they speak, it appears that the African student has difficulty following him. When they finish, I ask Assane if his French is too advanced for his friend.

"Oh, no, I wouldn't do that," Assane replies. "That would mean I am better than him, and I don't want to show off like that. So, I speak a lower-level French, although he could probably understand me because he went to college back home." Then he returns to his earlier criticism.

"The opportunities are not here," he says. "Because they don't let you get the opportunities. It's like they are afraid to let you have a chance. What are they afraid of?" He raises his voice. "I don't get it! This is the richest country in the world doing this."

Life, liberty, and the pursuit of happiness are values integral to the American dream, and this is in large part what attracts millions of immigrants to U.S. shores. Of course, striving for these goals without the proper standing or belonging renders these ideals illusory and out of reach. Yet these are not merely American values but a worldwide invitation, a clarion call, and a declaration of universal rights. Migrants like Assane have responded to those words emblazoned on a bronze plaque at the Statue of Liberty: "Give me your tired, your poor, your huddled masses yearning to breathe free." And thousands of West Africans are fleeing poor conditions, seeking freedom from economic depression. But so many have had their access to jobs severely curtailed in the United States. Assane understands all too well that citizenship is a major gateway to the American promise. Still, he questions the moral logic of allowing this requirement to supplant a basic human need. He is barely surviving, despite his sacrifice to stay in the country as a strategy to offer his family a better life. Most in his situation work several low-wage jobs that together barely pay the full salary of a decent one. Such a laborious lifestyle is a major shift for them, since their work and school schedules back home were punctuated with breaks to socialize or rest from a strenuous day.

The lives of these economic migrants are fractured and moving in multiple directions. And developing new friendships or maintaining old ones is virtually impossible. Ibrahima, a young man from Côte d'Ivoire, remembers his first month in America. "Everything was big," he says, "very fast, you know. I was living with a brother, and he knew me from before. He said, 'OK, everything is about money here. And you have to pay part of the rent, you got to pay part of the food, electricity. When I was in Africa, I had my own house and everything. But living with six to seven people in the same room, you know, it was not easy. And then they don't work at the same time; some work nighttime, some work daytime. And then people from Africa are calling, and you don't have rest." Ibrahima lowers his eyes in desperation as he prepares to continue. "Then you have to find work, and you're worrying about your status," he says. "You're in a country, you have a certain amount of time to stay, and then after that, you have to leave the country. All those things you have in your mind. But life here, it is not easy for nobody. There's no time for friendship here. Everybody's looking for something. Sometimes they're jealous because you have something, they don't have it. So they fake like they're happy for you, and at the end, they trick you. I can't really blame them, because some lost a lot back home and were expecting more here. They are disappointed, and sometimes they put that problem on other people."

Under such conditions, many experience acute social isolation and deep alienation. Their entire existence is defined by their economic production, because there is little room for much else. In fact, as a result of the social dislocation imposed on them, African Muslims say that "U.S.A." really means "U Suffer Alone." On one of my visits to L'Association des Sénégalais d'Amérique, Talla, a Senegalese official in his forties, proudly talks to me about innovations at the association office. Walls have been newly plastered with a coat of fresh paint. Even a new floor has been laid. After pointing out these improvements, he walks me over to a huge advertisement for a new housing development in Dakar. With the Atlantic Ocean in the background, it looks like condominiums or villas anywhere in the Caribbean or the South of France. As we talk, he mentions the benefit of having a place out of the country, somewhere in Africa.

Alim, another member at the office, sits on a bar stool about a foot away and peers at CNN on a small TV mounted near the ceiling. When Talla and I start talking about securing a home in Africa, Alim spins around.

"You can't live here!" he says with disdain.

"You just come here to work," Talla says, chiming in.

"It's like prison," Alim adds, giving me a stern look.

Their statements send my mind racing to Malcolm X speaking before a Detroit crowd. After revealing how he had been to prison, he paused, realizing that he could lose the respect of his audience. "[D]on't be shocked when I say that I was in prison," Malcolm said. "You're still in prison. That's what America means: prison."[41] In many respects, Malcolm's prophetic voice captures the Black condition in much of America. But I wonder if the same metaphor is able to describe the predicament of African Muslim immigrants forty years later? If nothing else, it clearly speaks to a similar struggle for self-determination. While they have made much progress, especially as a community, their attempt to integrate fully and reap the rewards America has to offer remains unfulfilled.

Fifth Avenue separates Harlem's east and west sides. While African Muslims have a commanding presence in the west, they are virtually absent on the other side. When they do appear, it's generally as security guards in clothing shops or variety stores owned by others. A few own one or two of the small shops wedged between much larger ones. They typically sell clothing or knickknacks. Similar to the rest of Harlem, the east side is changing. After the 1950s, a migration wave from Puerto Rico filled apartment buildings and tenements, transforming the area into Spanish Harlem. The 1970s, a period in which factory jobs abandoned inner cities for the suburbs, witnessed the rise of drugs and poverty.[42] Later, as gentrification spread, new stores began popping up everywhere. A new supermarket, Pathmark, spans a city block, and customers can park for two hours in its spacious lot free of charge. East Harlem began to sparkle with the coming of each newfangled store and brighter lights.

On one of my days in the area, I notice an older African American man, perhaps in his seventies, sitting in a wheelchair, twitching to images from "Beautiful," a Snoop Dogg music video featuring Pharrell Williams, projected on the side of a white truck. His bodily impulses are instructive, especially since the song is barely audible. The vehicle is a promotional van with a six-by-eight-foot panel. I begin thinking about how arresting these images must be, with Brazilian women gyrating throughout. They must be a source of consternation for African Muslims coming from a much more conservative environment.

But how do African Muslims in New York reconcile competing notions of morality? They would consider any public display of lascivious rap videos totally unacceptable. And they try to follow their own moral compass amid all sorts of distractions. But the massive effort it takes to combat what some regard as negative elements and still earn a living among them constitutes another dimension of their struggle. In response, African Muslims inscribe a sacred geography onto the streets of Harlem with an open display of *kufis* or other Islamic dress. Islamic stickers pepper their stands, taxis, or store windows with slogans such as "Islam Is the Answer." But sometimes the glitter of street life in commercial districts can easily drown out the counter discourse of these Islamic symbols. In *An Imagined Geography*, JoAnn D'Alisera observes the way Sierra Leonean Muslims in Washington, D.C., use their taxicabs and hot-dog stands to infuse messages about their Islamic identity into public space. Their engagement in this symbolic system does not merely announce their presence in America. Rather, it captures their complex experience as Sierra Leonean Muslims within the context of a broader Islamic community, here and abroad. "Sierra Leonean Muslims," D'Alisera states, "use religious goods to tell themselves and the world around them who they are, easing the burden of physical and cultural displacement."[43]

In late November, a Guinean merchant in East Harlem is managing a table of wooden and plastic necklaces, bracelets, and T-shirts near 125th and Park Avenue.

Mohamed, stocky and in his late thirties, typically wears a white *kufi* to signify his religious conviction. As I approach his table, I notice a White woman in her twenties talking to him. An African American man, also in his twenties, stands by her side. But they don't seem interested in buying. Like a puppeteer, the man seems to orchestrate her moves, straddling her on a catty-corner angle and pulling her arms one way or the other. Her blond hair, pale complexion, red blouse, and tight black pants augment the sidewalk drama. Suddenly, she flings her body around and begins tugging on his jacket, and their frolicking becomes more animated. Mohamed's face grows tense, and his lips tighten. He eases from behind the table and replaces a few items that have been knocked out of place by the couple. The young woman turns to Mohamed, backs up next to him, and wraps one arm around him. "Would you take a picture with me?" she says as her male friend raises a camera and attempts to focus. Mohamed frowns but says nothing. After the flash, he quickly pulls away. But then an even stranger thing occurs. The two move three feet away from the table and accost an African American man walking by. He slows his pace but doesn't stop. Her companion gestures to take a picture of him, while the woman reaches for his arm and positions her body next to his. He twists and turns, politely smiling, and tries to get away. He finally gives up, turning toward her, and she moves closer. His jeans and T-shirt littered with sawdust and specks of paint make no difference. The cameraman sets up the shot. "OK, put your arm around her!" he yells, standing with his feet apart and one arm extended to frame the picture. Just before the snap, she quickly kisses the passerby on the cheek, and the flash sparks. The two thank him and swiftly take two more steps, stopping yet another man, a heavy-set African American in his early twenties. He is bashful at first but doesn't need much coaxing. The woman and her new participant back up against a fence, she places one arm around him, and they smile, waiting for the flash. They thank the man and walk down the street.

It is unclear exactly what was going on or why, but I am more concerned with Mohamed and his response to all of this. "Why were they taking pictures of strangers?" I ask.

"I don't know," Mohamed says, frowning and shaking his head. Drops of rain fall, and he scrambles to pack up his merchandise. "I don't know why this woman wanted to take a picture with me," he repeats with added tension. "He wanted me to touch her. No! I don't do this! This is against my religion. I don't go around touching strange women!" As the rain picks up, Mohamed moves faster, stuffing items back into their bags. "The rain's coming!" he says.

I give him *salaam* and say good-bye. While this incident was clearly unusual, it does illustrate the kind of bizarre happenings that can frustrate the Islamic sensibility of these migrants. In many ways, this episode represents the outer struggle, the *jihad al-asghar*, that African Muslim vendors and others in the community encounter on a regular basis. Even if others might view the event as a harmless photograph with a young lady, some Muslim groups would consider it a religious violation on at least two levels. Those holding ultraconservative views believe that picture taking creates images, compromising their strict belief in God's authority as creator. This case perhaps reflects an extreme minority position; yet Mohamed was not disturbed about the photograph itself. His real concern, however, raises the second point. Many traditional Muslims believe that unnecessary touching of members of the opposite sex, if the person is not a relative, violates Muslim ethics. In Islam, the body has certain entitlements, and many believe that these include the right to engage in particular kinds of relations and not others. More important, what Muslims do or do not do with their bodies reflects the ethical principles within the religion. In the end, African Muslims in Harlem are engaged in a new *jihad*. As the next chapter shows, their effort to reconcile an un-Islamic work environment is another aspect of the struggle. But it is also an act of faith.

7

Doing Allah's Work

I

Rama is a young, professionally trained Senegalese woman. Rather than remaining in Harlem, she lives in Alphabet City in downtown Manhattan. I pull up in front of her building, a huge apartment complex amid twenty or so other tenements. Four African families live there among a Black and Latino majority. As I wait, I'm not sure what to expect, but I imagine she'll be draped in African wear. She finally emerges wearing an Arab-style *hijab*, a pink knitted cap, and a scarf with ends cascading down her front and back. As she walks toward me, I notice a purple and white dress peeking out from under her purple overcoat.

We greet each other, then decide to walk to the corner library to chat. On our way, Rama tells me about her decision to dress "more Islamically," at least when she is in public. This means she typically wears dark or monochrome colors, covers her hair with a *khimar* (headscarf), and wears a *jalabiyya* (loose robe) or *'ibaya* (overcoat). In Senegal, she worked as a physician in a large hospital, where she was frequently approached by friends about becoming more religiously conservative.

"They kept talking to me about it, and, I don't know, it just made sense after a while," Rama explains. "When I started wearing these clothes, my family started to call me Ibadou Rahman [servants of God] and asking what was wrong with me. 'Why would you want to become that?' they would ask me. 'Isn't the way we live Islam good enough for you?'" While she understands their concerns, Rama also seeks a deeper understanding of her faith, a spiritual knowledge beyond the scientific world that has occupied her life since college and medical school.[1]

While "Ibadou Rahman" might seem a praiseworthy title, its social significance is quite different. It actually reveals a kind of rupture exposing two versions of Islamic practice among West Africans in Harlem. On one side of the cultural border, Islam has virtually nothing to do with Arabs. For these Muslims, Arabic incantations ought to embody an African aesthetic. If Arab-style clothing is worn, it is customarily combined with African accessories, softening the hegemonic impact of a kind of Middle Eastern religiosity. In other words, West Africans who are not Ibadou Rahman practice Islam within an ethnic context. When the Qur'an is recited in Arabic during formal prayers, for example, an African-type recitation, Qalun, is chosen.[2] The Ibadou Rahman, on the other hand, are often ridiculed for "acting" Arab, characterized by an overuse of religious phrases in Arabic or donning Arab clothing as to indicate high devotion. This fact forces us to recognize the heterogeneity of Muslim cultures on the ground, in local places, and is a caution against ignoring important fissures within each group. In this case, terms such as *Arab* and *African* evoke powerful images for these communities, allowing members to distinguish one Islamic perspective from another.[3]

Although Ibadou Rahman might serve as a critique of religious practice within African faith communities, too many Westerners often associate such Arabized customs with terrorism. For outsiders, the *hijab* and public displays of Islamic rituals signal radical extremism. Yet in Harlem and elsewhere, there is a growing sentiment among African Muslims that using Arabic phrases, wearing Middle Eastern-style clothing, and routinely performing public prayers will increase their piety. The same people feel that an Arabic version of the religion is more authentic, and Ibadous are often made to feel that they are abandoning African culture or "selling out."[4] But Ibadous are doubly marginalized, ridiculed by other African Muslims and then profiled by outsiders.

As Rama and I walk, our conversation is interrupted by her waving to residents, particularly when we pass two elderly African American men reclining on beach chairs, chatting and listening to jazz from a nearby boom box. We enter the library and find children talking quietly, reading books in hushed tones, or reading aloud to one another in designated areas. The inside is one large, open space divided into sections. We decide to take a table in the back, placing us directly across from the main entrance. As we sit and begin talking, I notice a frail-looking Black security guard watching us intently. He wears a somewhat wrinkled blue uniform, and patches of woolly salt-and-pepper hair protrude from under his blue hat, while fluorescent ceiling lights reflect off the vinyl brim. He moves from one side of the room to the other, trying to find the best angle from which to observe us. He apparently wants us to know that we are under his surveillance.

Rama's eyes dart toward the man. "That guard's watching us!" she says. "Perhaps he thinks we're going to blow up the library or something," she adds scornfully, with a sly grin.

I look at her and notice a sense of weariness. "Yeah, perhaps," I say, trying to lighten the moment. But it is little consolation. "Ay," I say, "don't worry about him. We're not doing anything wrong, and this is a public library. So don't worry about it."

She agrees, but I realize that our meeting will be marred by "chronic stress," which is how sociologist Terry Williams describes the emotional state of poor Harlem residents braving the harshness of urban life.[5] As I sit there with Rama, it is hard to imagine her stress levels, especially as they have increased since she went from a highly respected medical position in Dakar to flipping burgers at a McDonald's in Manhattan. We discuss the triple burden of what it means to be discriminated against as a Black immigrant, profiled as a Muslim, and patronized as a woman.

On another occasion, I go to meet with Assetou. She lives in a five-story walkup on 135th Street. After parking several yards past her building, I begin walking back down the block. Icy winds whip around corners, between pedestrians, and into hallways. Several days after a winter blizzard, the city is covered with slush and dirty snow heaped against cars and piled high near crosswalks. It's early afternoon, but a few people wearily shuffle their feet across the frozen pavement. Others scurry about, tightly grasping the lapels on their coats. But no matter what the day is like, I expect Assetou, as always, to appear steady and unflappable. I look forward to seeing her today, because even with freezing weather, her good cheer is sure to be infectious.

Our visit has been scheduled during work hours, though Assetou is home baby-sitting African children while "looking for work." I walk up several flights, make my way to her apartment, and knock. The door opens slowly, and I find myself peering down at Jamilah, a nine-year-old girl with a bright smile.

"As-salaamu 'alaykum," I say. "Is Assetou here?"

"Yes, she is," she replies, pulling on the knob and stepping back. "Come in, she's back there."

I step in and go down a long, dank hallway that leads me past a tight kitchen and another small room on my left. The hall ends abruptly at the doorway of another room with a petite couch, a wooden armchair, and a small television propped on a three-foot tilted stand. A gauzy curtain screens off a bedroom on the other side of the chair.

"*As-salaamu 'alaykum!*" Assetou says jubilantly as she emerges from prayer and pulls back the cloth. She removes a large white scarf, exposing another head-wrap and a rust-colored African dress. "Have a seat," she says.

I put down my leather satchel and take a seat on the couch, and she shuffles over to the chair. Jamilah plops down on the floor between an infant and a toddler, both asleep on a single blanket. While the baby sleeps soundly, the other child occasionally wakens, crying, forcing Jamilah to scoop him up in her arms and rock him back to sleep. If this fails, she leans forward, tosses him onto her back, ties the two of them together with a yard of African fabric, and lightly bounces about until he falls asleep.

Assetou exhibits one of the unreconciled strivings among African Muslims in New York. For many, work is always punctuated by the five daily prayers. But unless one is self-employed, the American workplace rarely accommodates these obligations. In many Western, technologically advanced nations, religion is compartmentalized, reserved for specific times or days, and the sacred is typically removed from the workday altogether. As global capital and work travel much more effortlessly through time and space, it has become increasingly hard to designate even a single day for rest or worship. This is especially the case in a major metropolis like New York, where African immigrants often work around the clock, seven days a week. Those who are able to maintain their Islamic rites while working in secular, non-Muslim environments generally do so with much sacrifice. For there to be a large attendance at *jum'ah* prayers every Friday at midday, African workers must go to great lengths to adjust their job schedules or lose hard-earned pay. Because many have two or three jobs, their workweek is always full, except when they forgo a day's pay for special occasions.[6]

Assetou, a stocky, gentle woman in her late forties, was born in the central region of Côte d'Ivoire. Over the years, Muslim immigrants from Mali and Guinea have drastically increased her hometown's Islamic presence, outnumbering the substantial Christian population. She has been in the United States since 1997 but still finds it hard to adjust to not attending the *masjid* on a regular basis, as she did back home. Assetou lives in Harlem with her Ivoirian husband, and they have teenage and adult children in Côte d'Ivoire. But her parental obligations compel her to keep working in the United States. Like thousands of other African Muslims, she views work as *'amal*, a way to gain divine blessing and serve one's family. According to Islamic tradition, *'amal* or the act of earning money is not necessarily areligious or secular. On the contrary, Muslims are mandated by the Qur'an to enact *'amal saalih*, or wholesome work, labor considered divinely acceptable and duly rewarded. Among other things, what makes one's work *saalih*, or religiously sound, is one's engagement in Islamically permissible actions, on the one hand, and a firm intention to please God, on the other. By this measure, religious activity can become void of divine merit if it is performed for some ostentatious reason. But if a job prevents one from performing religious duties, many believe it ceases to be *'amal saalih*. A number of African Muslims in Harlem, then, seek to maintain their regular prayers and other religious rites in order to receive the full benefit of their sacrifice abroad. In fact, the belief that their arduous workloads, as they attempt to care for family members back home, are imbued with divine favor helps to lessen the strain of their hardship. Work in the New York context, therefore, matters little if it is merely for material gain and not linked to divine acceptance and familial well-being.

In the early 1900s, Italian immigrants in Harlem turned to the Madonna, their patron, asking to be healed from hardships associated with work. This could be a fear of losing a job or a dreadful panic over becoming destitute. Appeals were also made to the Madonna for better work, and benedictions were given to show gratitude for good jobs. "The devotion to the Madonna annually, and daily by means of the scapulars that the people took away with them," Robert A. Orsi writes, "reaffirmed the primacy of other values and reminded the people of the meaning of work and of the real nature of their mutual obligations."[7] For African Muslims, the prayers, fasting, and other daily liturgies they perform on their jobs help them avoid being reduced to mere chattel, and these religious practices give them a divine purpose, bolstering them against their mundane reality in Harlem. There is often a tendency to separate religion and work as sacred and profane spheres. But in this context, they are intimately related. And for most immigrants forced to take on undesirable or low-level positions—the jobs most native-born residents reject—religion helps to buffer them against the anxiety or adversity associated with these tasks.[8] However, for immigrants who arrive in the United States already well trained or educated, the trauma begins not on the job but with the realization that they must start at the bottom of the socioeconomic ladder.

Assetou's hometown was socially Islamic, and people there attended the *masjid* daily, even several times throughout the day. "Muslim religion," she says, "is one of our preoccupations." After high school, she graduated from a professional institute and obtained a certificate in secretarial and computer applications. This training allowed her to land a number of jobs with a few large companies in Abidjan and other Ivoirian cities. As a professional, she found religion infused into her workday, not separate, and she longs for ways to combine the two in New York. But her attempt to bring about this balance has been frustrated.

Assetou came to the United States following an economic downturn in Côte d'Ivoire. Although she is married, she feels obligated to care for her extended family, and her increased earning potential in New York justifies the hardship she faces. "I'm not happy," Assetou admits, "because I don't have my children with me." She has five children between the ages of eighteen and twenty-eight. "But at the same time," she says, "I'm also happy, because from here [New York], I can take care of my parents. That's the only good thing I can say. But to live without your children is . . . well, it doesn't make sense. But I can help my mother, my father, my sisters and brothers. I thought America was the best thing, but it's not easy."

As the economic climate in Côte d'Ivoire worsened, Assetou's determination to travel to the United States increased, especially since friends who went abroad to study would return with good jobs and "fat." "At that time," she says, "we think being fat was a good thing. So, when we see them, we say, 'My goodness! Look at me! I'm skinny! I have to go to America!'"

Since she had been working, Assetou earned enough to purchase a plane ticket and saved the rest to cover expenses. Her relatives performed benedictions, prayers for her safe travel and a blessed stay. An animal was slaughtered in her honor, with a portion of the meat reserved for charity, an act many perform to increase blessings and ensure a safe journey. "It was very hard for me," Assetou says. "Only God helped me. If not, I was going to say, 'No! I'm not going!' Because I have people crying, and my son, who was eight. Oh, my goodness! He was crying. Some were crying, and some were saying, 'Why cry? It's good for her. She's going to make money, and she's going to have a better life. She can take care of us.'"

Like many other Muslim immigrants from Africa, Assetou feels that the decision to migrate to America was the result of divine providence. "It's my destiny," she says resolutely. "For me, it was already a path God made for me. I'm just following it. Really!"[9]

African Muslims often become taxi drivers, open their own shops, or vend on the streets, because these jobs allow them the freedom to perform their religious duties with little interference. But this is not always the case, especially when they are up against the exigencies of a highly competitive labor market. And a seemingly less demanding task such as baby-sitting can impinge on Islamic practices as well. "Life in America is good, but it's hard," Assetou laments. "Even for Muslim people. Look at me! I don't have any papers to work, so I have to do baby-sitting. On Friday, you cannot go to the mosque [for *jum'ah* prayer], because if they come to the house and you're not here, that's not good." She takes a breath. "Babies!" she yells. "Monday, Tuesday, Wednesday, most of them are off. But Thursday, Friday, Saturday, you cannot have time off. And they say when you miss three Fridays together, you lose out. But that's not good for me, too." She stares off into space and then continues. "For me, I wish to be in Africa, because over there, you can go to every prayer, one o'clock, four o'clock, six, and eight. Because when you wake up, everybody is rushing to go to the mosque. But here, it is not the same. You have to have your own faith. If not, it's not easy."

The toddler she is baby-sitting starts to cry. Jamilah reaches over, begins rubbing his back, and alters his position on the blanket, trying to make him more comfortable. His twitching gradually subsides.

"You said you have to have your own faith?" I ask.

"Um-hm," Assetou replies.

"So," I say, "you live here as a Muslim individual, by yourself."

"Yes, most of the time," she says.

"Over there," I say, "in Côte d'Ivoire, everybody's together and—"

"All the time!" Assetou quickly interjects, shaking her head with eyes cast downward. "All the time," she repeats.

According to Islamic tradition, it is sacrilegious to neglect *jum'ah* prayer intentionally more than three times in a row. This is a major concern for African Muslim migrants when they are forced to work on Fridays without breaking for prayer. They are accustomed to behaving communally, where there is time to pray in congregation throughout the day, spend a few moments here and there with kin or friends, or return home for an hour or so. The pace in New York is devoid of these human moments and appears overwhelming. As they describe it, God and family, in their countries of origin, are interspersed in the workday. But in New York, they are hard pressed to find time for a single prayer. It is a tremendous source of stress, compelling many to move from one job to the next, seeking a more accommodating work schedule. While being self-employed provides some independence, working in non-Muslim environments can still be problematic.[10]

Assetou rises from her seat and walks over to the infant, who is still sleeping soundly, and makes sure that he is well covered. She returns to her chair with a mysterious gleam in her eye, a look that is at once far-off and very present.

"When I was in Africa," Assetou says, "I was working, but at prayer time, we are together. But here, I was helping one old lady as a home health aide. The first day the lady saw me, I had something on my head, and she asked me, 'Oh! How are you?' I said, 'I'm fine.' 'Where are you from?'" Assetou says, mimicking her former employer. "I said, 'I'm from Africa.' And she said, 'What type of Africa?' I said, 'I'm from West Africa.' And she asked me, 'Oh! Are you Muslim?' I said, 'Yes, ma'am, I'm Muslim.' She said, 'Ah! OK. Never pray in my house!' I said, 'OK. No problem, ma'am. I will never pray in your house.' I said it, but I know I'm not supposed to say that, because she's [mortal] like me. Just human, just dust and water. But I said that because at that time, she didn't have her legs. And she has two bedrooms. So, when it's time for me to pray, I'll go make my ablutions, go to the room, make my prayers, and come to the living room, because she was living in the living room."

Assetou pauses. "If I was in my country," she continues, "nobody would tell me, 'If you want my money, you don't have to pray in my house!' Because at that time, I need her money. That's the problem! I come to America to work. But by God, when it's time, I go to one of the rooms, I pray, and come in the living room. So, here, I say, it's a kind of slavery. So we're here to have money, and they say in America, time is money. So everybody's running after money. And that's not the best way to live. We have God watching us. We don't know what to do. It's not easy!"

Such a proscription against praying on the job is perhaps uncharacteristic of what most African Muslims experience.[11] Even so, finding sacred spaces to perform prayers is no easy task. While Islamic tradition states that the entire earth is a *masjid* of sorts and one can pray just about anywhere, there are conditions for the appropriateness of the place, particularly relating to its religious purity. The space designated for prayer (*musalla*), for example, should be clean from what Islamic law terms *najs*, defiling substances such as urine, feces, and blood.[12] Non-Muslim supplicants might find a private moment in a vacant restroom, but public toilets are unacceptable for the daily *salah*, because of the likely presence of *najs* or other unacceptable trace elements on the floor. Because of these stipulations, when a prayer area is chosen, it will typically be exposed and less private, although Muslims do try to find secluded corners or places with few passersby.[13]

For Assetou, her employment in America constitutes 'amal saalih, or "blessed work," and it links her to her family. In essence, it is the sole reason she remains in New York and puts up with so much hardship. At the same time, as economic migrants, she and many other Muslims from West Africa believe that their sojourn in the United States is divinely ordained. This fact gives her a great deal of resolve and allows her to remain steadfast and patient. But it is the periodic *salah*, the daily formulaic prayer, that helps to break up her ordinary workday. It counteracts an employer's domesticating gaze, an attempt to reduce her to a laborer and nothing more.

Since the five daily prayers are performed at specific times throughout the workday (dawn, noon, afternoon, sunset, and evening), African Muslim men have similar problems, especially when they work for someone else and particularly when they work for non-Muslims. The *salah* involves much more than a silent prayer. Rather, for able-bodied Muslims, it requires the full use of one's legs, arms, and torso—standing, bowing, and prostrating—not to mention a recitation of the Qur'an aloud (before dawn or at night). It begins with a statement of purpose in the heart, moves to a contemplative recitation of Qur'anic passages, and is enacted through bodily movement. These stipulations make the performance of *salah* on the job exceptionally challenging.

For Ismael, a thirty-five-year-old man from Côte d'Ivoire, remaining devout as an unskilled laborer takes a great deal of ingenuity. His first job was at a meat factory in Queens, where he worked in a freezer cleaning the ice off packed meat. He was given fifteen-minute breaks every hour, because his hands would be totally white from the cold. Getting to the plant was also arduous, requiring him to wake at three in the morning, catch two or three trains, then walk more than five blocks in order to reach his job by six. Being a dutiful Muslim under these conditions is very difficult. But when Ismael left this job for another one, he says he "went from a freezer to hell," quickly turning his American dream into a nightmare. His next job was uptown at Tutus, a huge establishment with a ground-floor restaurant and a bakery in the basement. As the new dishwasher, he worked from six in the morning till six at night, and he kept the position for over a year.

On a warm afternoon in July, Ismael and I are sitting in Masjid Salaam, and he begins to tell me about his experience at Tutus. "We are not allowed to eat!" he says, ashamedly lowering his head. "And you're not allowed to stop working. I was working like a slave. When you come in, he gives you some kind of social security [number] in your file. But all the tax returns come to him. One day, a lady cook, she gave me some food. We used to hide to eat. Once I forgot, and I didn't hide it. The boss came next to me, and he sees the food and looks down at me like I'm a dog. He goes like this"—Ismael's lips protrude to make a spitting sound—"next to the food."

"He spit next to the food?" I ask.

"Yes," Ismael says. "I didn't eat it. I put it in the garbage. And one day, we were hiding to pray. And in the basement, like, you see this stair going up? Behind the stair, there is a little space, and I was praying there one day. When he [the boss] goes to the basement, I was praying, but I don't move. He yelled out something, but I didn't move. He just saw something white, because I had a white deli uniform on. And Allah put in his heart that this thing is not a human being. And he runs upstairs!"

"He didn't know it was you?"

"He didn't see my face. He saw something standing with white clothes on. The boss saw my friend upstairs and told him to call me. I came upstairs, and he [the boss] said, 'OK, we're going to see something in the basement.' But he just sent the two of us down. We went and came back and told him, 'OK, we don't see nothing. Now you go!' Since that day, he never went down there again, and he doesn't know we pray there."

"He never went back downstairs again?"

"No, no, no. Because we didn't find that thing, he wouldn't go there," Ismael replies.

This type of miraculous intervention certainly does not work for all African Muslims. But what is worth noting is the type of sacrifices African Muslims endure just to be able to pray at work. Most are forced simply to leave one job for better religious conditions at another.[14] Abou, a graduate of Baruch College who was a high school teacher in Côte d'Ivoire, left one job as a bank teller for another bank because he wasn't allowed to pray at the first one. When he arrived in the United States in the late 1980s, he found a job at a fast-food establishment by scouring the bulletin board at a *masjid* in lower Manhattan. Because it was operated by a Pakistani Muslim, Abou could perform his prayers, and conditions were good. But the pay was inadequate, so he left. Ibrahim, an immigrant from Mali, encountered a slightly different situation. Like Abou's, Ibrahim's Moroccan coworkers were Muslim, so praying on the job was no problem. The trucking agency employing them delivered products to Connecticut, Virginia, and other states across the country. After missing *jum'ah* twice, Ibrahim became worried that his religious practice would continue to suffer. "This job is not for me," he says, repeating what he thought to himself at the time. "If I'm not careful, I'm not going to pray *jum'ah* anymore. I don't care about the money, but *jum'ah* is so important, if I can do it. Then I quit." Ibrahim and others feel that their presence in America is not a matter of their sheer desire to migrate. For them, coming to America is part of a divine decree, their destiny, or *qadr*, as Assetou says above. Viewing African Muslims in Harlem as mere economic migrants, then, misses the full range of their plight in America. Moreover, their migration is connected to a sacred devotion to family, close friends, and a deep struggle to earn *baraka*, God's favor. In this light, getting a job but losing religion constitutes failure. And while African Muslims have migrated to Harlem and other places in search of opportunities, many feel that these prospects must not come at the expense of their souls.

In the days following my conversation with Assetou, attending Masjid Aqsa isn't the same for me. It has acquired a different meaning. And Assetou helped me understand how Africans consider it not merely a sanctuary or a place to hide from the outside world but a space necessary to stabilize their work lives. African *masjids* in Harlem help Muslim immigrants maintain a crucial balance between the sacred and the profane, between work and family. In their home countries, *masjid* life offsets the everyday, inscribing sacral practices at both ends of the day and at various points in between. Moreover, these sequential breaks for congregational prayer place a premium on family, since friends and relatives are customarily in attendance. In Harlem, however, this religious and communal symmetry is harder to achieve. *Masjid* members are scattered throughout the city and across states, making their community an imagined one.

One afternoon at Masjid Aqsa, *thuhr* prayer ends, and half a dozen people rush to the entrance, scrambling to find their shoes. I stand nearby, waiting. On this

Breaking from work, African Muslims and others stand in *maghrib* (evening prayer) at
Masjid Aqsa. (Photo Sharjeel Kashmir)

warm day in November, many have taken advantage of the weather and turned out
in a striking array of African clothing.

"Africans like to look good, *akh* [brother]!" I hear someone say behind me.

I turn slowly to see Aziz's wide grin. An African American street merchant, he
sells perfume and incense and is a brawny six foot three. His long black beard with
specks of gray accents his motley gear of Middle Eastern- and African-style clothing.
Throughout the 1980s, he studied Islam in several Muslim countries but quickly
became enamored with Arabic.

"They dress the best out of the entire Muslim world," Aziz continues. "You see
them in their embroidered clothing. Hooked up! You should see them in Mali,
sitting out in the sun for hours, making one piece of clothing."

As we talk, I look over and see Omar sitting on the carpet not far from the
door. His hair is short and freshly cut, and his face is clean-shaven. His army-green
American suit complements his black crewneck knitted shirt. Just then, Imam
Konate joins us at the door, and Aziz sputters out a question in Arabic about the
grammatical structure of the phrase *min qabl*. Meanwhile, I continue to watch
Omar as he instructs another African man about where to sign a set of papers. After
completing their transaction, the two men stand and move toward the front. Like
the rest of us, Omar's client searches through a pile of shoes, then turns and snatches
his pair from the rack. I begin talking to Omar as he takes a seat to put on his
shoes.

"You look very familiar," I say.

"I look familiar," he repeats, looking up at me with a wily smile.

"Yeah," I say. "You look familiar."

"Well, he's my brother," Omar says, pointing to Imam Konate, who is now smiling widely. As Omar stands and prepares to leave, I have a better look at his suit. Its wide lapels and fitted cut resemble suits from the 1930s or '40s.

"Wow!" I say. "This is a nice suit. What do you do?"

Omar gives me the same smile but waits a few moments before responding. "What do I do?" he echoes. "I'm a truck driver!"

"A truck driver!" I say. "Boy, you're a sharp-looking truck driver."

"Of course, I'm not working now," he says. "But why should I look like a truck driver on my day off?"

Muslim men at other *masjids* across the New York metropolitan area often attend prayer in their work clothes. And Africans sometimes wear their professional clothing to prayer. But for many others, wearing traditional African attire or tailored apparel at the *masjid* is a way of totally removing themselves from the world of labor. Because African clothing designs are tailored to signify the ethnic belongings of the wearer, this sartorial practice at the *masjid* fosters an ancestral or familial bond as well. In other words, African Muslims, like many other people, clearly have all sorts of ways to defy the stigmatizing effects of their menial work lives.

II

A walk along 125th Street would not be the adventure it is without street vendors. Big retail chains mix in with specialty shops, but the sidewalks belong to the hustlers, suave traders hawking Afrocentric books and Islamic materials from groups such as the Ansarullah, the Nation of Islam, or the Moorish Science Temple of America.

"Readers are leaders!" cries Luke, a Black book vendor, twisting from side to side with a book in each hand. "And leaders read books! Come on, get your book today!"

Farther up the street and near the curb, huge posters line the sidewalk with images of mutilated victims of slavery and Jim Crow. Other life-size pictures show lynched Black bodies hanging from trees, and with the Apollo Theatre looming in the background, one can almost hear Billie Holiday's sultry voice singing "Strange Fruit."[15] Near the corners, vendors selling mango on a stick and roasted nuts fill the air with tropical delights. Emblazoned T-shirts, bootleg movies, and CDs jam fold-up tables, while shoppers stop to pose quickly and pay a few dollars for a photo with a friend.

Ibrahima stands behind his book table, packed with fiction and nonfiction, hardback and paperback titles. The arrangement appears haphazard, but he has ordered them just right, from the racy novels of Zane to more literary fare by Toni Morrison. The cerebral works of Cornel West are juxtaposed against Nathan McCall's poignant *Makes Me Wanna Holler.*

I cross the street and join Ibrahima near the corner. As I wait in front of his stand, he continues talking on his cell phone. He gazes at me through a pair of silver wire-framed glasses. His "homeboy" look—loose-fitting jeans, sneakers, casual shirt, and Kangol cap—belies his traditional upbringing in Côte d'Ivoire.[16]

"This is my brother in Ivory Coast," he tells me as he pulls the phone away from his ear and covers the mouthpiece.

I smile. "Oh, OK," I say, and he returns to his call.

His table is wedged between an African merchant selling natural soap, incense, and fragrant oils and an Arab food truck pushing barbecued chicken and wraps. Customers stroll up to the book table and look around while Ibrahima watches, waiting to respond to their queries. "Twenty dollars" is his prepared refrain when asked about a hardcover book. Some pause, think about the price, and pay. Others frown and continue down the street. Softcover books require a little more negotiation.

Ibrahima finally completes his call and turns toward me. Just then, an African American man walks up and slips behind the table.

"*As-salaamu 'alaykum*," I say.

He replies, "*Wa 'alaykum salaam*, my brother."

Ibrahima is respectful of the Muslim greeting but remains somewhat distrustful of unfamiliar Muslims, as a result of some bad experiences he had driving a cab in New York.

Along with jobs in restaurants or fast-food chains, driving taxis is a viable alternative. Because drivers are free from office or workplace constraints, they are more often able to attend the mosque between passengers or to perform their prayers without sanction. The pay is decent, and the hours are somewhat flexible, so they are able to shift their schedules in order to participate in Islamic functions. In fact, Muslim immigrants have saturated this industry in New York, so much that it is difficult to hail a cab on Fridays between one and two o'clock, when prayer is being held. During *jum'ah*, in Harlem or other parts of Manhattan, unmanned taxis line up outside *masjids*. The sight of yellow cabs double-parked and wrapped around blocks is arresting.

Driving taxis in poor neighborhoods, especially the so-called gypsy cabs—unlicensed private car services—has become deadly for hundreds of African immigrants.[17] Ibrahima himself was shot once, after a passenger entered his car, extended the Islamic greeting to gain his trust, and proceeded to rob him. In Washington, D.C.,

African Muslim cabbies from Sierra Leone have transformed their vehicles into *da'wa* (propagation) mobiles. As passengers enter their cabs, a recording of the Qur'an is played, and drivers distribute Islamic pamphlets to customers before they leave.[18] In their own way, they are engaged in *'amal saalih* (righteous work), where they have melded work and religion. While this behavior might certainly be viewed as discriminatory or religious harassment, it demonstrates how African Muslims attempt to insert an Islamic sensibility into their workday, contesting an American work ethic that tends to reduce them to mere laborers for eight or more hours. By contrast, certain Somali Muslim taxi drivers in Minnesota have refused to pick up passengers who are carrying liquor or have dogs with them (some conservative Muslims consider dog saliva to be religiously unclean). They have argued that to be in the company of either is against their religion. Commuters have charged them with discrimination, claiming that drivers have no right to refuse a passenger unless they sense imminent danger.[19] Unlike the situation in Minnesota, this does not appear to be an issue for African Muslim drivers in New York.

After Ibrahima and I complete our greetings, he describes how he began selling books. "Let me tell you, brother," he says. "I started with five hundred books. And I made seventy-five thousand dollars the first year. I help people eat!" he says proudly. "I hire people, and they go out and sell my books."

A young man with a beige T-shirt and blue jeans squeezes his brawny frame between the parked cars. He stands quietly and waits for Ibrahima to notice him. He looks exhausted, and the cart he is pulling has a manila box attached.

Ibrahima glances back. "Take this brother," he says. "He was in jail, didn't have a job, but wanted to work. I told him, 'Look, take these books. You take twenty percent, and I'll take the rest. I'm supplying you with the product—all you got to do is sell it.' He went to the hair salons, the barbershops, and other stores and came back with cash money! He earned about five dollars on every book he sold, and he sold all the books I gave him. About fifty. That's two hundred and fifty dollars. These guys make an average of six hundred dollars a week." Ibrahima yells, "People say Blacks and Africans don't work together!"

"What about this?" I say. "Who would think Black books could sell like that? People say Blacks aren't reading anymore, that people are just watching TV or are on the computer. But obviously, Black people are reading."

"Black people are reading," Ibrahima says. "But a lot of White people want to read these books, too."

"White people buy Black novels?" I ask.

"Yeah!" he shouts, looking around, staring up and down the street. "Yeah!" he repeats. "They wanna know, they wanna know about what's going on with Black people. And they get it in these books," he says. "Random House wants to buy it."

"Oh, really?" I say.

"Yeah, I get all kinds of letters from publishers. They all want Black books now," he says.

"You have more tables than this?" I ask.

"Oh, yeah, I have a couple of tables. We travel, and we sell in New Jersey and other places."

He turns and points to a garbage can plastered with the face of a new author. He walks over and beckons me to follow.

"Look at this," he says. "She wrote her own books, and now she just signed a two-million-dollar deal."

We stand and contemplate the shift in book sales. Two or three car honks interrupt our conversation. "Hey! Hey!" says the driver of a black Escalade.

Ibrahima's face sours. "That's her husband right there, riding around," he says in a low voice. Ibrahima turns toward the car, waves ceremoniously, and pivots back to continue talking.

He complains about his previous marriage to an Ivoirian woman and how she stole eighty thousand dollars from him. As he speaks, his lips turn up, and he squints. "I didn't even want to marry her," he says. "My mother made me marry her, because they wanted me to marry an African woman. And she robbed me! I was in Germany. I was seeing someone I really loved. But I have custody of my kids."

"Are they here in the States?" I ask.

"No," he replies. "I sent them to Africa."

"To Côte d'Ivoire?" I ask.

"Yeah, Côte d'Ivoire."

He walks to his van, fumbles through a black bag, and pulls out a thick wallet. He shows me pictures of his children, playing near a pool.

"This is the house I'm building in Africa," he says. Situated in what looks like a very upscale area, it's a multilevel house with spiral staircases winding up on both the right and left sides to the second floor. He flips through the pictures, and I notice a White woman with blond hair and blue eyes. She is embracing his children, and they hold on to her like family. Other shots of her reveal more smiles, posing, and silliness.

"Who is this?" I ask, pointing to the woman.

"Oh, that's my fiancée," he says. "She's from Sweden." Ibrahima moves on to other photos and stops once again. "This is the hospital I'm building," he says. "Well, I'm not building it, more like I'm trying to help it. Fix it up. The government's not taking care of it. And it's getting worse."

The 'amal animating Ibrahima speaks to a different religious sentiment altogether. In many ways, he represents what Luís León refers to as the "religious entrepreneur," the religiously motivated person whose mere presence in the world transforms those around him.[20] His enthusiasm for what is right, the *'amal saalih*, motivates others, allowing him to redeem people and rebuild structures. Moreover, his own life signifies how religious conviction and entrepreneurship merge and open alternative spaces where others benefit. As we talk, smoke bellows from the grill of the Arab food vendor, a man in his early thirties wearing jeans and a yellow cotton shirt. It doesn't seem to bother Ibrahima, but I am visibly upset, and this agitates him. I begin waving the smoke away from my face to breath.

"My God!" I say to Ibrahima. "How can you stand it?"

"Yeah, I know," he says. "He didn't use to be here. He just started coming around, and many customers complain. I've told him about it." The fumes move across his table, covering the books in a misty film. "His grill is dirty," Ibrahima says as smoke blows into our eyes. "That's the problem. He doesn't clean it. I told him about it, but he doesn't listen." He moves closer to the Arab merchant, perhaps so he can overhear his remarks. The vendor sees Ibrahima pointing at the food cart.

"What's wrong?" he yells, peering at Ibrahima with arms outstretched.

Ibrahima ignores him and keeps talking, making hand gestures toward the food truck.

"Ibrahima! Ibrahima! What's wrong?" he pleads. "Did I do something wrong?"

"*Hatha haram* [This is Islamically unlawful]," Ibrahima says in Arabic.

"What?" the Arab says in English. "You shouldn't say that!" he yells.

"*La! Hatha haram* [No! This is unlawful]," Ibrahima repeats. "*La! Laysa ta'am, wa lakin ad-dukhan* [No! Not the food but the smoke]. *Hatha haram!*"

"No! No! Ibrahima, don't say that!" He lowers his voice to a more sympathetic tone. "Why you saying that?"

"You drive away my customers," Ibrahima replies, and he turns toward me. "*Halal* [lawful] is not just the meat," he says. "You are polluting the streets. This is not *halal*. This is not healthy."

"Don't say that, Ibrahima!" the Arab vendor shouts. "This is not fair. That's not right. Don't say this in front of my customers!" he yells once more.

While religious bodily practices in the workplace are less relevant here, Ibrahima evokes an important principle of Islamic ethics to criticize the business behavior of the Arab merchant. And he enacts it using Islamic Arabic, giving his pronouncements much more weight. Ibrahima is fluent in a number of languages, including German, which he claims is even better than his English, but he also admits that his Arabic is not fluent. Still, rather than appealing to the moral sensibility of the Arab vendor, an approach he has attempted several times before, he puts forth a Muslim precept to address what constitutes good business etiquette in

Islam. This is not to suggest that Ibrahima's book dealership is religiously *halal*, either, since many of the books contain very graphic material, including books he himself has written. But his verbal action against the blinding smoke coming from the food grill reflects a prophetic edict to stop wrongdoing by one's hand, by one's words, or, at the very least, by abhorring it in one's heart. Not only does migration interject "African voices into the marketplace," as Ogbu Kalu asserts, but immigration from all over the Middle East, Africa, and South Asia increases Muslim diversity within an already multireligious city like New York.[21] This intrareligious pluralism also ensures that Islam will enter the market in various places and in unprecedented ways.

In *Money Has No Smell*, Paul Stoller finds that Nigerien Africans in New York have adopted a similar approach to business. While some Muslim migrants from Niger might be less concerned with the explicit content of their products, selling caps that read "Fuck Off," many strive to uphold their religious integrity by informing customers about the true quality of their merchandise.[22] For these Muslim merchants, honesty in business is an Islamic mandate that they are bound to follow, and they say it fosters trust and strengthens relationships.[23] At the same time, adhering to these moral principles in their home country as well as in New York is not so simple.

When Ismael grew up poor back in Abidjan, and although he was a practicing Muslim, he hustled to survive, committing minor infractions such as stealing here and there. As a van caller, he would ride in the passenger's seat and call commuters to the van when it stopped at bus depots. Sometimes he would collect money from passengers for the driver, keeping a little for himself. "That's the bad part about it," he says. "Because if you find yourself in poverty, it comes a time you don't even know stealing is bad. And I would never encourage it, for my family or any Muslim to do such a thing." The idea that he would not be forced to continue this illicit behavior is what attracted him and others to America. In fact, they were led to believe that jobs were simply waiting for them. "They would tell us a fake story," Ismael says. "You know when you go to the airport, and limousine drivers are waiting for planes, holding up signs with people's name on it? When people see this on the TV, they said big businessmen are looking for people to work for them. I said, 'Wow! Is there a country asking you to come work for them? That's beautiful!' And when I went back home and told them I wasn't working, they said, 'Don't tell me you're not working now! We see the TV, we see all those bosses waiting for people to work for them.' I start laughing, because I know the reality now."

For other religious groups, their spiritual beliefs are deemed incompatible with American culture and altered or even abandoned. Thomas J. Douglas argues that the religious practices of Cambodian immigrants in Long Beach, California, and Seattle, Washington, are being transformed by the pressures of a capitalist economy.

Ibrahima Sidibe straightens books at his stand not far from the famous Apollo Theatre. (Photo Zain Abdullah)

He relates the sentiments of one Cambodian man, saying that "Buddhism could not survive in America because in the U.S., a person had to be aggressive, and Buddhism taught passivity."[24] Some African Muslims in New York share a similar view. Imam Bah Algassim, the Guinean leader of the Futa Islamic Center on Eighth Avenue near 138th, discusses the difficulty of continuing religious and cultural practices in America.

"We have a proverb that says, 'You cannot travel with a tradition,'" he says.

"What would you say this means?" I ask.

"Because traveling is not easy, sometimes you must leave that tradition somewhere. That's why if you are traveling, Islam will remove many, many loads from you, because the Prophet said that traveling is a piece of punishment. You must go under some rules you don't know. So, sometimes you must do something you don't like to survive."

According to Islamic tradition, the supplication of the *musaafir* (traveler) is always accepted by God, but one can only retain this migrant status for two weeks. Imam Algassim's statement reflects an important mood that many other African Muslim immigrants share. While they have been living in the United States for five, ten, or twenty years, many still consider themselves *musaafir*, and America remains a transient place. The "myth of return," which upholds their belief of sudden wealth and an easy return home, is a dream that only a relative few have attained. In the meantime, more are attempting to bring their religion to work, in the form of either rituals or principles, and it seems that the borderland separating the two will continue to be contested.

III

Most Senegalese Muslims in New York belong to the Murid Sufi order. After their annual Cheikh Amadou Bamba Day parade in Harlem, participants and spectators are invited to attend talks at the United Nations. People pile into the chamber hall, and several Senegalese speakers take seats at the head table. One talk in particular addresses the "work ethic" in Muridism. "Muridiyya," the speaker says, "has been depicted as a secular organization or a religious group concerned only with collecting wealth." He argues that this is incorrect, surmising that because European researchers gather data from secondary sources rather than the writings of Bamba, they are misled. He makes a clear distinction between 'amal and *khidma*. While the former means work, he explains, the latter connotes a type of service, which can be viewed as a sacrament or a way of gaining divine favor. The choice of words, he argues, is crucial. In his view, *khidma* means that Murid followers structure their lives in service to Allah, the Prophet, the Muslim community, and the world.

"The main idea behind *khidma*," he says, "is to keep one's mind and body worshipping Allah by way of prayer, *thikr* [remembrance], or working for one's livelihood, so one does not wander off the divine path or stray from God due to idleness." According to the speaker, colonial administrators in Senegal reduced Bamba's message to a simple work ethic, and Murid *taalibes* have internalized this meaning.

In *Fighting the Greater Jihad*, Cheikh Anta Babou offers an intriguing exploration of the word *khidma*, examining its usage in a number of Bamba's earliest writings. While Babou argues that one of the original meanings of *khidma* involves the service a disciple performs for a *marabout*, its purpose is to solidify an enduring relationship between the student and the spiritual guide.[25] Babou also explains how *khidma* comes in many forms for demonstrating one's commitment to Muridiyya, including the earning of wealth as a way to empower the brotherhood.[26] In the overall scheme of things, however, *khidma* implicates all Murids, *cheikhs* and disciples alike.[27] In fact, the Murid founder, Cheikh Amadou Bamba, is famously called *khadimou rasoul* or "the one in service to the Prophet," which vicariously inducts all Murids into a long line of devotees. It is this principle, the speakers at the forum announce, that allows them to raise six hundred thousand dollars quickly to purchase their four-story brownstone. While the term *khidma* does not appear in the Qur'an, its esoteric connotation is deeply embedded in the Islamic spirit. Fulani Muslims employed the same concept to collect one hundred thousand dollars in a single week in order to rent and renovate their building in Harlem. Shortly thereafter, they raised another three hundred thousand dollars to buy a building for a new *masjid* in the Bronx. Representing three distinct areas in Guinea, Fulani migrants from each region are likewise represented in the greater New York area. Appealing to each of the three groups, Imam Algassim charged them each with raising one hundred thousand dollars, and within three weeks, the entire sum was deposited. This *khidma* activity is not limited to men. According to Jacob K. Olupona, a woman led a fund raiser to build a Nigerian *masjid* in Miami, amassing more than one million dollars.[28]

Unlike the concept of *'amal* or *'amal saalih*, which is much more focused and goal-oriented, *khidma* can create an ecstatic energy, collapsing the religious and the everyday into a single moment. In other words, with *'amal*, the workday becomes punctuated with religious rites such as prayers or verbal incantations. By comparison, *khidma* encompasses the total round of one's activities, both secular and religious, blurring any distinctions between them, since its focus is to transform all actions into divine service. In this sense, African Muslims moving swiftly around Harlem might appear frantic. But this is because their duties are much more exaggerated in the New York context. Not only are they working more than one job, but this is combined with the herculean task of building a new Islamic community.

In *Fires in the Mirror*, Anna Deavere Smith constructs a series of monologues about a clash between Blacks and Jews in Crown Heights, Brooklyn.[29] The conflict erupted in 1991, when an African American boy was killed by an errant car in a rabbi's motorcade. In the play, Smith brilliantly incorporates excerpts from interviews with nearly thirty individuals, including Black and Jewish residents and ideologues. Her depiction of a Reverend Dr. Heron Sam, pastor of St. Mark's Episcopal Church, is worth noting for his view of how the Hasidim and their leaders move around Crown Heights: "The Grand Rebbe, he says, 'gotta be *whisked*!' You know like a President. He says he's an intuhnational figuh like a Pope! I say then, 'Why don't you get the Swiss guards to escort you rather than using the police and taxpayers' money?' He's gotta be *whisked*! Quickly through the neighborhood. Can't walk around."

This excerpt reveals more than the jaundiced view of how outsiders see others within ethnically diverse neighborhoods such as Brooklyn. It also helps us recognize a cultural distinction among different kinds of movement. When the *cheikh* of the Murid order arrives in New York, for example, he is certainly "whisked" around, from the airport to cars, from *masjids* to homes, and from one event to another. An imposing entourage accompanies him on the streets and even inside buildings. This type of "whisking" is the movement of *khidma*, a religious enactment propelling members into complete service. But this religious motion does not necessarily emulate a similar action in Senegal. For all intents and purposes, the scope and range of this action, not to mention its level of complexity and intensity, correspond to the way space and time are experienced in Harlem.

This point comes up during my chat with Jabril, a twenty-two-year-old African American Murid who spent his teenage years in Senegal. Jabril and I have just left a gathering in which the head of the Murid order, Cheikh Mor Mbacke, was royally carted from place to place.

"I noticed African Muslims here seem like they're always rushing somewhere," I say to Jabril as we stroll down the street. "Have you noticed that?" I ask.

"Yeah, definitely!" he replies.

"Why do you think that's the case?"

"Well, they rush in Senegal, too," he says. "Yeah, they rush there, too. But it's not like here. This society makes you rush! So you gotta rush here. They work a lot more here than back home. They have to!"

While Jabril is a Murid *taalibe*, fluent in Senegal's national language, Wolof, he was born and partially raised in Harlem, and he can appreciate the important temporal nuance distinguishing the two worlds.

African Americans intimately exposed to the lifeways or work habits of West African Muslims have their own perspective on what their presence means, especially as it relates to a new kind of street hustle. Kenny, for example, has lived in Harlem for all of his thirty years. From time to time, he sells old LPs and other items on the street, but this is only a "hustle" to supplement his income. His steady work is with a moving company. His thin, wiry frame makes me doubt his ability to move heavy appliances. But sometimes, he says, he gets involved in "boostering" (another word for shoplifting). He says that a "White fellow is a master booster. He goes into stores and comes out with a bookbag full of goods. But I give the community a great price." Kenny is very articulate and speaks with excitement and the suaveness of a skilled salesman. "Two for five!" he says. "That's the cost of toothpaste. You can't beat that," he adds with a sly grin. "Two for five! But the Africans come in and give a better price."

Kenny also says that he has problems with Africans in the community, because they "treat you nasty." While he dislikes their attitude toward him and other non-Africans, he has worked in a few of their restaurants, and they have treated him well. "They like the way I work," he says, explaining why he receives better treatment. Because of his rapport with them, Kenny claims that he can "get work or a meal from them anytime." He stares at me. "You know, they are slick, very slick!" He describes their shrewd behavior and business dealings. "They sure know how to hustle and move products," he says. While Kenny is not a Muslim, he believes that another Muslim "would probably have an advantage with them." And this final point is worth noting, because it illustrates at least one motivating factor that pushes Africans in Harlem. This is, in large measure, the energy that impresses Kenny. And this is very much the essence of how *khidma* is reenacted in Harlem.

Outside this Islamic environment, however, Murids grapple with the secular nature of the labor market, and they face similar challenges when trying to negotiating the line between religion and work. Rama's story, discussed earlier in this chapter, illustrates this point. Although she was a highly educated and successful physician in Senegal, she is ineligible to do this type of work in the United States. And even though she was granted a work visa because her brother had entered her name in the lottery while she was in Senegal, the only real jobs available to her are in the fast-food industry.

As we sit at the table in the local library, she raises her right hand above her left, holding them about a foot apart. "You have to start at the bottom of any country and climb slowly to the top," she says, indicating the social distance an immigrant must traverse.

She talks about a Muslim friend from Ghana, an English-speaking country in West Africa. He was a lawyer back home but took a job as a baker in the United States. "I was surprised," she says. "I couldn't believe it. He had to show me a picture. He had the white top and the big pointy hat." She holds her hand high above her head. "But he got himself together and returned back home all right. People won't believe what I'm doing here," she continues. "The job I have here, after being what I was back home. Ahh! They tell me, 'What? You mean to tell me that this is what you do?' Yeah, well, you have to survive here."

"Why do you think Africans are not able to continue being doctors or something else here?" I ask. "Is it because of the kind of visa they have?"

"No," she says, and her lips turn up. "You have to take all the examinations all over again!" Her tone rises. "At the same time, you have to take care of your family. It's too hard. By the time you do this, you're too tired."

Some dispute the claim of one researcher who states that Igbo immigrants in Washington, D.C., have fared much better because they don't send as much money to their families back home. Still, African Muslim professionals are often inundated with working several jobs to pay high rents in urban areas, remit money to their families, and pay a great deal of money for escalating school fees if they are preparing to retake examinations or obtain other degrees.

On another occasion, a Muslim from Sudan laments that while he worked as highly successful gynecologist in several places, including Egypt and East Africa, he is suffering in the United States because he can't manage the time to study and retake the medical examination. He works at a few low-paying jobs and lives in Jersey City, a concentrated urban environment just outside New York.

"You don't know," he tells me. "My family has a large house, like a mansion, and a lot of land. But here, I live in a tiny apartment with rats and roaches. It's crazy!"

Again, his problem is not that he is unable to pass the examination, even with certain minor language constraints. But the effort it takes to earn a decent living in the New York area, particularly with low-paying jobs and while sending money abroad, drains him. He simply has no energy for study. Moreover, because Africans often emigrate from countries where they were in the majority, entering an underclass position in the United States is a huge stigma to bear and taxes them emotionally. In other words, the combination of becoming a racial minority and an immigrant in a hostile climate severely limits their economic mobility and life chances. The difficulty is increased when Africans are forced to compete with millions of other immigrants or natives for the same low-wage positions in service industries. The slim chances they face in the larger economy generally force them into the informal sector or back within their own ethnic niches. And of course, this says little about the religious discrimination they encounter on the job.

Rama leans forward and places her elbows on the table. "It's hard, if you really, really want to respect your religion here," she says. "Like, if you don't want to miss the *jum'ah*. But you have to miss that here, because of your job. That's not how it is back home, because they know *jum'ah* is for a Muslim to go pray. So you can leave your job and go pray *jum'ah*. But here, it's something you can't really do."

Many Muslims in the United States are unable to attend *jum'ah* prayers. At the same time, thousands crowd into renovated *masjids* and newly built mosques every week. In fact, these congregations are growing much faster than Muslim communities are able to accommodate. Islamic tradition dictates that men are obligated to attend, while encouraging women to be present (or, depending on the gender politics at a particular *masjid*, discouraging them). This means that the Friday prayer is predominated by males. But while employers might adjust a worker's schedule around lunchtime and breaks to comply with an hour of *jum'ah* prayer on Fridays, others are less tolerant when it comes to Islamic rites.

"There's a big difference," Rama continues. "And you know, for fasting Ramadan, some jobs really don't understand that."

"What do you mean?" I ask.

"Like, there are some jobs where you really don't have a time for lunch. When it's time for you to cut [break] your fast, because I remember my first job here. I used to work at the McDonald's, and my supervisor was very mean. So I remember during the fasting, when she gave me a break, I told her, 'I don't want to take my break now, because I'm fasting. So I want to stay later, then I can cut my fast.' She said, 'No, you have to take your break now, because it's your time!' I said, 'What about later, if I need to fast?' 'Well,'" Rama says, echoing her manager, "'if you need to fast, it's your business! But you have to work, 'cause I'm not gonna give you another time for your fast.' Back home, when it's Ramadan, everybody knows it's Ramadan. So, before they need to cut the fast, most of the Muslims are home— to pray and catch the Ramadan [activities]. But here, you don't really see that."

While working under these conditions is difficult for African Muslim women, particularly those who desire to uphold their religious rites, the recourse is often to work for an African hair-braiding shop, especially since most newcomers lack adequate language skills for the broader market.

"When I first came in October," Rama says, "I was living with one of our Senegalese girls for three weeks. She was so nice. I came here one Wednesday, and that Monday, she had me a job."

"What job?" I ask.

"African hair braiding," she replies. "She took me to one shop and told the lady, 'OK, she's a newcomer. Do you need help?' And the lady says yes. I start working for her for one week, and she paid me seventy dollars."

"For the week?"

"Yeah, for the week! So I didn't want to stay there. So she [her friend] got me something else a week later, at another hair-braiding place."

"But how did you learn how to braid hair?" I ask. "Did you learn in Senegal?"

"No," Rama replies, leaning back in her chair. "She told me to come and help her, that's how I learned. She say, 'When she starts in the beginning, you do this end—you do the end like you see here. Now, you finish the job.' I do that with another girl, one week, then I quit."

"Then you went to another hair-braiding salon?" I ask.

"Yes," she says. "There were no jobs—only braiding."

As Cheikh Anta Babou discovered in his research on African hair braiding throughout the United States, many salons established during the early 1980s were able to fill a crucial gap in the market.[30] Rama arrived in New York in the late '90s, and the industry was already becoming saturated. The pay was low, the hours were long, and the work was extremely tedious. Because of fierce competition, there was little time for much else, and her Islamic practice suffered as well. She tried baby-sitting, and, unlike the constraints Assetou experienced, her Monday and Wednesday fasting regime and regular prayers impressed her employer, an Irish American woman married to an nonobservant Malian Muslim.

While hair-braiding salons have undoubtedly been lucrative for some shop owners, Rama claims that many African female workers are forced into it.[31] Hair braiding is often their first exposure to the job market.

Not accustomed to this type of work and strenuous schedule, Rama opted to become a home health aide like many of her countrywomen. It was also closer to her field. "When I find a job," she says, "I have to have time for my religion. I'm a home health aide, and everywhere they send me, the first thing I tell my patient is, 'I'm Muslim. I have to pray. Five times a day. It's not taking much time—like five or ten minutes.' I always tell them that, and when it's time, I tell them, 'OK, it's time for me to pray. Give me only five minutes.' They never refuse."

Rama has certainly been fortunate in this regard. Many clients might not appreciate her religious commitment on the job. But facing these challenges is not as hard as changing class positions in one's adopted country. This is particularly the case for well-educated African migrants forced to take jobs doing menial or low-level tasks, as teachers with master's degrees in Dakar are reduced to being dishwashers in midtown Manhattan. In fact, the class lines separating the educated or highly skilled in their countries of origin disappear when they arrive in the United States. This is a major source of consternation for African professionals who are unable to find commensurate work in America.

In Senegal, Aliou earned his master's degree and landed a job as a high school teacher, a plum position with high esteem. He came to New York seven years ago to increase his earning potential, allowing him to take better care of his wife, children, and extended family. When he first arrived, he was unable to find adequate work, though his condition has improved somewhat, since he has been employed as a substitute teacher in the public schools.

"In your mind," Aliou tells me, "it's very difficult to accept some jobs when you come from a high position." He stops and stares at me with deep anguish. "When you come in United States the first time, you go look for a job. They ask you to mop, to clean, all this stuff. You're not prepared for that! And you're going to work at the same level with someone who just came from the village—someone who doesn't even know how to read his name! I just come here, because I want to get opportunities for my family, not particularly for me." He pauses again, then snaps, "But for my family!" After thinking, he continues. "You know, in my country now, when people finish their studies, you're a doctor, you're an engineer, but you're not sure if you'll get a job. You spend a lot of money for your studies, and it's frustrating when you spend twenty years finishing college, and after that, you stay home. OK? That's why more people who used to stay in the country are now getting out. And what's worse is that they come here and work like they've never been to school! That's a big, big problem. Come over here, and for eight hours, from the morning to the evening, you are mopping with someone who came here with nothing to lose. It's horrible! You left a society very, very different, and you come to a society . . ." He turns his head away. "No one knows, no one! You understand! You are at the same level with everyone. How would Americans feel, if they had to do this? And this is going on month after month, year after year! It's something very, very hard to accept."

For Aliou, Rama, and hundreds of other middle-class African immigrants, the greater difficulty is having to tell their families back home what they do for a living. Given the high hopes their parents and relatives have for these expatriates, most find it extremely hard to reveal the nature of their work. The situation is even more complicated, because they also have trouble themselves coming to grips with their inverted status.

"The job you would *never* do in your country," says Rama, "you have to do that here. Like, you know, home-care people. If people back home told me, 'Look, one day you will go and wash somebody's butt.' It's, like, 'No! Me? Never!' Go wash a woman, clean an old man or young man. It's, like, no, no, never! But here, you have to do it." She diverts her eyes.

"Yeah, that's a really important point," I say.

"There's a lot of things you have to do just to survive, you know," she replies. "It's not easy. No, it's not easy," she repeats. "Yeah, like, back home, a lot of people have their own maids. And then they have to leave everything, come here, and be maids!"

"Really?" I say.

"There's a lot of African people in that situation right now," Rama says. "They have to do something they never thought they will have to do. And you're really, really stressed out! You say to yourself, 'OK, I'm coming to a big country and have an easy life. But then it's a hard life. And if you don't have papers, your work status, they pay you less. But you have to do it! You have no choice! And your people back home don't know. People have to hide the type of job they're doing here from their family."

"Why are they hiding it?" I ask.

"It's a shame, you know," she says. "Oh, I left everything, and then look what kind of job I'm doing here. So they have to hide that from the family."

"Well, what do they say when their relatives ask about their work?"

"They say, 'Look, I'm in America, and that's it.' Or 'I work, that's it,'" she says, echoing typical responses. "'What kind of job do you do?'" Rama says, quoting a question from relatives. "'I work!'" She pauses and smiles and cannot help chuckling.

"What happens when people come to visit them?" I ask. "What do they do?"

"I guess they tell them not to come," Rama replies. "Yeah, that's it—don't come! But now, I think, people understand. In many African countries, people are starting to see the reality of coming to other countries. But before, people who were here, like, ten, fifteen, or twenty years ago, they were hiding the jobs they were doing here. Since everybody's here now, you can try to hide that from your family. But somebody you know will see you and tell them what kind of job you are doing. It's better to say it. Because sometimes you call [home], oh, this person will see you and say you're doing that and that and that. They tell it on 125th and 116th, you know, Little Africa? And the news goes like this, very fast."

"They call it the African grapevine," I say.

"Yeah," Rama replies. "The news goes very fast there."

Advances in telecommunications have altered the migration space. African immigrants have entered transnational fields, spaces where the distance between two or more nations has imploded into what may be considered a single place. What happens on 116th Street is instantly sent to African cities and relayed back to New York, forming a revolving circuit. While it is harder for relatives to receive the latest news on their diasporic family members, operating under a certain cloak of anonymity has enabled them to enter the American job market in ways that would be improbable at home. As one African Muslim explains, being away from the watchful eye of his family and friends, he was free to take any job he found, regardless of the social or cultural stigma attached to it.[32] In his case, after working at several cleaning and taxi jobs, he owns and operates a very successful Guinean restaurant in Harlem and is the head chef. At the same time, his culinary endeavors are unacceptable in his West African hometown because of the taboo against men cooking.

Rama mentions her concern for fellow hair braiders, who during these tough times are sometimes forced to scour the streets, the subways, and the shopping districts, looking for customers, especially during the slow winter months. This dire situation is quite different from what they experienced in their own hair salons in their countries of origin, she says, and these women expected a great deal more when they arrived in America. Many feel stuck, with no option to return home, since the American dream was their only hope. They also expected "easy money" but have found what Aliou calls "hard money." They justify their sojourn in the United States, because while their work conditions are nearly intolerable, they have been granted work and sometimes more than one job. Moreover, the exchange rate between the American dollar and, say, the Senegalese franc is certainly high enough to improve the economic status of family members back home.

Still, this is a tremendous change from their chances in African countries, where regular employment eludes even the highly educated, much less the unskilled. Because so many African Muslim women are married at a young age, they become housewives early in their adolescence and either never complete their schooling or never go, leaving them completely illiterate. As migrants in New York, these women have no option other than hair braiding, at least until they can find a way to gain other skills. But their ultimate reason for making such sacrifices has much more to do with their ability to perform *khidma*. Aliou always says that his sole reason for migrating to America was to increase the economic standing of his family. And although the U.S. economy doesn't appear to be fully utilizing this newly arrived African "human capital," thousands are able to alter the life conditions of multiple households in their home countries. Many women working as home health aides, including Rama, see their training as a prelude to becoming qualified nurses and bringing these skills back home to help others. In her work on gender relations in African churches, Regina Gemignani writes about the importance of paraprofessional and nursing positions for the economic empowerment of African women, defying the stereotype that they are all struggling on the streets as trailing spouses.[33] But when African Muslim women take full advantage of health-related fields, even as home health aides working on the bottom rung in the profession, they are able collectively to remit thousands of dollars, enriching their families in New York and back home. Moreover, they are poised to repatriate valuable services upon their return, which is a major way to repair the massive brain drain devastating African nations. Despite their arduous plight in America or even the spiritual blessings they strive to earn, their story ends with what has driven them so far away from home: family. But family in Africa and Black America is not static, and the next chapter explores this murky ground.

8

Family Matters

I

It's a week before Cheikh Amadou Bamba Day. A Senegalese professor at the United Nations event speaks about the need to create bridges between Murids and others. "What we do as a community," he tells the crowd, "will depend on what we do in a shared community." When a conference participant asks how Murids plan to become a part of the Harlem community, one of the panelists, Niang, another professor from Senegal, offers three approaches.[1] First, by opening legitimate businesses and demonstrating their economic empowerment, Murids hope to earn the respect of Harlem locals. Because they are in a capitalist society, he argued, "economic power" is a crucial symbol of success. Second, Niang feels that their religious brotherhood is a prime example of the kind of "unity" and "solidarity" the community lacks. He advocates that Murids become positive role models and urges members to "share" their fellowship with others. And third, he and others strongly encourage intermarriage, particularly among continental Africans and Black Americans. This final precept is the most striking of the three. Immigrant communities in America have long sought economic self-sufficiency, and often ethnic enclaves have resulted from the emergence of specialty stores and hometown restaurants. So, the call to economic empowerment has been typical. Moreover, while Muslim immigrants have long been engaged in Islamic propagation (which has entered a new phase with the aid of technology and the Internet), their proselytizing can conceivably fit a model that researchers now call reverse mission, which recognizes new ways in which Christian immigrants are preaching to their irreverent coreligionists in the West.[2] In other words, in a role similar to the one Christian migrants play by evangelizing native-born Western residents, Muslim newcomers evangelize members of the host society by calling the irreligious to the faith. A call to intermarriage, however, appears to be a unique model for immigrant incorporation. Individual immigrants obviously become attracted to longtime residents and eventually wed, and, of course, fraudulent unions occur. But this approach is unique as a group strategy for mass integration.[3]

The proposition of cross-cultural marriage strikes me as an important way to understand African Muslims and their sense of belonging in Harlem. Moreover, the very fact that intermarriage is suggested as a mode of integration also speaks to how they imagine family and thus construct community. But the way African Muslims in Harlem think about family is not necessarily compatible with the Black notion of it.

I once drove Abdoulaye, a Murid official, back to Harlem from Newark, New Jersey, and we discussed these differences. "I remember we were talking about African and African American marriages," I say.

"Oh, yeah, oh, boy," he replies, squirming in his seat somewhat. "There's a lot there," he says.

"What do you mean?" I ask.

"Well, African men are having a lot of problems with African American women. It's cultural," he asserts.

"What do you mean, 'cultural'?" I ask.

"Well, everything is all right until the men want to go back to Africa."

"Why?"

"Because the women don't want to go to Africa. They think Africa is a jungle and backward. They refuse to go back with them, so, they split up," Abdoulaye explains. "If the African man brings her to Africa first," he says, "and she sees how it is, then he marries her, there are less problems." Abdoulaye then takes up another aspect of the topic. "African American women like it when African men take care of the bills and give them money—like back home. But when they need to share a bank account, African men say, 'Oh, no, we're not doing that!'"

"Why do they need to share a bank account?" I ask.

"Immigration wants to see a shared bank account to prove marriage, and the African man doesn't want to share it with the African American woman, because she will take all his money," he replies.

Of course, if this is a marriage of convenience, or a "green-card marriage," in which the union is merely to help an African immigrant obtain legal status and the woman is paid for the service, a high level of distrust is clearly understandable. While these illegal matrimonies certainly occur, many others are legitimate and involve genuine courtship and nuptials.

"African women are looking to get married, too," Abdoulaye says, and I dart my eyes toward him, glancing at his gaping grin, then return my attention to the road.

"Oh, really," I say.

"Yeah! It's easy," he says.

Since Abdoulaye has already asserted that family matters most to African Muslim migrants—stating, in fact, that their family was the sole reason they came to America—I wonder what is involved in this process. What forms does it take in Harlem? And in what ways does it inform their experience in New York? More to the point, how do Muslim men and women in this migrant culture go about dating and courtship? Does passionate love, or even sexual compatibility, have anything to do with it?

Some researchers claim that under the sway of globalization and modernity, marriage and sex are becoming secularized, not just in Western societies but in other places as well. For Africanists such as Göran Therborn, the secularization of sexuality and matrimony constitutes a blurring of the line between formal and informal unions (or what is religiously or socially approved as legal or illegal cohabitation) as a result of changing conditions and the exigencies of a new world.[4] For many Muslims, sexuality is both a private and a public affair, charging both the couple and the community with maintaining some sense of propriety. A formalized sanction of sexual activity means that some form of marriage ought to be the place for sexual intercourse. In many respects, the act of strict gender segregation (which can include a visual separation of the sexes by donning loose-fitting outfits) is often an attempt to prevent the temptation toward illicit sex. Over time, Muslims have recognized various marital arrangements such as *nikah* (civilly contracted marriage), *zawaj al-'urfi* (informal/customary marriage), *zawaj al-misyar* (marriage in transit), and *mut'a* (time-limited marriage).[5] This is not to say that sexuality does not have other legally recognized outlets. In her intriguing work on Muslim sexuality, Kecia Ali writes that "marriage was not the exclusive mode of licit sexual relationship in most Muslim societies"[6] and that "throughout Islamic history, slave concubinage was practiced by those men who could afford it."[7] While Ali claims that slavery was abolished by the nineteenth and twentieth centuries, it appears that not all Muslim countries have outlawed its practice, and Muslims still dispute its illegality, which sharply brings into question the practice of nonmarital sex between slave and owner in present-day Muslim nations.[8]

In theory, consent (both individual and social or ecclesiastical) is at the center of these sexual unions, with the possible exception of arranged marriages involving minors and enslaved persons.[9] If, however, Therborn is correct when he argues that the secularization of marriage is on the rise, we might also witness a change in the traditional mode of dual consent. In such cases, informal cohabitation will rely solely on the couple's consent without outside approval. This could also mean that the sex-marriage link will be broken, and sexuality will be relegated to new spaces offering alternative sanctions. But while Therborn argues that these changes appear to be occurring at a slower pace among African Muslims, Ali recognizes a dual trend moving in opposite directions. On the one hand, most Muslim nations have outlawed slavery and concubinage, many have officially constrained polygyny, and others have established a system to register couples and distribute marriage licenses, essentially legitimizing *nikah* as the single mode of cohabitation. On the other hand, temporary marriage in the form of *mutʻa* is becoming popular, along with *zawaj al-misyar* and *zawaj al-ʻurfi*. "The rise in these informal marriage practices," Ali argues, "as well as what is likely to be a rising incidence of sex outside of marriage, is attributable in part to a large and increasing gap between sexual maturity, beginning at puberty, and social maturity, the age at which it is socially reasonable to get married."[10]

Many African Muslims in Harlem are in their late thirties and forties and either haven't seen their family in years or have never married. But some live sexually between two worlds, a purportedly married-traditional one in their home country and a single-modern one in Harlem. In studying Muslim migrants from Niger in New York, Paul Stoller found that "they sometimes present themselves to local women as single men in search of companionship."[11] And although Issifi, a street merchant and one of Stoller's primary respondents, explained to Monique, his African American girlfriend, that he was married and fully committed to his family in Africa, they still became romantically involved. Many other married men who are devout Muslims remain monogamous and shun sexual infidelity. Some single African Muslim men befriend numerous women, including European female tourists who come around year after year.[12] "Many of the men," Stoller argues, "especially if they are traveling, believe it is their inalienable right to have sexual relationships with other women. As Muslims, moreover, they have the right, if they choose and are financially able, to marry as many as four women."[13] Polygyny, however, or marriage to several women at the same time, proves highly contentious in the American context. Similar incidences can be found among Muslim migrants from Senegal, Côte d'Ivoire, and Guinea in Harlem. However, single men, and many women, find that the fellowship they receive at local *masjids* helps them stave off loneliness and the lascivious atmosphere of New York City.

Asra Q. Nomani, author of the widely publicized work *Standing Alone in Mecca: An American Woman's Struggle for the Soul of Islam*, daringly questions the need for religion or government to regulate the sexual activity between two consenting, committed adults. Because women are generally unevenly burdened with the guilt and stigma of illicit sex, the eighth principle of her "Islamic Bill of Rights for Women in the Bedroom" states, "Women have an Islamic right to exemption from criminalization or punishment for consensual adult sex."[14] In light of Therborn's argument above, does Nomani's proposition represent an unraveling of sexuality and marriage as a result of secularization? Or do positions like hers reflect an uneasy alliance between the classical sources and new Muslim realities? Either way, many majority-Muslim nations are engaged in some form of negotiation regarding their involvement in the sexual lives of adults, and countries such as Egypt, which is home to Al-Azhar University, one of the citadels of Islamic learning, do not prosecute matters of sexuality.[15] In March 2005, legal scholar and philosopher Tariq Ramadan put forth a controversial call for a moratorium on medieval punishments (hudud) for sexual impropriety such as stoning to death or one hundred lashes.[16] This attitude shift means, at the very least, that present-day Muslims are raising new questions about their sexuality, their social condition, and the interpretation of religious precepts. "Nomani's statement," Kecia Ali reasons, "crystallizes a widespread but largely inchoate sentiment among many contemporary Muslims: consent matters."[17] This new challenge requires deep personal reflection and open intellectual debate, a problem-solving approach already stipulated in the Qur'an and prophetic traditions. Changes in sexual outlook for Muslims or any other group will not merely vanish or remain hidden behind age-old platitudes on morality.[18]

Pardis Mahdavi writes about a recent sexual revolution among youth in Iran, while Marddent Amporn investigates the prominence of a sexual culture among young Muslim immigrants in Bangkok.[19] In many respects, questions about sexuality and mutual consent necessarily underscore assumptions about who gets to define faith. As religious studies scholar Aminah Beverly McCloud notes in her book on Islam and immigrants in the United States, Muslim migrants from more than eighty countries and American converts (all with various allegiances and orientations) will in the coming years wrestle with issues of Islamic authenticity, proper representation, and suitable religious authority.[20] To be sure, this doesn't suggest a total change in religious attitudes among Muslims the world over; it does, however, provide a clue to where the modern discourse on Islam and sexuality is heading. Even so, African Muslims in Harlem overall strive to adhere to commonplace, religious interpretations of sexuality and attempt to remain chaste until marriage. Sex and religion are often strange bedfellows but perhaps not in a place like New York. Ethnographic works such as that of Moshe Shokeid on a gay and lesbian synagogue in lower Manhattan, which was considered the largest one in America, remind us how urban congregations can complicate the interplay between sexuality and the sacred.[21] As the work of anthropologist Tom Boellstorff reveals, multiple sexualities do exist within Muslim communities around the world. And while Islam is viewed as a "sex-positive" faith, "in the sense that sexuality is regarded as a gift from God and the right of every person," he argues that the fusion of homosexual and Muslim identities is "incommensurate" or incompatible with the Islamic public sphere of Indonesia.[22]

For African Muslims and others within Islamic communities, sexuality is linked to the social order in that, first, they believe that its proper place is in marriage, and, second, wedlock is not an individual choice but a legal accord linking many households and families, essentially permeating the entire social system. In this sense, sexuality has traditionally been a community concern for Muslims, particularly as it pertains to the procreation of children and issues of paternity and inheritance. The sexual conservatism of the African Islamic community makes the possibility of being both gay and Muslim "ungrammatical," in the language of Boellstorff, or at least publicly unacceptable.

An African *imam* describes for me how in the early days Africans were physically attacked by local residents. They woke each morning, he says, wondering "which cab driver or African was killed last night." As Africans, they are easy prey, because their immigrant or undocumented status makes them vulnerable. But the worst days are long gone, and conditions have certainly improved. "Today," the *imam* says, "it's beautiful to be African and Muslim. Africans in Harlem today have five *masjids*, thirty-five *masjids* in Bronx area, a couple in Brooklyn area, Staten Island, New Jersey. I have all addresses here, you see?" He points to a piece of paper on his desk. "The United States is going to change," he says.

"What do you mean, 'change?'" I ask.

"The local government, federal government, all of them, they used to be with the Christians, the Jewish synagogue. But the past five years now, they're coming to the *masjid*. Two weeks ago, the police commissioner was here."

"The government is trying to work with you now?" I ask.

"Coming to Muslims now, because they don't find gay *imam*. Gay *imam*, you don't see that," he says.

Our conversation coincides with the heavy news coverage of the child-molestation cases involving the Catholic church, and, like most people, the *imam* has been following the stories closely.

"*Imam* using drug," he continues, "you don't see that, because if the *imam* does, the Muslims would stop him and fire him. We don't play that game, and they know that for sure. That's why they know these people [African Muslims] are good people. That's why they are coming to us now. Believe me!"

I wonder how sexuality can make someone a good person or a bad one. There doesn't appear to be any easy answer. But one thing, at least, is certain. What it means to be African and Muslim in Harlem is part of how these people navigate their sexuality in this society. In other words, more than mere taboos, ideas of homosexuality or nonmarital sexuality help to construct a canvas against which

African Muslims come to understand what it means to be a "good" Muslim or, in some cases, a good person. But the playing field for working out this link between one's sexuality and moral respectability is often murky. Even so, locals have their own views of Islamic sexuality, particularly as it relates to polygyny.

As one of the yearly Cheikh Amadou Bamba Day parades meanders up Adam Clayton Powell Boulevard, I walk beside it, snapping pictures from as many angles as possible. Each position will give me a different point of view, so I jump up onto the street divider a few blocks before 125th. I notice an African American woman in her late fifties already there, and she greets me with a smile. Born and raised in Harlem, Gloria spent twelve years down South, but now she is back. Her round face is radiant; as she stands still, only her head moves from side to side, like a child unable to decide what to watch next. After a few shots, I begin a conversation.

"What do you think of all this?" I ask, lowering my camera and smiling at her.

"What you think?" she shoots back, turning to look at me with the same expression.

"Well," I say, not wanting to lead her on or sound flippant, "some like it, and some don't. What about you?"

"Humm." She sighs and thinks. "Some of us feel like they're invading, like, you know?"

"Oh, really? What do you mean?"

"Well," she says, "then again, they got American kids and shit. So I guess you can say they're American, really. You know, they're hot? The men fuck whatever moves. They don't have African women—they get our women, or they get Latino women."

"They do marry African American women," I say.

"What you call us now?" She snaps her head toward me, still smiling. "Were not African!" she yells before I can respond. "African American, Black American, whatever. We're not them!" she concludes.

After the parade ends at the Harlem State Office Building, I decide to double back down Seventh Avenue to talk to residents. Two Jamaicans are hanging out under a scaffolding near the corner of 123rd. I approach them, and one speaks first.

"Yeah, man, OK, man," he says, with his arms flung backward and wrapped around one of the poles. Strands of gray hair run through a few pieces of his heavily matted brown and black dreadlocks. The rest of his hair is neatly tucked under a blue knitted hat, while a long, scraggly beard extends down the front of an over-sized T-shirt. The other, younger man has a trimmed mustache and no beard. His wide black shades fit neatly under an orange and white baseball cap.

"Hey, what's up?" I say.

We talk freely, but their thick island accent makes it difficult to follow at first. I try to remain patient, nodding from time to time.

As we all relax a bit more, I decide to ask a question. "Did you see the African parade today?"

"No, no," the older one says, projecting his body from the rail. "What parade, man? There was a parade?"

"Yeah," the other man says. "There was a parade today—a little while ago," he adds in a stodgy manner. The other one frantically peers up and down the street, as if he can reimagine it.

"I'm writing a story on the march, and I'm trying to get some feedback from folks in Harlem." They both remain silent. "I just want to know what people think," I say. Their stillness makes me nervous, so I turn to look at the younger one. "Do you have any thoughts about it?"

"No, not really," he replies, looking straight ahead. A few seconds later, he adds, "I don't know. What do you mean?"

"Well," I say, "do you think it was good, bad, or something else?" As he thinks, I add, "Just in general."

Finally, he says, "It was nice."

"Nice in what way?" I ask. "What did you like about it?"

"It was nice seeing men, women, and children marching together," he says. "It's good seeing the family like that. Strong families!"

"They're organized," the older man says, chiming in. "That's good. Yeah, even dem Irish march, and dem wear those little skirts. Gays march—but they need to keep that shit down there!" He waves his hand toward downtown. "We don't want to see that shit!"

"Even Bush don't come up here without a bulletproof car," the younger one quips.

"And guards on the roof," the other adds.

"Oh, Bush came here?" I ask.

"No," the older one replies. "He's just driving through, that's all. He don't like New York, ya know? New York's Democrat, ya know?"

What is striking about these two episodes is how a similar conversation about the same event can invoke sexuality as a marker for two entirely different boundaries. For Gloria, Africans are "invading" the Harlem community, and their perceived promiscuity marks a boundary between them and Black residents. While the *imam* speaks of homosexuality as an indicator of impropriety and social unacceptability, Gloria views marital or nonmarital engagement with multiple women as morally reprehensible. More important, her evaluation of their sexuality becomes a way to differentiate Africans from African Americans. While she is not entirely sure how the separation works, she is absolutely certain that a difference exists and presumes that the hypersexuality of African men helps to mark it. In contrast, the two Jamaican men put forth a different view of the African Muslims' parade and their presence in Harlem. Perhaps their favorable perspective also speaks to a shared immigrant sensibility along with insider/outsider notions of belonging as Black migrants. For the two of them, the children, women, and men represent strong families and Black solidarity. Moreover, their depiction of African wholesomeness is juxtaposed against the Irish with little skirts (as another marker of difference) and the kind of "shit" that occurs in the Gay Pride parade. Again, race, in their description of the Irish, and sexuality, as it relates to the Gay Pride parade, intersect yet obviously cut across each other in opposite directions. Despite the fact that marchers carry huge banners with Islamic slogans and chant in Arabic, it is doubtful that their Muslim identity factors into these observations. As it relates to African Muslims in Harlem, however, their presence as Black people and sexual beings, with or without families, remains a frontier they will be forced to reconcile. In the meantime, their social compass and religious practice are very much animated by their need to construct new notions of family in the diaspora.

II

Following a religious event at Masjid Touba, the Murids serve their customary dish, *thiebou jen*, to all of their guests. Before eating, everyone performs *thuhr*, the afternoon prayer. Attendees scatter to different rooms throughout the brownstone. They spread out newspaper to cover the carpeted areas, and people move into position. With four or six to a section, everyone surrounds each station, dropping down to sit on the floor with legs folded or extended. In the ground-floor *musalla* (prayer area), the room is of modest size, and people are squeezed into any available space. Women position themselves across from men, but with such a crowd, there can be no real gender separation. Most women, however, sit against the main wall, and the men (who outnumber them significantly) occupy the middle of the room. Soon, some men move in swiftly, carrying huge aluminum containers of orange-colored broken rice, fish and lamb, pieces of cooked carrots, white yams, steamed cabbage, and eggplant. Like an assembly line, they quickly move in and out of the kitchen, plopping dishes down into the middle of each section. Some, both men and women, are still at the nearby *wudu* station at the rear of the room, and we hear water splashing as they take turns cleaning their hands.

I stake out a spot near the center of the room and sit down on my left foot, with my right leg up, a posture from the prophetic texts. Each person says a personal blessing, and right hands dive into the containers. A few moments later, a young

African man, Mamadou, joins us and starts taking food. "*As-salaamu 'alaykum*," he says.

"I think we met," I say as I grab more fish and rice.

"Yes, you're right," he replies.

"Do you live in Harlem?" I ask.

"No, in D.C., but we met when I was up here last year," he says. "And we talked at Balozi's house in New Jersey."

"Oh, yeah," I say.

Several small groups of African women are eating at their own separate stations throughout the room. As I look around, one woman in her mid-thirties watches me from the far left side. She takes breaks between handfuls, sitting up occasionally and leaning against the wall. I pretend not to notice and continue my conversation with Mamadou. Suddenly, people begin speaking aloud in Wolof, addressing the man sitting next to me. The men begin to grumble. One admonishes the woman who is staring at me, and she unleashes a fierce reply. Something is clearly wrong.

Mamadou shifts his body in my direction. "She wants to know if you want to get married," he says discreetly, leaning toward me.

"What?" I lift my eyes from the food and stare at him.

"She wants to know if you want to get married," he repeats. "But this other guy asked what was wrong with her, because she's a married woman. She says it's not for her but for her sister. But he asked her, 'What sister? You don't have a sister.'"

"Does she have a sister?" I ask.

"I don't know," he says, shrugging his shoulders. "Maybe she's talking about her friend," he says as the uproar settles down. A few moments pass, and I continue to eat as if nothing happened.

"So, do you?" Mamadou asks, glancing at me while I take another bite.

"Who is she talking about?" I say, leaning back from the food.

"I don't know," he replies. "Are you married?"

I wondered when that question would pop up. "Well, I am in a relationship," I say, leaning forward to resume eating.

"Well, you know," Mamadou says, "you can have more than one wife."

"But I don't even know who she's talking about," I say.

"I think you're scared!" he says.

"Scared of what?" I ask, incredulous.

"You brothers are scared!" he says, apparently referring to African American men.

Our pan of food is down to a few morsels, and we get up to wash our hands. Mamadou and I walk toward the back.

"How do you all do this sort of thing back home?" I ask.

"What do you mean?" he says.

"How do you know who to marry? Do you date first, you know?"

"Oh," he says. "Back home, our families are involved. But in this case, she is offering you a chance to marry her sister or her friend—we don't know which one."

As we talk, people finish their meal and begin moving toward the washroom. A few men gather up dirty newspapers and begin to move empty containers to the kitchen. One fellow, about six feet tall and in his late twenties, stops cleaning, walks over and addresses me. "You know, brother," he says, "it's really a blessing." Mamadou and I turn to listen. "I don't know if you see it that way," he continues. "You see, look at me. I'm Senegalese, working every day, and I want a wife. But she didn't ask me. She asked you! I wish someone would ask me. So, it's really a big blessing." His words are so passionate and sincere. I thank him for sharing them and face Mamadou.

"How do I know if this woman is looking to get married for a green card or money?" I ask.

"Yeah," he says, "I see what you mean."

"How do I know?" I repeat.

"Just tell her and the family you don't have any money," he says. "You're just a poor person, and if she still wants to get married, that's fine."

"Yeah," I reply, "but how does that work for someone like me, who has a decent job and lives in America? People aren't going to believe that."

"What you do is tell her you are not going to live in America, you're going to keep her in Africa, and you don't want to return," he answers as we stand there thinking. "You do have to be careful," Mamadou says.

As Mamadou mentions, entire families are very much involved in the mate-selection process in Senegal. The choice of a spouse is not an individual decision, although urban couples have greater latitude. Even so, extended-family members often preside over the entire courtship. In many cases, matchmaking is endoga-mous, restricting eligible partners to paternal or maternal cousins. But paternal cousins have preference, some believe, because of the heavy influence of patriarchal values within Islam and Christianity.[23] "In Africa," a woman named Kadiatou has told me while we discussed dating in Côte d'Ivoire, "you're not getting married to a person. You're getting married to a family. If my husband asks me to marry him, he won't come to me directly, although we both know what we want. He has to go to his father; his father has to go to his family; then my parents. My parents have to come to me with the proposal. You see how it goes? And then if I say yes, it has to go back around. You understand me? It doesn't happen between two people—it has to be between everybody."

The marriage offer in the *masjid*, however, underscores how the African Muslim community in Harlem constitutes a surrogate, extended family, and it also demonstrates how it has adopted a kind of familial responsibility for finding adequate mates. While this procedure is far from what generally occurs in their home countries, a proposal for courtship was made by way of the religious brotherhood, and it was brought to me by an associate from the community.

Adjusting to American-style dating is a major challenge. For some, like Moussa, a thirty-year-old Ivoirian Muslim who arrived as a teenager, traditional courtship, requiring sexual abstinence before marriage, is not an option. Although he comes from a somewhat religious family, Moussa doesn't consider himself a "strong believer" and claims that many Muslim youths will "never wait until they get married." He also believes that even a devout Muslim might become romantically involved. The extent of one's religious upbringing can play a major part in the decision, but he feels that it is ultimately an individual choice and based on one's beliefs.

For African women seeking an African spouse, the choice to become sexually active before marriage is much more difficult, because most men expect their future brides to be virgins. And it is a source of great pride for the entire family. When Hawa migrated to the United States from Côte d'Ivoire several years ago, she became intimate with a man from her country. Their relationship resulted in a pregnancy, and while her son is the joy of her life, Hawa finds it hard to handle the social stigma from back home and the ridicule of her compatriots in New York.

This clearly does not suggest that premarital or nonmarital sex is nonexistent in African Muslim or Muslim-majority countries. In Côte d'Ivoire, N'Dri Thérèse Assié-Lumumba writes, "there has been a trend toward an increased number of informal unions."[24] But marriage in these traditionally Muslim societies is a central component of the social fabric, and extramarital affairs receive a heavy sanction.

"Sex," says Laye, a Senegalese salesman from Dakar, "isn't widespread, but when it starts, people kind of index you—you understand? Everybody knows, and they start to see you as somebody out of control, unless you hide it, which, to tell you the truth, was my case. If you're pregnant before getting married, man, it's a bitch! It's a bitch for your family. Even in Dakar," he adds, "which is basically a modern town, and even though little by little, the social and cultural barriers are starting to erode, they're not giving up to the modern world."

In New York, however, far away from their families' glare, the decision to remain celibate is hard.[25] At the same time, it is equally hard for African Muslims in Harlem who have chosen to maintain the customary rules of courtship. Besides the absence of relatives with firsthand knowledge of the prospective mate, the migrant must bear the high cost of planning a wedding for families and friends on two continents. Under these circumstances, some may wait many years to return to their home country for a spouse. But migrating back home remains a myth for most, and they are left to search for available prospects in the United States.

One April evening, *maghrib* prayer has just ended at Masjid Aqsa, and I notice Bakary hanging out in his usual spot, sitting with his back against the left wall. He is six foot two, and his slender build, cropped hair, and ready smile give him a youthful appearance. Instead of African attire, he wears a long monochrome Saudi *thobe* (robe), with a Nehru collar and without embroidery. He is extremely cordial and has a magnetic personality. When greeting someone, he holds the other's hand comfortably yet firmly, with a warm stare, as though no one else matters. He drives a taxi and spends his time off teaching children Arabic and Islam. He also performs small maintenance tasks at the *masjid* and locks up at night.

"This is where I am all the time—in the mosque," he says proudly.

I make my way over to him and sit down. "How are things going?" I ask, immediately sensing his uneasiness.

"Yeah, *al-hamdu lillah* [praise Allah], everything's all right," he answers, and he begins rubbing his right foot vigorously.

"So, how are things?" I say, repeating my initial question.

"For four years," he says unexpectedly, "I've been trying to get married. But they don't want somebody like me."

"Why?" I ask.

"They say, 'You better not marry somebody like him, he'll have you at home all day, and he'll make you wear that stuff.'"

"That's what they say about you?"

"Yeah!"

"How do you know?" I ask.

"Two sisters were talking here in the *masjid*, and I was trying to get married to her sister. She told her sister, 'If you marry to this guy, you will have a problem, because he's so religious.' I hate that," Bakary says, raising his voice somewhat and grimacing. "People see you're so related to Islam, you're always in the mosque, you're so religious. People are scared of you. They think when you marry their daughter, you're going to ask their daughter to wear *hijab* [headscarf/veil] all the time, you're going to ask their daughter to stay at home—no school, no job. And they look at you. 'You're young; what you doing always in the *masjid*?' They say, 'Maybe something wrong with him.' Maybe they will say, 'You don't know how to work, you lazy, you got some mental problem?' But anytime they see you, they will say something different. 'Oh, you love Islam, oh, I wish my kids can be like you, oh, I wish I have a daughter, I give her to you.' I talked to at least six sisters about marriage. There are a lot of African women here, but it's hard to find a good one. They want to stay in the streets! This is our biggest problem here. People are getting married here every day, even in this mosque. But most of them don't marry because they love you or you're Muslim or you're doing this. They get married for what you have. They're going to look at you, how your apartment looks, what kind of job you have, what kind of car you have, how you're going to be in the future. Because everything now is money," he says, even though he has a good job and rents a two-bedroom apartment. "But I have to thank Allah," he says, "for teaching me about the community and for showing me I don't have to get married. The time didn't come. If the time comes, *inshallah* [Allah willing], it will be good."

This conversation echoes others I've had. And it illustrates some important points about courtship for Muslims at African *masjids*. While the *masjid* plays a very important role in the lives of these migrants, the overwhelming majority did not come to America for Islam or to improve their religious practice. Bakary lived a very religious life in Mali before migration. In fact, he only came to the United States because of a sponsorship he received from a wealthy businessman, and even then, he had to be cajoled by relatives. Of course, like his countrymen, he was curious about America and its promise of unimaginable opportunities. But his primary vocation was the religious life. It is little wonder that his expectation of others and his efforts to find compatibility among his coreligionists have gone astray. This Muslim community in Harlem is fueled by the continuous flow of economic migration from Côte d'Ivoire and other West African nations. Because these countries offer no real state aid for the elderly or indigent, income-producing adult children are a family's greatest asset. For Côte d'Ivoire, N'Dri Thérèse Assie-Lumumba points out, because of "the global economic crisis and the erosion of the economic power of even the 'middle class,' women's work is a sheer necessity, needed to sustain the family." She goes on to say that "working outside the home is not a simple economic exercise. It is a cultural factor located in an African world vision that does not confine women in the private sphere while men alone can work outside for wages."[26] Many African Muslim men in Harlem expect their wives to conform to traditional or idealized homemaker roles and be stay-at-home mothers. However, much of this has changed significantly even in Africa, especially in urban locales.

My conversation with Bakary also illustrates a shift in the premarital expectations of African Muslim women in New York. African female entrepreneurs or those working for wages require a different marital arrangement from what was readily accommodated in Africa. Because many are "in the streets," as Bakary notes, working to care for needy families back home, even before they get married, their lives as economic migrants will necessarily challenge any traditional form of family. In this sense, their idea of family must be renegotiated in the New York context and must adjust to the realities of American life. But because the African notion of family includes extended relations and operates beyond the confines of two individuals, the readjustment will involve a major cultural shift or the reconceptualization of family life itself. However, even if African Muslim

Far away from their country of origin, West African Muslim women at Aqsa maintain a faith-based extended-family network in New York. (Photo Soulaymane Konate)

families become more nuclear, focused around the immediacy of a husband, wife, and children, this does not mean that they are disconnected from multiple households in Harlem or abroad.[27] Under such conditions, African men might discover the need to alter their roles as sole breadwinners and participate in domestic chores and child rearing, as African women are being advised to look for mates who are willing to make these changes.[28] But this is clearly easier said than done. And the situation is compounded depending on whether or not Africans marry each other, intermarry with American Muslim converts, or wed non-Muslims.

III

Khady and I have arranged to meet at Masjid Touba for an interview. I have promised to bring the few photographs I took of her at *jum'ah* a week ago and at the Bamba Day parade. As I drive toward the *masjid*, I reach the corner of St. Nicholas and 125th, and my cell phone rings. I recognize Khady's number and answer.

"*As-salaamu 'alaykum*, Khady!"

"*Wa 'alaykum salaam*, brother. Where are you?" she says with a single breath.

"I'm in Harlem, at St. Nicholas, on my way up the street," I answer.

"I have something for you," she says. "Something you'll really like."

"Oh, really," I say.

"Yeah! So don't mess this up, brother! It's really good!"

I arrive at Touba and find a parking spot in front. I get out and head to the trunk for my bag filled with interview equipment—a cassette recorder with blank tapes, two lavalier microphones, wire and connection accessories, two notepads, and several black and red ink pens.

"She's here!" Amadou shouts down to me from his seat at the third-floor hallway window. "Yes," he calls again, "she's here—waiting for you."

I thank him and walk in through the ground-floor entrance where he's now waiting. "*As-salaamu 'alaykum*," he says sternly. "Come on, this way! They're over here." I follow him past the *musalla* on the right and through the doorway, and we pause in front of the kitchen. He takes a left, where stairs lead to a different part of the house, and stops. "Right up there," he says. I thank him again. "You're welcome," he says, then turns to leave.

I ease my way up the narrow stairwell. Before reaching the top, I see a landing without a door. I stop and announce my presence. "*As-salaamu 'alaykum!*" I yell out. "*Wa 'alaykum salaam*" echoes back. At the top, the stairway opens to a golden-colored carpeted area with deep yellow walls, a couch, a love seat, and a sizable window letting in plenty of light. A large framed picture of Cheikh Mourtalla

Moustafa Mbacké, the Murids' late spiritual leader, looms on the far wall. On this late afternoon in August, a clanking air conditioner and a small oscillating fan do little to abate the sweltering heat. "Hey, you're here," Khady says. Karima and Amina, two African American Murid women, sit on the couch and the floor, respectively.

Khady, dressed in an all-black *khimar* and gown, immediately sticks out her hand. "OK," she says. "Where's my pictures?" I give her the envelope, and she reaches in and eagerly pulls out all four. "Oh, brother!" she says. "These are beautiful! These are absolutely beautiful," she repeats, then passes them to Amina, as Karima scoots over to see.

"Oh, Khady," Amina says, "these *are* beautiful."

Khady's face beams as she inspects the last one. "You brought me beautiful pictures," she says.

"Yes, Dr. Zain," Karima remarks, "these are very nice."

"Now I have to find you a wife, a beautiful wife," Khady says.

A wife! I think to myself. *I guess it's just her way of expressing gratitude.* We laugh, and I laugh the loudest, trying desperately to ease an awkward moment.

A prospective wife is what Khady meant when she spoke of something she had for me, something I'd really like. During and after our session, she goes to great lengths to put me in contact with Fatou, a young Senegalese lady who owns an African hair-braiding salon in Brooklyn.

Later that day, standing outside, I am surprised to learn that Omarou, a middle-aged Senegalese man dressed in Western attire, condones Khady's matchmaking. I had assumed that his business suit indicated a departure from time-honored approaches to mate selection.

"Khady has somebody for you, huh?" Omarou says.

"Yes, she does," I reply, naively wondering how he knows.

"She's a good sister," he says, referring to Fatou. "She's really a good sister," he repeats.

On a different occasion, Konate, the Ivoirian *imam* at Masjid Aqsa, and I are standing on the corner of 116th and Eighth. "You know," he tells me, "it's important to have a good Muslim wife. When you're ready for a good Muslim woman, just let me know."

Of course, offers like these are flattering, especially because they appear to be authentic attempts to build family.[29] While African Muslim women have been hesitant to marry Black American men, especially since Muslim women are expected to marry within the faith, some of this reluctance appears to be subsiding, and they are beginning to seek out African American Muslim spouses. A major cause for this shift is that more progressive, well-educated, or affluent African businesswomen feel that many African men will never tolerate their new status. "African men," says

Ami, a thirty-year-old professional woman from Senegal, "are very traditional and want a traditional woman who will do everything for them." Still, the majority of marriages in these communities are between African men and women and then, to a much lesser extent, African men and African American women.

After my interview with Khady, Amadou walks in and begins spreading out newspaper. When he is finished, another young Senegalese man, Thierno, enters carrying a huge container of *yassa*, broken colored rice and grilled chicken. Khady moves over to one side of the dish.

"You want to eat?" she says, calling me over with an insistent wave of her hand.

By this time, Amina, with her back against the couch, and Karima, on her right, have already surrounded the *ma'ida* (eating place).

"Come on, brother," Khady says. "Come and eat with us."

"*Al-hamdu lillah*, OK, sure," I reply, and take a seat on the floor facing the sofa. As we begin eating, another Senegalese man, Moustafa, appears halfway up the stairs and stands there peering into the room.

"Please, come and join us," Khady says, twisting around to glance at him.

He smiles. "No, no, later," he says shyly.

"Come on," she repeats.

He continues smiling and pops back downstairs.

"There seems to be less of a separation here," I say as we break off pieces of chicken with our forks and spoons. "I mean, between men and women. It feels more like family than other places."

"Well," Amina says, "some places are separate. Men eat in one place, women eat in another, and children in another."

"But," Karima adds, "they all eat at the same time, though. When I was single, I didn't eat with men. But we're all married."

"Yeah," Khady says. "We're all married. That's different."

"That's right," Amina says.

"So we're kind of off limits," Karima interjects.

"Before I was married," Khady says, "guys used to push up on you all the time. You know how you guys do." We all laugh. "When you're married," she repeats, "you're off limits!"

It approaches six o'clock, and I explain that I have another appointment and must leave.

"You can't go!" Khady blurts out. "She's on her way!"

"Who?" I ask.

Khady sucks her teeth, then snaps her head to the right. Amina, sitting behind her, leans forward, anticipating a conversation, but Khady says nothing. "She's coming from New Jersey," Khady says.

"She lives in New Jersey?" I ask.

Khady spins around, unfolding her legs, and abruptly gets up from the floor. "Let me walk you out," she says. "Let's talk!"

Outside, we walk a few yards to the corner. Khady doesn't say a word, just dials a number on her cell phone. She urges Fatou to leave her shop immediately so we can meet, but her attempts fail. Khady begins to make her case for the courtship.

"Yeah, well, she owns her own hair-braiding shop, and she doesn't want to be out here alone. She wants to do the right thing."

"OK," I answer. "That's good, but—"

"Look," she says, cutting me off. "Let me tell you, she picked *me* out of many sisters to help her. Other sisters do other things, but she wanted me to find her a husband."

Khady's phone rings, and it's Fatou. She holds out the phone, and we stare at each other briefly. I take her phone, and Fatou and I exchange pleasantries, suggesting a longer conversation at a different time. I then thank Khady and leave for my next meeting.

Early marriage in Senegal is a social norm, although with increased urbanization and the secularization of family life or the slow shift toward informal cohabitation, research has indicated that even eligible African men and women have been waiting longer to marry.[30] Illustrating this point, a dated but relevant study in 1986 revealed that 91 percent of Senegalese women between forty and forty-four years old were married, while only 4 percent were widows and 5 percent were divorced.[31] For Senegalese Muslims, this marital practice "is probably a holdover from African custom," the study's authors write, "which maintains that marriage is compulsory for both genders and that an adult women must be married and integrated into a family unit. If she is made single by divorce or widowhood, it is her family's obligation to make sure that she remarries in order to maintain her social status."[32] Moreover, childbearing appears to be highly regarded in Senegal, and women are exalted for having many children.[33] In Harlem, though, the African Muslim women's relatives back home cannot be closely involved in this part of their lives, so Fatou has asked Khady, a respected figure in the African community, to play this guardianship role for her. At this point, we can see a crucial pattern emerging, one that underscores the foundation of family life and community formation for African Muslims in New York City. Abdoulaye, Mamadou, Imam Konate, Khady, and others are part of a brotherhood-sisterhood network. They are marriage guardians within the immigrant community, and they adopt the role that an extended-family member would play by vetting all available suitors. As Khady mentions above, other "sisters" are assigned other tasks, but her duty is mate selection. This network is at the heart of family formation for these African Muslims, particularly in the way it helps to facilitate marriages that are either monogamous, cross-cultural, or polygynous.

Khady, Karima, and Amina all say that they are married, but each has a very different arrangement. Khady's monogamous relationship is typical for African men and women in Harlem. Although Khady holds the traditional view that men ought to be "first," something she claims to have learned growing up in Senegal, she will not tolerate polygyny.[34] "If you see me today," she says, "you think I just came from Senegal yesterday. But when I came to this country, I was young, and I cannot take a man having two wives—I cannot take that part." Many African couples have loving, caring relationships. Many others, however, undergo harsh breakups, and seasoned community members such as Khady and African *imams* act as marriage counselors. "I said to myself," Khady says, "I need a tape to help the ladies stay out of trouble, a tape that can help them with their husband, stick together for their marriage and help their kids." Each year, Khady has purchased more taped lectures on the Islamic virtues of Mame Diarro Bussou, Cheikh Amadou's mother, describing her exemplary character as a pious Muslim, wife, and mother. During the past five years, she claims to have bought and distributed more than three hundred tapes. "Sometimes you give someone a tape," she says, "and then another year, they pull your arm and say, 'Sister Khady, I pray for you, because one night my husband and I get into a fight, and I think of the tape.'"

Other African women in the community act as cultural translators between couples and the state, especially when there are allegations of spousal or child abuse. "DYFS [Division of Youth and Family Services] is involved, and African families don't know how to deal with this cultural conflict," says Zeinab, a Sudanese immigrant and cofounder and executive director of the African women's advocacy group Sauti Yetu. "The state says, 'Just stop doing that!' They [Africans] say, 'Well, this is the way we do it back home.'" She imitates the state agency's response: "'You're in America now, and you can't do that here!'" Zeinab stops to look at me, then says passionately, "But that's not going to solve this problem! You have to appeal to their cultural values and find ways to bridge the gap." In the Guinean Muslim community, Imam Bah Algassim of the Futa Islamic Center advises his members to contact the *masjid* when marital conflicts erupt, especially before the authorities are called. "If we come before police," Imam Algassim says, "we will talk to them and leave them in peace, they sleep in peace. But if the police come over before us, they break the marriage, because they will tell the husband, whether he's wrong or not, 'You have to go to jail.' And the day they release you, they tell you to stay fifty blocks away from your house. It means the marriage is collapsed."

But while African Muslim couples struggle to retain their traditional customs, cross-cultural marriages are almost an entirely different case. Karima, an

African American who also embraces her Native American heritage, is in her late thirties. She grew up in a middle-class Roman Catholic family in Kansas City, Missouri, but converted to Islam about seven years ago. She ended up in New York some time after her conversion and became a member of the Murid community. The group appealed to her because of her early Afrocentric upbringing and spirituality. Her yearlong marriage to Amadou, a Senegalese migrant and member of Masjid Touba, tells a different story from Khady's. Intermarriage between Africans and African Americans is occurring more frequently in Harlem, but it is fraught with its own unique challenges. When these marriages do occur, they are primarily between African Muslim men and Black American Muslim women, although African men do at times marry African American Christians and, much less frequently, Latinas. When these intermarriages go awry and conflict occurs, most blame irreconcilable cultural differences. But as it relates to marriage and the family, identifying a dissimilar culture as a problem is no simple matter.

In theory, Islam encourages cross-cultural encounters. What matters most is the maintenance of particular ethical practices.[35] "Everything is about respect," says Kadiatou, an Ivoirian businesswoman and owner of a hair salon. "That's the way I was raised. Every time my father got home, my mother was always there." As an entrepreneur and a working woman, she knows how difficult this is in a city like New York. Still, she says, as a wife, she makes a conscious effort to "give him his time." African Muslims in Harlem frequently mention respect as a central value for all of their relationships.

"Well, to me," Karima says, discussing her relationship with her Senegalese husband, "it's not really so much different because I come from a very old-fashioned way of dealing with relationships. There's still a common courtesy that wives have for taking care of their husbands, or a husband taking care of his wife." She admits that "you don't hear people talking like that a whole lot these days. Like, people will say, 'Oh, well, that person is grown, they better take care of themselves.' But we have a responsibility to each other, and we have a certain level of respect and kindness and tenderness for each other. That is very much needed these days—how we talk to each other, to care for each other's feelings, and even the tone of our voice when we talk to each other. I don't think we realize the impact of how we're communicating."

Karima also speaks candidly about the importance of religious understanding for transcending cultural differences between African and African American couples. Religious or, more exactly, spiritual compatibility, she says, is critical to helping culturally diverse couples overcome marital difficulties. "I'm not even looking at it like I crossed a culture," she says. "Even though I have. I'm seeing it in a very different way, because I'm seeing the spirituality of that person as greater than the culture, even though the culture does have a strong influence. And there are different things that are expected, responsibilities, obligations, roles, and duties that are expected because of the cultural upbringing of my spouse."

Other African American Muslim women, however, feel that culture is paramount. "What people don't understand," says Jalsa, an African American Muslim woman raised in Harlem, "is that culture is a big deal. A *big* deal! It's not a small thing." She goes on to say that "there are so many little things. You have to respect my culture and my history, and you have to have a Nation of Islam background, because certain things that I hold dear, you have to respect that. You're not going to tell me that Elijah Muhammad's a *kafir* [disbeliever] and you're standing in my house," she asserts, even though she is presently a Sunni (orthodox) Muslim and is no longer affiliated with the Nation.

"I have a sister I know," Jalsa continues, speaking about a friend with an African spouse. "She woke up one morning, and she said there was a village in her living room. She said to her husband, 'There's all these West African people in my house. What's going on?' He said, 'Oh, they're from my village. They're staying for two months.'" Comparing Africans and African Americans, Jalsa says, "Black folks, they try not to have anybody in their house that long. That's where the difference comes. African women are more docile than African American women, because they always see their men being in charge. We haven't had that experience. So they're not used to dealing with a sister with the necks and snapping the fingers and the whole thing. To them, that's disrespectful. That's why they get into a lot of arguments. Whereas we're, like, 'Get a grip!' Black men have developed ways of being. Like my husband, he'll tease me if I get too sassy. That breaks everything down, because I understand what he's doing. They don't have that mechanism, because they never had to do it. It's hard enough to be with each other, you know? But two different cultures—that's light years away."

Jalsa's comments underscore the need to understand Blackness as a multiethnic category. Cultural or ethnic differences can be as real (or imagined) as racial ones. Her reference to having a spouse who understands or respects her Nation of Islam background points out another crucial area to consider. Without subsuming religion under the broad rubric of culture or ethnicity, both members of an African and African American couple can be Muslim, but they also might have very different religious orientations. This alone can be problematic, unless, of course, they are willing and able to work out some sort of a compromise. In Harlem, one African and African American Muslim couple attends two separate *masjids*. While the African man belongs to Masjid Aqsa, the African American woman was advised by her husband to join the African American-based, Mosque of Islamic Brotherhood. Moreover, the way each person understands the notion of family itself is important. Jalsa's friend most likely did not completely understand her African husband's notion of family. More important, she also seemed not to fully grasp the extent to which African relatives are thoroughly integrated into the lives of married couples, and how they are fully involved across households. In this way, the centrality of family is so important that one is not expected to have an individual identity, or at least one totally separate from one's familial identity.[36] Something not discussed explicitly but often alluded to by both Africans and African Americans is the problem of language. For cross-cultural marriages, this is crucial, and the fact that most African Muslims in Harlem are not very proficient in English prevents much-needed communication.

Karima and other African American Murid women married to Senegalese men have established a formal circle where they can compare matrimonial notes. Many have voiced concerns that they might not be treated with the same regard reserved for a Senegalese bride. Most women from back home are given hefty dowries of gold jewelry and financial entitlements. When some complain to their husbands about this disparity, they are told that these practices are reserved for "virgin" brides. Most African American women married to African men, however, want some assurance that their marriages are what Karima calls "solid." "By solid," she says, "I mean they want to make sure their marriages are recognized in the community and respected in the community, as well as by their families abroad." Even several African men have verbally rebuked their compatriots who disregard their African American spouses once the marriage papers are complete. In fact, Africans increasingly advise prospective American mates to visit Africa before the marriage, making certain to learn as much as possible about their future spouses' culture, relatives, and expectations. Some African American wives tell stories about the pressure their husbands received from African women, attempting to dissuade them from marrying Black Americans. Obviously, some African women have been threatened by the competition for eligible African men in the diaspora. In addition, some African American women talk about concerns that African men might be infected with sexually transmitted diseases such as AIDS or HIV, because the problem is so widespread in sub-Saharan Africa. While concerns about disease loom large, there are many stereotypes on both sides, and each views the other with skewed, exotic, and erotic notions. Since polygyny is a major practice throughout West Africa, and particularly Senegal, many American women are concerned that they might be cajoled into becoming cowives. But other African and American Muslim women have accepted a polygynous relationship for their own reasons.

When I meet Amina at the interview with Khady, she is in her forties. She was raised in a single-family house in Rhode Island, but she came to Harlem in her late twenties. Her first real exposure to Islam was as a teenager. African Muslims from Tanzania resided in her Rhode Island neighborhood, and she was introduced to their Pan-African rhetoric and Islamic practices. After leaving her hometown for New York, however, her religious interests faded. Then, when she met Yaya, her life took another turn.

Yaya worked as a street merchant in downtown Brooklyn, and Amina would pass by his stand during her lunch break. "I never speak to anyone really, or give out my number," she says. "If I do, I give out a different number, not my real number. And for some reason, when I passed this guy, and he said, 'Miss, miss, please one minute, one minute,' I turned around, and we started talking."

During this time, Amina was working two jobs, but Yaya was persistent and kept calling, leaving messages. They eventually had many telephone conversations and learned a great deal about each other. "His accent was very hard to catch, and I don't know, but my heart opened up, his heart opened up," she says. At the same time, Yaya began teaching her about Islam. "He was telling me the do's and the don'ts, what he can do and what he cannot do. 'Although I like you, Amina,'" she says, repeating Yaya's words to her, "'I would like you to be my wife, and I can't come to your house. I can't do any of these things because I'm not respecting Islam.' So my conditioning was, like, what are you talking about? Is he gay? But that was one of the things that was appealing to me. How humble and respectful and true he was to his faith. Although we wanted to be together, he said we have to marry first."[37]

Yaya was also honest with her about his other wife and family. They eventually had an Islamic engagement ceremony and prepared to travel to Africa to meet his family. "He said, 'I want to take you home, then you're going to really know who I am.' When I first went over, I'm open, because I already know about everything," Amina says. "But how am I going to be received? So I'm coming with some paranoid conditioning—that Americanism. But she [Yaya's first wife] was such a model of affection and love. They were just so genuinely humble and sweet, but it was more than that. The sisterly bond! I have never had it unconditional like that. I mean, we lived together, ate together, prayed together. She demonstrated everything you can do to please your husband in an African, Islamic way. She became a great mentor to me, and she's younger than I am. But our connection became even bigger than him."

Clearly, I am more than a little stunned that Amina, a Black American woman born and raised, could speak so passionately about polygynous relationships and embrace her cowife as a sister in faith. It is surely a curious thing. But while some countries on the continent, such as Côte d'Ivoire, have moved to ban plural marriage officially, it appears to predominate throughout Africa. Göran Therborn notes that even for "the Christian half of Ghana where a fourth of Christian women were in polygynous unions, . . . polygyny is, above all else, an African institution, recently legitimized by the advanced egalitarian South African legislation, . . . although a rare formal practice there."[38] And while polygyny is a significant part of

Muslim and African life in many West African nations, 60 percent of the urban Senegalese population is monogamous (50 percent in rural areas in the late 1980s).[39] Polygyny continues to be much more of a rural practice than an urban one, particularly as a way to solidify farm work, reunite widows, or create alliances between vying ethnic groups. "My father lost his younger brother," says Ibrahima, a Muslim street merchant from Côte d'Ivoire. "And he didn't want his family to go away, so he accepted her [married the brother's widow], but they never had a sexual relationship. He wanted to keep her in the family and keep the children."[40]

For Amina, though, it appears that her polygynous arrangement is based not merely on her relationship with her husband but also on a spiritual realization and an acculturation into an entire familial system. "It's different, and it's a universal level," Amina says. "I love Yaya, but I love him as my brother, my friend, and my husband. So it's not possessive at all. I only speak for myself. I mean, the relationship that me and my husband have, again, because of where I'm at mentally, I'm able to look at him as my brother if I have to. As my husband if I have to. And as my friend. So, that helps a lot. I mean, if I say, 'Oh, this is my husband,' I can't communicate what I need to communicate, you know? So, I have to take it down a notch and say, 'OK, you're my brother, I'm your sister.' And we get some stuff out. In relationships, before I became Muslim," she admits, "the guy was always cheating on me anyway. Always! I mean, it was always some kind of static. This is great, I know everything, she knows everything. We have no problem. But it takes a very unique individual to balance that relationship, because we're there together. In Africa, the houses are huge, and there's communal living. Nobody's bumping heads. He's able to make each one feel, like, 'Yeah, I treat you both equally,' without that static or anything."

Housing arrangements typically vary for polygynous families—from a large, compound setting in rural environments to separate houses for cowives while the husband has his own residence, essentially visiting his wives. "There's a huge house," Amina says, explaining their living arrangements in Africa. "So he has his room, she has her room, I have my room, the kids have their room. And then his father and brother's house is attached, so it's just really huge, right? And so no affection is displayed throughout the day. But on your night to go to his room, you discuss whatever you're going to do. Discuss all your issues, whatever it is that happened that you didn't like or whatever. Next night, it's her turn. But it's respectful and peaceful. And because I think there's no flesh around, you're able to stay focused. Nobody's being provocative, and it makes it a lot easier."

I ask, "Do you see more marriages between Africans and African Americans occurring?"

"I would love to see that," Amina says. "I have some friends who are non-Muslim, and they have observed my relationship with my husband over the years.

Although they don't agree on everything, but they do like the respect they see in our relationship. And if I can just be an example, I'm happy."

IV

What is illuminating about the nature of family among West African Muslims in Harlem is its complexity and fluidity. From formal marriage and its various expressions to informal cohabitation and its nuances, the institution of family is clearly multilayered and not reducible to any simplistic model. More important, familial ties here operate across cultures and identities, either faltering around issues of ethnic diversity and varying notions of Blackness or transcending these constructs under the sway of spiritual values. Even with all of this, nonmarital relationships—or the ability to embrace nonblood relatives as kin—also occur in this space. And African immigrants employ this flexible notion of family to connect with local residents.

The distance between the Mosque of Islamic Brotherhood on 113th and African Kine restaurant on 116th is relatively short, yet a walk along this stretch tells a unique story about Harlem. Youngsters propel tennis balls against apartment stoops. Sidewalks are taken over by girls jumping rope or hopping in and out of chalked rectangles for hopscotch. People hang out, leaning against fences, scaffolding bars, and railings as rendezvous points. Each street represents a distinctive community, a familial space where people find a sense of belonging. The bond people share as members of a street community—or "street neighborhood," as Jane Jacobs labeled it—in certain respects relates to their physical residence and their collective experience in Harlem.[41] This is not to say that residents do not share other types of attachments or affiliations. But by and large, what typifies their sense of inclusion or kinship, whether real or imagined, in street communities is their residential membership.

From Seventh Avenue, a stroll up 116th to African Kine on Eighth reveals a new version of the urban theme. At Masjids Salaam and Aqsa, African women stand behind their vending tables, selling an assortment of drinks made from ginger, tamarind, or hibiscus. Yogurt-millet snacks are stacked high in clear containers. Tube socks, scarves, and other clothing items appear on top and in nearby boxes. African children run behind the stands, playing peekaboo and other games, while others dodge between African men standing like poles on a concrete playground. Some bob and weave between pedestrians, never running into them and always careful not to venture too far out of *masjid* range. Yet street play in both residential and commercial areas domesticates the bustling traffic and appears to soften the pavement. Just as Robin D. G. Kelley considers city streets or play areas to be arenas where gender identities are constructed and rehearsed, Black American and African children engage in play as a way to demonstrate belonging, reenacting a type of neighborhood kinship.[42]

While Africans live here, their presence is dwarfed by that of the African American majority. Unlike many Black Americans who foster a communal sensibility by hanging out and swapping stories on their apartment steps, the African presence in Harlem is still scattered and not concentrated in any one neighborhood. One exception was during the early 1980s, when most Africans rented rooms in several single-room-occupancy hotels.[43] They filled these SROs to such capacity that French-speaking West Africans began calling them "Ghetto Afrique." After they began finding their own apartments, their living has been scattered, and so African Muslims in Harlem have not yet formed any significant settlement clusters in residential areas. Instead, they form familial bonds with one another in the commercial district along 116th Street. African *masjids*, agencies, and businesses breed an associational life for them, and, unlike their marginal presence within street communities, their collective belonging and filial bonds are fostered through their religious, social, and business activities and the relationships they engender.

Just as the random mingling and idle chatter of street life produce an atmosphere of sociability and mutual rapport, the casual gathering of Africans in front of shops and *masjids* produces camaraderie and fellowship. Even the colorful dress worn by Muslim women moving about seems to soften the commercialism of bright neon signs flashing in store windows. In fact, the centrality of the *masjids*, Islamic supply shops, and religiously sanctioned restaurants becomes a distinctive marker separating street neighborhoods from the communal district of 116th Street. For the majority of African Muslims in the area, their associational life underscores the African value of extended family and an Islamic mandate to sustain kin relations. In contrast, while street communities often exhibit some level of affinity or fictive kinship, their relationships are essentially secular, and religion rarely factors into their association. In other words, while street neighborhoods are primarily based on secular notions of belonging, the commercial district along 116th Street is a space where religion and African ideals intersect, informing their ties as blood relatives and extended-family members.

Overall, relations between Africans and Blacks in Harlem have been less than cordial. Some early African migrants, however, tapped into preexisting notions of the Black extended family. When Abdoulaye first arrived in the early 1980s, he faced a hostile environment and contemplated leaving Harlem altogether. As his father back in Senegal instructed him, he made greater efforts to become acquainted with the children, paying special attention to those from woman-headed, single-parent households. His plan was to foster a fictive kin-ship with the community, and he would occasionally intimate to neighborhood youngsters that he was their "father" and that they should see him if they needed anything. One midweek afternoon, Abdoulaye describes how a young boy ques-tioned him about his claim.

"You're my father?" the boy asked.

"Yes!" Abdoulaye says he replied. "I am your father."

"OK," said the youngster. "I want a bike, 'cause all my friends have bikes."

"When is the next time you're out of school?" Abdoulaye asked.

"Oh, on the weekend."

"OK, ask your mother if it is all right," Abdoulaye told him, "and I'll take you to the store and buy you one."

The boy received permission, and they both went to the store to purchase a bicycle that Saturday.

As he rode his new bike up and down the sidewalk, one of the boy's friends noticed. "Hey! Who got you that bike?" the friend yelled.

"My father!" the boy answered.

Besides the role of fatherhood, Abdoulaye would attempt to use other kinship terms such as *uncle* in order to make a connection with neighborhood youth.

"I used to tell them, 'I'm your uncle,'" Abdoulaye says. "'Oh, my uncle passed away!'" he says they would respond. "I said, 'I come back. I was in Africa, and I come back.' I'd buy them candy, and he'd go tell his mama. Because they're kids, their mama said, 'No, no.' I said, 'It's OK, that's my children.' She said, 'No, I don't know you!' I say, 'I know you don't know me, but these kids belong to my skin, we have the same skin.' Or I make them African clothes and give to them. The mother loves it, and they come back and talk to me."

It might be true that, today, too many Black fathers reside away from their children.[44] However, it would be wrong to assume that a father figure of some sort is absent from the lives of Black youth. In other words, the absenteeism of a Black father might refer to his irregular or nonexistent presence. But it should not imply the absence of one or more positive male role models. A host of uncles, cousins, and close friends who become fictive relatives might provide a nurturing image of manhood for one or many households, essentially mitigating the loss of a single male parent. This is not to suggest that such networks can supplant the natural father. It does illustrate, however, how maleness as a vital component for balanced families need not emerge from a single home. By the same token, it does not stand to reason that the mere presence of the father (or mother, for that matter) fore-shadows a well-adjusted household, either. It is an unfortunate fact that two-parent households might be more dysfunctional than single-parent ones.[45] African

Americans and African immigrants in Harlem, however, share a concept of an extended family. They also imagine it quite differently.

When West African Muslim migrants talk about their families back home with outsiders, they are forced to rethink their own traditional categories. "For Malinke people," Mariam says, explaining the notion of family in Côte d'Ivoire, "we don't have cousin. It is brother or sister, no cousin! Over there, when you say, 'My cousin,' they say, 'Oh! You're white now! You have a cousin?' No! It's brother, brother, or brother, sister."

"This is pretty much Malinke?" I ask.

"Everybody," Mariam says. "But the family thing, that is for Muslim people. You know, when I saw the American people's behavior, I'm not surprised."

"Why is that?"

"I'm not surprised," she repeats, "because the Christian people in my country, they live a little bit like American people. They think only about their [immediate] family. They're not thinking about uncles, aunties, cousin. No! Only Muslim people think like this. That's our education."

For Mariam, the designation *cousin* creates too much distance for the communal character of extended family. Since it is typical for African Muslims in countries such as Côte d'Ivoire to share one large house with aunts and uncles, their offspring, grandparents, other relatives (blood and imagined), cowives in polygynous marriages, and even close associates, all of the children in the household are considered the brothers and sisters of one another. That is, for the sake of a cohesive family unit, they are all customarily viewed as siblings with no further distinction. By the same token, all adults are equally responsible for parenting a child, regardless of the genetic link between the youngster and the adult. But this arrangement doesn't imply inflexibility. Rather, other factors such as age within a system of intergenerational relations can alter kinship categories.

During one of our conversations, Khady says, "When I first came, one of my cousins—" She stops abruptly to address a cultural gaffe. "I call him 'uncle,' but from the American way, you call him 'cousin.' This is the African way."

"You call your cousin 'uncle'?" I ask. "Why is that?"

"Because in this country, what they call cousin is cousin, but sometimes, what we call uncle you guys call cousin. When I talk to my [American] friends, they say, 'Oh, this is my cousin.' But to us, it's not your cousin. It's an uncle."

"It's an uncle?" I repeat, wrinkling my forehead.

"Yeah," she replies.

"For us," I say, "the uncle is either your mother's—"

"Brother!" she interjects. "OK, but that's the *real* uncle. We also have that. But to us, sometimes just an older person is like an uncle to you, because you respect him. If I find that someone is older, and I don't know his name, and I don't want to disrespect him, I say, 'Oh, my uncle,' and he will answer, because he knows he's older than me. It's about respect."

At the same time, "real" uncles are often expected to be more than just congenial males in the bloodline. The cultural logic of what constitutes family is based on a wide range of shared obligations and mutual concerns. The maintenance of family is not the sole duty of a single couple and their offspring but extends to other relatives and the larger community. "Back home," Khady announces, "you're not raised by only one person. You're raised by a family! You see, in Africa, family is bigger, it's wider than in America. And family is not about parents and kids. It's about aunts, uncles, and even neighbors. Everybody must correct the kids, when they see something wrong, and his own parents have nothing to say about that. You understand?" Khady explains that "everybody knows how it works, because life is not only organized in small groups—small families like Western communities. You know? If you touch someone, everybody is concerned. You're even going to see someone coming from far away, you know, asking for reparation and demanding that a wrong deed be corrected."

"Why do you think this is important?" I ask.

"Responsibility," she says. "It is not just a responsibility for his kids or for his wife—because life is not limited to that. Life is wider! So everybody has to do what he can."[46]

A Masjid Touba official performs the role of uncle or community elder. (Photo Zain Abdullah)

While the pronouncements of Abdoulaye, Mariam, and Khady speak to grand notions of social morality and collective rectitude where the all-too-familiar "village" raises a child dictum is recognized, it is crucial here not to romanticize the process or underestimate how women and young people fare under these systems. The extended family is clearly a central part of the social structure in much of West Africa, including Senegal and Côte d'Ivoire.[47] But many are troubled by a familial system in which the coupling of institutionalized patriarchy and age handicap women (especially since many women marry men more than twice their age), adolescents, and even adult children. Because of the weakness or lack of social services in many African countries, working women in both rural and urban areas and industrious children provide a valuable safety net for aging relatives and destitute families. Still, African customary laws and sexist readings of Islamic codes have tended to support male dominance over women, even reducing their rights of inheritance.[48] While South Africa began to advance efforts to enact legislation for the rights of children in the 1990s, this is the exception on the continent. Some argue that greater access to technology and globalization is weakening the stronghold of male supremacy and seniority. Rather than relying on the knowledge of older gatekeepers, some are finding that the "acquisition of education and of 'information' has overtaken the experience of age."[49] To be sure, familial structure in Senegal alone is not simple. And major differences in family life exist, from monogamy to polygyny, between rural and urban locales, across numerous ethnic customs, and gender relations can differ significantly between a husband and a wife within each category.[50]

In Harlem, family matters in different ways. But what tends to matter less is any strict notion of blood ties or direct ancestry. In Senegal, consanguinity or a blood relationship is in absolute terms no requirement for kinship, and many see Black Americans in Harlem as a part of a larger family, and, when possible, they extend mentorship and care the way a relative would.[51]

"I used to have friends, and their mother used to drink a lot," Khady says. "I used to go to their house and talk to their mothers like I'm the mother. That time I was young, and you should not do this. I said, 'If you're drinking so much, how's your daughter going to become?' They would say, 'Yes, but, you know, my husband do this.' I said, 'Forget about your husband—he's gone.' She used to fight with the daughter, every single day, and she's going to call the police, she going to throw her out. I said, 'Don't do that, this is your only daughter.' So then I reach the daughter. It took a long time, but it was the first time she ever hugged her mother. They both cried for maybe twenty minutes." Khady describes her conversation with a Black teenager about her sexual activity. "I said to her, 'These days, men can cook, they can clean, they pay rent, they work for themselves. So, there's only one thing men don't have. It's you! And if you make yourself cheap, who can give you something important he would want?' I said, 'Do you love him?' She says, 'Yeah.' I say, 'Then make sure you're very important to him.' She says, 'How do you do it?' I said, 'Don't sleep with him! If you do already, stop! If he love you, he's going to come back. If he don't love you, he don't come back, and that mean he just want to use you.' They still want me to go to their house today. Yeah. It's a blessing, I think."

While there are many conflicts between African Muslim migrants and Black residents in Harlem, there are also many collaborations, spaces where they are finding ways to connect as family. Family matters, but it matters differently from what is commonly understood in the Western sense (not that American or European notions of family have been simple, either). During difficult times, both African and African American communities need flexible and cooperative familial struc-tures—especially when they cannot find the assistance they require from state or federal agencies. And it is for this reason, if no other, that the family will always matter. As we will see, this fact continues to give them hope, although their sense of it is somewhat different.

9

Epilogue: In Pursuit of Hope

In a commencement speech she gave at Simmons College, novelist Amy Tan offered a few writing tips.[1] Rather than a typical talk about the state of the world and the grand potential of new graduates in it, she hoped her approach would force her audience to think more deeply about their lives. She urged students to focus in their writing on what she believed were the important questions. Any good story, Tan argued, has a moral, encouraging us to ask one or two major questions about our humanity and the meaning of life: "What is love?" "What is loss?" "What is happiness?" or "What is faith?" These are the things that appear to matter most. They are the stuff of life. In thinking about this, I wonder what big question would emerge in this story about West African Muslims in the United States. That is, at this unique stage of their sojourn in Harlem, what matters most? What are the big questions that animate their presence in America? When I ask this question directly, most respondents talk about their "family." Many others discuss their "struggle" in New York. And quite a few raise concerns about "unity" and the need to better avail themselves of the opportunities before them. But what stands out for me is the notion of hope. It is an idea that seems to encompass their responses and tap into the core of my observations. But what does hope mean in this context? And what difference does it make in their lives at this moment?

America itself is "selling hope," according to one Senegalese Muslim. And thousands have migrated to its shores in search of it. This is where we return to my original point that African Muslims are a new blues people in Harlem. A major thrust of the blues is to force us to acknowledge our plight in the world. When one is facing hard times, the blues impulse is to bear witness to the struggle and name the difficulties. But to say that African Muslims are a blues people is not to associate them with musical blues artists. Nor do I mean to speak of them and their trials as literary scholars speak of blues poems or a blues voice in literature, though what African Muslims face in America could certainly include elements from both.[2] Their religious practices incorporate a blues sensibility because the blues are rooted in their day-to-day activities. Their fight for a better life, struggles for spiritual fulfillment, workplace conflicts, and battles to maintain families near and far reflect their blues story. But it is a blues story that is intimately linked to hope. Some might believe that the blues are only about despair. "They [the blues] are despair," theologian James H. Cone argues, "only in the sense that there is no attempt to cover up reality. . . . But there is also hope in what Richard Wright calls the 'endemic capacity to live.' This hope provided the strength to survive, and also an openness to the intensity of life's pains without being destroyed by them."[3] African Muslims are imbued with this blues-drenched sense of hope. For them, struggle is a prerequisite of faith. But they find solace in the fact that hope is intimately connected to the blues they encounter.

In the Western tradition, philosophical debates rage over the differences among ultimate hope, fundamental hope, ordinary hope, or absolute hope and how these varieties differ from notions of desire, expectant waiting, or optimism.[4] But this is typically a secular, mundane analysis of the topic, one divorced from spiritual yearning. By contrast, Muslim scholars such as Seyyed Hossein Nasr claim that because Islamic philosophy has remained connected to religion, its exploration of the term has an otherworldly dimension.[5] "Those who believe," the Qur'an states, "and those who suffer migration and exile [*hijrah*] and struggle in the path of God—they have *hope* [*rajaa'*] of the mercy of God; and God is all forgiving, all merciful" (2:218). Just as this Qur'anic passage addresses the trials of migration and the expectation of hope, African Muslim life in Harlem represents the combination of a blues reality, religious yearning, and hope.

As global forces and new technologies continue to shrink our world, making it easier to migrate to Western nations such as the United States, the West African Muslim population in cities like New York will grow exponentially. This ongoing migration augments their numbers and complexity, and since many are unable to return after their arrival, their exile foreshadows the possibility that the first generation will remain dominant, at least for now. While earlier migrants have become entrenched in Harlem and are discovering alternative ways to enter new social sectors, a constant flow of newcomers will undoubtedly stretch the limits of local *masjids*, African associations, and state and municipal agencies. Moreover, the politics of poverty and governmental corruption in many African countries appears to fuel an exodus from the continent, exacerbating a seemingly implacable brain drain, a process by which Africa's most talented professionals abandon their countries for more lucrative opportunities abroad. Still, most African Muslims migrating to New York City are unskilled or semiskilled laborers. Even educated migrants without adequate competence in English or Western credentials are forced to work their way up the socioeconomic ladder. And without the proper orientation to an Anglophone world and American life, all will quite conceivably face an arduous reception upon their arrival, unless receiving communities, African Islamic organizations, and community fellowships are able to pick up the slack. Easing this initial phase of migration, however, hardly seems likely, especially when newcomers work around the clock and are put to work the first or second day after they arrive. Not only do their job schedules prevent them from adequately improving their English, but most are also trapped within the ethnic enclaves of their countrymen and -women and rarely find chances to acclimate themselves to the larger community.

Besides remitting thousands of dollars to build multilevel homes or expand health clinics in their countries of origin, many African Muslims are beginning to shift their interest toward a more viable future for Africa. And more are talking about ways to invest in the continent, for example, by setting up businesses that might forestall massive emigration in the future. For African immigrants charged with caring for their families abroad, the sense of hope is a very active one and obviously transnational. While some talk about returning with newly acquired health skills as a way to give back to underdeveloped areas, others contemplate ways to bring back a "modern" work ethic, allowing them to operate well beyond traditional business hours. Armed with new cosmopolitan sensibilities and global resources, African professionals in the diaspora appear to be gaining for themselves what Matt Meyer and Elavie Ndura-Ouédraogo call "seeds of new hope."[6] There is also a growing remorse among those who left good jobs or sold their homes to pay for the journey. And with major fluctuations in the American economy, more than a few have begun to question the logic of their stay abroad, not to mention the huge cost (emotional and otherwise) they pay to reap the opportunities they seek. As Muslim migrants faced with daunting challenges, their religious practices ('amal or khidma) and faith (iman) produce the hope (rajaa') that they need to survive and succeed.

In a post-9/11 world, Africans have begun to close ranks with other Muslims (mostly at the behest of their Arab and South Asian counterparts). But this does not mean that sectarian differences are nonexistent.[7] In fact, the theological or ethnic divisions among Muslims in America are inevitable, particularly given the fact that these immigrants come from numerous countries and represent even more ethnicities. But the persistence of such a politically charged climate could jeopardize the stability and peaceful coexistence of Muslims and their neighbors, especially if there are conflicting messages about the nature of Islamic practice or the place of Muslims in American society. And West African Muslims have come under much closer scrutiny prior to migration and during their time in the United States. More strenuous background checks for Africans with noticeably Muslim names have slowed down the processing of visas considerably. In Harlem, many report feelings of angst followed by bouts of depression, when pundits publicly excoriate their religion and its prophet, essentially charging all Muslims with outright terrorism or, at the very least, belonging to a hate-filled faith.

Bintou, from Senegal, now speaks of a "double paranoia." On the one hand, she used to read her Arabic Qur'an on the bus or train before the 9/11 attacks, just as one might see a Christian reading a pocket-sized Bible while in transit. Given the high alert of a post-9/11 world, however, she has become extremely nervous, discontinuing the practice altogether to avoid suspicion. On the other hand, when she travels to Muslim countries abroad and is asked to present her American passport, she suffers the indignation of those opposed to the escalation of an American-led global war on terror. Public condemnation is weighty enough for any immigrant, but it is especially daunting for these newcomers who are already fearful of criminal violence, racial profiling, or police brutality, in addition to a widespread anti-Muslim backlash. By the same token, African *masjids* were completely filled or overflowing in the weeks immediately following the attacks. Apparently, many more have chosen to enter the fray by "Stamping the Earth with the Name of Allah," as Pnina Werbner would have it, or coming out to stake their claim for their faith.[8] In this regard, West Africans have also actively sought to educate the community and local authorities about tolerance and nonviolence in Islam. They are also working with federal agencies as the first line of defense against terrorism, albeit with some caution against the possibility of entrapment and community suspicion.[9] These actions illustrate their ongoing efforts to defend their religion against what they feel are gross misrepresentations from both outsiders and members.

With the high cost of upscale development and rising rents, African *masjids* struggle to remain in a gentrified Harlem. Unless they are able to take advantage of lowering prices resulting from the recent economic crisis, there doesn't appear to be any relief in sight. Because of religious restrictions, they have chosen not to acquire interest-bearing loans, and this has stretched their resources to the limit. Most *masjids* have building funds, and while one community reportedly offered a landlord a quarter of a million dollars in cash to acquire a building, many property owners are holding out for more money, since even decaying storefronts are now worth nearly two million dollars—buildings that were, according to one Realtor, purchased for around four hundred thousand dollars two decades ago. The irony, of course, is that it was African entrepreneurs and their religious institutions that greatly helped to revive the area and subsequently to attract middle- and upper-class buyers and investors. If the closing of Masjid Salaam on 116th Street is any indication of the future, what will remain in its place once African Muslims are completely pushed out? As it stands now, members of Salaam decided to join their sister *masjid* at Aqsa in order to stave off mounting expenses. But it is hard to imagine how these *masjids* will be able to continue paying high rents every month. The hope is that they will be able to stay in Harlem, and they have been desperately seeking a solution. Without bank support or the help of other financial institutions, even vacant lots are outside their price range. With African cuisine, clothing, entertainment, social events, and a round of Islamic activity within easy reach, they say that West Harlem has become like Senegal, Côte d'Ivoire, or Guinea. Their extended families, the ones for whom they work so hard, are the only missing element. But now much of this is slowly being undermined.

The Murids at Masjid Touba were advised in the mid-1980s to buy their four-story brownstone, and they purchased it from Balozi Harvey, an African American Murid convert and past president of the Murid Islamic Community of America, with approximately six hundred thousand dollars in cash. As they continue to get settled in their newly renovated space, the Murids already have plans to find a larger place to accommodate their fast-growing community. Because of their deep religious commitment and strong work ethic, which, according to Scott L. Malcomson, "can make Protestants look like pikers," the Murids will most likely continue to make economic strides and, by strengthening their transnational networks, secure a better place for themselves in the U.S. economy.[10] With the influx of many more Murids from Senegal, the earning potential of the community will undoubtedly increase. Their hierarchical leadership style also improves their efforts to galvanize the resources they need not only to survive as a viable religious community but also to foster new growth and development. But while Harlem is the point of entry for most African Muslims, many are relocating to other major cities such as Philadelphia, Atlanta, Houston, and Los Angeles. In fact, at the annual Cheikh Amadou Bamba Day parades, delegations from these and other places are well represented, and the whole affair resembles a national convention, with each group lined up behind its regional sign. Although Murid communities are springing up across the nation, their religious and organizational center remains in Touba, Senegal. This fact will most likely afford them a tremendous opportunity to continue mobilizing group members as they seek greater integration into American society.

Besides the diligent work of street vendors and traders, Murid intellectuals and professionals have been organized in New York since the late 1980s.[11] And they have been working to introduce Muridiyya to the American middle class, which could accelerate their incorporation into the mainstream. But conflicts over interpretations of Muridism and Bamba's teachings, especially as they relate to hereditary

After combining *masjids*, members of Salaam and Aqsa find their blues impulse and seek new hope in Harlem. (Photo Soulaymane Konate)

With a global network and members nationwide, Murids in America continue to make strides toward integration. (Photo Zain Abdullah)

leadership reserved for Bamba's descendants, might bring about some changes in their organizational structure and how their message is understood. Some see Bamba's message as an "unfinished prophecy," in the words of Senegalese scholar Mamadou Diouf.[12] This class distinction, I would argue, has a direct impact on how Muridiyya is practiced and realized in America. Unlike the formidable educated class in France, a Murid intelligentsia is just emerging in America. A growing contingent of professors and intellectuals is beginning to publish in English and disseminate ideas to the American public. At the same time, a working-class force from the brotherhood has struggled to maintain and promote traditional interpretations of Muridism. While some change is perhaps inevitable, West African Murids will undoubtedly remain attached to the conventional wisdom they have inherited from Touba.

It is evident that West African Muslims will continue reinventing their religious and cultural traditions in the United States. What is less apparent is the result this will yield. While West African Murids have already developed a presence for themselves, one they transported from Senegal and reshaped in New York, their Africanness is heavily nuanced with Islamic and Black overtones that appear to operate on a somewhat equal footing. Other African *masjids*, however, appear much more universalistic, attempting to foreground an Islamic orthodoxy against the backdrop of an African ethos. Appropriating this type of religious orientation is perhaps understandable, especially when we consider the premigration status of many Africans from *masjids* with Ivoirian members. Islam helped to delineate differences between them—as Muslim minorities in their own countries—and their Christian and ethnic counterparts. Moreover, appealing to a universal Islam helped them transcend their own internal fissures. In the Harlem context, their appeal to an "ummatic" or global Islam will most likely continue, since their communities are much more ethnically diverse than the Wolof-based Murids.[13] Even so, it will be interesting to see what forms their identities take as they become more ensconced in Black locales across America.

Despite conflicts between Blacks and Africans in Harlem, African Muslims are marrying American Muslims as well as some Black and Latino Christians. And while cultural differences do point to serious fault lines between them, African Americans and continental Africans are forging alliances. Old tensions appear to be waning. At the same time, these rifts must not be trivialized or reduced to mere misunderstandings, problems to be solved through meet-and-greet sessions. Each group has its own relationship with municipal and state agencies, wrestles with its unique social position, and manages competing worldviews. All of this precludes quick fixes or simple solutions. Still, West African Muslims claim that they are "not going anywhere." And there are clear indications that whether they clash, pass each other in the night, or actively work together, they are certainly learning each other's ways. But with the fast pace of gentrification under way, there is no telling who will be able to stay in Harlem. While these problems may appear intractable, some believe that the solution lies with the second generation.

One major question that African immigrant families face is whether to send their children to Africa once they reach school age. African Muslim parents obviously want their children to have the proper religious upbringing, and they also talk about making sure they are raised with specific African values. Others argue that since their children were born in New York and have already begun their young lives in America, they "belong" in the United States. Because they still want their children to experience the culture of their parents, they try to send them home for extended summer visits. There are clearly problems on both sides of the issue. For the second generation remaining in the United States, their parents cannot be certain that their Islamic practices will be transferred, especially when African Muslims are marrying Americans (both Muslims and non-Muslims). Even for those who bring brides to New York from their home countries, pressures to maintain a two-parent income have undermined the necessary time needed to pass on traditions.

For some, polygyny (having a wife in the United States and another in Senegal or Côte d'Ivoire) is the answer. Still, this does not solve the problem. Many immigrants fail to realize that when they come to the United States for its economic or educational opportunities, they, too, are being transformed in the process. The extent to which this change happens might be debatable. Nonetheless, while parents are adjusting to life abroad, their children are raised by relatives back home with old-country ways, and, accordingly, major problems often occur when they are reunited.[14] On the other hand, most African children attend public schools, and many have encountered their own problems deflecting Black prejudice against Africans. In fact, the situation became so bad that the *Umoja* Media Project, under the auspices of the *Harlem* Children's Zone, had to be created to help dispel stereotypes and ease tensions. This was frequent during the early period, but things appear to be getting better.

For most West African Muslim associations in the diaspora, parent organizations already existed in the country of origin. But the leadership structure of African Muslims from Côte d'Ivoire, Guinea, Mali, and a few other countries is more horizontal and decentralized. This is not to suggest, however, that they have not formed important alliances. And because they face such a hostile economy and harsh political climate, there is every reason to believe that they will form even tighter bonds and reach out to communities with other ethnic or religious affiliations. To this end, they have already created a loosely organized national association designed to mobilize West African Muslims under a single umbrella. As more become permanent residents and U.S. citizens, they will become concerned with their political rights and civic duties. The political campaign of Sadique Wai is a case in point. In 2001, Wai, a Sierra Leonean Muslim and reportedly the first continental African to run for political office in the United States, was supported by a West African Muslim leadership group called Association des Imams Africains de New York (Association of African Imams of New York). During a meeting, the members agreed that a *masjid*-sponsored voter-registration drive for a West African Muslim candidate was not only important but crucial for their continued survival. While Wai's city council bid for the 35th District seat in central Brooklyn was unsuccessful, his run signaled increasing involvement in the political process and the power dynamics of the city.

At the same time, African *imams* participate in a *majlis ash-shura*, an Islamic consultative body addressing a number of issues affecting Muslims citywide. There appears to be little coordination between Murids and other African Muslims in Harlem, but given strenuous times and their shared religious affiliation, more collaboration is likely. For now, the Murid civic organization, L'Association des Sénégalais d'Amérique (the Senegalese Association of America), mainly caters to group members, and its efforts are geared toward transnational ties between Senegal and the United States. While the African American-led Mosque of Islamic Brotherhood and Masjid Aqsa have a system for a rotating *khateeb* (speaker) for the *jum'ah* prayer, whereby they sometimes give sermons at each other's *masjid*, the Murids have established the African and African American Relations Committee. Moreover, a Senegalese-sponsored African Cultural Committee holds an annual event featuring traditional music and dance as a way to expose the Harlem community to African culture and build bridges. By the same token, Imam Konate from Masjid Aqsa, for example, has joined with some neighborhood groups to improve relations and increase their profile in the larger community.

All in all, the attempts by African Muslims to sustain viable *masjids* and religious practices, to incorporate themselves into the city's social and cultural fabric, and to maintain relations abroad demonstrate their need to survive and their constant pursuit of hope. Beyond this, the presence of African Muslims in Harlem and other U.S. cities has changed our world forever. In the process, they, too, have changed. The diversity they bring to our religious landscape challenges our sense of the sacred and how we have come to understand Islam and Muslims. Their presence as new Black immigrants also promises to frustrate our notions of race overall and, in particular, Blackness itself. No matter what the future holds for them and their neighbors, African Muslims—and the Black Mecca they have created—tell yet another story of what it means to live, struggle, and hope in Harlem, U.S.A.

Glossary

Al-hamdu lillah	Praise Allah; God is the sole source of all good fortune.
Allah	Arabic name for God; the one God according to strict monotheism.
'amal	Work, action, practice.
'amal saalih	Religiously sanctioned actions; righteous behavior for a common good.
asr	Afternoon; the afternoon prayer; considered the middle prayer of the day.
As-salaamu 'alaykum	May [God's] peace be with you; one of Allah's divine names is *as-salaam*, "the Peace."
athan	The call to prayer; also spelled *adhan* or *azan*.
ayah	A single verse in the Qur'an; literally means "a sign" or "a symbol."
baraka	Blessing, grace, or divine favor; divine fortune believed to emanate from a Sufi or spiritual master.

Barcelone aw barzakh	Barcelona or the grave; the word *aw* means "or," and *barzakh* means "grave" in Arabic.
boubou	A wide-sleeved robe worn mostly in West Africa; also known by other names such as *agbada* in Yoruba and *babariga* in Hausa.
Ça va?	French greeting for "How are you?" or "How's everything?"
Ça va bien?	French reply for *Ça va?* meaning "It goes well" or "I'm fine."
cheikh	An honorific title for a male elder but indicates high respect for one's learning or nobility; also rendered *sheikh, sheik, shaykh,* or *shaikh*
daanu leer	A Wolof term for spiritual ecstasy.
dahira	A Murid religious circle or gathering for performing certain religious acts or devotional service; also written *daira* or *da'ira*.
dar al-harb	The place of war; non-Islamic territory, lands hostile to Muslims; translated as "outsider" for the Harlem context.
dar al-Islam	The place of peace; Islamic territory, lands under Muslim control; translated as "insider" for the Harlem context.
da'wa	Religious propagation; Muslim missionary work.
dua	A personal or collective invocation or prayer to Allah.
du'at	Muslim missionaries; singular *daa'e*.
fajr	Dawn or dawn prayer.
Fula	A language spoken by the Fulbe or Fulani people in Guinea and other West African countries.
griot	A West African praise singer, poet, or oral historian; pronounced "gree-o"; another term is the Manding *jeli*.
hadith	A saying of the Prophet Muhammad; also a general reference to the various collections of recorded behavior on what the Prophet said, did, or approved after observing an action without comment.
hajj	The annual pilgrimage to Mecca, Islam's holiest site; a religious visit required of all Muslims once in a lifetime if able.
halal	Religiously permissible; lawful products or actions.
haram	Religiously impermissible; unlawful or sinful actions.
hijab	To cover, separate, or screen; a Muslim female head covering.

hijrah   Migration; the first exile of Muslims in Mecca to Medina, a journey marking the beginning of the Muslim calendar. Also spelled *hijra* or *hegira*.

imam   Religious leader; pronounced "e-mame"; someone who leads the prayer but may also perform clerical duties like a minister, particularly in Western nations, or a divinely sanctioned leader like a priest among the Shia.

insha-allah   If Allah wills; an oft-repeated phrase recognizing the divine decree in all events.

iqama   The position for standing in prayer; the call to stand for prayer.

isha   Night; night prayer and the last one of the day before *fajr*.

Islam   Means peace and religious submission; monotheistic belief system beginning with the prophetic revelation of Muhammad ibn Abdullah in Arabia in 610; believed to be a continuation of the original divine message of Abrahamic faiths such as Judaism and Christianity; reportedly has one billion followers worldwide.

jalabiyya   Long, flowing robe, also called *thobe*.

jihad   Struggle, effort; a struggle against bad habits or unjust conditions.

jihad al-akbar   The greatest struggle; an internal effort against evil and destructive temptations or personal behaviors.

jihad al-asghar   The lesser or secondary struggle; an external effort to correct social injustice or community wrongdoing.

jum'ah   Friday, congregation prayer; the weekly communal service replacing *thuhr*, the noon prayer; includes a sermon.

khassaïd   The religious poetry of Cheikh Amadou Bamba.

khidma   Religious service to others; helping others for divine favor.

khimar   Muslim female headscarf.

khutba   Sermon given at *jum'ah* but also at other religious events.

kufi   Various cloth hats with no brim worn by Muslim men; part of traditional costume but carries no religious obligation.

le sans-papiers   The paperless; French term for undocumented migrants.

maghrib   Evening or sunset prayer.

Malinke   People of Côte d'Ivoire and other West African countries who speak various languages of the Mande linguistic branch such as Bambara, Soninke, and Dyula (pronounced "jula").

Mame Diarra Bousso	The mother of Cheikh Amadou Bamba; *Mame* is an honorific title; Diarra is pronounced "jara."
Mangi fe	I'm fine; reply to *Nangadef?* in Wolof, a major language in Senegal.
masha-allah	Allah is pleased; it pleases Allah.
masjid	Place of prostration or worship for Muslims; *mosque* is a non-Arabic term for *masjid*; plural is *masajid*.
musaafir	Traveler.
musalla	Prayer area; also prayer rug.
Muslim	Follower of Islam; words such as *Mohammedan* are incorrect.
mut'a	Time-limited and contracted marriage.
najs	Religiously impure substances such as urine, feces, and blood.
Nangadef?	How are you?; a greeting in Wolof, Senegal's popular language.
nikah	Conventional and contracted marriage without time limitations.
passeurs	Human traffickers.
pateras	Small fishing boats; also called *pirogues* (local dialect), *cayucos* in Spanish, and *lothios*.
qadr	Divine destiny or providence.
qalun	A style of Qur'an recitation with an African tone; it is the third most popular style in some parts of North Africa.
Qur'an	The holy book of Islam; with 114 chapters, it was revealed over a twenty-two-year period to Muhammad ibn Abdullah from 610 to 632; believed to be the final revelation after others like the Suhuf of Abraham, the Torah, the Psalms, and the Gospel.
rajaa'	Hope; hope for divine mercy.
rizq	Livelihood; sustenance.
sadaqa jara	Perpetual charity; good deeds for which one is rewarded in the hereafter; Arabic rendering *sadaqa jaariya*.
Salafi	A member of an ultraconservative movement arguing that the "ancestors" of early Islam should be followed as exemplary models for correct belief and behavior; the term *salaf* means "predecessor" or "ancestor."
salah	Formal prayer; the five daily prayers performed by Muslims; also written as *salat*.

serigne An Wolof honorific title like *cheikh* for people of great religious merit or nobility.

Sufi A person who follows the principles of Sufism or a particular order or *tariqa* (spiritual group or path) in Sufism.

Sufism Islam mysticism; the branch of Islam focusing on spiritual development, purity of heart, and closeness to God; *tasawwuf* in Arabic.

sunnah Customary practices of the Prophet Muhammad; religious acts that are voluntary such as extra prayers or fasting outside Ramadan.

Sunni Orthodox Islam/orthodox Muslim; the Muslim majority believing it adheres to the example of the Prophet and his early followers.

sura A chapter of the Qur'an; also written *surah* or *surat*.

taalibe Disciple; student or follower of a religious tradition.

takbir To say "*Allahu Akbar*," "God is the Greatest!"; to magnify God.

taqiyya God-consciousness; also a Shia concept allowing believers to conceal their faith when under threat.

thikr Remembrance; reciting a religious formula; also spelled *zikr* or *dhikr*.

thuhr Noon prayer; also spelled *zuhr*.

ummah The Muslim community worldwide; also the early faith community in Medina.

Wa 'alaykum salaam And may [God's] peace be with you; a response to *As-salaamu 'alaykum.*

Wolof The native language of the Wolof people; they are prominent in Senegal and also reside in Gambia and Mauritania.

wudu Ablution; ritual washing prior to prayer.

zawaj al-misyar Marriage in transit.

zawaj al-'urfi Informal/customary marriage.

Notes

CHAPTER 1

1. Sanna Feirstein, *Naming New York: Manhattan Places and How They Got Their Names* (New York: New York University Press, 2001), 153.

2. Amy Waldman, "Killing Heightens the Unease Felt by Africans in New York," *New York Times*, February 14, 1999, A1; Sam Roberts, "More Africans Enter US Than in Days of Slavery," *New York Times*, February 21, 2005, A1.

3. Ralph Ellison, "Richard Wright's Blues," *Antioch Review* 5:2 (Summer 1945): 199. This essay also appears in Ralph Ellison, *Shadow and Act* (New York: Vintage International, 1995).

4. Gomez asserts that "of the estimated 481,000 Africans imported into British North America during the slave trade, nearly 255,000 came from areas influenced by Islam. It is therefore reasonable to conclude that Muslims arrived in North America by the thousands, if not tens of thousands." See Michael A. Gomez, *Black Crescent: The Experience and Legacy of African Muslims in the Americas* (New York: Cambridge University Press, 2005), 166. For similar works, see Michael A. Gomez, *Exchanging Our Country Marks: The Transformation of African Identities in the Colonial and Antebellum South* (Chapel Hill, N.C.: University of North Carolina Press, 1998); Allan D. Austin, *African Muslims in Antebellum America: A Sourcebook* (New York: Garland, 1984) and, significantly reduced from this 759-page book, Allan D. Austin, *African Muslims in Antebellum America: Transatlantic Stories and Spiritual Struggles* (New York: Routledge, 1997); Sylviane A. Diouf, *Servants of Allah: African Muslims Enslaved in the Americas* (New York: New York University Press, 1998).

5. Gomez, *Exchanging Our Country Marks*, 79. For a fuller account, Gomez refers to William S. McFeely, *Frederick Douglass* (New York: Norton, 1991).

6. Diouf, *Servants of Allah*, 200.

7. For cultures in which scriptures are chanted or rhythmically preached, as in many Black churches, the influence of religious practice on popular music is quite conceivable. This is particularly the case when we consider how a number of Blacks began singing in church and became popular artists who appropriated religious elements, such as Ray Charles. For example, see Teresa L. Reed, *The Holy Profane: Religion in Black Popular Music* (Lexington: University Press of Kentucky, 2003). For the connection between West Africa and the blues, see Paul Oliver, *Savannah Syncopators: African Retentions in the Blues* (New York: Stein and Day, 1970); Gerhard Kubik, *Africa and the Blues* (Jackson: University Press of Mississippi, 1999); Ronald Radano and Philip V. Bohlman, eds., *Music and the Racial Imagination* (Chicago: University of Chicago Press, 2000). For the link between Islam and the blues, see Fatima El Shibli, "Islam and the Blues," *Souls* 9:2 (2007): 162–170; Jonathan Curiel, *Al' America: Travels through America's Arab and Islamic Roots* (New York: New Press, 2008).

8. LeRoi Jones (Amiri Baraka), *Blues People: Negro Music in White America* (New York: Perennial, 1999 [1963]), ix.

9. Cornel West, *Hope on a Tightrope: Words & Wisdom* (Carlsbad, Calif.: SmileyBooks, 2008), 114.

10. Ellison, "Richard Wright's Blues," 199. Cornel West would refer to this Black sense of resilience as a tragicomic blues or "the ability to laugh and retain a sense of life's joy—to preserve hope even while staring in the face of hate and hypocrisy." See Cornel West, *Democracy Matters: Winning the Fight against Imperialism* (New York: Penguin Books, 2004), 16, 21.

11. The announcement "*Sadaqa Jara*" is based on a prophetic tradition in Islam, which refers to the Arabic phrase *sadaqa jaariya*, or the kind of charity that reaps heavenly rewards long after one dies.

12. Based on a strict interpretation of an Islamic tradition, it appears that Muslims have been urged not to clap in applause the way pre-Islamic Arabs would do in praise of their idols. Snapping the fingers is a compromise. It is interesting to note that snapping for applause is also done by audiences at poetry performances. However, I am not aware of any connection or of how this practice started.

13. See also El Shibli, "Islam and the Blues," 165–168; Curiel, *Al' America*, 26–27. Moreover, Dick Weissman mentions several reasons the blues have become popular: (1) guitar styles, referring to the voice as an instrument in Islam, (2) soulfulness of singing, and (3) expressiveness of lyrics. But more specifically, Islam or Arabic culture, he argues, contributed "vocal shakes" and vibrato and the lengthening of particular notes, which are both heard in the *athan* (call to prayer) five times daily and in Qur'anic recitation. See Dick Weissman, *Blues: The Basics* (New York: Routledge, 2005), 1, 10.

14. Sue Monk Kidd, *Firstlight: Early Inspirational Writings* (New York: Guideposts Books, 2006), 19.

15. Ibid., 16.

16. For a succinct explanation of multisited ethnography in anthropology, see George E. Marcus, "Ethnography in/of the World System: The Emergence of Multi-sited Ethnography," *Annual Review of Anthropology* 24 (1995): 95–117.

17. While the three African *masjids* constituted my main research sites, there are at least two others in Harlem and many more throughout New York, especially in Brooklyn, Queens, and the Bronx. For an example of how Douglas E. Foley tracked "ethnographic portraits" in his study of Mexican Americans and "Anglos" in Texas, see Douglas E. Foley,

Learning Capitalist Culture: Deep in the Heart of Tejas (Philadelphia: University of Pennsylvania Press, 1990).

18. For a discussion on using the real names of respondents, see Mitchell Duneier's "Appendix: A Statement on Method," in Mitchell Duneier, *Sidewalk* (New York: Farrar, Straus and Giroux, 1999).

19. Min Zhou, "Segmented Assimilation: Issues, Controversies, and Recent Research on the New Second Generation," in Charles Hirschman, Philip Kasinitz, and Josh DeWind, eds., *The Handbook of International Migration: The American Experience* (New York: Russell Sage Foundation, 1999).

20. For the projected growth of the American Muslim community, see Yvonne Yazbeck Haddad and John L. Esposito, *Muslims on the Americanization Path?* (Atlanta: Scholars Press, 1998).

21. Aminah Beverly McCloud, *Transnational Muslims in American Society* (Gainesville: University Press of Florida, 2006), 2; John L. Esposito, *What Everyone Needs to Know about Islam* (New York: Oxford University Press, 2002), 169. African American Muslims are estimated to represent approximately 30 percent to 40 percent of the Islamic community in the United States. Thousands of White Americans, Latinos, and Native Americans are also converting. See also Jane I. Smith, *Islam in America* (New York: Columbia University Press, 1999).

22. Barack Obama, *Dreams from My Father: A Story of Race and Inheritance*, rev. ed. (New York: Three Rivers Press, 2004). For Ellison's swearing-in ceremony, see Amy Argetsinger and Roxanne Roberts, "The Reliable Source," *Washington Post*, January 3, 2007. For a scholarly source on Jefferson's Qur'an, see Kevin J. Hayes, "How Thomas Jefferson Read the Qur'an," *Early American Literature* 39:2 (2004): 247–261. As the first Muslim to hold congressional office from Indiana, Carson assumed the seat after it became vacant upon the death of his grandmother Julia Carson. He won in a special election.

23. Jacques Barou, "In the Aftermath of Colonization: Black African Immigrants in France," in Hans C. Buechler and Judith-Maria Buechler, eds., *Migrants in Europe: The Role of Family, Labor and Politics* (New York: Greenwood Press, 1987). For an overview of African immigration to the United States, see Zain Abdullah, "West Africa," in James Ciment, ed., *Encyclopedia of American Immigration* (Armonk, N.Y.: M. E. Sharpe, 2001), 1070–1078; and Zain Abdullah, "African 'Soul Brothers' in the 'Hood: Immigration, Islam and the Black Encounter," *Anthropological Quarterly* 82:1 (Winter 2009): 41–44.

24. Donna L. Perry, "Rural Ideologies and Urban Imaginings: Wolof Immigrants in New York City," *Africa Today* 44:2 (1997): 234.

25. For an excellent history of Muridiyya in Senegal, see Cheikh Anta Babou, *Fighting the Greater Jihad: Amadu Bamba and the Founding of the Muridiyya of Senegal, 1853–1913* (Athens: Ohio University Press, 2007).

26. U.S. Bureau of the Census, *Characteristics of the Foreign-Born Population in the United States* (Washington, D.C.: U.S. Government Printing Office, 2000); U.S. Bureau of the Census, *Characteristics of the Foreign-Born Population in the United States* (Washington, D.C.: U.S. Government Printing Office, 1990); U.S. Bureau of the Census, *Current Population Survey* (Washington, D.C.: U.S. Government Printing Office, 2000).

27. Perry, "Rural Ideologies and Urban Imaginings," 229. While my research did not include Bambara speakers from Mali, it is quite evident that they are beginning to show up in sizable numbers in Harlem.

28. Scott L. Malcomson, "West of Eden: The Mouride Ethic and the Spirit of Capitalism," *Transition: An International Review* 6:3 (1996): 30; see also Cheikh Anta Babou, "Brotherhood Solidarity, Education and Migration: The Role of the Dahiras among the Murid Muslim Community of New York," *African Affairs* 101 (2002): 151–170.

29. Will Herberg, *Protestant, Catholic, Jew: An Essay in American Religious Sociology* (Garden City, N.Y.: Doubleday, 1955).

30. For the quote on Harlem as "Little Africa", see Waldman, "Killing Heightens the Unease,." Mecca, as the holiest site in Islam and the spiritual center of the Muslim world, is in Saudi Arabia, and it has been used as a metaphor (particularly among non-Muslims) to identify a place representing the core of any activity. During the Harlem Renaissance of the 1920s, Wallace Thurman dramatized Harlem by dubbing his coauthored play *Black Mecca*. See Amritjit Singh and Daniel M. Scott III, eds. *The Collected Writings of Wallace Thurman: A Harlem Renaissance Reader* (New Brunswick, NJ: Rutgers University Press, 2003), 371–75.

CHAPTER 2

1. Ed Robinson, "Rescue at Sea," *New York Post*, February 2, 2007.

2. In order to protect the identity and privacy of this volunteer, I use the name Robert as a pseudonym.

3. In *sura an-Nisaa*, or chapter 4:97, the passage states: "Lo! as for those whom the angels take [in death] while they wrong themselves, they [angels] will ask: In what were you engaged? They will say: We were oppressed in the land. They [angels] will say, 'Was not Allah's earth spacious that ye could have migrated therein?' As for such, their habitation will be hell, an evil journey's end." For a good English version of the Qur'an, see Abdullah Yusuf Ali, *The Qur'an: Text, Translation and Commentary* (Elmhurst, N.Y.: Tahrike Tarsile Qur'an, 2005).

4. One respondent told me the amount for a visa is around two thousand dollars.

5. Victoria Burnett, "To Curb Illegal Migration, Spain Offers a Legal Route," *New York Times*, August 11, 2007, http://www.nytimes.com/2007/08/11/world/europe/11spain.html.

6. Khadim Mbacké, *Sufism and Religious Brotherhoods in Senegal* (Princeton, N.J.: Markus Wiener, 2005), 67.

7. The name of the catamaran is from David Usborne, "Senegalese Men Rescued Trying to Sail to New York," *Independent*, February 3, 2007, http://www.independent.co.uk/news/world/americas/senegalese-men-rescued-trying-to-sail-to-new-york-434799.html.

8. For a story about recovered African bodies and how a Spanish couple helped to return them for burial, see Rafael Estefania, "From Shipwreck to Solidarity," BBC News, September 10, 2008, http://news.bbc.co.uk/2/hi/africa/7586597.stm.

9. Belachew Gebrewold, ed., *Africa and Fortress Europe: Threats and Opportunities* (Burlington, Vt.: Ashgate, 2007); Dirk Kohnert, "African Migration to Europe: Obscured Responsibilities and Common Misconceptions," German Institute of Global and Area Studies Working Paper 49 (May 2007): 5–24. See also BBC News, "Spain in Senegal Migration Deal," October 11, 2006, http://news.bbc.co.uk/go/pr/fr/-/2/hi/africa/6039624.stm.

10. For several news accounts on these fourteen Senegalese Muslim men, see Leslie Ann Murray, "14 Senegalese Men Search for Economic Freedom," *New York Amsterdam News*, March 29–April 2, 2007, 6; Robinson, "Rescue at Sea"; U.S. Customs and Border Patrol Protection, "Fourteen Senegalese Refugees Rescued at Sea," http://www.cbp.gov/xp/cgov/newsroom/news_releases/archives/2007_news_releases/022007/02012007_1.xml; *USA Today*, "Africans' Sea Voyage

to NYC Ends in Rescue Hundreds of Miles Offshore," February 1, 2007, http://www.usatoday.com/news/nation/2007-02-01-africans-at-sea_x.htm; Jeca Taudte, "Fourteen Senegalese Join the Exodus to Europe and Beyond," *Columbia Journalist*, May 7, 2007, http://columbiajournalist.org/article.asp?subj=international&course=The_International_Newsroom&id=1523.

11. Gebrewold, *Africa and Fortress Europe*; Kohnert, "African Migration to Europe, 5–24. See also BBC News, "Spain in Senegal Migration deal."

12. Vicky Short, "Spain Strengthens Borders against African Refugees," *World Socialist*, June 2, 1999, http://www.wsws.org.

13. Ibid.

14. Ibid.

15. A CNN quote is instructive: "More than 38,000 people have made the perilous journey across the Gulf of Aden from Somalia to Yemen during the first 10 months of this year, a 'considerable increase from the 29,500 who made the same journey during the whole of last year,' UNHCR [U.N. High Commissioner for Refugees] said Tuesday." See CNN.com, "African Refugee Situation Getting Worse, U.N. Says," November 4, 2008, http://www.cnn.com/2008/WORLD/africa/11/04/un.refugees.africa/index.html.

16. Emma Daly, "African Refugees Are Rescued after 2-Week Ordeal," *New York Times*, February 22, 2003, http://www.nytimes.com.

17. Graham Keeley and Robert Hooper, "Grim Toll of African Refugees Mounts on Spanish Beaches," *Guardian*, July 13, 2008, http://www.guardian.co.uk/world/2008/jul/13/spain/print.

18. CNN.com, "African Refugee Situation Getting Worse."

19. Kohnert, "African Migration to Europe," 13. *Pirogues* is a word from the local dialect. They are called *cayucos* in Spanish.

20. Keeley and Hooper, "Grim Toll of African Refugees."

21. Kohnert, "African Migration to Europe," 12. See also BBS News, "Key Facts: Africa to Europe Migration," July 2, 2007, http://news.bbc.co.uk/2/hi/europe/6228236.stm. The cost ranges between one thousand and sixteen thousand euros, depending on the point of departure and the destination, but this is obviously an extremely dangerous way to travel.

22. Qur'an 2:156.

23. Meg Bortin, "Desperate Voyage, Destination Spain: For Young African, Risks Seem Worth It," *International Herald Tribune*, May 31, 2006, http://www.iht.com/articles/2006/05/28/news/senegal.php.

24. Ibid.

25. Manthia Diawara, *We Won't Budge: A Malaria Memoir* (New York: Basic Civitas Books, 2003), 169.

26. BBC News, "In Pictures: Immigrant Boats," September 11, 2006, http://news.bbc.co.uk/2/hi/in_pictures/5335062.stm.

27. Tidiane Sy, "Mother's Battle against Senegal Migration," BBC News, November 6, 2006, http://news.bbc.co.uk/2/hi/africa/6109736.stm.

28. Nicolas van de Walle, Nicole Ball, and Vijaya Ramachandram, eds., *Beyond Structural Adjustment: The Institutional Context of African Development* (New York: Palgrave Macmillan, 2003).

29. The phrase heading each chapter of the Qur'an is "*Bismillah ar-rahman ar-raheem*" ("In the Name of God, the Merciful, the Compassionate"). The English translation of these terms misses the important nuances alluded to in the text.

30. The Qur'an states, "Reverence God, through whom you demand your mutual rights, and reverence the wombs that bore you. Verily God is always watching over you" (4:1).

31. Paul Stoller, *Money Has No Smell: The Africanization of New York City* (Chicago: University of Chicago Press, 2002), 28.

32. For a discussion of the Magal and its meaning, see Christian Coulon, "The Grand Magal in Touba: A Religious Festival of the Mouride Brotherhood of Senegal," *African Affairs* 98 (1999): 195–210.

33. Manthia Diawara, *In Search of Africa* (Cambridge, Mass.: Harvard University Press, 1998), 99–100.

34. BBC News, "Key Facts."

35. For enslaved Africans in early America, the Middle Passage—the transatlantic slave trade linking Africa with the New World—was considered a bridge back home. There was a belief that upon death, the African soul would fly back to Africa along this bridge. See Carl Pedersen, "Sea Change: The Middle Passage and the Transatlantic Imagination," in Werner Sollors and Maria Diedrich, eds., *The Black Columbiad: Defining Moments in African American Literature and Culture* (Cambridge, Mass.: Harvard University Press, 1994).

36. Diawara, *We Won't Budge*, 226.

37. Ibid., 228.

38. The literature on the early presence of African Muslims in the Americas is growing, and several examples are very good. See Gomez, *Black Crescent*; Diouf, *Servants of Allah*; and Austin, *African Muslims in Antebellum America*.

39. For a portrait of these African Muslims in early America, see Austin, *African Muslims in Antebellum America*.

CHAPTER 3

1. Countee Cullen, "Heritage," in Manning Marable, Nishani Frazier, and John Campbell McMillian, eds., *Freedom on My Mind: The Columbia Documentary History of the African American Experience* (New York: Columbia University Press, 2003 [1925]).

2. Employers can also reinforce identity boundaries, for example, by the way they emphasize the "higher" work ethic of West Indian workers compared with that of African Americans. See Mary C. Waters, *Black Identities: West Indian Immigrant Dreams and American Realities* (Cambridge, Mass.: Harvard University Press, 1999).

3. The "perfect beat" is a hip-hop reference to what DJs and rappers are trying to achieve. See Kurt B. Reighley, *Looking for the Perfect Beat: The Art and Culture of the DJ* (New York: Pocket Books, 2000).

4. In similar versions of this story, I have used the pseudonym Rob to protect the identity of Jamal. However, because his first name is Muslim, I thought it would be a good idea to reveal this fact in the book, since it helps to demonstrate how African American culture in Harlem is heavily influenced by Islamic naming customs. For a somewhat different version, see Abdullah, "African 'Soul Brothers' in the 'Hood," or Zain Abdullah, "African 'Soul Brothers' in Harlem: Immigration, Islam, and the Black Encounter," in Manning Marable and Hishaam Aidi, eds., *Black Routes to Islam* (New York: Palgrave Macmillan, 2009).

5. Robert C. Smith, *Mexican New York: Transnational Lives of New Immigrants* (Berkeley: University of California Press, 2006), 167.

6. John L. Jackson Jr., *Harlemworld: Doing Race and Class in Contemporary Black America* (Chicago: University of Chicago Press, 2001), 43.

7. Tibbett Speer, "The Newest African Americans Aren't Black," *American Demographics* 16:1 (January 1994): 9–10.

8. Gaining access or maintaining rapport in these ethnographic situations involves a consideration of dress. So, issues of reflexivity or what kinds of cultural messages researchers bring to the fieldwork must be taken seriously.

9. For some time now, researchers have been using the term *transmigrant* instead of *immigrant*, since many migrants are no longer considered to be tied to a single society. See Nina Glick Schiller, Linda Basch, and Cristina Szanton Blanc, "From Immigrant to Transmigrant: Theorizing Transnational Migration," *Anthropological Quarterly* 68:1 (January 1995): 48–63.

10. There is substantial literature on whether immigrants hurt or help the places where they settle. For a discussion on immigration and its impact on Black residents, see Ewa Morawska, "Immigrant-Black Dissensions in American Cities: An Argument for Multiple Explanations," in Elijah Anderson and Douglas S. Massey, eds., *Problem of the Century: Racial Stratification in the United States* (New York: Russell Sage Foundation, 2001), 47–95. See also Steven Shulman, ed., *The Impact of Immigration on African Americans* (New Brunswick, N.J.: Transaction, 2004).

11. For an excellent discussion of the way Harlem is imagined and historicized as a Black space, see Jackson's *Harlemworld*, chapter 1. For Harlem as a Black capital and its gentrification, see Monique M. Taylor, *Harlem between Heaven and Hell* (Minneapolis: University of Minnesota Press, 2002).

12. For a look at the relationship between identity and place, see Steven Feld and Keith H. Basso, *Senses of Place* (Seattle: University of Washington Press, 1996). For a discussion on belonging as it relates to African identity, see Mineke Schipper, *Imagining Insiders: Africa and the Question of Belonging* (New York: Cassell, 1999).

13. See Oscar Zeta Acosta, *Revolt of the Cockroach People* (San Francisco: Straight Arrow Press, 1973), and Pedro Pietri, "Suicide Note of a Cockroach in a Low Income Project" in *Loose Joints* (Folkways Records, 1979). Current conditions in many Black neighborhoods resemble those in underdeveloped nations. Jonathan Kozol, for example, discusses the disparities between Black and White communities, describing in horrific detail how some public schools in cities such as New York have been forced to ration toilet paper. These situations are absolutely intolerable for any democracy and deplorable statistics for a wealthy nation. See Jonathan Kozol, *Savage Inequalities: Children in America's Schools* (New York: Harper Perennial, 1992).

14. For a discussion on how Malcolm X and Martin Luther King Jr. were moving ideologically toward each other before their assassinations, see the renowned Christian theologian James H. Cone's *Martin & Malcolm & America: A Dream or a Nightmare* (Maryknoll, N.Y.: Orbis Books, 1991).

15. For a review of the Nation culture in Harlem, see *The Autobiography of Malcolm X* (New York: Ballantine Books, 1999). For a history of the Nation of Islam, see Edward E. Curtis IV, *Islam in Black America: Identity, Liberation, and Difference in African-American Islamic Thought* (Albany: State University of New York Press, 2002); Richard Brent Turner, *Islam in the African American Experience*, 2nd ed. (Bloomington: Indiana University Press, 2003); Gomez, *Black Crescent*.

16. It is shocking still to find books that identify the Muslim world and exclude the marvels of West African Muslim empires, including the great learning and legacy of Timbuktu.

17. Some scholars recognize how the pluralization of Muslim practices and beliefs translates into "Islams" by the way it adapts to local places and realities. See Aziz Al-Azmeh, *Islams and Modernities*, 2nd ed. (New York: Verso, 2009); and Leif Manger, ed., *Muslim Diversity: Local Islam in Global Contexts* (Surrey, U.K.: RoutledgeCurzon, 1999).

18. The number of scholarly works on the various religious orientations of Islam among African Americans has been growing exponentially. For a survey, see, among others, Manning Marable and Hishaam Aidi, eds., *Black Routes to Islam* (New York: Palgrave Macmillan, 2009); Edward E. Curtis IV, *Black Muslim Religion in the Nation of Islam, 1960–1975* (Chapel Hill: University of North Carolina Press, 2006); Gomez, *Black Crescent*; Sherman A. Jackson, *Islam and the Blackamerican* (New York: Oxford University Press, 2005); Turner, *Islam in the African American Experience*; Robert Dannin, *Black Pilgrimage to Islam* (New York: Oxford University Press, 2002).

19. Taxi and livery drivers or gypsy cab drivers have been the biggest victims. Imam Konate and many others recount numerous stories about how they would send a body home almost daily. And the news in the street was about who was the next victim. For example, see Frank Bruni, "Invisible, and in Anguish: A Slain Driver's Service Brings Attention to Senegalese," *New York Times*, November 18, 1997, B1.

20. For some African Muslim youth, conflict with their African American peers is reason enough to start "acting" Black in order to avoid attack. By contrast, Arab Muslims with lighter complexions seeking racial inclusion could try "passing" for white and move into America's suburbs. Acting Black, however, means wearing hip-hop gear, listening to rap, walking with an exaggerated swagger, and speaking Black slang. For some, this translates into joining gangs for fast money and, undoubtedly, protection. For African Americans, the act of passing occurred mostly in the late nineteenth and early twentieth centuries. When the skin color of an African American approximated that of Whites, the former could relocate to a White neighborhood, as long as the individual's true identity would not be discovered, and lead a very different life. See Joel Williamson, *New People: Miscegenation and Mulattoes in the United States* (Baton Rouge: Louisiana State University Press, 1995). Whether passing for White or acting Black, both processes involve strategies for racial inclusion. Of course, the social rewards for either passing or acting are different.

21. The word *imam* is an Arabic term that generally translates as "leader." The Arabic plural is pronounced "a-emma." Many Arabic words are being anglicized as they are adopted in the everyday speech of English-speaking Muslims. It has become commonplace to speak of *imams* with an *s* added for pluralization. For a discussion of the emergence of Islamic English in Western societies, see Barbara Daly Metcalf, "Toward Islamic English? A Note on Transliteration," in Barbara Daly Metcalf, ed., *Making Muslim Space in North America and Europe* (Berkeley: University of California Press, 1996); and Isma'il Raji al-Faruqi, *Toward Islamic English* (Herndon, Va.: International Institute of Islamic Thought, 1986).

22. Jackson, *Harlemworld*, 43.

23. Ann Miles, *From Cuenca to Queens: An Anthropological Story of Transnational Migration* (Princeton, N.J.: Princeton University Press, 2004), 32–33.

24. Robert Moran, Gaiutra Bahadur, and Susan Snyder, "Residents Say Beating Fits Widespread Pattern," *Philadelphia Inquirer*, November 3, 2005.

25. English translations of the Qur'an vary between the use of old English and modern language. But the Arabic version remains the primary source of the holy book and serves as the sacred text of the faith.

26. Verse 13 of *sura al-hujarat* reads: "O People! We have created you from a single pair of male and female and made you all into *tribes* and *nations*, so you might know one another. Truly, the most righteous among you in the sight of Allah is the one with the most faith. And Allah is all-knowing, all-aware" (49:13).

27. Sylviane Diouf-Kamara writes about a Senegalese graduate of the University of Chicago, Mohammed Diop, who returned to the United States and started Homeland, an African products business with thirty employees and an annual sales of $8 million. See Sylviane Diouf-Kamara, "Senegalese of New York: A Model Minority?" *Black Renaissance/Renaissance Noire* 1:2 (Summer-Fall 1997).

28. As part of the fieldwork experience, ethnographers—researchers gathering data from live subjects—must be prepared to make all sorts of compromises with respondents. I've purchased dinners for people, paid for transportation tokens or cards, loaned money, given rides, made donations to causes, and, on a request from Lee, bought a lottery ticket, something some would deem un-Islamic. In *All Our Kin*, Carolyn B. Stack talks about how she had to give her respondents rides to the grocery store, which allowed her access to this population, since they would otherwise not have the time to talk to her. However, when her fieldwork was complete and she needed to write up her notes, she was forced to dispose of the car, because continued demands for rides prevented her from writing. See Carolyn B. Stack, *All Our Kin: Strategies for Survival in a Black Community* (New York: Harper & Row, 1974).

29. Ruth Frankenberg, *White Women, Race Matters: The Social Construction of Whiteness* (Minneapolis: University of Minnesota Press, 1993).

CHAPTER 4

1. This episode was described to me by Mohamed during one of our interviews.

2. In Islam, what language will be spoken in *jannah* (heaven) or the heavenly paradise in the afterlife is debatable. Based on a weak tradition, some say it will be Arabic, the language of the Qur'an. The Qur'an itself simply says there will not be any *laghaw* or idle talk but only *salaaman* (peace). See chapter Maryam (19:61–62).

3. With hundreds of parades in New York City, obtaining a permit for a new one can be a daunting task. Mohamed fought hard and was granted one just in time for the inaugural date of August 5, 2007. Unlike the Cheikh Amadou Bamba Day parade (discussed here in the chapter 3), which is religious in nature and includes mostly Senegalese Murids, or the commercialism of the African American Day parade, the African Day parade is a cultural celebration bringing together a range of people across the African diaspora.

4. Carola Suárez-Orozo, Marcelo M. Suárez-Orozo, and Irina Todorova, *Learning a New Land: Immigrant Students in American Society* (Cambridge, Mass.: Belknap Press, 2008), 156.

5. Beyond French, others have linguistic skills in German, Italian, Spanish, or even Russian. This is for two reasons. While many choose English as their mandatory second language in high school, several other languages are offered. Because a large number of Africans have migrated to Germany and Russia for educational and job opportunities, these linguistic patterns have become a part of their world.

6. For Cote d'Ivoire, see *Ethnologue* and its Web site, http://www.ethnologue.com/ show_country.asp?name=CI. For Nigeria, see David Crozier and Roger Blench, *An Index of Nigerian Languages*, 2nd ed. (Abuja, Nigeria, and Dallas: Nigerian Language Development Centre, University of Ilorin, and Summer Institute of Linguistics, 1992); see also Roger Blench, "The Status of the Languages of Central Nigeria," in M. Brenzinger, ed., *Endangered Languages in Africa* (Köln: Köppe Verlag, 1998), 187–206, http://www.rogerblench.info/ Language%20data/Africa/Nigeria/Language%20Death%2in%20Nigeria.pdf.

7. Suárez-Orozco, Suárez-Orozo, and Todorova, *Learning a New Land*, 158. Besides background and exposure, the authors recognize a combination of factors in second-language learning, such as motivation, cognitive aptitude (including age), and quality of instruction.

8. According to some Islamic sources, Muslim women should not travel alone but must be accompanied by a *mahram*, a male companion who is a close relative and unmarriageable.

9. Apparently, there is a *hadith* telling Muslims to multiply, perhaps in the biblical sense of "go forth and multiply." Supposedly, the Prophet Muhammad will delight on the day of judgment when he sees the large size of the Muslim *ummah* (community).

10. While we can be certain that the Senegalese community was very small in the mid-1980s, the 1990 U.S. Census recorded that there were more than two thousand Senegalese in the entire United States. Like most Africans, Aissatou belongs to a network of Senegalese Muslims in Harlem, and she and her associates were definitely in the first wave to arrive in the States after the 1965 Immigration Act. Her statement that there were ten Senegalese in the country undoubtedly referred to people in her immediate circle.

11. It's difficult to speculate about the reason Aissatou singled out Muslim women in this statement. However, Sunni (orthodox) Muslims tend to believe that the role Muslim women play as mothers and educators of a new generation is extremely important. I can only assume that this is at least partially what she intended.

12. Paul Stoller, *Jaguar: A Story of Africans in America* (Chicago: University of Chicago Press, 1999), 14. I use this research-based, fictional account instead of a similar story in Stoller's ethnography because the former highlights the French language as an important network. The latter focuses on fellowship among African immigrants. See Stoller, *Money Has No Smell*, 154.

13. Donald Martin Carter, *States of Grace: Senegalese in Italy and the New European Immigration* (Minneapolis: University of Minnesota Press, 1997), 79.

14. Ibid., 79–80.

15. While tourists might stroll into the Harlem Market from time to time and busloads disembark to look for the exotic, African vendors apparently receive the bulk of their income from repeated sales to local customers.

16. Katherine S. Newman, *No Shame in My Game: The Working Poor in the Inner City* (New York: Vintage Books and Russell Sage Foundation, 1999), 145.

17. In *sura al-an'am*, the Qur'an states, "Whoever brings a good deed shall have ten times the like thereof to his credit, and whoever brings an evil deed shall have only the recompense of the like thereof, and they will not be wronged" (6:160). For Muslims, this verse illustrates God's generosity and kindness, reminding them to extend the same to others.

18. The Qur'an instructs the faithful to extend a courteous greeting to one another and if one is received, to give one even better (*an-nisa*, 4:86). At the same time, the Qur'an gives

a parable of the dwellers of heaven and states that their greeting is "*salaamu 'alaykum*" (*al-a'araf*, 7:46), which elevates the status of this greeting. Even so, the prophetic traditions expound on this process and provide a bit more detail.

19. One tradition, according to Abu Dharr, states that the Prophet said, "And your smiling in the face of your brother is charity, your removing of stones, thorns, and bones from people's paths is charity, and your guiding a person gone astray in the world is charity for you." See the collection of Muhammad ibn Isma'il Bukhari, *Sahih al-Bukhari: The Translation of the Meanings of Sahih al-Bukhari* (Medina: Dar al-Fikr, 1981).

20. The city of Newark is just twelve minutes from Manhattan by train and is part of the New York metropolitan area.

21. Among Qur'anic passages and *hadith* (prophetic traditions), Muslims read the following verse as a dictate to call people to Islam with ingenuity and, as it were, the proper skills: "Call to the way of thy Lord with wisdom and beautiful preaching; and debate with them in ways that are best and most gracious; for thy Lord knows best who has strayed from the path and who has been guided" (*an-nahl* 16:125).

22. Newman, *No Shame in My Game*, 158–159.

23. Some claim that Nigerians have the highest level of education of all immigrants, including Asians. See April Gordon, "The New Diaspora—African Immigration to the United States," *Journal of Third World Studies* 15:1 (1998): 79–103.

24. Diawara, *We Won't Budge*, 88.

CHAPTER 5

1. For a more detailed discussion on the parade, see Zain Abdullah, "Sufis on Parade: The Performance of Black, African, and Muslim Identities," *Journal of the American Academy of Religion* 77:2 (June 2009): 1–39. The word *thikr* is also spelled *zikr* or *dhikr*, but I prefer to use *th* as pronounced in the word *that*, because it approximates the corresponding letter in Arabic. *Thikr* beads are similar to traditional Roman Catholic rosary beads. Muslims use ninety-nine or one hundred beads strung together to keep track of Islamic recitations or formulaic chants.

2. After New York, proclamations have been declared in cities such as Newark, Baltimore, Atlanta, and Washington, D.C. For Newark, Baltimore, and Washington, see Malcomson, "West of Eden," 41. The New York and Atlanta proclamations have been reproduced in their entirety in Monika Salzbrunn, "The Occupation of Public Space through Religious and Political Events: How Senegalese Migrants Became a Part of Harlem, New York," *Journal of Religion in Africa* 34:4 (2004): 482, 483.

3. In July 2001, the parade began at the Harlem State Office Building at Seventh Avenue (Frederick Douglass Boulevard) and 125th Street and proceeded to 110th Street at Central Park North. The paraders made supplications and held a rally at the park entrance. In 2003, the order was reversed, allowing paraders to end the prayer at the Harlem State Office Building with a huge rally of delegates and spectators. This shift made sense, especially for the attention it gained at a major Harlem intersection.

4. Setha Low, ed., *Theorizing the City: The New Urban Anthropology Reader* (New Brunswick, N.J.: Rutgers University Press, 1999), 20.

5. For a discussion on the concept of "suspect community," see Paddy Hillyard, *Suspect Community: People's Experience of the Prevention of Terrorism Acts in Britain*

(London: Pluto, 1993). With what is undoubtedly a minority view among traditionalists, some believe the act of picture taking is *haram* (religiously forbidden), since it is believed to mock God's creative powers.

6. *Allahu Akbar* is Arabic for "Allah (God) is the greatest." It is used in prayers and considered a major theme in the life of a Muslim, since it orients the faithful to make God one's priority.

7. Ibrahima Faal, a contemporary and follower of Cheikh Amadou Bamba, is the central figure in the influential Baye Faal movement. For more information, see Neil J. Savishinsky, "The Baye Faal of Senegambia: Muslim Rastas in the Promised Land?" *Africa: Journal of the International African Institute* 64:2 (1994): 211–219.

8. The Arabic word *athan* (sometimes written and pronounced *azan* or *adhan*, with the *dh* pronounced like the th in the word *the*) is the Muslim call to prayer.

9. Clare Corbould, "Streets, Sounds and Identity in Interwar Harlem," *Journal of Social History* 40:4 (Summer 2007): 861.

10. Corbould (ibid.) quotes Zora Neale Hurston's fictional account to describe how Black workers were treated under Jim Crow, America's legalized segregation laws, which lasted approximately from 1876 to 1965. See Zora Neale Hurston, *Their Eyes Were Watching God: A Novel* (London: Virago Press, 1986 [1937]), 9, 862.

11. Any place where individuals come in contact with the divine can be considered pure. In Islam, for instance, not only should places of worship such as *masjids* maintain a state of ritual purity, but the devotee's body, as a sacred site of divine communication, must likewise be ritually pure during prayers. "As a place of communication with divinity," Joel P. Brereton asserts, "a sacred space is typically a place of purity because purity enables people to come into contact with the gods." See Joel P. Brereton, "Sacred Space," in Lindsay Jones, ed., *Encyclopedia of Religion*, 2nd ed. (Detroit: Macmillan Reference, 2005), 7981. For an ironic twist on how New York's Halloween parade in the Village attains a similar purity because it occurs at night and lacks many commercial and political features, see Jack Kugelmass, *Masked Culture: The Greenwich Village Halloween Parade* (New York: Columbia University Press, 1994), 21.

12. Susan G. Davis, *Parades and Power: Street Theatre in Nineteenth-Century Philadelphia* (Philadelphia: Temple University Press, 1986), 7. Sociologist Arnold van Gennep believed that ritual behavior or rites of passage occurred in three stages: (1) *separation* (from the group or society), (2) *liminality* (a transition into a new state), and (3) *incorporation* (or a reincorporation into society). See Arnold van Gennep, *The Rites of Passage* (Chicago: University of Chicago Press, 1960 [1908]). Victor Turner, a British anthropologist, advanced Gennep's idea for his understanding of the ritual process, especially the liminal stage. See Victor Witter Turner, *The Ritual Process: Structure and Anti-Structure* (Chicago: Aldine, 1969), 94–113, 125–130. Influenced by the social process model of British social anthropologist and Africanist Max Gluckman, Turner argued that during the liminal state (antistructure), the limitations of social structures are relaxed and allow practitioners to create new identities or alter old ones. See Max Gluckman, *Custom and Conflict in Africa* (Oxford: Blackwell, 1955) and *Order and Rebellion in Tribal Africa: Collected Essays* (London: Cohen & West, 1963). The ritual behavior of carnival is an example of how masqueraders incorporate masks to invert identities. A good example of this process appears in Efrat Tseëlon, ed., *Masquerade and Identities: Essays on Gender, Sexuality, and Marginality* (New York: Routledge, 2001). Once the liminal state is complete,

members are strengthened by a new expression of solidarity, a concept Turner termed *communitas*. In true Durkheimian form, the final stage of reincorporation describes the way society averts the revolutionary nature of the liminal state and maintains its own equilibrium. For Emile Durkheim's notion of social equilibrium, see Emile Durkheim, *The Division of Labor in Society* (New York: Free Press, 1964 [1933]). I borrow the concept of liminality as a way to describe the kind of space paraders enter during these public events.

13. This statement is not to suggest that the Cheikh Amadou Bamba Day parade is devoid of subaltern voices or competing messages. Parades and processions give the appearance of uniformity by means of their very structure and military-style formation. However, because these public displays are made up of individuals and subgroups, all with their own agendas, internal differences generally go unnoticed by spectators.

14. Allen F. Roberts and Mary Nooter Roberts, *A Saint in the City: Sufi Arts of Urban Senegal* (Los Angeles: UCLA Fowler Museum of Cultural History, 2003), 38.

15. Susan Slyomovics, "The Muslim World Day Parade and 'Storefront' Mosques of New York City," in Barbara Daly Metcalf, ed., *Making Muslim Space in North America and Europe* (Berkeley: University of California Press, 1996), 206.

16. Barbara Kirshenblatt-Gimblett and Brooks McNamara, "Processional Performance: An Introduction," *Drama Review* 29:3 (1985): 2.

17. An English rendition would be: "The Annual Visit of the Honorable Mourtalla Mbacke, Son of [Bamba] the Disciple of the Messenger to the United States from July 25 through August 3, 2001—Hosted by the Murid Islamic Community with the Participation of Assurances CNART—the Assistance of Taxa Wu—Guarantees Adaptees [underwriting] for All Your Needs—With Assurances CNART, You Can Navigate the World."

18. This identity work reflects what Judith Byfield means when she says: "In the United States, cities like New York have become home to significant numbers of Nigerians, Ethiopians, and Senegalese as well as Jamaicans, Haitians, and Dominicans. All can be claimed as part of the African diaspora, but their relationship to Africa, to each other, and to black Americans is mediated by national and ethnic identities, gender, and class. Together they have forged multinational, multi-ethnic urban black communities of overlapping diasporas with both shared and competing interests." See Judith Byfield, "Introduction: Rethinking the African Diaspora," *African Studies Review* 43:1 (April 2000): 6.

19. See Ali Mazrui, *The Africans: A Triple Heritage* (Boston: Little, Brown, 1986).

20. For an early treatise on the concept of glocalization, see Roland Robertson, *Globalization: Social Theory and Global Culture* (London: Sage, 1992).

21. In his discussion on this ongoing dissension, Mamadou Diouf writes: "The triumph of the *modu-modu* [non-Western-educated merchants and traders] as representative of the Murid community took place in the second half of the 1980s at the expense of another group much more active in the 1970s, the Murid intellectual—students and Senegalese professionals living in Western countries, particularly in France. While there has never been any direct confrontation between the two groups, a competition between them is at the heart of tensions and conflicts that afflict the Murid brotherhood. The stakes are the management and supervision of Touba, on one hand, and questions of how to interpret, dramatize, and act out the Murid heritage and the founder's message, on the other." See Mamadou Diouf, "The Senegalese Murid Trade Diaspora and the Making of a Vernacular Cosmopolitanism," *Public Culture* 12:3 (2000): 697.

22. For a poll on how American Muslims feel in a post-9/11 climate, see John L. Esposito and Dalia Mogahed, *Who Speaks for Islam? What a Billion Muslims Really Think* (New York: Gallup Press, 2007).

23. Roberts and Roberts, *A Saint in the City*, 25.

24. For a discussion on *baraka*, see Clifford Geertz, *Islam Observed: Religious Development in Morocco and Indonesia* (New Haven, Conn.: Yale University Press, 1968), 44; Babou, *Fighting the Greater Jihad*, 8–9.

25. Victoria Ebin, "Making Room versus Creating Space: The Construction of Spatial Categories by Itinerant Mouride Traders," in Barbara Daly Metcalf, ed., *Making Muslim Space in North America and Europe* (Berkeley: University of California Press, 1996), 100.

26. Ibid.

27. Joseph Sciorra, "'We Go Where the Italians Live': Religious Processions As Ethnic and Territorial Markers in a Multi-ethnic Brooklyn Neighborhood," in Robert A. Orsi, ed., *Gods of the City: Religion and the American Urban Landscape* (Bloomington: Indiana University Press, 1999), 520. See also Linda Racioppi and Katherine O'Sullivan See, "Ulsterman and Loyalist Ladies on Parade: Gendering Unionism in Northern Ireland," *International Feminist Journal of Politics* 2:1 (Spring 2000): 1–29. Women, however, play different roles and occupy various positions. For British Muslims of Pakistani descent, for example, only men march in the Urs procession, while women come to witness the *zikr* (chants), prayers, and other festivities. See Pnina Werbner, "Stamping the Earth with the Name of Allah: Zikr and the Sacralizing of Space among British Muslims," in Barbara Daly Metcalf, ed., *Making Muslim Space in North America and Europe* (Berkeley: University of California Press, 1996), 169. In fact, this exclusion mirrors the absence of women marchers in Pakistan. Pakistani women do participate in the Shi'i Karbala procession in Canada, but they are stationed in the rear. See Vernon James Schubel, "Karbala As Sacred Space among North American Shi'a: 'Every Day Is Ashura, Everywhere Is Karbala," in Barbara Daly Metcalf, ed., *Making Muslim Space in North America and Europe* (Berkeley: University of California Press, 1996), 198. At other fairly religious parades such as the one for Saint Patrick's Day in New York, gender separation has been common, with the men's contingent preceding the women's group, each with "its own marshal and set of aides." See Jane Gladden Kelton, "New York City St. Patrick's Day Parade: Invention of Contention and Consensus," *Drama Review* 29:3 (Fall 1985): 95.

28. Adriana Piga, *Dakar et les orders soufis: Processus socioculturels et développement urbain au Sénégal contemporain* (Paris: L'Harmattan, 2002), 238.

29. Kugelmass, *Masked Culture*, 21.

30. Roberts and Roberts, *A Saint in the City*, 161.

31. For mixed-gendered *dahiras*, see Barbara Callaway and Lucy Creevey, *The Heritage of Islam: Women, Religion, and Politics in West Africa* (Boulder, Colo.: Lynne Reiner, 1994), 48. For all-female circles, see Codou Bop, "Roles and the Position of Women in Sufi Brotherhoods in Senegal," *Journal of the American Academy of Religion* 73:4 (December 2005): 1108.

32. Along with social and other forms of capital, I include "religious capital" to mean the ways in which sacred beliefs and practices create networks that not only have value but also produce resources influencing one's real or imagined life chances. For a discussion of other forms of capital, see Pierre Bourdieu, "The Forms of Capital," in John G. Richardson, ed., *Handbook of Theory and Research for the Sociology of Education* (New York: Greenwood Press, 1986), 241–258.

33. Arjun Appadurai, *Modernity at Large: Cultural Dimensions of Globalization* (Minneapolis: University of Minnesota Press, 1996), 55–58.

34. Christian Coulon, "Women, Islam, and Baraka," in Donal B. Cruise O'Brien and Christian Coulon, eds., *Charisma and Brotherhood in African Islam* (Oxford: Clarendon Press, 1988).

35. Roberts and Roberts, *A Saint in the City*, 159.

36. Cheikh Anta Babou claims that there were perhaps thirty *dahiras* in New York City in 2001, which was an increase from fourteen in 1996. See Babou, "Brotherhood Solidarity, Education and Migration," 164–165.

37. Ibid., 162.

38. Babou, *Fighting the Greater Jihad*, 9.

39. Edward C. Zaragoza, *St. James in the Streets: The Religious Processions of Loíza Aldea, Puerto Rico* (Lanham, Md.: Scarecrow Press, 1995), 80.

40. Coulon, "Women, Islam, and Baraka," 118.

41. Piga, *Dakar et les orders soufis*, 241.

42. Bop, "Roles and the Position of Women," 1112–1116.

43. For a history of Islamic thought and ideology among African Americans, see Curtis, *Islam in Black America*.

44. Turner, *Islam in the African American Experience*, 198–199.

45. This is a pseudonym to protect my respondent's identity and privacy.

46. Among many other works on the Black middle class, see Mary Pattillo-McCoy, *Black Picket Fences: Privilege and Peril among the Black Middle Class* (Chicago: University of Chicago Press, 1999); Mary Pattillo, *Black on the Block: The Politics of Race and Class in the City* (Chicago: University of Chicago Press, 2007); and Patricia A. Banks, *Represent: Art and Identity among the Black Upper-Middle Class* (New York: Routledge, 2009).

47. On the rise of an underclass in America, see Douglas S. Massey, *American Apartheid: Segregation and the Making of the Underclass* (Cambridge, Mass.: Harvard University Press, 1998).

48. Rebecca Sullivan, "Breaking Habits: Gender, Class and the Sacred in the Dress of Women Religious," in Anne Brydon and Sandra Niessen, eds., *Consuming Fashion: Adorning the Transnational Body* (New York: Berg, 1998), 109, n. 1.

49. Spelman College is an exceptional liberal arts college for women in Atlanta, one of the HBCUs (Historically Black Colleges and Universities). It reportedly ranks among the seventy-five best liberal arts colleges according to *U.S. News & World Report* in 2007.

50. Choosing respondents during fieldwork is at times difficult, because the researcher might be forced to make choices to distance himself/herself from social undesirables, especially if he/she wants to maintain some rapport with so-called respectable members of the community.

51. Mamadou is referring to Muhammad ibn Salih al-'Uthaymin, one of the prominent members of the Salafiyyah movement. This is an ultraconservative group whose members believe that Muslims must follow the Salaf as-Salah (righteous ancestors) as dictated by a set of rules in the *minhaj* (program) and *'aqeedah* (belief) of the group, including elements of dress and personal appearances such as facial hair, in order to "return" to the correct path of God.

52. Scholars of Islamic studies see this dichotomy as a Muslim innovation that deviates from the principles of the religion. I have decided to translate these Arabic terms as "outsider" and "insider," respectively, because a literal rendering would miss the way they

are meant to act as well-defined frontiers in Harlem. In a literal sense, they would be translated as *dar al-harb* (abode of war) and *dar al-Islam* (abode of Islam). Contrary to its religious role, Islam in this context is used as an organizing principle, a bifurcated way of looking at the world and those who inhabit it.

CHAPTER 6

1. Jane Jacobs, *The Death and Life of Great American Cities* (New York: Random House, 1961).

2. For a discussion on Harlem as a distinct place, culturally separate from the rest of Manhattan, see Jackson, *Harlemworld*, 1–10.

3. While the term *barrio* is Spanish and refers to a particular district or neighborhood with a largely Latino population, *barrios* and ghettos have historically been heterogeneous places, shot through with class, racial, and religious diversity. In the post-civil rights era, this diversity has changed somewhat, as middle-class minorities have gained greater access to suburban living and corporate jobs.

4. The art piece is a terra-cotta mosaic entitled *Minton's Playhouse/Movers and Shakers*. The quote is from the artist, Vincent Smith, who created the subway art at 116th Street and Lenox Avenue. Along with other similar art works at 125th and 135th Streets, they complete a particular story about Black history. See the Metropolitan Transportation Authority (MTA) Web site, http://www.nycsubway.org/perl/artwork.

5. Shelby Steele and Thomas Lennon, *Seven Days in Bensonhurst* (film), Frontline, WGBH Educational Foundation, Boston, 1990.

6. Reynolds Farley et al., "Continued Racial Residential Segregation in Detroit: 'Chocolate City, Vanilla Suburbs' Revisited," *Journal of Housing Research* 4:1 (1993): 1–38.

7. Robin D. G. Kelley, "Disappearing Acts: Harlem in Transition," in Jerilou Hammett and Kingsley Hammett, eds., *The Suburbanization of New York: Is the World's Greatest City Becoming Just Another Town?* (New York: Princeton Architectural Press, 2007), 66.

8. See Robert E. Park, *The City* (Chicago: University of Chicago Press, 1968 [1928]).

9. Michael Dunlop Young, *Family and Kinship in East London* (London: Routledge, 1957). See also Peter Marris, *Family and Social Change in an African City: A Study of Rehousing in Lagos* (Evanston, Ill.: Northwestern University Press, 1962).

10. See Lisa Redfield Peattie, *The View from the Barrio* (Ann Arbor: University of Michigan Press, 1972); Susan D. Greenbaum, "Housing Abandonment in Inner-City Black Neighborhoods: A Case Study of the Effects of the Dual Housing Market," in Robert Rotenberg and Gary McDonogh, eds., *The Cultural Meaning of Urban Space* (Westport, Conn.: Bergin & Garvey, 1993).

11. Jacobs, *The Death and Life of Great American Cities*, 117.

12. Jerilou Hammett and Kingsley Hammett, eds., *The Suburbanization of New York: Is the World's Greatest City Becoming Just Another Town?* (New York: Princeton Architectural Press, 2007).

13. Kelley, "Disappearing Acts," 67.

14. Jerilou Hammett and Kingsley Hammett, "Preface," in Hammett and Hammett, *The Suburbanization of New York* 19.

15. Ibid., 20.

16. Ralph Ellison, *Invisible Man* (New York: Random House, 1952).

17. For the link among identity, conversation, and code switching or the use of more than one language or linguistic varieties, see Peter Auer, ed., *Code-Switching in Conversation: Language, Interaction and Identity* (New York: Routledge, 1998).

18. Duneier, *Sidewalk*.

19. Ibid., 8.

20. Jacobs, *The Death and Life of Great American Cities*, 68. See also Duneier, *Sidewalk*, 6–8.

21. Deneier, *Sidewalk*, 8. For a different look at street corners as social realms of activity, see the work of William Foote Whyte, who wrote about gang activity and the nature of street-corner life for first- and second-generation Italian immigrants in a Boston slum. See his classic *Street Corner Society: The Social Structure of an Italian Slum*, 4th ed. (Chicago: University of Chicago Press, 1993 [ORIG. 1943]).

22. Jackson briefly explores the role conspiracy theories play in constructing identity. See his *Harlemworld*, 123–125, and *Real Black: Adventures in Racial Sincerity* (Chicago: University of Chicago Press, 2005), 105–109.

23. I realize that many departments are including innovative courses that allow for a much more free-flowing exchange of ideas, and I applaud these efforts. Many courses in the humanities, cultural anthropology or sociology, and interdisciplinary fields such as cultural studies, feminist studies, African American and African studies, to name a few, also employ works that allow students to unpack a range of concerns, affording them a more critical way of understanding the world. It is not my intention to discredit these attempts.

24. Harriet A. Washington, *Medical Apartheid: The Dark History of Medical Experimentation on Black Americans from Colonial Times to the Present* (New York: Doubleday, 2006).

25. The Tuskegee syphilis experiment is well known. In addition to Washington's work (ibid.), see James H. Jones, *Bad Blood: The Tuskegee Syphilis Experiment* (New York: Free Press, 1981); Susan M. Reverby, *Tuskegee's Truths: Rethinking the Tuskegee Syphilis Study* (Chapel Hill: University of North Carolina Press, 2000). Denny also refers us to an interesting Web site, http://www.boydgraves.com.

26. Michael Roemer and Robert Young, *Nothing but a Man* (film), CCM Films, 1964. The film is a story about an African American man and his wife dealing with the trials of racism in the South.

27. Peter Bate, *White King, Red Rubber, Black Death* (film), ArtMattan Productions, New York, 2004.

28. This brief exchange of farewells is instructive for the way each greeting speaks to a different ideology and way of seeing the world. The Islamic "*as-salaamu 'alaykum*" for African American Muslims does not merely emulate a similar one extended by Arab or South Asian Muslims. For Black Muslims, the "*salaams*," as it is sometimes called, validate their invisible presence within a larger Black minority, recentering their marginal status. For African Americans, especially Black males, the greeting of "Peace" signifies a level of Black consciousness, underscoring a love for the Black self, and psychologically repudiates notions of Black-on-Black crime. "Hotep" reflects a Pan-Africanist philosophy and envisions Black identity in terms of the great civilizations of Egypt and the Nile Valley. The term itself refers to Imhotep, considered the father of medicine from ancient Egypt, and it could mean peace. It is certainly intended to combat notions of Black inferiority, linking African American

identity and culture to this important legacy. As it relates to the reality of multiple worlds in Harlem, the simple act of extending farewell requires three separate gestures, each with its own cultural perspective.

29. The idea of "emotional truth" is borrowed from an interview with an amazing new female Nigerian writer, Chimamanda Ngozi Adichie. She was discussing her recent work, *Half of a Yellow Sun* (New York: Alfred A. Knopf, 2007), a fictionalized account based on the Nigerian-Biafran war of 1967–1970. While she made sure that the major political events were presented accurately, her primary concern was what she called "emotional truth," because she "wanted this to be a book about human beings, not a book about faceless political events." See "The Story Behind the Book" at http://www.halfofayellowsun.com/content .php?page=tsbtb&n=5&f=2.

30. For a brief treatment of how African Muslims shift the boundaries of these identities, see Zain Abdullah, "Negotiating Identities: A History of Islamization in Black West Africa." *Journal of Islamic Law and Culture* 10:1 (2008): 5–18.

31. For an interesting discussion of transnationalism and the differences between the old and new immigration in New York City, see Nancy Foner, "Introduction: New Immigrants in New York," in Nancy Foner, ed., *New Immigrants in New York*, updated ed. (New York: Columbia University Press, 2001), 1–31.

32. Diawara, *We Won't Budge*, 62.

33. For an insightful look at discrimination among Muslim girls in Paris, see Trica Danielle Keaton, *Muslim Girls and the Other France: Race, Identity Politics, and Social Exclusion* (Bloomington: Indiana University Press, 2006).

34. Stoller, *Money Has No Smell*, 145.

35. Jacob K. Olupona, "Communities of Believers: Exploring African Immigrant Religion in the United States," in Jacob K. Olupona and Regina Gemignani, eds., *African Immigrant Religions in America* (New York: New York University Press, 2008), 27–46.

36. Ibid., 29.

37. Ogbu U. Kalu, "The Andrew Syndrome: Models in Understanding Nigerian Diaspora," in Jacob K. Olupona and Regina Gemignani, eds., *African Immigrant Religions in America* (New York: New York University Press, 2008), 73–78.

38. W. E. B. DuBois, *The Souls of Black Folk* (New York: Signet Classic, 1995 [1903]), xxxiv.

39. Karen Armstrong, *The Spiral Staircase: My Climb Out of Darkness* (New York: Anchor Books, 2004), 23–24.

40. For an extraordinary yet concise treatment of Muslim immigrant communities in the United States, see McCloud, *Transnational Muslims in American Society*. For an intriguing documentary film about contested gender relations within immigrant Muslim communities in the United States and Canada, see Zarqa Nawaz, *Me and the Mosque*, National Film Board of Canada, 2005.

41. George Breitman, ed., *Malcolm X Speaks: Selected Speeches and Statements* (New York: Grove Weidenfeld, 1990), p. 8.

42. For an intriguing ethnography about Spanish Harlem and the impact of drugs on the community, see Philippe Bourgois, *In Search of Respect: Selling Crack in El Barrio*, 2nd ed. (New York: Cambridge University Press, 2003).

43. JoAnn D'Alisera, *An Imagined Geography: Sierra Leonean Muslims in America* (Philadelphia: University of Pennsylvania Press, 2004), 80.

CHAPTER 7

1. Linda Beck refers to a similar situation in which "Ibadous," as she calls them, constitute a reformist movement among Senegalese youth and women. They are a more conservative group, and the relationship between Ibadous and other Muslims, particularly Sufis, has been strained. Beck feels this tension has been transported to Harlem. See Linda Beck, "West African Muslims in America: When Are Muslims Not Muslims?" in Jacob K. Olupona and Regina Gemignani, eds., *African Immigrant Religions in America* (New York: New York University Press, 2008), 186.

2. Imam Soulaymane Konate from Masjid Aqsa says that he prefers to recite the Qur'an in the Qalun style because of its African character. According to Ahmad Ali al-Imam, Qalun is the third most popular style in some parts of North Africa. For this and other information on Qur'anic recitation, see Ahmad Ali al-Imam, *Variant Readings of the Qur'an: A Critical Study of Their Historical and Linguistic Origins* (Herndon, Va.: International Institute of Islamic Thought, 1998), 48.

3. In a different religious context, however, this type of condescension can move in the opposite direction. As a journalist in Saudi Arabia, Imam Konate, an Ivoirian, told me that although his Qalun recital of the Qur'an was recognized as religiously authentic, it was nonetheless ridiculed as African. The dreadlocks he decided to wear while working in Saudi Arabia were chided as sacrilegious, and his colleagues even called him "*ash-shaytan*" (the devil).

4. Yushau Sodiq writes about Nigerian Muslims in Texas who accuse their Arabocentric members of forsaking Yourba culture. See his "African Muslims in the United States: The Nigerian Case," in Jacob K. Olupona and Regina Gemignani, eds., *African Immigrant Religions in America* (New York: New York University Press, 2008), 320.

5. For how Terry Williams employs "chronic stress," see Jonathan Stack, Terry Williams, and Susanne Szabo Rostock, *Harlem Diary: Nine Voices of Resilience* (film), Discovery Channel, Gabriel Films, and Films for the Humanities & Sciences, Princeton, N.J., 2003 [1993]. The film is based on Williams's Writers' Crew project. See Terry Williams and William Kornblum, *The Uptown Kids: Struggle and Hope in the Projects* (New York: Putnam, 1994), and also their earlier work, *Growing Up Poor* (Lexington, Mass.: Lexington Books, 1985).

6. For a dated yet interesting discussion on urban anthropology and how cities construct time, see Robert Rotenberg, *Time and Order in Metropolitan Vienna: A Seizure of Schedules* (Washington, D.C.: Smithsonian Institution Press, 1992). In contrast with Francophone African Muslims in Harlem, Yushau Sodiq writes that Nigerian Muslim immigrants in Houston, Texas, meet regularly on Sundays rather than Fridays, because "Sunday is a weekend and everyone is free." Sodiq, "African Muslims in the United States," 313. In either case, the uneasy fit between Islamic daily liturgies and an American workplace is quite an adjustment for immigrants from Muslim countries. By comparison, it is equally difficult for Westerners trying to adjust to a Muslim schedule while living abroad.

7. Robert A. Orsi, *The Madonna of 115th Street: Faith and Community in Italian Harlem, 1880–1950* (New Haven, Conn.: Yale University Press, 2002), 201–202.

8. For a similar discussion on how Islam helps African Muslims from Niger brave harsh social and economic conditions in New York, see Paul Stoller, "West Africans:

Trading Places in New York," in Nancy Foner, ed. *New Immigrants in New York*, updated ed. (New York: Columbia University Press, 2001), 246.

9. Assetou's perspective on destiny speaks to the Islamic concept of *qadr*, or a Muslim belief that God's power prevails over all situations and, in the overall scheme of things, that the major events in one's life are preordained. While the physical form might be altered through supplication or other kinds of religious intervention, the value remains constant. This idea is typically illustrated by referring to a miraculous event, the Night of Ascension, when the Prophet Muhammad received the dictate for Muslims to pray fifty times a day. As legend has it, during his journey through the heavens, Muhammad was advised by other prophets to ask God to reduce the number until the prayers were five a day, but the value of fifty prayers remains. This religious tradition is supported by the Qur'anic verse stating that each good deed is multiplied tenfold.

10. Each *salah* (formal prayer) in Islam is appointed at a particular time of the day, but each prayer can also be performed within a period of so many hours. For example, the time allotted for the noon prayer, *thuhr*, begins after the sun has passed its zenith and lasts until the afternoon, or when one's shadow has doubled in length (depending on season and region). During the summer months, this could be three or four hours. With less daylight in the winter, the time between prayers is shortened. The prayer itself takes approximately five minutes to perform, and a Muslim can pray anytime within the allotted period. The *athan* (call to prayer) indicates the beginning of each prayer time. And most American *masjids* that are open for the daily prayers (some are open only in the evenings and for the weekly *jum'ah* services) tend to perform the *salah* collectively about fifteen minutes after the *athan* is called, allowing attendees enough time to perform *wudu* (ablution) first.

11. Albeit with very little success, some Muslim women in America have attempted to sue their employers for religious discrimination. See Yvonne Yazbeck Haddad, Jane I. Smith, and Kathleen M. Moore, *Muslim Women in America: The Challenge of Islamic Identity Today* (New York: Oxford University Press, 2006), 107–110. For a similar type of discrimination against praying on the job for Sierra Leonean Muslim women in Washington, D.C., see D'Alisera, *An Imagined Geography*, 90–91.

12. Other places, such as graveyards, are deemed unacceptable for the formal *salah*, according to various Muslim jurists. Some might include the need to exclude images from the *musalla* (prayer area). See Sabiq al-Sayyid, *Fiqh us-Sunnah, Supererogatory Prayer*, vol. 2, trans. by Muhammad Sa'eed Dabas and Jamal al-Din M. Zarabozo (Indianapolis: American Trust Publications, 1989), 74–79.

13. In *Jaguar*, Paul Stoller creates a fictionalized account based on his ethnographic fieldwork in New York among Africans from Niger. In the opening chapter, he illustrates the challenges they face when attempting to perform *wudu* (ablution) and find adequate places to pray. See Stoller, *Jaguar*, 3–4.

14. Before being hired as full-time leaders of their communities, three prominent African *imams* in Harlem recounted their stories about having to make up all of their prayers at night once they returned from work. Imam Soulaymane Konate of Masjid Aqsa said he made a firm decision one day that he had to "save his life" and quit working at an Arab Muslim-owned bodega selling alcohol and pork, items Muslims customarily avoid. Today, Imam Konate, who is from Côte d'Ivoire, along with the *imam* of Masjid Touba, Bassirou Lo from Senegal, and the *imam* of the Futa Islamic Center, Bah Algassim from Guinea, are all employed full-time as Muslim clerics. Imam Lo and two of his assistant *imams* all have

diplomatic status, as they are paid by the Senegalese government. To my knowledge, however, Imam Konate and Imam Algassim are largely supported by community donations.

15. Released in 1939, the song "Strange Fruit" condemned American racism and the lynching of African Americans throughout the South and other parts of the United States. It was most famously sung by Billie Holiday, and her version was inducted into the Grammy Hall of Fame in 1978. Apparently, it was originally written as a poem by a Jewish high school teacher, Abel Meerpol, who worked in the Bronx. Meerpol was moved to write the ode upon seeing a 1930 photograph of two lynched African American men, Thomas Shipp and Abram Smith. His work was published in the union magazine *New York Teacher* in 1936. For more information, see David Margolick, *Strange Fruit: The Biography of a Song* (New York: Harper Perennial, 2001).

16. The term *homeboy* or *homegirl* generally refers to a reliable friend from the same neighborhood. For Black immigrants embracing urban hip-hop styles in New York City, Manthia Diawara uses "homeboy cosmopolitan." Speaking of the slain Guinean Muslim Amadou Diallo, Diawara states that he "was a 'homeboy cosmopolitan,' dressed in his down jacket, baseball cap, and tennis shoes. He hustled videos outside of a storefront in Manhattan and counted his money at the end of the day, with his mind full of every immigrant's dream of making it in this land of unlimited opportunities." See Diawara, *We Won't Budge*, viii.

17. Richard Marosi, "One of the Most Dangerous Jobs in New York: Gypsy Cab Driver," Columbia University News Service, http://www.taxi-library.org/marosi.htm.

18. Before *jum'ah* services, Sierra Leonean taxi drivers often give free rides to their co-religionists heading to the *masjid* for prayer. Their cars create a religious circuit as they communicate the latest Islamic news and distribute paraphernalia to other Muslim street vendors. D'Alisera, *An Imagined Geography*, 17, 77–78, 89, 103.

19. See Deborah Block, "Somali Taxi Drivers in Minnesota in Dispute over Passengers with Pets, Alcohol," Voice of America, April 4, 2007, http://www1.voanews.com/english/news/a-13-2007-04-04-voa62.html; Associated Press, "Muslim Cabdrivers May Have to Signify Alcohol-Free Cars," October 1, 2006. A similar case has occurred in Australia. See *West Australian*, "Muslim Taxis Refuse to Carry Guide Dogs," October 8, 2006, http://au.news .yahoo.com/thewest. According to contemporary scholars such as Khalid Abou El Fadl, early students of Islam were apprehensive about dogs and deemed them unclean. Even so, Muslims were still allowed to retain dogs for specific reasons such as hunting or to guard property. See Khaled Abou El Fadl, *The Search for Beauty in Islam: A Conference of the Books* (Lanham, Md.: Rowman & Littlefield, 2006), chap. 20.

20. Luís León, "Born Again in East LA: The Congregation as Border Space," in R. Stephen Warner and Judith G. Wittner, eds., *Gatherings in Diaspora: Religious Communities and the New Immigration* (Philadelphia: Temple University Press, 1998), 177.

21. Kalu, "The Andrew Syndrome," 80.

22. Stoller, *Money Has No Smell*, xi.

23. Ibid., 37–38, 172.

24. Thomas J. Douglas, "Changing Religious Practices among Cambodian Immigrants in Long Beach and Seattle," in Karen I. Leonard, Alex Stepick, Manuel A. Vasquez, and Jennifer Holdaway, eds., *Immigrant Faiths: Transforming Religious Life in America* (Lanham, Md.: AltaMira Press, 2005), 138.

25. Babou, *Fighting the Greater Jihad*, 85–86, 90–92.

26. Ibid., 92, 178

27. Ibid., 92.

28. Olupona, "Communities of Believers," 38.

29. Anna Deavere Smith, *Fires in the Mirror: Crown Heights, Brooklyn and Other Identities* (New York: Anchor Books, 1993), 75. While the book is a fascinating read, plays are appreciated much more when they are performed onstage. The video version, however, is certainly worth viewing. See Anna Deavere Smith, George C. Wolfe, and Cherie Fortis, *Fires in the Mirror: Crown Heights, Brooklyn and Other Identities* (film), Monterey Video and Hipster Entertainment, Thousand Oaks, Calif., 2003. The film depicts the experiences of eighteen African American and Jewish residents.

30. Cheikh Anta Babou, "Migration and Cultural Change: Money, 'Caste,' Gender, and Social Status among Senegalese Female Hair Braiders in the United States," *Africa Today* 55:2 (2009): 3–22.

31. In the documentary film *Dollars and Dreams: West Africans in New York*, Belgisse Zoungrana has traveled much of the world as a performing artist with a French dance troupe before her arrival in America from West Africa. In New York, she works up to twelve hours a day braiding hair and might earn as little as thirty-five dollars a day. When she first tells her family she is braiding hair, they refuse to believe her, because this is not her custom. But Zoungrana quickly explains how she was forced to do this to survive, even though she doesn't mind the arduous work, since she enjoys her coworkers, and they have become a surrogate family. See Jeremy Rocklin, *Dollars and Dreams: West Africans in New York* (film), Documentary Educational Resources, Watertown, Mass., 2007.

32. For a similar account of an African immigrant hiding his job as a dishwasher from his family, not to mention the harsh treatment and racism he faced, see Diawara, *We Won't Budge*, 252–262.

33. Regina Gemignani, "Gender, Identity, and Power in African Immigrant Evangelical Churches," in Jacob K. Olupona and Regina Gemignani, eds., *African Immigrant Religions in America* (New York: New York University Press, 2008), 135–137. Moreover, some African Muslim women (and some African Muslim men) admit that before working in the health field, they were reluctant to go to hospitals because they didn't like seeing blood or handling needles. But after gaining experience as home health aides and being exposed to this side of caretaking, many have even considered careers in nursing.

CHAPTER 8

1. The actual name of this professor has been changed to protect his identity.

2. For discussions on reverse mission among African immigrants, see Akintunde Akinade, "Non-Western Christianity in the Western World: African Immigrant Churches in the Diaspora," in Jacob K. Olupona and Regina Gemignani, eds., *African Immigrant Religions in America* (New York: New York University Press, 2008), 89–101; Elias Bongmba, "Portable Faith: The Global Mission of African Initiated Churches," in Jacob K. Olupona and Regina Gemignani, eds., *African Immigrant Religions in America* (New York: New York University Press, 2008), 102–129.

3. For cross-cultural marriage in various societies, see Rosemary Breger and Rosanna Hill, eds., *Cross-Cultural Marriage: Identity and Choice* (Oxford: Berg, 1998).

4. Göran Therborn, "African Families in a Global Context," in Göran Therborn, ed., *African Families in a Global Context* (Uppsala: Nordiska Afrikainstitutet, 2004), 38–44.

5. Kecia Ali, *Sexual Ethics and Islam: Feminist Reflections on Qur'an, Hadith, and Juris-prudence* (Oxford: Oneworld Publications, 2006), 58, 92.

6. Ibid., 37.

7. Ibid. For Qur'anic passages referring to sexual intercourse with enslaved persons, see verse 24 in *sura an-Nisa* (the Women). It uses the term "right hand possess," or *milk al-yamin* in Islamic law. Some popular interpretations argue that engaging in sex with enslaved captives (whether or not they are currently married, since the act of war ostensibly dissolves previous civil ties) is allowed only when a Muslim marries the bondswoman. For a brief example of this argument in an English translation of the Qur'an, see Muhammad Asad, *The Message of the Qur'an* (Gibraltar: Dar al-Andalus, 1980). However, Asad's position does not seem to be clearly supported in the original text or overwhelmingly supported in the scholarly or juristic literature, as Kecia Ali has so painstakingly presented. See Ali, *Sexual Ethics in Islam*, chap. 3.

8. For a comprehensive treatment, see William Gervase Clarence-Smith, *Islam and the Abolition of Slavery* (New York: Oxford University Press, 2006).

9. This dual consent is similar to some Christian wedding ceremonies when the religious official publicly asks if there is anyone who objects to this union, let them speak or remain silent. While the couple has already consented, such a statement seeks a public consensus as well.

10. Ali, *Sexual Ethics and Islam*, 58. Ali goes on to say that this "does not mean that illicit sex (premarital intercourse, extramarital liaisons, etc.) was unknown in the past or is not practiced in Muslim majority societies today, often without discovery or punishment." In fact, she argues that the tenor of Islamic law regarding illicit sex is "don't ask, don't tell." This is especially the case when one considers the fact that in order to report a publicly punishable sexual transgression in Islamic law, there must be four eyewitnesses who all saw the actual sexual penetration, not just one person lying on top of another.

11. Stoller, *Money Has No Smell*, 21.

12. Ibid., 161–162; for more on Issifi and Monique, see 2–4.

13. Ibid., 160.

14. Asra Q. Nomani, *Standing Alone: An American Woman's Struggle for the Soul of Islam* (New York: HarperSanFrancisco, 2005), 295. See also "An Islamic Bill of Rights for Women Mosques," app. A.

15. Ali, *Sexual Ethics and Islam*, 68.

16. Tariq Ramadan, *Radical Reform: Islamic Ethics and Liberation* (New York: Oxford University Press, 2009), 274–277.

17. Ali, *Sexual Ethics and Islam*, 71.

18. In addition to an intellectual debate, I am also referring to the process of *ijtihad* (rigorous, scholarly deliberation). The Qur'anic spirit for settling differences with beautiful argumentation can be illustrated in this passage: "Invite people to the way of your Lord with wisdom and a beautiful exhortation; and argue with them in the most kind manner: for your Lord knows best who have strayed from the Lord's path and who has received guidance" (*an-Nahl*, or the Bee, 125). While this might initially speak to an approach in interfaith dialogue, it certainly informs the kind of compassion Muslims are encouraged to have for one another. Indeed, the presence of varying views among Muslims is seen as a divine favor, as in the prophetic saying "Difference of opinion in my faith community is a mercy." Regarding the need for deep internal reflection when it comes to matters of faith

and righteous behavior, the prophetic saying is, "On the authority of Wabisa ibn Ma'bad who said, 'I came to the messenger of Allah and he said, 'You have come to ask about righteousness?' I said, 'Yes.' He said, 'Consult your heart! Righteousness is that about which the soul feels tranquil and the heart feels tranquil, and wrongdoing is that which wavers in the soul and moves to and fro in the breast even though people again and again have given you their legal opinion.'" See Ahmad ibn Muhammad ibn Hanbal, *Al-Musnad* (Beirut: Mu'assasat al Risālah, 2008); Abd Allah ibn Abd al-Rahman Darimi, *Musnad al-Dārimī* (Riyadh: Dar al-Mughni, 2000). For a religious *sharh* (interpretation) of this tradition, see Mustafa Deeb Bugha, *Al-Wafi fi sharhal-Arba'in al-Nawawiyah* (Damascus: Dar ibn Kathir, 1989).

19. Pardis Mahdavi, *Passionate Uprisings: Iran's Sexual Revolution* (Stanford, Calif.: Stanford University Press, 2009); Marddent Amporn, *Sexual Culture among Young Migrant Muslims in Bangkok* (Bangkok: Silkworm Books, 2007).

20. McCloud, *Transnational Muslim in American Society*, chap. 10, "Global Islam in America: The Mix and the Challenges."

21. Moshe Shokeid, *A Gay Synagogue in New York* (Philadelphia: University of Pennsylvania Press, 2002). My observations and discussions in the field were on heterosexual relationships. Since homosexuality among Muslims was not a part of my research design, I also did not ask questions about gay and lesbian Muslim behavior, and, as I recall, these issues were typically not raised by my respondents. However, my lack of exposure does not mean that homosexual activity was not a factor in these communities, and this research area appears to be growing.

22. Tom Boellstorff, "Between Religion and Desire: Being Muslim and Gay in Indonesia," *American Anthropologist* 107:4 (2005): 578.

23. Loretta E. Bass and Fatou Sow, "Senegalese Families: The Confluence of Ethnicity, History, and Social Change," in Yaw Oheneba-Sakyi and Baffour K. Takyi, eds., *African Families at the Turn of the 21st Century* (Westport, Conn.: Praeger, 2006), 94. Bass and Sow also state that the "decision of when and whom to marry typically rests with parents, and 42 percent of marriages are endogamous or take place with partners in the extended family, typically cousins" (91).

24. N'Dri Thérèse Assié-Lumumba, "Structural Change and Continuity in the Ivoirian Family," in Yaw Oheneba-Sakyi and Baffour K. Takyi, ed., *African Families at the Turn of the 21st Century* (Westport, Conn.: Praeger, 2006), 122.

25. Manthia Diawara discusses courting in Mali and the case of a friend, Maï, who began pregnant and ostensibly died from the trauma. See Diawara, *We Won't Budge*, 106–112.

26. Assié-Lumumba, "Structural Change and Continuity in the Ivoirian Family," 119–120.

27. Ibid., 123.

28. Jacob K. Olupona and Regina Gemignani, eds., *African Immigrant Religions in America* (New York: New York University Press, 2008), 12.

29. If African women are looking to marry simply for a green card, I am told, they generally are upfront and speak of this directly. And of course, it will never involve consummation.

30. Therborn, "African Families in a Global Context," 38–42.

31. Bass and Sow, "Senegalese Families," 91.

32. Ibid., 87.

33. Ibid., 95.

34. In fact, after interviewing a large number of African Muslims in Harlem about their upbringing, it became evident that almost everyone had been raised with some connection to a polygynous household, eventually forcing me to begin asking the question outright. Many Muslims might see this practice as normal because of their own cultural background, and they also lay claim to it as a noble gesture, since the polygynous husband is required to support each family at the same economic level, not to mention the requirement that he give them an equal share of his time.

35. The passage in the Qur'an promoting human diversity is as follows: "O mankind! Surely you have been created from a single pair of male and female, and made into separate populations and groups so you will come to know (understand) each other. Truly the most honored of you in the sight of God is the most moral. And God has complete knowledge of all things" (al-hujurat, the Inner Domain, 49:13).

36. For a discussion on similar issues for Ghanaian and African American marriages, see Yvette Alex-Assensoh and A. B. Assensoh, "The Politics of Cross-Cultural Marriage: An Examination of a Ghanaian/African-American Case," in Rosemary Breger and Rosanna Hill, eds., Cross-Cultural Marriage: Identity and Choice (Oxford: Berg, 1998), 101–112. Moreover, Paul Stoller writes about how his respondents from Niger feel that African Americans do not realize how Africans understand the concept of family. See Stoller, Money Has No Smell, 4. During one of my discussions with Mohamed, an Ivoirian activist and businessman, he talks about the link between one's individuality and the family. "When the family is strong," Mohamed says, "you look good. But if the family is not strong, even if you're rich, you're going to have a bad name. Nobody will look at you as a good person. In Africa, it's like when somebody succeeds a lot, that means his family's really strong." That is, one's success is intimately tied to the condition of one's extended family.

37. American Muslims grapple with dating issues in their own way, as Asma Gull Hasan, a second-generation Pakistani, notes in an essay where she discusses how the faithful might handle courtship in the United States. In her view, Muslim dating falls into three categories. "Strict Muslims," as she calls them, engage in halal (religiously permissible) dating. They are well educated and savvy, and, rather than arranged marriages, they find suitable mates on their own or through suggestions from relatives or friends. During outings, a chaperone is always present. Premarital sex is barred, and holding hands is similarly off limits. Besides supervised get-togethers, the couple learns about each other, Hasan says, through telephone conversations and the Internet. On the other side of halal dating is what Hasan dubs "Sex and the City-style" haram (religiously impermissible) dating. This is everything halal dating is not, including free-wheeling sex with one or many partners. Between these two classifications are the "Eid Muslims." Lenient in their ritualistic observance, they typically attend the masjid for major celebrations. While they date without chaperones, there is no sex, though touching is limited and parents heavily monitor the relationship. In Amina's description of Yaya, his approach to courtship was to replicate traditional dating habits from back home. See Asma Gull Hasan, "Halal, Haram, and Sex and the City," in Michael Wolfe, ed., Taking Back Islam: American Muslims Reclaim Their Faith (Emmaus, Penn.: Rodale, 2002), 117–121.

38. Therborn, "African Families in a Global Context," 32–33.

39. Ibid., 86, 94.

40. Regarding the use of polygynous marriages as symbolic unions, see ibid., 36; Bass and Sow, "Senegalese Families," 95; Assié-Lumumba, "Structural Change and Continuity in the Ivoirian Family," 108.

41. Jacobs, *The Death and Life of Great American Cities*, 117.

42. Robin D. G. Kelley, "Playing for Keeps: Pleasure and Profit on the Postindustrial Playground," in Wahneema Lubiano, ed., *The House That Race Built* (New York: Vintage, 1998), 205.

43. For an informative note about SRO hotels in New York City, see Stoller, *Money Has No Smell*, 201, n. 10.

44. It would be incorrect to assume that father absenteeism has always been a problem for Black families. In fact, Black communities retained a higher rate of two-parent households and a lower divorce rate than the nation as a whole until the 1950s. See Obie Clayton, Ronald B. Mincy, and David Blankenhorn, eds., *Black Fathers in Contemporary American Society: Strengths, Weaknesses, and Strategies for Change* (New York: Russell Sage Foundation, 2003).

45. The African American cultural studies scholar "bell hooks" (spelled with lower-case letters) remembers a time growing up in the segregated South when the Black men around her were divested from the patriarchal ideal. There was Felix, "a hobo who jumped trains, never worked a regular job, and had a missing thumb." Others included Kid, a hunter living outside town whose wild game they would enjoy at dinner, and Daddy Gus, "who spoke in hushed tones, sharing his sense of spiritual mysticism." She remembers these men because of their kindness and overall concern for people, not for their presumed manly control over others. They "loved folks," she says, "especially the women and children. They were caring and giving. They were black men who chose alternative lifestyles, who questioned the *status quo*, who shunned a ready made patriarchal identity and invented themselves." Because of her exposure to them, she has "never been tempted to ignore the complexity of black male experience and identity." See bell hooks, *Black Looks: Race and Representation* (Boston: South End Press, 1992), 88. For a more recent and extensive reflection on this topic, see bell hooks, *We Real Cool: Black Men and Masculinity* (New York: Routledge, 2004).

46. As I have been informed by numerous respondents, natural uncles often assume parental duties as part of their collective responsibility. In these cases, the biological parents of the child will completely defer to the relative, especially if he is a paternal uncle or older, even for life decisions such as marriage.

47. See Bass and Sow, "Senegalese Families," 83–102; Assié-Lumumba, "Structural Change and Continuity in the Ivoirian Family," 103–127.

48. Bass and Sow, "Senegalese Families," 87, 97–98; Assié-Lumumba, "Structural Change and Continuity in the Ivoirian Family," 112–115.

49. Therborn, "African Families in a Global Context," 26.

50. Bass and Sow, "Senegalese Families."

51. Ibid., 90.

CHAPTER 9

1. Amy Tan, *The Opposite of Fate: Memories of a Writing Life* (New York: Penguin Books, 2003), 297.

2. For a blues impulse in poetry, see Kevin Young, ed., *Blues Poems* (New York: Alfred A. Knopf, 2003); and for a blues voice in literature, see Houston A. Baker Jr., *Blues, Ideology,*

and Afro-American Literature: A Vernacular Theory (Chicago: University of Chicago Press, 1984).

3. James H. Cone, *The Spirituals and the Blues* (New York: Orbis Books, 1991 [1972]), 125.

4. See Bernard Schumacher, *A Philosophy of Hope: Josef Pieper and the Contemporary Debate on Hope*, trans. by D. C. Schindler (New York: Fordham University Press, 2003); Jayne M. Waterworth, *A Philosophical Analysis of Hope* (New York: Palgrave Macmillan, 2004).

5. See the published interview "Seyyed Hossein Nasr: Islam and the Philosophy of Hope," in Michael Tobias, J. Patrick Fitzgerald, and David Rothenberg, eds., *A Parliament of Minds: Philosophy for a New Millennium* (Albany: State University of New York Press, 2000).

6. Matt Meyer and Elavie Ndura-Ouédraogo, eds., *Seeds of New Hope: Pan-African Peace Studies for the Twenty-first Century* (Trenton, N.J.: Africa World Press, 2009).

7. Beck, "West African Muslims in America."

8. Werbner, "Stamping the Earth with the Name of Allah."

9. Bradley Hope, "To Gain Immigrants' Trust, Police Reach Out to African Imams, Revive Dormant Unit," *New York Sun*, January 12, 2007, 3; Michael Moss and Jenny Nordberg, "A Nation at War: Muslims, Imams Urged to Be Alert for Suspicious Visitors," *New York Times*, April 6, 2003, B15.

10. Malcomson, "West of Eden," 41.

11. Diouf, "The Senegalese Murid Trade Diaspora."

12. Mamadou Diouf, "Preface," trans. by Dominic Thomas, in Roberts and Roberts, *A Saint in the City* 12.

13. My reference to "ummatic" comes from the Islamic concept of *ummah*, which refers to a Muslim's membership in the global faith community of Islam irrespective of other group affiliations.

14. For a discussion on how this separation affects Caribbean immigrant families, see Waters, *Black Identities*.

Bibliography

Abdullah, Zain. "African 'Soul Brothers' in Harlem: Immigration, Islam, and the Black Encounter." In Manning Marable and Hishaam Aidi, eds., *Black Routes to Islam*. New York: Palgrave Macmillan, 2009.

——. "African 'Soul Brothers' in the 'Hood: Immigration, Islam and the Black Encounter." *Anthropological Quarterly* 82:1 (Winter 2009): 41–44.

——. "Negotiating Identities: A History of Islamization in Black West Africa. *Journal of Islamic Law and Culture* 10:1 (2008): 5–18.

——. "Sufis on Parade: The Performance of Black, African, and Muslim Identities." *Journal of the American Academy of Religion* 77:2 (June 2009): 1–39.

——. "West Africa." In James Ciment, ed., *Encyclopedia of American Immigration.* Armonk, N.Y.: M. E. Sharpe, 2001, 1070–1078.

Acosta, Oscar Zeta. *Revolt of the Cockroach People.* San Francisco: Straight Arrow Press, 1973.

Adichie, Chimamanda Ngozi. *Half of a Yellow Sun.* New York: Alfred A. Knopf, 2007.

——. "The Story Behind the Book." http://www.halfofayellowsun.com/content. php?page=tsbtb&n=5&f=2.

Akinade, Akintunde. "Non-Western Christianity in the Western World: African Immigrant Churches in the Diaspora." In Jacob K. Olupona and Regina Gemignani, eds., *African Immigrant Religions in America.* New York: New York University Press, 2008.

Al-Azmeh, Aziz. *Islams and Modernities*, 2nd ed. New York: Verso, 2009.

Al-Faruqi, Isma'il Raji. *Toward Islamic English.* Herndon, Va.: International Institute of Islamic Thought, 1986.

Al-Imam, Ahmad Ali. *Variant Readings of the Qur'an: A Critical Study of Their Historical and Linguistic Origins.* Herndon, Va.: International Institute of Islamic Thought, 1998.

Al-Sayyid, Sabiq. *Fiqh us-Sunnah, Supererogatory Prayer*, vol. 2. Trans. by Muhammad Sa'eed Dabas and Jamal al-Din M. Zarabozo. Indianapolis: American Trust Publications, 1989.

Alex-Assensoh, Yvette, and A. B. Assensoh. "The Politics of Cross-Cultural Marriage: An Examination of a Ghanaian/African-American Case." In Rosemary Breger and Rosanna Hill, eds., *Cross-Cultural Marriage: Identity and Choice.* Oxford: Berg, 1998, 101–112.

Ali, Abdullah Yusuf. *The Qur'an: Text, Translation and Commentary.* Elmhurst, N.Y.: Tahrike Tarsile Qur'an, 2005.

Ali, Kecia. *Sexual Ethics and Islam: Feminist Reflections on Qur'an, Hadith, and Jurisprudence.* Oxford: Oneworld Publications, 2006.

Amporn, Marddent. *Sexual Culture among Young Migrant Muslims in Bangkok*. Bangkok: Silkworm Books, 2007.

Appadurai, Arjun. *Modernity at Large: Cultural Dimensions of Globalization*. Minneapolis: University of Minnesota Press, 1996.

Argetsinger, Amy, and Roxanne Roberts. "The Reliable Source." *Washington Post*, January 3, 2007.

Armstrong, Karen. *The Spiral Staircase: My Climb Out of Darkness*. New York: Anchor, 2004.

Asad, Muhammad. *The Message of the Qur'an*. Gibraltar: Dar al-Andalus, 1980.

Assié-Lumumba, N'Dri Thérèse. "Structural Change and Continuity in the Ivoirian Family." In Yaw Oheneba-Sakyi and Baffour K. Takyi, eds., *African Families at the Turn of the 21st Century*. Westport, Conn.: Praeger, 2006.

Associated Press. "Muslim Cabdrivers May Have to Signify Alcohol-Free Cars." October 1, 2006).

Auer, Peter, ed. *Code-Switching in Conversation: Language, Interaction and Identity*. New York: Routledge, 1998.

Austin, Allan D. *African Muslims in Antebellum America: A Sourcebook*. New York: Garland Publications, 1984.

———. *African Muslims in Antebellum America: Transatlantic Stories and Spiritual Struggles*. New York: Routledge, 1997.

Babou, Cheikh Anta. "Brotherhood Solidarity, Education and Migration: The Role of the Dahiras among the Murid Muslim Community of New York." *African Affairs* 101 (2002): 151–170.

———. *Fighting the Greater Jihad: Amadu Bamba and the Founding of the Muridiyya of Senegal, 1853–1913*. Athens: Ohio University Press, 2007.

———. "Migration and Cultural Change: Money, 'Caste,' Gender, and Social Status among Senegalese Female Hair Braiders in the United States." *Africa Today* 55:2 (2009): 3–22.

Baker, Houston A., Jr. *Blues, Ideology, and Afro-American Literature: A Vernacular Theory*. Chicago: University of Chicago Press, 1984.

Banks, Patricia A. *Represent: Art and Identity among the Black Upper-Middle Class*. New York: Routledge, 2009.

Barou, Jacques. "In the Aftermath of Colonization: Black African Immigrants in France." In Hans C. Buechler and Judith-Maria Buechler, eds., *Migrants in Europe: The Role of Family, Labor and Politics*. New York: Greenwood Press, 1987.

Bass, Loretta E., and Fatou Sow. "Senegalese Families: The Confluence of Ethnicity, History, and Social Change." In Yaw Oheneba-Sakyi and Baffour K. Takyi, eds., *African Families at the Turn of the 21st Century*. Westport, Conn.: Praeger, 2006.

Bate, Peter. *White King, Red Rubber, Black Death* (film). ArtMattan Productions, New York, 2004.

BBC News. "In Pictures: Immigrant Boats." September 11, 2006). http://news.bbc.co.uk/2/hi/in_pictures/5335062.stm.

———. "Key Facts: Africa to Europe Migration." July 2, 2007. http://news.bbc.co.uk/2/hi/europe/6228236.stm.

———. "Spain in Senegal Migration Deal," October 11, 2006. http://news.bbc.co.uk/go/pr/fr/-/2/hi/africa/6039624.stm.

Beck, Linda. "West African Muslims in America: When Are Muslims Not Muslims?" In Jacob K. Olupona and Regina Gemignani, eds., *African Immigrant Religions in America*. New York: New York University Press, 2008.

Blench, Roger. "The Status of the Languages of Central Nigeria." In M. Brenzinger, ed., *Endangered Languages in Africa*. Köln: Köppe Verlag, 1998, 187–206. http://www.rogerblench.info/Language%20data/Africa/Nigeria/Language%20Death%20in%20Nigeria.pdf.

Block, Deborah. "Somali Taxi Drivers in Minnesota in Dispute over Passengers with Pets, Alcohol." Voice of America, April 4, 2007. http://www1.voanews.com/english/news/a-13-2007-04-04-voa62.html.

Boellstorff, Tom. "Between Religion and Desire: Being Muslim and Gay in Indonesia." *American Anthropologist* 107:4 (2005): 575–585.

Bongmba, Elias. "Portable Faith: The Global Mission of African Initiated Churches." In Jacob K. Olupona and Regina Gemignani, eds., *African Immigrant Religions in America*. New York: New York University Press, 2008.

Bop, Codou. "Roles and the Position of Women in Sufi Brotherhoods in Senegal." *Journal of the American Academy of Religion* 73:4 (December 2005): 1099–1119.

Bortin, Meg. "Desperate Voyage, Destination Spain: For Young African, Risks Seem Worth It." *International Herald Tribune*, May 31, 2006. http://www.iht.com/articles/2006/05/28/news/senegal.php.

Bourdieu, Pierre. "The Forms of Capital." In John G. Richardson, ed., *Handbook of Theory and Research for the Sociology of Education*. New York: Greenwood, 1986, 241–258.

Bourgois, Philippe. *In Search of Respect: Selling Crack in El Barrio*, 2nd ed. New York: Cambridge University Press, 2003.

Breger, Rosemary, and Rosanna Hill, eds. *Cross-Cultural Marriage: Identity and Choice*. Oxford: Berg, 1998.

Breitman, George, ed. *Malcolm X Speaks: Selected Speeches and Statements*. New York: Grove Weidenfeld, 1990.

Brereton, Joel P. "Sacred Space." In Lindsay Jones, ed., *Encyclopedia of Religion*, 2nd ed. Detroit: Macmillan Reference, 2005.

Bruni, Frank. "Invisible, and in Anguish: A Slain Driver's Service Brings Attention to Senegalese." *New York Times*, November 18, 1997, B1.

Bugha, Mustafa Deeb. *Al-Wafi fi sharhal-Arba 'in al-Nawawiyah*. Damascus: Dar ibn Kathir, 1989.

Bukhari, Muḥammad ibn Isma'il. *Sahih al-Bukhari: The Translation of the Meanings of Sahih al-Bukhari, Arabic-English*, trans. Muḥammad Muhsin Khan), 9 vols. Medina: Dar al-Fikr, 1981.

Burnett, Victoria. "To Curb Illegal Migration, Spain Offers a Legal Route." *New York Times* (11 Aug 2007) http://www.nytimes.com/2007/08/11/world/europe/11spain.html.

Byfield, Judith. "Introduction: Rethinking the African Diaspora." *African Studies Review* 43:1 (April 2000): 1–9.

Callaway, Barbara, and Lucy Creevey. *The Heritage of Islam: Women, Religion, and Politics in West Africa*. Boulder, Colo.: Lynne Reiner, 1994.

Carter, Donald Martin. *States of Grace: Senegalese in Italy and the New European Immigration*. Minneapolis: University of Minnesota Press, 1997.

Clarence-Smith, William Gervase. *Islam and the Abolition of Slavery*. New York: Oxford University Press, 2006.

Clayton, Obie, Ronald B. Mincy, and David Blankenhorn, eds. *Black Fathers in Contemporary American Society: Strengths, Weaknesses, and Strategies for Change*. New York: Russell Sage Foundation, 2003.

CNN.com. "African Refugee Situation Getting Worse, U.N. Says," November 4, 2008. http://www.cnn.com/2008/WORLD/africa/11/04/un.refugees.africa/index.html.

Cone, James H. *Martin & Malcolm & America: A Dream or a Nightmare*. Maryknoll, N.Y.: Orbis, 1991.

———. *The Spirituals and the Blues*. New York: Orbis Books, 1991 [1972].

Corbould, Clare. "Streets, Sounds and Identity in Interwar Harlem." *Journal of Social History* 40:4 (Summer 2007): 859–894.

Coulon, Christian. "The Grand Magal in Touba: A Religious Festival of the Mouride Brotherhood of Senegal." *African Affairs* 98 (1999): 195–210.

———. "Women, Islam, and Baraka." In Donal B. Cruise O'Brien and Christian Coulon, eds., *Charisma and Brotherhood in African Islam*. Oxford: Clarendon Press, 1988, 113–135.

Crozier, David, and Roger Blench. *An Index of Nigerian Languages*, 2nd ed. Abuja, Nigeria, and Dallas: Nigerian Language Development Centre, University of Ilorin, and Summer Institute of Linguistics, 1992.

Cullen, Countee. "Heritage." In Manning Marable, Nishani Frazier, and John Campbell McMillian, eds., *Freedom on My Mind: The Columbia Documentary History of the African American Experience*. New York: Columbia University Press, 2003.

Curiel, Jonathan. *Al' America: Travels through America's Arab and Islamic Roots*. New York: New Press, 2008.

Curtis, Edward E., IV. *Black Muslim Religion in the Nation of Islam, 1960–1975*. Chapel Hill: University of North Carolina Press, 2006.

———. *Islam in Black America: Identity, Liberation, and Difference in African-American Islamic Thought*. Albany: State University of New York Press, 2002.

D'Alisera, JoAnn. *An Imagined Geography: Sierra Leonean Muslims in America*. Philadelphia: University of Pennsylvania Press, 2004.

Daly, Emma. "African Refugees Are Rescued after 2-Week Ordeal." *New York Times*, February 22, 2003. http://www.nytimes.com.

Dannin, Robert. *Black Pilgrimage to Islam*. New York: Oxford University Press, 2002.

Darimi, Abd Allah ibn Abd al-Rahman. *Musnad al-Dārimī*. Riyadh: Dar al-Mughni, 2000.

Davis, Susan G. *Parades and Power: Street Theatre in Nineteenth-Century Philadelphia*. Philadelphia: Temple University Press, 1986.

Diawara, Manthia. *In Search of Africa*. Cambridge, Mass.: Harvard University Press, 1998.

———. *We Won't Budge: A Malaria Memoir*. New York: Basic Civitas Books, 2003.

Diouf, Mamadou. "Preface," trans. by Dominic Thomas. In Allen F. Roberts and Mary Nooter Roberts, eds., *A Saint in the City: Sufi Arts of Urban Senegal*. Los Angeles: UCLA Fowler Museum of Cultural History, 2003.

———. "The Senegalese Murid Trade Diaspora and the Making of a Vernacular Cosmopolitanism." *Public Culture* 12:3 (2000): 679–702.

Diouf, Sylviane A. *Servants of Allah: African Muslims Enslaved in the Americas*. New York: New York University Press, 1998.

Diouf-Kamara, Sylviane. "Senegalese of New York: A Model Minority?" *Black Renaissance/Renaissance Noire* 1:2 (Summer-Fall 1997).

Douglas, Thomas J. "Changing Religious Practices among Cambodian Immigrants in Long Beach and Seattle." In Karen I. Leonard, Alex Stepick, Manuel A. Vasquez, and Jennifer Holdaway, eds., *Immigrant Faiths: Transforming Religious Life in America*. Lanham, Md.: AltaMira Press, 2005.

DuBois, W. E. B. *The Souls of Black Folk*. New York: Signet Classic, 1995 [1903].

Duneier, Mitchell. *Sidewalk*. New York: Farrar, Straus and Giroux, 1999.

Durkheim, Emile. *The Division of Labor in Society*. New York: Free Press, 1964 [1933].

Ebin, Victoria. "Making Room versus Creating Space: The Construction of Spatial Categories by Itinerant Mouride Traders." In Barbara Daly Metcalf, ed., *Making Muslim Space in North America and Europe*. Berkeley: University of California Press, 1996.

El Fadl, Khaled Abou. *The Search for Beauty in Islam: A Conference of the Books*. Lanham, Md.: Rowman & Littlefield, 2006.

El Shibli, Fatima. "Islam and the Blues." *Souls* 9:2 (2007): 162–170.

Ellison, Ralph. *Invisible Man*. New York: Random House, 1952.

———. "Richard Wright's Blues." *Antioch Review* 5:2 (Summer 1945): 199.

———. *Shadow and Act*. New York: Vintage International, 1995 [1964].

Esposito, John L. *What Everyone Needs to Know about Islam*. New York: Oxford University Press, 2002.

Esposito, John L., and Dalia Mogahed. *Who Speaks for Islam? What a Billion Muslims Really Think*. New York: Gallup Press, 2007.

Estefania, Rafael. "From Shipwreck to Solidarity." BBC News Online, September 10, 2008. http://news.bbc.co.uk/2/hi/africa/7586597.stm.

Ethnologue. http://www.ethnologue.com/show_country.asp?name=CI.

Farley, Reynolds, C. Steeh, T. Jackson, M. Krysan, and K. Reeves. "Continued Racial Residential Segregation in Detroit: 'Chocolate City, Vanilla Suburbs' Revisited." *Journal of Housing Research* 4:1 (1993): 1–38.

Feirstein, Sanna. *Naming New York: Manhattan Places and How They Got Their Names*. New York: New York University Press, 2001.

Feld, Steven and Keith H. Basso. *Senses of Place*. Seattle: University of Washington Press, 1996.

Foley, Douglas E. *Learning Capitalist Culture: Deep in the Heart of Tejas*. Philadelphia: University of Pennsylvania Press, 1990.

Foner, Nancy. "Introduction: New Immigrants in New York." In Nancy Foner, ed., *New Immigrants in New York*, updated ed. New York: Columbia University Press, 2001, 1–31.

Frankenberg, Ruth. *White Women, Race Matters: The Social Construction of Whiteness*. Minneapolis: University of Minnesota Press, 1993.

Gebrewold, Belachew, ed. *Africa and Fortress Europe: Threats and Opportunities*. Burlington, Vt.: Ashgate, 2007.

Geertz, Clifford. *Islam Observed: Religious Development in Morocco and Indonesia*. New Haven, Conn.: Yale University Press, 1968.

Gemignani, Regina. "Gender, Identity, and Power in African Immigrant Evangelical Churches." In Jacob K. Olupona and Regina Gemignani, eds., *African Immigrant Religions in America*. New York: New York University Press, 2008, 133–157.

Gluckman, Max. *Custom and Conflict in Africa*. Oxford: Blackwell, 1955.

———. *Order and Rebellion in Tribal Africa: Collected Essays*. London: Cohen & West, 1963.

Gomez, Michael A. *Black Crescent: The Experience and Legacy of African Muslims in the Americas*. New York: Cambridge University Press, 2005.

———. *Exchanging Our Country Marks: The Transformation of African Identities in the Colonial and Antebellum South*. Chapel Hill: University of North Carolina Press, 1998.

Gordon, April. "The New Diaspora—African Immigration to the United States." *Journal of Third World Studies* 15:1 (1998): 79–103.

Graves, Boyd E. http://www.boydgraves.com.

Greenbaum, Susan D. "Housing Abandonment in Inner-City Black Neighborhoods: A Case Study of the Effects of the Dual Housing Market." In Robert Rotenberg and Gary McDonogh, eds., *The Cultural Meaning of Urban Space*. Westport, Conn.: Bergin & Garvey, 1993.

Haddad, Yvonne Yazbeck, and John L. Esposito. *Muslims on the Americanization Path?* Atlanta: Scholars Press, 1998.

Haddad, Yvonne Yazbeck, Jane I. Smith, and Kathleen M. Moore. *Muslim Women in America: The Challenge of Islamic Identity Today*. New York: Oxford University Press, 2006.

Hammett, Jerilou, and Kingsley Hammett, eds. *The Suburbanization of New York: Is the World's Greatest City Becoming Just Another Town?* New York: Princeton Architectural Press, 2007.

Hasan, Asma Gull. "Halal, Haram, and Sex and the City." In Michael Wolfe, ed., *Taking Back Islam: American Muslims Reclaim Their Faith*. Emmaus, Penn.: Rodale, 2002, 117–121.

Hathaway, Heather, Josef Jarab, and Jeffrey Melnick, eds. *Race and the Modern Artist*. New York: Oxford University Press, 2003.

Hayes, Kevin J. "How Thomas Jefferson Read the Qur'an." *Early American Literature* 39:2 (2004): 247–261.

Herberg, Will. *Protestant, Catholic, Jew: An Essay in American Religious Sociology*. Garden City, N.Y.: Doubleday, 1955.

Hillyard, Paddy. *Suspect Community: People's Experience of the Prevention of Terrorism Acts in Britain*. London: Pluto, 1993.

hooks, bell. *Black Looks: Race and Representation*. Boston: South End Press, 1992.

———. *We Real Cool: Black Men and Masculinity*. New York: Routledge, 2004.

Hope, Bradley. "To Gain Immigrants' Trust, Police Reach Out to African Imams, Revive Dormant Unit." *New York Sun*, January 12, 2007, 3.

Hurston, Zora Neale. *Their Eyes Were Watching God: A Novel*. London: Virago Press, 1986 [1937].

Ibn Hanbal, Ahmad ibn Muhammad. *Al-Musnad*. Beirut: Mu'assasat al Risālah, 2008.

Jackson, John L., Jr. *Harlemworld: Doing Race and Class in Contemporary Black America*. Chicago: University of Chicago Press, 2001.

———. *Real Black: Adventures in Racial Sincerity*. Chicago: University of Chicago Press, 2005.

Jackson, Sherman A. *Islam and the Blackamerican*. New York: Oxford University Press, 2005.

Jacobs, Jane. *The Death and Life of Great American Cities*. New York: Random House, 1961.

Jones, James H. *Bad Blood: The Tuskegee Syphilis Experiment*. New York: Free Press, 1981.

Jones, LeRoi (Amiri Baraka). *Blues People: Negro Music in White America*. New York: Perennial, 1999 [1963].

Kalu, Ogbu U. "The Andrew Syndrome: Models in Understanding Nigerian Diaspora." In Jacob K. Olupona and Regina Gemignani, eds., *African Immigrant Religions in America*. New York: New York University Press, 2008, 73–78.

Keaton, Trica Danielle. *Muslim Girls and the Other France: Race, Identity Politics, and Social Exclusion*. Bloomington: Indiana University Press, 2006.

Keeley, Graham, and Robert Hooper. "Grim Toll of African Refugees Mounts on Spanish Beaches." *Guardian*, July 13, 2008. http://www.guardian.co.uk/world/2008/jul/13/spain/print.

Kelley, Robin D. G. "Disappearing Acts: Harlem in Transition." In Jerilou Hammett and Kingsley Hammett, eds., *The Suburbanization of New York: Is the World's Greatest City Becoming Just Another Town?* New York: Princeton Architectural Press, 2007.

———. "Playing for Keeps: Pleasure and Profit on the Postindustrial Playground." In Wahneema Lubiano, ed., *The House That Race Built*. New York: Vintage, 1998, 195–231.

Kelton, Jane Gladden. "New York City St. Patrick's Day Parade: Invention of Contention and Consensus." *Drama Review* 29:3 (Fall 1985): 93–105.

Kidd, Sue Monk. *Firstlight: Early Inspirational Writings*. New York: Guideposts, 2006.

Kirshenblatt-Gimblett, Barbara, and Brooks McNamara. "Processional Performance: An Introduction." *Drama Review* 29:3 (1985): 2–5.

Kohnert, Dirk. "African Migration to Europe: Obscured Responsibilities and Common Misconceptions." German Institute of Global and Area Studies Working Paper 49 (May 2007): 5–24.

Kozol, Jonathan. *Savage Inequalities: Children in America's Schools*. New York: Harper Perennial, 1992.

Kubik, Gerhard. *Africa and the Blues*. Jackson: University Press of Mississippi, 1999.

Kugelmass, Jack. *Masked Culture: The Greenwich Village Halloween Parade*. New York: Columbia University Press, 1994.

León, Luís. "Born Again in East LA: The Congregation as Border Space." In R. Stephen Warner and Judith G. Wittner, eds., *Gatherings in Diaspora: Religious Communities and the New Immigration*. Philadelphia: Temple University Press, 1998.

Low, Setha, ed. *Theorizing the City: The New Urban Anthropology Reader*. New Brunswick, N.J.: Rutgers University Press, 1999.

Mahdavi, Pardis. *Passionate Uprisings: Iran's Sexual Revolution*. Stanford, Calif.: Stanford University Press, 2009.

Malcolm X. *The Autobiography of Malcolm X*. New York: Ballantine, 1999 [1965].

Malcomson, Scott L. "West of Eden: The Mouride Ethic and the Spirit of Capitalism." *Transition: An International Review* 6:3 (1996): 24–43.

Manger, Leif, ed. *Muslim Diversity: Local Islam in Global Contexts*. Surrey, U.K.: RoutledgeCurzon, 1999.

Marable, Manning, and Hishaam Aidi, eds. *Black Routes to Islam*. New York: Palgrave Macmillan, 2009.

Marcus, George E. "Ethnography in/of the World System: The Emergence of Multi-sited Ethnography." *Annual Review of Anthropology* 24 (1995): 95–117.

Margolick, David. *Strange Fruit: The Biography of a Song*. New York: Harper Perennial, 2001.

Marosi, Richard. "One of the Most Dangerous Jobs in New York: Gypsy Cab Driver." Columbia University News Service. http://www.taxi-library.org/marosi.htm.

Marris, Peter. *Family and Social Change in an African City: A Study of Rehousing in Lagos*. Evanston, Ill.: Northwestern University Press, 1962.

Massey, Douglas S. *American Apartheid: Segregation and the Making of the Underclass*. Cambridge, Mass.: Harvard University Press, 1998.

Mazrui, Ali. *The Africans: A Triple Heritage*. Boston: Little, Brown, 1986.

Mbacké, Khadim. *Sufism and Religious Brotherhoods in Senegal*. Princeton, N.J.: Markus Wiener, 2005.

McCloud, Aminah Beverly, *Transnational Muslims in American Society*. Gainesville: University Press of Florida, 2006.

McFeely, William S. *Frederick Douglass*. New York: Norton, 1991.

Metcalf, Barbara Daly. "Toward Islamic English? A Note on Transliteration." In Barbara Daly Metcalf, ed., *Making Muslim Space in North America and Europe*. Berkeley: University of California Press, 1996.

Metropolitan Transportation Authority (MTA). http://www.nycsubway.org/perl/artwork.

Meyer, Matt, and Elavie Ndura-Ouédraogo, eds. *Seeds of New Hope: Pan-African Peace Studies for the Twenty-first Century*. Trenton, N.J.: Africa World Press, 2009.

Miles, Ann. *From Cuenca to Queens: An Anthropological Story of Transnational Migration*. Princeton, N.J.: Princeton University Press, 2004.

Moran, Robert, Gaiutra Bahadur, and Susan Snyder. "Residents Say Beating Fits Widespread Pattern." *Philadelphia Inquirer,* November 3, 2005.

Morawska, Ewa. "Immigrant-Black Dissensions in American Cities: An Argument for Multiple Explanations." In Elijah Anderson and Douglas S. Massey, eds., *Problem of the Century: Racial Stratification in the United States*. New York: Russell Sage Foundation, 2001, 47–95.

Moss, Michael, and Jenny Nordberg. "A Nation at War: Muslims, Imams Urged to Be Alert for Suspicious Visitors." *New York Times*, April 6, 2003, B15.

Murray, Leslie Ann. "14 Senegalese Men Search for Economic Freedom." *New York Amsterdam News*, March 29–April 2, 2007, 6.

Nawaz, Zarqa. *Me and the Mosque* (film). National Film Board of Canada, 2005.

Newman, Katherine S. *No Shame in My Game: The Working Poor in the Inner City*. New York: Vintage Books and Russell Sage Foundation, 1999.

Nomani, Asra Q. *Standing Alone: An American Woman's Struggle for the Soul of Islam*. New York: HarperSanFrancisco, 2005.

Obama, Barack. *Dreams from My Father: A Story of Race and Inheritance*, rev. ed. New York: Three Rivers Press, 2004.

Oliver, Paul. *Savannah Syncopators: African Retentions in the Blues*. New York: Stein and Day, 1970.

Olupona, Jacob K. "Communities of Believers: Exploring African Immigrant Religion in the United States." In Jacob K. Olupona and Regina Gemignani, eds., *African Immigrant Religions in America*. New York: New York University Press, 2008, 27–46.

Olupona, Jacob K., and Regina Gemignani, eds. *African Immigrant Religions in America*. New York: New York University Press, 2008.

Orsi, Robert A. *The Madonna of 115th Street: Faith and Community in Italian Harlem, 1880–1950*. New Haven, Conn.: Yale University Press, 2002.

Park, Robert E. *The City*. Chicago: University of Chicago Press, 1968 [1928].

Pattillo, Mary. *Black on the Block: The Politics of Race and Class in the City*. Chicago: University of Chicago Press, 2007.

Pattillo-McCoy, Mary. *Black Picket Fences: Privilege and Peril among the Black Middle Class*. Chicago: University of Chicago Press, 1999.

Peattie, Lisa Redfield. *The View from the Barrio*. Ann Arbor: University of Michigan Press, 1972.

Pedersen, Carl. "Sea Change: The Middle Passage and the Transatlantic Imagination." In Werner Sollors and Maria Diedrich, eds., *The Black Columbiad: Defining Moments in African American Literature and Culture*. Cambridge, Mass.: Harvard University Press, 1994, 42–51.

Perry, Donna L. "Rural Ideologies and Urban Imaginings: Wolof Immigrants in New York City." *Africa Today* 44:2 (1997): 229–259.

Pietri, Pedro. "Suicide Note of a Cockroach in a Low Income Project." In *Loose Joints: Poetry by Pedro Pietri*. Folkways Records, 1979.

Piga, Adriana. *Dakar et les orders soufis: Processus socioculturels et développement urbain au Sénégal contemporain*. Paris: L'Harmattan, 2002.

Racioppi, Linda, and Katherine O'Sullivan See. "Ulsterman and Loyalist Ladies on Parade: Gendering Unionism in Northern Ireland." *International Feminist Journal of Politics* 2:1 (Spring 2000): 1–29.

Radano, Ronald, and Philip V. Bohlman, eds. *Music and the Racial Imagination*. Chicago: University of Chicago Press, 2000.

Ramadan, Tariq. *Radical Reform: Islamic Ethics and Liberation*. New York: Oxford University Press, 2009.

Reed, Teresa L. *The Holy Profane: Religion in Black Popular Music*. Lexington: University Press of Kentucky, 2003.

Reighley, Kurt B. *Looking for the Perfect Beat: The Art and Culture of the DJ*. New York: Pocket Books, 2000.

Reverby, Susan M. *Tuskegee's Truths: Rethinking the Tuskegee Syphilis Study*. Chapel Hill: University of North Carolina Press, 2000.

Roberts, Allen F., and Mary Nooter Roberts. *A Saint in the City: Sufi Arts of Urban Senegal*. Los Angeles: UCLA Fowler Museum of Cultural History, 2003.

Roberts, Sam. "More Africans Enter US Than in Days of Slavery." *New York Times*, February 21, 2005, A1.

Robertson, Roland. *Globalization: Social Theory and Global Culture*. London: Sage, 1992.

Robinson, Ed. "Rescue at Sea." *New York Post*, February 2, 2007.

Rocklin, Jeremy. *Dollars and Dreams: West Africans in New York* (film). Documentary Educational Resources, Watertown, Mass., 2007.

Roemer, Michael, and Robert Young. *Nothing but a Man* (film). CCM Films, 1964.

Rotenberg, Robert. *Time and Order in Metropolitan Vienna: A Seizure of Schedules*. Washington, D.C.: Smithsonian Institution Press, 1992.

Salzbrunn, Monika. "The Occupation of Public Space through Religious and Political Events: How Senegalese Migrants Became a Part of Harlem, New York." *Journal of Religion in Africa* 34:4 (2004): 468–492.

Savishinsky, Neil J. "The Baye Faal of Senegambia: Muslim Rastas in the Promised Land?" *Africa: Journal of the International African Institute* 64:2 (1994): 211–219.

Schiller, Nina Glick, Linda Basch, and Cristina Szanton Blanc. "From Immigrant to Transmigrant: Theorizing Transnational Migration." *Anthropological Quarterly* 68:1 (January 1995): 48–63.

Schipper, Mineke. *Imagining Insiders: Africa and the Question of Belonging*. New York: Cassell, 1999.

Schubel, Vernon James. "Karbala As Sacred Space among North American Shi'a: 'Every Day Is Ashura, Everywhere Is Karbala." In Barbara Daly Metcalf, ed., *Making Muslim Space in North America and Europe*. Berkeley: University of California Press, 1996.

Schumacher, Bernard. *A Philosophy of Hope: Josef Pieper and the Contemporary Debate on Hope*, trans. by D. C. Schindler. New York: Fordham University Press, 2003.

Sciorra, Joseph. "'We Go Where the Italians Live': Religious Processions As Ethnic and Territorial Markers in a Multi-ethnic Brooklyn Neighborhood." In Robert A. Orsi, ed., *Gods of the City: Religion and the American Urban Landscape*. Bloomington: Indiana University Press, 1999.

Shokeid, Moshe. *A Gay Synagogue in New York*. Philadelphia: University of Pennsylvania Press, 2002.

Short, Vicky. "Spain Strengthens Borders against African Refugees." *World Socialist*, June 2, 1999, http://www.wsws.org.

Shulman, Steven, ed. *The Impact of Immigration on African Americans*. New Brunswick, N.J.: Transaction, 2004.

Singh, Amritjit, and Daniel M. Scott III, eds. *The Collected Writings of Wallace Thurman: A Harlem Renaissance Reader*. New Brunswick, NJ: Rutgers University Press, 2003.

Slyomovics, Susan. "The Muslim World Day Parade and 'Storefront' Mosques of New York City." In Barbara Daly Metcalf, ed., *Making Muslim Space in North America and Europe*. Berkeley: University of California Press, 1996.

Smith, Anna Deavere. *Fires in the Mirror: Crown Heights, Brooklyn and Other Identities*. New York: Anchor, 1993.

Smith, Anna Deavere, George C. Wolfe, and Cherie Fortis. *Fires in the Mirror: Crown Heights, Brooklyn and Other Identities* (film). Monterey Video and Hipster Entertainment, Thousand Oaks, Calif., 2003.

Smith, Jane I. *Islam in America*. New York: Columbia University Press, 1999.

Smith, Robert C. *Mexican New York: Transnational Lives of New Immigrants*. Berkeley: University of California Press, 2006.

Sodiq, Yushau. "African Muslims in the United States: The Nigerian Case." In Jacob K. Olupona and Regina Gemignani, eds., *African Immigrant Religions in America*. New York: New York University Press, 2008.

Speer, Tibbett. "The Newest African Americans Aren't Black." *American Demographics* 16:1 (January 1994): 9–10.

Stack, Carolyn B. *All Our Kin: Strategies for Survival in a Black Community*. New York: Harper & Row, 1974.

Stack, Jonathan, Terry Williams, and Susanne Szabo Rostock. *Harlem Diary: Nine Voices of Resilience* (film). Discovery Channel, Gabriel Films, and Films for the Humanities & Sciences, Princeton, N.J., 2003 [1993].

Steele, Shelby, and Thomas Lennon. *Seven Days in Bensonhurst* (film). Frontline, WGBH Educational Foundation, Boston, 1990.

Stoller, Paul. *Jaguar: A Story of Africans in America*. Chicago: University of Chicago Press, 1999.

———. *Money Has No Smell: The Africanization of New York City*. Chicago: University of Chicago Press, 2002.

———. "West Africans: Trading Places in New York." In Nancy Foner, ed., *New Immigrants in New York*, updated ed. New York: Columbia University Press, 2001.

Suárez-Orozo, Carola, Marcelo M. Suárez-Orozo, and Irina Todorova. *Learning a New Land: Immigrant Students in American Society*. Cambridge, Mass.: Belknap Press, 2008.

Sullivan, Rebecca. "Breaking Habits: Gender, Class and the Sacred in the Dress of Women Religious." In Anne Brydon and Sandra Niessen, eds., *Consuming Fashion: Adorning the Transnational Body*. New York: Berg, 1998.

Sy, Tidiane. "Mother's Battle against Senegal Migration." BBC News, November 6, 2006. http://news.bbc.co.uk/2/hi/africa/6109736.stm.

Tan, Amy. *The Opposite of Fate: Memories of a Writing Life*. New York: Penguin Books, 2003.

Taudte, Jeca. "Fourteen Senegalese Join the Exodus to Europe and Beyond." *Columbia Journalist*, May 7, 2007, http://columbiajournalist.org/article.asp?subj= international&course= The_International_Newsroom&id=1523.

Taylor, Monique M. *Harlem between Heaven and Hell*. Minneapolis: University of Minnesota Press, 2002.

Therborn, Göran. "African Families in a Global Context." In Göran Therborn, ed., *African Families in a Global Context*. Uppsala: Nordiska Afrikainstitutet, 2004, 38–44.

Tobias, Michael, J. Patrick Fitzgerald, and David Rothenberg. "Seyyed Hossein Nasr: Islam and the Philosophy of Hope." In Michael Tobias, J. Patrick Fitzgerald, and David Rothenberg, eds., *A Parliament of Minds: Philosophy for a New Millennium*. Albany: State University of New York Press, 2000.

Tseëlon, Efrat, ed. *Masquerade and Identities: Essays on Gender, Sexuality, and Marginality*. New York: Routledge, 2001.

Turner, Richard Brent. *Islam in the African American Experience*, 2nd ed. Bloomington: Indiana University Press, 2003.

Turner, Victor Witter. *The Ritual Process: Structure and Anti-Structure*. Chicago: Aldine, 1969.

U.S. Bureau of the Census. *Characteristics of the Foreign-Born Population in the United States*. Washington, D.C.: U.S. Government Printing Office, 1990.

———. *Characteristics of the Foreign-Born Population in the United States*. Washington, D.C.: U.S. Government Printing Office, 2000.

———. *Current Population Survey*. Washington, D.C.: U.S. Government Printing Office, 2000.

U.S. Customs and Border Patrol Protection. "Fourteen Senegalese Refugees Rescued at Sea." http://www.cbp.gov/xp/cgov/newsroom/news_releases/archives/2007_news_releases/022007/02012007_1.xml.

USA Today. "Africans' Sea Voyage to NYC Ends in Rescue Hundreds of Miles Offshore." February 1, 2007, http://www.usatoday.com/news/nation/2007-02-01-africans-at-sea_x.htm.

Usborne, David. "Senegalese Men Rescued Trying to Sail to New York." *Independent*, February 3, 2007. http://www.independent.co.uk/news/world/americas/senegalese-men-rescued-trying-to-sail-to-new-york-434799.html.

Van de Walle, Nicolas, Nicole Ball, and Vijaya Ramachandram, eds. *Beyond Structural Adjustment: The Institutional Context of African Development*. New York: Palgrave Macmillan, 2003.

Van Gennep, Arnold. *The Rites of Passage*. Chicago: University of Chicago Press, 1960 [1908].

Waldman, Amy. "Killing Heightens the Unease Felt by Africans in New York." *New York Times*, February 14, 1999, A1.

Washington, Harriet A. *Medical Apartheid: The Dark History of Medical Experimentation on Black Americans from Colonial Times to the Present*. New York: Doubleday, 2006.

Waters, Mary C. Black Identities: West Indian Immigrant Dreams and American Realities. Cambridge, Mass.: Harvard University Press, 1999.

Waterworth, Jayne M. *A Philosophical Analysis of Hope*. New York: Palgrave Macmillan, 2004.

Weissman, Dick. *Blues: The Basics*. New York: Routledge, 2005.

Werbner, Pnina. "Stamping the Earth with the Name of Allah: Zikr and the Sacralizing of Space among British Muslims." In Barbara Daly Metcalf, ed., *Making Muslim Space in North America and Europe*. Berkeley: University of California Press, 1996.

West, Cornel. *Democracy Matters: Winning the Fight against Imperialism*. New York: Penguin, 2004.

———. *Hope on a Tightrope: Words & Wisdom*. Carlsbad, Calif.: SmileyBooks, 2008.

West Australian. "Muslim Taxis Refuse to Carry Guide Dogs." October 8, 2006. http://au.news.yahoo.com/thewest.

Whyte, William Foote. *Street Corner Society: The Social Structure of an Italian Slum*, 4th ed. Chicago: University of Chicago Press, 1993.

Williams, Terry, and William Kornblum. *Growing Up Poor*. Lexington, Mass.: Lexington Books, 1985.

———. *The Uptown Kids: Struggle and Hope in the Projects*. New York: Putnam, 1994.

Williamson, Joel. *New People: Miscegenation and Mulattoes in the United States*. Baton Rouge: Louisiana State University Press, 1995.

Young, Kevin, ed. *Blues Poems*. New York: Alfred A. Knopf, 2003.

Young, Michael Dunlop. *Family and Kinship in East London*. London: Routledge, 1957.

Zaragoza, Edward C. *St. James in the Streets: The Religious Processions of Loíza Aldea, Puerto Rico*. Lanham, Md.: Scarecrow Press, 1995.

Zhou, Min. "Segmented Assimilation: Issues, Controversies, and Recent Research on the New Second Generation." In Charles Hirschman, Philip Kasinitz, and Josh DeWind, eds., *The Handbook of International Migration: The American Experience*. New York: Russell Sage Foundation, 1999.

Index

CPSIA information can be obtained
at www.ICGtesting.com
Printed in the USA
BVHW02s0015100118
504881BV00002B/31/P